THE DEVELOPMENT OF TROPICAL LANDS

THE DEVELOPMENT OF

TROPICAL LANDS:

POLICY ISSUES IN LATIN AMERICA

MICHAEL NELSON

Published for Resources for the Future, Inc.
by The Johns Hopkins University Press,
Baltimore and London

RESOURCES FOR THE FUTURE, INC.
1755 Massachusetts Avenue, N.W., Washington, D.C. 20036

Resources for the Future is a nonprofit corporation for research and education in the development, conservation, and use of natural resources and the improvement of the quality of the environment. It was established in 1952 with the cooperation of the Ford Foundation. Part of the work of Resources for the Future is carried out by its resident staff; part is supported by grants to universities and other nonprofit organizations. Unless otherwise stated, interpretations and conclusions in RFF publications are those of the authors; the organization takes responsibility for the selection of significant subjects for study, the competence of the researchers, and their freedom of inquiry.

Michael Nelson, a research associate with RFF at the time this book was written, is now program adviser in agriculture to the Mexican office of the Ford Foundation. The book was edited by Tadd Fisher. Maps and charts were drawn by Clare and Frank Ford, and the index was prepared by Helen Eisenhart.

RFF editors: Mark Reinsberg, Vera W. Dodds, Nora E. Roots, Tadd Fisher.

Copyright © 1973 by The Johns Hopkins University Press
All rights reserved
Manufactured in the United States of America

The Johns Hopkins University Press, Baltimore, Maryland 21218
The Johns Hopkins University Press Ltd., London

Library of Congress Catalog Card Number 72-12363
ISBN 0-8018-1488-X (cloth)

Library of Congress Cataloging in Publication data will be found on the last printed page of this book.

FOREWORD

The humid tropics of Latin America have long held a special fascination for a wide variety of men—explorers, statesmen, novelists, land speculators, and soldiers. Each has had his own vision of the meaning and promise of this vast region; none has doubted its importance. In recent decades attention has been fixed increasingly on the region's potential for economic development. Although sparsely populated, the humid tropics are endowed with enormous expanses of forest, ample water, rich mineral deposits, and, in many places, fertile land. Some public officials and private entrepreneurs, seeing virtually no limits to the region's potential, have envisioned development at a breathtaking pace and scale. Others, more cautious, have emphasized the enormous investments that would be required to harness the potential of the tropics and have worried that the scope of the effort would exceed the capacity of the countries involved to manage it.

Constructive consideration of the development potential of the humid tropics has been hampered by a lack of well-grounded technical and economic information. Consequently it has been difficult to distinguish imaginative flights of fancy from realistic analysis. Michael Nelson's study will help to make this distinction. Through detailed examination of twenty-four land development projects, he attempts to sort out the principal issues involved, to roughly assay their relative importance, to establish some ground rules for judging the success or failure of such projects, and to identify the main factors contributing to success or failure. Because of the immensity and diversity of the region his conclusions are necessarily tentative. Nevertheless we believe he has provided a body of information and a perspective on development issues in the humid tropics that will greatly enrich future discussion of this important subject.

Dr. Nelson's study is the result of a program of research undertaken jointly by the Instituto Latinamericano de Planificación Económica y Social (ILPES) and Resources for the Future. Other studies published under this program are *The Water Resources of Chile* by Nathaniel Wollman, *Natural Resource In-*

v

formation for Economic Development by Orris Herfindahl, and *Agricultural Development and Productivity: Lessons from the Chilean Experience* by Pierre Crosson. The Wollman and Herfindahl books have been published in Spanish by ILPES as *Los recursos hidráulicos de Chile* and *Los recursos naturales en el desarrollo económico.*

Raúl Prebisch, Director
Latin America Institute for
  Economic and Social Planning

Joseph L. Fisher, President
Resources for the Future

ACKNOWLEDGMENTS

This study, carried out over the period 1967–69, has involved travel throughout much of Latin America north of the Tropic of Capricorn and discussions with people in many different fields, including highway construction, forestry, colonization, and agricultural industries in the forest frontier regions and capital cities of the continent. I have learned much from those who have shared their knowledge with me, and I am indebted to Resources for the Future (RFF) and the Instituto Latinamericano de Planificación Económica y Social (ILPES) for providing the opportunity for me to undertake this inquiry.

The collection of data required about twelve months in the field. During that time I was wholly dependent on the generosity of agencies (public, private, and international) and individuals to provide ideas, access to data, and the opportunity to see new-land development projects. Ample time was made available for discussion and for helping me to search for appropriate materials, and in many cases transportation and staff were put at my disposal at considerable cost to the institutions concerned. Thus while I accept full responsibility for the opinions expressed in this volume—many of which are controversial and not widely shared—my analysis has been drawn from the experience of others. Born in New Zealand on a temperate island 9,000 miles from the Amazon jungles, I could hardly be said to be familiar with tropical land development, nor, considering the range and depth of knowledge to which I have been exposed, can I claim much originality of thought. Those who have sponsored and assisted my endeavor, however, are in no way culpable for the shortcomings of the study, nor is any implication intended that they are necessarily in agreement with the findings.

The research topic was suggested by Hans Landsberg of RFF, who in 1966 became concerned about apparent contradictions in the literature on humid tropical land development in Latin America. Throughout the study he has been a source of ideas and encouragement.

During the course of my research I was fortunate to be associated with the Inter-American Development Bank (IDB), and credit is due to numerous staff members, both in Washington, D.C., and in the field, with whom I worked for ten months. Thomas Carroll, Juan Casals, Jacques Kozub, Claudio Meira, Harold Jorgensen, Frederick Mattson, and Hector Morales all contributed to my thinking on the subject, particularly as it has been expressed in chapters 5 and 7.

I am especially indebted to Pierre Crosson of RFF for comments based on his careful review of the preliminary draft and to Paul Mandell of Stanford University for his thorough evaluation of a revised version. In addition I have received valuable ideas from Sterling Brubaker, Marion Clawson, Delbert Fitchett and Orris Herfindahl of RFF and from Michael Brewer, formerly of RFF and now president of the Population Reference Bureau. Jack Condliffe and Robert Spiegelman of the Stanford Research Institute also made a number of constructive comments on the original research proposal.

Estevam Strauss, Carlos Plaza, Francisco León, and Jesús González of ILPES and Janos Hrabovszky of the Food and Agriculture Organization (FAO) reviewed the manuscript and made detailed and helpful criticisms. A number of FAO specialists took time to discuss the problem and to suggest materials; among them were L. B. Kristjansen, Barry Nestel, and Rudi Dudal. In the formulation of the problem, field work, and analysis, Arthur Domike of FAO helped in terms of both discussions and data; his collaboration enabled me to obtain information on projects in Mexico, Costa Rica, Peru, and Bolivia that otherwise would have been unavailable. I am also grateful to Henry Ergas of the FAO-World Bank Programme for the opportunity to work with his staff on a paper dealing with tropical colonization lending policy. During this collaboration the incisive comments of Edward Quicke were of great value, and I also am indebted to Peter Brumby and John Hancock for sharing their experience with me.

Guillermo Gallo Mendoza of the FAO-IDB Programme carried out field work pertinent to this study, prepared material on seven of the Bolivian projects evaluated, and provided many original ideas. In the studies of the Papaloapan River basin in Mexico, Professor Carlos Inchaustegui of the Instituto Nacional Indigenista and Juan Ballesteros Porta of the Centro de Investigaciones Agrarias made valuable contributions.

Of the many people who generously gave their time for discussion and who accompanied me on field trips, special recognition must be given to Reynaldo Massi, president of the Sociedade de Melhoramentos e Colonização (Brazil); Harold Knowles of the FAO Amazon forestry project in Santarém, Brazil; Joseph Tosi of the Tropical Science Research Center in Costa Rica; Guiherme Mayer of the Colonizadora Noreste Matogrossense in Brazil; Walter Knowles of Le Tourneau del Perú; Hernán Zeballos of the Bolivian Instituto Nacional de Colonización; Franco Carrasco of the Papaloapan Commission in Mexico; Julio Chavez of the Instituto Ecuatoriano de Reforma Agraria y Colonización (Ecuador); Abram Hiebert of the Mennonite Social and Economic Committee (Paraguay); Atilio González of the Peruvian Coporación de

Financiamiento de la Reforma Agraria; and Rubens Rodriguez Lima of the Brazilian Instituto de Pesquisas e Experimentação Agropecuarias do Norte, in Belém.

Alden Gaete carried out the library research and preliminary calculations at ILPES in 1968. In the later stages of the work Carlos Sepúlveda was my research assistant, although his contribution went well beyond that normally associated with such a position. Finally I must place on record the excellent support provided by ILPES and RFF throughout the study.

June 1972   Michael Nelson

CONTENTS

LIST OF TABLES

LIST OF MAPS

LIST OF FIGURES

INTRODUCTION

Latin America today is similar to Canada in the early 1900s—a sleeping giant, basically underpopulated, whose potential rests on the exploitation of enormous land, forest, mineral, and water reserves. For five centuries the mystique associated with the untapped wealth of the Amazon basin has persisted, despite the lack of major development and despite pessimistic predictions about the hopeless plight of colonists practicing shifting agriculture and the dire consequences of wholesale forest destruction. Over sixty years ago it was said that the twentieth century belonged to Canada.[1] The same might have been said about the vast tropical regions of the Western Hemisphere, and there are those who would say it even now in the eighth decade of the century.

In some quarters it is an article of faith that the great forested heartland of South America can and must be utilized if Latin America is to realize its development goals. This belief rests squarely on the premise that the mere existence of unused forest and land resources is sufficient reason to warrant the investment of capital and labor in their exploitation. Such an approach runs counter to the widely held economic doctrine that natural resource endowment is far less vital to development than the rate of sociotechnical change that extends resources through substitution, alters the location of economic activity, and provides a climate for the adoption of new techniques or the application of existing ones.[2]

This study is an examination of the economic basis underlying investment and policy for the development of new lands for agriculture and forestry in Latin America. The area under consideration is limited to the humid tropical lowlands and uplands and the semiarid Chaco[3]—approximately 12 million

[1] Remark attributed to Sir Wilfrid Laurier, Premier of Canada from 1896 to 1911, who was responsible for a vigorous campaign to attract settlers and open up the Canadian West.

[2] See Harold J. Barnett and Chandler Morse, *Scarcity and Growth: The Economics of Natural Resource Availability* (Johns Hopkins Press for Resources for the Future, 1963).

[3] In the balance of the text mention of the humid tropics always includes the Chaco, a region that consists of parts of Argentina, Bolivia, and Paraguay.

1

square kilometers (km), or 60 percent of Latin America. (See map 1.) Within this region an area approaching 0.7 million square km is under some form of permanent or shifting agricultural exploitation. Most of this agricultural enterprise is found within 100 km of the coast; in south central Brazil, it emanates from the core region of São Paulo and Rio de Janeiro within a radius of 500 km. Additionally, about 1 million square km of native pastures are used for cattle.

Before discussing the study further it is important for the reader to have an understanding of the following terms as they are used in this book:

1. *Humid tropics.* These are lands lying principally between the Tropic of Capricorn and the Tropic of Cancer. Most are below 500 meters in elevation, have a mean temperature in the coldest month of over 21° C and an annual rainfall in excess of 1,000 millimeters, and are forested in the virgin state except for savanna (25 percent of the area), which is generally subject to extended annual flooding. The *cerrado*—about 15 percent of the area—is transitional between forest and savanna.

2. *Land resources.* In addition to land itself these include the associated forest, wildlife, and water resources that govern alternative uses and methods of development.

3. *New lands.* The logical interpretation to be expected is that "new" denotes a wholly unexploited resource. In fact practically all lands are exploited to some extent—for hunting, gathering, or twenty-five-year forest-fallow where only one hectare in twenty-five would be in production at any given time. The critical factor is the degree of exploitation as measured by the amount of labor and capital associated with the land in the production process. If this degree is to be quantified, one must establish the production functions for the various land classes. The preparation of these functions requires specification of the physical input-output relationships, the level of management, and the prices of the inputs and outputs. Under these specifications the problem of new-land development becomes indistinguishable from that of the deepening of capital and the intensification of labor use in the exploitation of land already considered developed. In order to make the distinction, new land is defined in terms of the principal development procedures that are expected to result in a major transference of population and a quantum jump in production. As a general rule the major identifying procedure is forest clearing. By definition, increased production in frontier areas must be attributable almost entirely to expansion of the area in cultivation.

4. *Development procedures.* These procedures include public and private investments in infrastructure, forest clearing, land settlement, hydraulic works for flood control or drainage, and wood and agricultural processing industries in forest frontier regions. Such capital projects may also be supported by public measures and production or social services designed to accelerate the flow of capital and population.

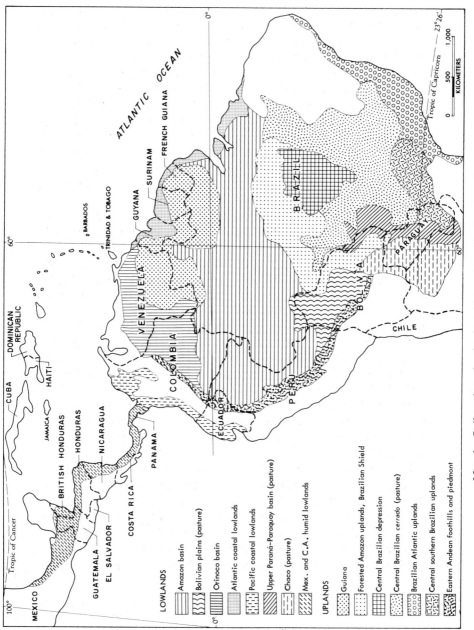

LOWLANDS

▤ Amazon basin

▨ Bolivian plains (pasture)

▥ Orinoco basin

▦ Atlantic coastal lowlands

▨ Pacific coastal lowlands

▧ Upper Paraná–Paraguay basin (pasture)

▤ Chaco (pasture)

▨ Mex. and C.A. humid lowlands

UPLANDS

⬚ Guiana

⬚ Forested Amazon uplands, Brazilian Shield

▦ Central Brazilian depression

▤ Central Brazilian cerrado (pasture)

▦ Brazilian Atlantic uplands

▨ Central southern Brazilian uplands

▨ Eastern Andean foothills and piedmont

Map 1. Soil regions in the humid tropics of Latin America.

The transformation of agriculture, although fraught with problems, is seen as a prerequisite to development throughout Latin America. Difficult questions related to the agrarian structure must be resolved, however, before agriculture can make its full contribution. Improvements in public administration are needed to correct many shortcomings. For example, means must be found to enable the processing of land title registrations and to protect property rights. Inadequate tax systems and ineffective enforcement of tax laws, which result in inefficient production or failure to redistribute land and income, must be corrected. Planning and the allocation of state funds to agriculture for research, extension, credit, education, and infrastructure in rural areas must be made more efficient; and state regulation of the market must become more effective in order to prevent monopoly, misallocation of resources through inept control of product and input prices, and excessive spoilage of agricultural products.

Within the agricultural sector, policy makers must allocate their resources for the improvement of the standard of living in rural areas; for the application of technology and management to increase efficiency on lands already in production; for hydraulic works for irrigation, drainage, and flood control; and for the development of new lands. There are sharp differences of opinion about these allocations. Arthur Lewis expressed the view that in most countries with unexploited land "increases in agricultural output come more easily from larger acreage than from higher productivity."[4] In contrast Wright and Bennema believe that "it is clear that the greatest increases in agricultural production may be expected from more intensive use of humid temperate zone soils rather than new agricultural endeavor on the soils of the humid tropics."[5] Pleading for less emphasis on production and more attention to income distribution, Schatan and Barraclough have stressed that "new technology will almost inevitably lead to a rise in the average wage on modernizing farms while labor income will remain stagnant or decline in traditional agriculture."[6]

No attempt is made in this study to explicitly confront the problem of allocation posed in the statements above. The purpose of the study is to increase the understanding of the role that development of new lands in the humid tropics plays in economic development. It is hoped that this information, combined with data on how to increase efficiency on lands already exploited, the control and distribution of water, and the response to investment in education of the rural population, will provide an improved basis for

[4]W. A. Lewis, *Development Planning* (London: George Allen and Unwin, 1966), p. 48.

[5]A. C. S. Wright and J. Bennema, *The Soil Resources of Latin America*, FAO/UNESCO Project, World Soil Resources Report no. 18 (Rome: FAO, 1965), p. 115.

[6]Jacobo Schatan and Solon Barraclough, "Technological Policy and Agricultural Development" (FAO Project, Santiago, Chile, May 1970, mimeo.).

government planning of development objectives in the tropical countries of Latin America.

It is beyond dispute that new-land development on the plains and valleys of the gulf coast of Mexico; the Caribbean coast of Central America, Colombia, and Venezuela; and the Guayas River basin of Ecuador, has had significant impact on agricultural output over the past thirty to forty years. The same is true of subtropical areas in south central Brazil and southern Paraguay and at Santa Cruz in Bolivia. Consolidation in these areas undoubtedly will have high priority in the future, and the result will be the incorporation of significant new areas, whether by forest clearing or reduced bush-fallow. Current debate, however, centers on the viability of new-land development in other areas of Latin America and the potential consequences of attempting further expansion toward interior tropical forest regions or of converting native pasture to crops. Expansion may take the form of (1) a progressive pushing out of the frontier, such as the northern movement in Mato Grosso, Goiás, and Minas Gerais in Brazil; the eastern extension toward the lowland areas from the Andean foothills and piedmont, or the inland penetration from some coastal areas in Mexico, Central America, and Venezuela and Amapá and Pará in Brazil; or (2) major thrusts aimed at massive settlement of virgin territory and dependent on ambitious highway projects such as the Transamazónico, Carretera Marginal de la Selva, Cuiabá-Acre, or Cuiabá-Santarém.[7]

It is evident that experience in the development of new lands in the humid tropics has been very mixed. There is no clear understanding of why some areas seem to have prospered and others have stagnated. Only in Brazil has any attempt been made to assess how new land in the humid tropics contributes to the overall development process. There is no record of what has happened as a result of previous land development investments and policies nor of their economic, social, and political objectives and the extent to which these objectives have been achieved. We have only fragmented knowledge about the requirements for capital, managerial talent, and foreign exchange and about how the agrarian structure affects the results of investments.

What is the influence of noneconomically determined motivation? How much time will elapse before investments pay off, and who will be the beneficiaries? Who should pay? What are the forward and backward linkages? Does scale of operations influence economic performance? How much direct and indirect employment will result, and where? In what ways do public administration and the provision of government services affect the results? How important are mechanization and new technology? And how serious is erosion?

Answers to such questions should contribute to more rational policy formulation. The exercise of deliberate public policy in the settlement of new

[7] See map 11.

land implies that social and economic goals will be achieved more readily if governments apply systematic controls and influence resource allocation rather than allow unrestrained operation of the free market. In this study an attempt is made to identify the goals and to determine the degree to which the state, by providing capital and enterprise, may intervene effectively in the process of expanding the agricultural land frontier. A primary focus is on criteria with respect to the achievement of economic or social goals, trade-offs between large-scale operations and income distribution or employment, who receives benefits and who bears costs, the choice of areas and the timing of intervention, and project design. These aspects are evaluated by means of a survey of twenty-four development projects, all of which involve the settlement of small farmers. No attempt is made to evaluate the rather unusual Brazilian model, where large tracts are developed as a single unit by experienced and well-capitalized entrepreneurs, nor is consideration given to the question of regional master planning of land use.

The specific objectives of this study are:

1. To trace the sequence of events, cash flows, and economic performance of selected cases of land development in the humid tropics and to present the different institutional and environmental conditions characterizing each case and the range of activities that in varying degrees are susceptible to public policy.

2. To identify the principal factors that have influenced the results.

3. To indicate the various bases for strategy formulation in new-land development under given national or regional policies for expansion of the agricultural frontier in the humid tropics.

4. To outline the data requirements and to suggest appraisal techniques for the provision of an economic basis for government planning, investment decisions, and policy related to land development in these regions.

5. To define the kind of documentation of future land development projects needed to assure systematic analysis and to provide useful indicators of needed change in procedures and policy. It must be emphasized that the study of a few cases of land development can shed light only on some of the principal issues when the area involved is as large and physically heterogeneous as the humid tropics of Latin America and where development is governed by diverse political, institutional, social, and economic factors.

In order to achieve a degree of comparability between countries and between investments over time, prices throughout the study have been adjusted to 1967–68 U.S. dollars, using International Monetary Fund indexes of exchange and inflation.[8] While this procedure has obvious shortcomings for

[8] IMF, *International Finance Statistics*, vol. 7, no. 12 (December 1954); vol. 14, no. 12 (December 1961); and vol. 22, no. 12 (December 1969).

estimating real consumption, it was deemed the most appropriate way of handling the situation.

The first three chapters of the study deal with the current theory and practice of humid tropical land development in Latin America. An evaluation of projects is presented in the following five chapters and is used to derive implications for both investment policy and project design in chapter 9.

THE ROLE OF
TROPICAL LANDS
IN DEVELOPMENT
IN LATIN AMERICA

In order to place the humid tropical land reserves of Latin America in per-spective with regard to their potential role in overall development of the region, it is necessary to have an idea of the productive potential of the resources and of the general development policies in recent decades, the problems in their implementation, and the relative importance they assign to tropical lands. These matters will be taken up in this chapter, as well as the sociopolitical and institutional factors that guide development policy in the agricultural sectors of the tropical countries. In addition the ways in which the agricultural sector affects economic development and employment in these countries will be examined.

Land Capability for Agriculture

The 12 million square kilometers (km) of the area under consideration—the humid tropical lowlands and uplands and the semiarid Chaco—have been classified into fifteen soil regions, which are shown in map 1 and further described in table 1.[1] Soil surveys at various levels of precision have been carried out for about 8 percent of the humid tropics, and exploratory studies have been made for an additional 25 percent. On the basis of this material and miscellaneous observations, the Food and Agricultural Organiza-tion (FAO) has estimated the land capability in the humid tropics of Latin America (see table 2). No data are available on the area that is currently being exploited, nor is there any information on the extent to which the present use is incompatible with the various types of soils.

[1] For a description of the physical characteristics of land and forest resources, see K. J. Beek, *Soil Map of South America 1:5,000,000*, FAO/UNESCO Project, World Soil Resources Report no. 34 (Rome: FAO, November 1968); A. C. S. Wright and J. Bennema, *The Soil Resources of Latin America*, FAO/UNESCO Project, World Soil Resources Report no. 18 (Rome: FAO, 1965); and L. R. Holdridge, *Life Zone Ecology* (San Jose, Costa Rica: Tropical Science Center, 1967).

For six of the principal tropical countries of South America[2] it has been estimated that there are about 3.4 million square km of unused arable land (virtually all in the humid tropics), which is five times the exploited area in these countries.[3] Indications are that as much as 50 percent of this potential cropland may be in native pasture. Thus if FAO criteria are used to give a global estimate of unused land in the humid tropics of Latin America, it would appear that an additional 3-4 million square km may be available for cultivation and 4-5 million square km for the development of pastures.

FAO's *Indicative World Plan*[4] represents the first systematic attempt to locate the potential source of the increased agricultural and forest production needed to meet projected demand. Estimates for new-land development during the period 1962-85 for the seven principal tropical countries of South America are shown in table 3. Total investment is projected at $3.26 billion over the twenty-three-year period to clear about 39 million hectares (ha) of forest—32 million ha for pasture and 7 million ha for crops—and to convert 7 million ha of pasture into cropland.[5]

Two conclusions may be drawn from these statistics and projections.[6] First, it is probable that only about 2 percent of the vast area covered by the humid tropics is currently being exploited for crops and that 10 percent is in pasture (see table 4), although it appears that as much as 80 percent may be considered suitable for agricultural development. FAO projections call for the exploitation of 6 percent of the estimated arable area and about 30 percent of the pasture potential by 1985. Second, although the relative proportion of land to be developed is small, the absolute areas and the investments involved are enormous. The prospect of clearing jungle at a rate of about 2 million ha per year presents formidable problems in regard to area selection, dispersion in relation to infrastructure, and the fate of forest resources.

Land Capability for Forestry

The extent of the forest resources in the humid tropics of Latin America is shown in map 2. About 70 percent of the region is classified as forest—8.5-9 million square km—of which over 95 percent is broadleaved seasonal and equatorial rain forest (see table 5). Since only about 5 percent of this area has

---

[2] Bolivia, Brazil, Colombia, Ecuador, Peru, and Venezuela. These countries account for 86 percent of the humid tropical lands in Latin America.

[3] FAO, *Indicative World Plan for Agricultural Development to 1975 and 1985, South America*, vol. 1 (Rome, 1968), p. 81.

[4] Ibid.

[5] FAO, *Indicative World Plan*, vol. 2, p. 50.

[6] For the purpose of making global estimates, land classes in tropical Central America and Mexico have been assumed to be the same as those in South America. Since these areas make up only 4 percent of the Latin American humid tropics, this assumption is unlikely to affect the overall figures significantly.

Table 1. Broad Soil Regions of the Humid Tropics of Latin America

(*million hectares*)

Soil region[a]	Mexico	Central America	Venezuela	Colombia	Ecuador	Peru	Bolivia	Brazil	Guianas	Paraguay	Argentina	Total
Lowlands												
Amazon basin	–	–	–	22.0	4.0	44.0	2.0	224.0	–	–	–	296.0
Bolivian plains	–	–	–	–	–	4.0	33.0	4.0	–	–	–	41.0
Orinoco basin	–	–	34.0	40.0	–	–	–	–	–	–	–	74.0
Atlantic coastal lowlands, northern South America	–	–	–	–	–	–	–	14.0	15.0	–	–	29.0
Pacific coastal lowlands, northern South America	–	–	–	18.0	7.0	–	–	–	–	–	–	25.0
Upper Paraná–Paraguay basin	–	–	–	–	–	–	6.0	18.0	–	16.0	6.0	46.0
Chaco	–	–	–	–	–	–	7.0	–	–	10.0	25.0	42.0
Mexican and Central American humid lowlands	18.0	27.0	–	–	–	–	–	–	–	–	–	45.0
Total lowlands	18.0	27.0	34.0	80.0	11.0	48.0	48.0	260.0	15.0	26.0	31.0	598.0

Uplands

Guiana uplands	–	32.0	–	–	–	–	46.0	29.0	–	–	107.0
Forested Amazon uplands of the Brazilian Shield	–	–	–	–	–	16.0	78.0	–	2.0	–	96.0
Central Brazilian depression	–	–	–	–	–	–	48.0	–	–	–	48.0
Central Brazilian *cerrado* uplands	–	–	–	–	–	–	169.0	–	2.0	–	171.0
Brazilian Atlantic uplands	–	–	–	–	–	–	55.0	–	–	–	55.0
Central southern Brazilian uplands	–	–	–	–	–	–	30.0	–	9.0	–	39.0
Eastern Andean foothills and piedmont	–	–	6.0	5.0	22.0	6.0	–	–	–	–	39.0
Total uplands	–	32.0	6.0	5.0	22.0	22.0	426.0	29.0	13.0	–	555.0
Total humid tropics	18.0	27.0	86.0	16.0	70.0	70.0	686.0	44.0	39.0	31.0	1,153.0

Note: Dashes indicate "not applicable."

[a]See map 1.

Sources: A. C. S. Wright and J. Bennema, *The Soil Resources of Latin America*, FAO/UNESCO Project, World Soil Resources Report no. 18 (Rome: FAO, 1965); and K. J. Beek, *Soil Map of South America 1:5,000,000*, FAO/UNESCO Project, World Soil Resources Report no. 34 (Rome: FAO, November 1968).

Table 2. Inventory of the Humid Tropical Land Resources of Latin America, by Country

(million hectares)

Country	Soil areas according to suitability								
	Cropping						Pasture or plantations[f]	Forestry or reserve	Total
	Alluvial[a]	Hydromorphic[b]	Good upland[c]	Marginal-low fertility[d]	Marginal-shallow or steep[e]	Total			
Mexico	—	—	—	—	—	←—— 6.7 ——→	11.4	—	18.1
Central America	—	—	—	—	—	←—— 2.3 ——→	5.2	18.5	26.0
South America									
Colombia	3.6	6.3	1.5	20.2	0.4	32.0	69.4		101.4
Ecuador	0.1	0.6	0.4	4.8	0.1	6.0	15.3		21.3
Peru	0.1	2.7	1.6	17.2	0.4	22.0	55.1		77.1
Bolivia	0.7	10.8	0.6	12.3	2.2	26.6	52.2		78.8
Argentina	2.7	2.3	3.1	5.7	1.7	15.5	15.2	6.5	37.2
Paraguay	0.7	2.8	4.2	7.1	0.7	15.5	14.8	10.4	40.7
Brazil	3.2	25.4	21.8	174.4	18.5	243.3	333.3	170.1	746.7
Venezuela	0.2	5.7	2.3	17.1	5.0	30.3	6.1	18.7	55.1
Total South America	11.3	56.6	35.5	258.8	29.0	391.2	←—— 767.1 ——→		1,158.3

Sources: A. C. S. Wright and J. Bennema, *The Soil Resources of Latin America*, FAO/UNESCO Project, World Soil Resources Report no. 18 (Rome: FAO, 1965); and K. J. Beek, *Soil Map of South America 1:5,000,000*, FAO/UNESCO Project, World Soil Resources Report no. 34 (Rome: FAO, November 1968).

Note: Dashes indicate "not available."

[a] Soils developed from recent deposits and located in flood-plains or deltas. Characteristics of the soils depend on their parent material.

[b] These soils are found on flat or depressed landscapes with little or no runoff where drainage presents a problem.

[c] These soils occur on undulating or level topography, are well drained, are not susceptible to serious erosion, and have medium-high natural fertility.

[d] These soils are of the upland type but with very low natural fertility. With appropriate crops and fertilizer, reasonable yields may be expected.

[e] These soils pose special problems for agricultural use due to shallowness or slope, heavy texture or sandiness. They occur primarily in highland areas and are susceptible to severe erosion.

[f] These soils are unsuited to normal crop production because of major limiting factors such as steep topography, poor drainage, low fertility, sandiness, heavy texture, and rock outcrops or stones.

Table 3. New-Land Development and Investments in Seven Tropical South American Countries, Projected for the Period 1962–1985

Country	Development of new lands							Total investment[c]
	Cropland (dry and irrigated)[a]					Pasture from forest	Total forest clearing	
	Irrigated	Dry land	From pasture[b]	From forest	Total			
	(-- million hectares --)							($ million)
Colombia	0.3	1.7	1.0	1.0	2.0[d]	6.6	7.6	440
Ecuador	0.1	0.6	0.35	0.35	0.7	0.85	1.2	93
Peru	0.3[e]	0.8	0.4	0.4	0.8	0.7	1.1	70
Bolivia	0.3	0	0.15	0.15	0.3[d]	4.15	4.3	120
Paraguay	0	0.4	0.2	0.2	0.4	3.7	3.9	147
Brazil	0.4	9.4	4.9	4.9	9.8	12.2	17.1	2,120
Venezuela	0.3	0.1	0.2	0.2	0.4[d]	3.8	4.0	270
Total	1.7	13.0	7.2	7.2	14.4	31.7	39.2[f]	3,260

Source: FAO, Indicative World Plan for Agricultural Development to 1975 and 1985, South America, vol. 1 (Rome, 1968).

[a] Irrigated land derived 50 percent from pasture and 50 percent from dryland crop area.

[b] Assumption that 50 percent of new cropland will be derived from existing pasture.

[c] Investment in development of new lands not associated with irrigation, drainage, or flood control, at 1962 prices.

[d] Total area in nonirrigated crops in Colombia is projected to increase by 1.7 million ha. The additional 0.3 million compensate for projected irrigation of currently nonirrigated pasture and croplands. Increases of 0.3 million ha are made for both Bolivia and Venezuela in similar compensation.

[e] Irrigated land derived from desert.

[f] Annual rate of forest clearing would be 1.75 million ha.

Table 4.   Approximate Area of Humid Tropical Lands in Latin America
in Crops and Pasture

(million hectares)

Country	Crops[a]	Pasture[b]	Total[c]
Mexico[d]	4.1	5.5	9.6
Central America[e]	0.4	0.8	1.2
Colombia[f]	1.6	8.5	10.1
Ecuador[g]	0.9	0.8	1.7
Peru[h]	0.3	0.4	0.7
Bolivia[i]	0.3	4.7	5.0
Argentina[j]	0.7	6.6	7.3
Paraguay[k]	0.2	0.8	1.0
Brazil[l]	17.2	82.2	99.4
Venezuela[m]	0.5	13.2	13.7
Total	26.2	123.4	149.6

Note: The most recent data available from individual countries all fall within the 1961–68 period, except in the case of Paraguay (1956).

[a]No data are available on the area cropped twice or on crops undersown. It is assumed that figures refer to cultivated area rather than to area in crops.

[b]No distinction is made between native and improved pasture, nor do the statistics indicate whether any unexploited savannas are included.

[c]Bush-fallow is so vaguely defined that it is not normally reported in national censuses, and the area is excluded in the total here.

[d]Secretaría de Industria y Comercio, Dirección General de Estadística, México, *Anuario estadístico compendiado 1964* (1965). Includes the states of Veracruz, Tabasco, Campeche, and Chiapas.

[e]SIECA, unpublished data, March 1965.

[f]Departamento Administrativo Nacional de Estadística República de Colombia, *Encuesta agrícola nacional 1966* (1968). No data are available on the states of Chocó, Guapira, Aranca, Vichada, Vaupés, Caquetá, Putumayo, and Amazonas.

[g]Unpublished material from the Ministerio de Agricultura, Junta de Planificación, 1969. Includes the Pacific coastal lowlands and Amazon basin.

[h]Ministerio de Agricultura y Universidad Agraria, *Estadísticas agrarias Perú 1965*, Resumen Nacional (Lima, 1966), p. 34.

[i]República de Bolivia, Ministerio de Hacienda, Dirección Nacional de Estadística, *Censo agropecuario 1950* (La Paz, March 1956); and unpublished data of the Ministerio de Planificación, 1970. Includes the provinces of Pando, Beni, Santa Cruz, and part of La Paz and Cochabamba.

[j]CIDA, *Land Tenure Conditions and Socio-Economic Development of the Agricultural Sector, Argentina* (Washington: Pan American Union, OAS, 1965). Includes only the northeast region.

[k]Dirección Nacional de Estadística y Censo, *Censo agropecuario del Paraguay (1956)* (Asunción, 1960), p. 202.

[l]IBGE, *Anuario estadístico de Brasil 1968* (Rio de Janeiro, 1968), p. 139. Excludes the northeast and the states of Paraná, Santa Catarina, and Río Grande do Sul.

[m]Ministerio de Fomento, Dirección General de Estadística y Censos Nacionales, *Compendio estadístico de Venezuela*, data of the III Censo Agropecuario 1961 (Caracas, 1968), p. 188. Includes states of Apure, Barinas, Portuguesa, Cojedes, Guárico, Anzoátegui, Monagas, Bolívar, Territorio Delta Amacuro, and Territorio de Amazonas.

Map 2. Vegetation regions in the humid tropics of Latin America.

Table 5. Forest Resources of the Humid Tropics of Latin America

(million hectares)

Country	Tropical wet evergreen forest	Seasonal tropical forest	Tropical coastal swamp forest	Subtropical araucaria forest	Caribbean pine forest	Semi-arid formations	Tropical savanna	Total
Mexico	13.3	–	–	–	–	–	3.7	17.0
Central America	20.2	–	–	–	5.8	–	–	26.0
Colombia	47.0	13.6	–	–	–	–	27.2	87.8
Ecuador	8.2	–	–	–	–	–	–	8.2
Peru	44.1	1.0	–	–	–	–	2.4	47.5
Bolivia	0.5	36.6	–	–	–	4.8	25.9	67.8
Argentina	–	6.2	–	–	–	31.0	–	37.2
Paraguay	–	7.8	–	–	–	23.2	2.4	33.4
Brazil	319.2	161.5	11.2	22.5	–	18.7	210.7	743.8
Venezuela	28.2	21.4	7.3	–	–	–	27.2	84.1
Guianas	31.2	–	6.8	–	–	–	6.8	44.8
Total	511.9	248.1	25.3	22.5	5.8	77.7	306.3	1,197.6[a]

Sources: K. J. Beek, Soil Map of South America 1:5,000,000, FAO/UNESCO Project, World Soil Resources Report no. 34 (Rome: FAO, 1965); C. V. Plath, Uso potencial de la tierra, informe a los gobiernos de: Costa Rica, El Salvador, Guatemala, Honduras, Nicaragua, Panama, FAO Report no. AT 2234 (Rome: FAO, 1966), p. 21; and Russell Ewing, ed., Six Faces of Mexico (University of Arizona Press, 1966).

Note: Dashes indicate "not applicable."

[a]Difference of 40,000 square km (0.03 percent) between this total and that in table 2 is due to slight variations in areas classified according to soils and those classified according to vegetation.

been covered by forest inventories, estimates of capability must necessarily be rather general.

Studies of the equatorial forests in Brazil[7] indicate that there are more than 700 species, and that on any one hectare there are approximately 1,000 trees over 5 centimeters (cm) in diameter at breast height (DBH), representing about 100 species on the average. The standing volume of all trees over 25 cm DBH is estimated to be in excess of 200 cubic meters per hectare. Of the 1,000 trees per hectare, about 40 would qualify as commercial size (more than 45 cm DBH), with a standing volume of 150 cubic meters;[8] 10 of these would be species that may be classified as commercially acceptable in current markets, with a standing volume of about 45 cubic meters. Estimates of the commercial volume technically available range between 15 and 60 cubic meters per hectare.[9] However, since 60-70 percent of the tropical forest area is inaccessible at the present time and in much of what is accessible products are still subject to laborious and expensive transport to markets over high mountain passes or down tortuous rivers, these figures by no means represent the marketable volume. The forest is considered to be in "balanced climax"; that is, the species composition is stable and annual growth equals annual losses. The annual increment in standing volume is estimated at 3-10 cubic meters per hectare, which, in effect, is the amount available for extraction without depletion of the resource if harvesting is organized to eliminate losses. With the introduction of management programs to change the species composition, the volume may approach 20-25 cubic meters per hectare on a sustained-yield basis.

If the unit figures above are used as general indicators, the standing volume of wood in trees of commercial size would be about 120 billion cubic meters, with an annual increment of about 5 billion cubic meters—about three times the projected world consumption in 1975.[10] Assuming a land-clearing rate of 1.75 million ha[11] annually over the period 1962-85, the potential volume of wood available from commercial-sized trees would be about 250 million cubic meters per year, over three times the projected level of Latin American consumption (of temperate and tropical woods) in 1975, or the equivalent of total world import demand in that year.[12] This calculation in no way is

[7] See O. H. Knowles, *Investment and Business Opportunities in the Forest Industrial Development of the Brazilian Amazon, 1968*, FAO, Forestry and Forest Industries Division (Rome, March 1969).

[8] The estimate for all South American forests is 105 cubic meters of growing stock volume per hectare. See FAO, *Indicative World Plan* .

[9] Allan Randal, "Forest Surveys for Economic Development," in *Physical Resource Investigations for Economic Development* (Washington: OAS, 1969), p. 185.

[10] FAO, *La madera: tendencias y perspectivas mundiales*, Estudio Básico no. 16 (Rome, 1967), pp. 33-34.

[11] See table 3.

[12] FAO, *La madera*, pp. 2-3.

meant to imply that these resources should or could be utilized; it merely indicates the present high level of forest destruction and nonutilization.

Realization of the forestry potential of the region is seriously handicapped by the heterogeneous nature of most tropical forests, the low volume of marketable trees per unit area, technical difficulties in milling or processing a wide range of hardwoods for lumber and particle board, costly processes for pulp and paper manufacture from mixed tropical hardwoods, and the lack of information on the physical properties of many species. The most valuable tropical forests are the pine areas in southern Brazil, southeastern Paraguay, northern Honduras, and northeastern Nicaragua, which account for 1 percent of the total forested area.[13] In fact FAO recommends that Brazil, a country with 260 million ha of unexploited equatorial rain forest, should plant 400,000 ha to conifers by 1985.[14]

Aside from wood and its derivatives, the forest resources can also be used for the conservation of wildlife and for recreation and tourism. In addition the maintenance of forest cover, either undisturbed or through sustained-yield management, could contribute to watershed protection or even to the maintenance of the climatic regime.

Development Policies

Along with most other developing areas, Latin America is generally considered to have had an unsatisfactory record of economic and social progress over the past two or three decades.[15] Many reasons are given, including high rates of population growth, low rates of capital formation and economic growth, unemployment, mushrooming urban slums, social inequities, structural deficiencies, civil disorders, political instability, deteriorating terms of trade, a widening gap in productivity and living standards between the region and the developed nations, and the unfavorable consequences of dependency on such nations.

Historically, natural resources have played a preeminent role in development in Latin America, leading to urban and infrastructure investment oriented to international trade and not necessarily adapted to industrialization and mobility of the factors of production within the continent. A further consequence of the natural resource orientation has been a high level of instability in the economy stemming from the volatile commodity prices on the world market and the relative importance of the basic export activities

[13] FAO, *World Forest Inventory, 1963* (Rome, 1963), pp. 62–63.

[14] FAO, *Indicative World Plan*, vol. 1, p. 206.

[15] See Raúl Prebisch, *Transformación y desarrollo, la gran tarea de América Latina*, ILPES-BID (Santiago, Chile, 1970), chaps. 1 and 4; Osvaldo Sunkel and Pedro Paz, *El subdesarrollo latinoamericano y la teoría del desarrollo* (Mexico, D.F.: Siglo XXI Editores, S.A., 1970), pp. 366–80; and Economic Commission for Latin America, *Economic Survey of Latin America* (Santiago, Chile), annual issues from 1951 to 1969.

as a source of public revenues.[16] In the case of commodities from tropical lands, notoriously unstable markets have ruled for coffee, rubber, sugar, and cocoa.

Since the depression of the 1930s various policies have been formulated to bring about the "take-off." Industrialization was planned with emphasis on import substitution. Then the Alliance for Progress called for massive foreign assistance between 1961 and 1970 to support basic structural reforms in land tenure, taxation, and public administration. Finally regional and subregional integration were designed to achieve factor mobility, specialization, and economies of scale.[17]

A number of development policies have been proposed over the past ten years that direct attention to the unused tropical land resources. One traditional approach is that summarized by John Karlik, which, in principle, takes the Malthusian thesis as the point of departure. Major emphasis is placed on birth control, agricultural research, and "an integrated transportation system throughout the heart of South America."[18] The provision of an adequate diet is seen as an important prerequisite of development.[19] The approach is oriented to liberal tariff policies in order to reap the benefits of trade through international specialization and operation of the principle of comparative advantage, while embracing all the reform objectives proposed by the Alliance for Progress.

This policy contains the essential elements of what may be regarded as the "official" prescription put forward by the developed countries of the West. As a result of an analysis undertaken by the Comisión Económica para América Latina (CEPAL) in the 1950s, a major challenge to this thesis came from Raúl Prebisch. In his celebrated article in 1961[20] Prebisch stated that prevailing trade conditions have a detrimental effect on the economic development of Latin America because of the developed nations' monopoly of both goods and factor markets.[21] His position has since been elaborated into

[16] Joseph Grunwald and Philip Musgrove, *Natural Resources in Latin American Development* (Johns Hopkins Press, 1970), pp. 25–42.

[17] Victor L. Urquidi, *Viabilidad Económica de América Latina* (Mexico, D.F.: Fondo de Cultura Económica, 1962), pp. 125–36.

[18] John Karlik, *The Long-Range Potential of Latin America: A Year 2000 Ideology* (Hudson Institute, November 1967), pp. 1–5, 60–67.

[19] In the specific case of tropical South America, however, only in Bolivia and Ecuador (7 percent of the population) were supplies less than 95 percent of requirements for both calories and protein on an overall national basis. Such figures obviously conceal distribution deficiencies. See FAO, *Indicative World Plan*, p. 48.

[20] Raúl Prebisch, "El desarrollo económico de la América Latina y algunos de sus principales problemas," *Boletín Económico para América Latina* (CEPAL), vol. 7, no. 1 (February 1961), pp. 1–24.

[21] The Prebisch thesis is not universally accepted. See C. P. Kindleberger, "Terms of Trade for Primary Products," in Marion Clawson, ed., *Natural Resources and International Development* (Johns Hopkins Press for Resources for the Future, 1964),

a theory of underdevelopment characterized by external dependency.[22] This dependency can be technological, economic, political, or cultural. It may manifest itself in a variety of ways—heavy reliance on foreign trade; the concentration of export items or sources of imports; prejudicial trade agreements; the volume and conditions of external debts; foreign ownership of production factors (capital goods and land) and the orientation of such production toward export or domestic markets; the introduction of unsuitable technology; and the structure of the foreign ownership, i.e., single plant organization or multiplant, multiproduct, multinational holding companies.

The focus on the causes of underdevelopment has led to a demand for policies to be reformulated to reduce the dependence of the region on foreign capital, technology, and markets and to emphasize the creation of new poles of development in the interior. These poles would be based on the generation of capital through the use of the vast underemployed labor force and the unexploited land, forest, water, and mineral resources along the Caribbean coast of Mexico and Central America and the interior basins of the Amazon, Orinoco, and Paraná rivers in South America. This theory rests on the following premises:

1. The limited financial resources available will yield a lower capital-output ratio in the interior than elsewhere because of the existence of virgin natural resources.
2. The exploitation of these resources (particularly land) will occupy the unemployed labor force with a minimum cash requirement; an important consideration where opportunities for providing employment in existing urban centers are not available in sufficient measure.
3. The autonomous creation of capital from labor and natural resources and the formation of industrial complexes will generate the much-needed internal demand to reduce the instability of a dependent externally oriented economy.
4. Unless the program is undertaken on an integrated basis aimed primarily at industrialization, it will probably fail since the extraction of raw materials (tropical agricultural and forestry products, or minerals) will be accompanied by the traditional problems—high transport costs,

---

pp. 341–49, and Harry G. Johnson, *Economic Policies toward Less Developed Countries* (Brookings Institution, 1967), pp. 249–50.

[22] For a discussion of the thesis of external dependency, see Celso Furtado, *Subdesarrollo y estancamiento en América Latina* (Buenos Aires: Editorial Universitaria de Buenos Aires, 1966), pp. 28–57; Osvaldo Sunkel, "Política nacional de desarrollo y dependencia externa," *Estudios internacionales* (Santiago), vol. 1, no. 1 (May 1967); Andre Gunder Frank, *Capitalism and Underdevelopment in Latin America* (New York: Monthly Review Press, January 1967), pp. 98–120 and 162–74; and Arturo Israel, "Teoría del subdesarrollo y dependencia externa" (Instituto de Economía, Universidad de Chile, January 1969, mimeo.).

unstable and competitive world markets, and the extension of subsistence agriculture.

5. The need is for the creation of a wholly new development pole that has a greater capacity to grow and to generate satellite activities than large old urban centers that reflect diseconomies of scale requiring enormous expenditures in renewal. At the same time it will stimulate a more creative and dynamic mentality that would foster capital accumulation and technological advance.[23]

The proposal carries enormous popular appeal since it suggests the possibility of creating another American "Midwest." Like the other schemes, however, it is marred by impracticalities and a number of imponderables. What would be the financial and real resource requirements of new-land development schemes launched on a scale sufficient to have significant impact? What mix of public and private finance and enterprise would offer the best chance of success? To what extent would the administrative capacity of government agencies limit the scope and success of such schemes? What sort of basic institutional reform (e.g., in land tenure, rural credit, and agricultural marketing) would be necessary to assure that project benefits would be reaped by the intended clientele—small farmers and landless workers? These are some of the key policy questions. The author does not pretend to have found answers to them in this study. An attempt has been made, however, to illuminate some of the major issues that must be addressed in the search for answers.

Tropical Land Development and Increased Crop Production

A priori it can be asserted with considerable confidence that the development of new lands in certain humid tropical areas has had a major impact on overall development in Latin America. In Brazil 84 percent of the increased crop output between 1948 and 1962 has been attributed to the incorporation of additional area.[24] Between 1950 and 1967 an estimated 9 million ha were added to the crop area in the humid tropical regions relative to an addition of 7 million ha in other areas.[25] If this proportion is used for the period 1948–62 and it is assumed that the average value of production per hectare is equal in both regions, new lands in the humid tropics would account for about 50 percent of the expansion in Brazilian crop output over the fifteen

[23]Carlos Matus Romo, "El desarrollo del interior de América Latina," in ILPES, *Dos polémicas sobre el desarrollo de América Latina* (Santiago, Chile: Editorial Universitaria, S.A., October 1970), pp. 1–85.

[24]USDA, *Changes in Agriculture in 26 Developing Nations, 1948 to 1963*, Foreign Agricultural Report no. 27 (1965), p. 19.

[25]IBGE, *Anuario estadistico do Brazil* (Rio de Janeiro, 1955 and 1970).

years. Obviously this figure is qualified by the assumption on equal values of production per hectare above and by the absence of any data on how much of the new area may have been a result of reducing the bush-fallow ratio or of cultivating lands that were previously in pasture. The question of allocating the increase in cattle production[26] between area increase and yield improvement remains unresolved. Nevertheless it appears that new lands in the tropics have made an impressive contribution to Brazil's agricultural output over the past twenty years.

The conditions under which Brazil has developed its agriculture set it apart from the rest of tropical Latin America. From the days of early settlement the opening up of humid tropical lands has been carried out on a relatively large scale in Brazil. A cadre of land developers has arisen, plus a mobile campesino (rural worker or small farmer) group to whom the forest frontier causes no anxiety. In contrast, for three centuries the primary focus of agricultural development in the other tropical countries was on the highlands and on irrigation of arid zones. Except for cattle development—which involved very few people—in the Llanos (savanna in Venezuela and Colombia), the Beni plains of Bolivia, and the Chaco, there has been considerable resistance to large-scale migration from highland regions to the humid tropics. Thus while 17 percent of Colombia's increased crop production from 1948 to 1962 was attributed to new land,[27] interpretation of this figure poses difficulties. How much of this area was derived from new irrigation, new lands or pasture in temperate zones, or reduction in the fallow ratio in nonhumid tropical regions? What proportion of the additional land in crops in the tropics is due to a reduction in the bush-fallow ratio or to the substitution of pasture? In Bolivia the increase in annual gross agricultural output as a result of tropical land settlement in the Yungas region and in Santa Cruz between 1950 and 1968 amounted to about $25 million, or 80 percent of the total increase in the agricultural sector over this period.[28] It may be safely assumed that at least 90 percent of the increase from the tropics was due to a land expansion of about 190,000 ha.[29]

No attempt is made here to resolve the statistical problems of defining country by country the actual expansion in cropland, pasture, and bush-fallow over the past twenty years in humid tropical areas and the value of

[26] A 45 percent expansion between 1950 and 1967, according to IBGE, *Anuario estadistico* (1970).

[27] USDA, *Changes in Agriculture*, p. 19.

[28] CEPAL, *Boletín Estadístico de América Latina*, Publicación N E/S/70/II/G/5 (Santiago, 1970), p. 158; CEPAL, *Producto interno bruto de los países de América Latina*, Publicación N E/CN.12/L/51, pt. 1 (Santiago, 1970), p. 10; CEPAL, *Análisis socioeconómico de la región de Santa Cruz de la Sierra*, Anexo C (Santiago, November 18, 1970), p. 3, and the case studies in chapter 5.

[29] Eighty percent of the increase in tropical output was derived from the Santa Cruz region.

production attributable to this expansion. Suffice it to say that apparently significant, and probably economically viable, development of new lands has been achieved in the tropical coast areas of all countries[30] and in certain interior regions, the most notable being south central Brazil, southern Paraguay, and Santa Cruz. In other regions where new lands have been developed—Amazonia[31] and the Andean piedmont in Bolivia, Peru, Ecuador, Colombia, and Venezuela[32]—progress appears to have been slow and the impact indeterminate. The balance of this chapter deals with some of the principal problems of tropical agriculture in Latin America that are particularly relevant to new-land development policy.

The Structure of Agriculture

In order to appraise how the humid tropical lands affect development policies in the countries covered in this study, it is necessary to examine the amount and quality of capital, labor, and management applied to land in general and the elements that govern the combination of productive factors in agriculture and forestry. It is also important to recognize the two basic objectives for new-land development: (1) the achievement of greater and more efficient production to improve nutrition levels and provide raw materials for domestic industry, exports, and adequate cheap food for urban dwellers; and (2) the creation of productive employment to absorb labor that cannot be effectively handled by the manufacturing and service sectors, at the same time augmenting rural consumption and effective demand.

The economies of these countries have a number of important characteristics in common. First, they have a virtually unlimited labor supply, i.e., population is so large in relation to capital (capital invested in skilled human resources as well as in physical plant and inputs) that the marginal productivity of labor is low.[33] In 1970, 48 percent of the population of the eighteen

---

[30]With the exception of Peru, Bolivia, and Paraguay, which have no humid tropical lands on the coast.

[31] Interior plains and uplands of the Amazon basin.

[32] Indications are that new land development in the humid tropics of Venezuela may have been of the same relative order of importance as in Brazil—85 percent of the increase in agricultural output between 1948 and 1962 has been assigned to land expansion. USDA, *Changes in Agriculture*, p. 19.

[33] As stated by W. Arthur Lewis in "Economic Development with Unlimited Supplies of Labour," *Manchester School of Economic and Social Studies*, vol. 22, no. 2 (May 1954), p. 56: ". . . an unlimited supply of labour may be said to exist in those countries where population is so large relative to capital and natural resources that there are large sectors of the economy where the marginal productivity of labour is negligible, zero, or even negative." For a discussion of the doctrine of zero-valued labor and unemployment in agriculture, see Charles H. C. Kao, Kurt R. Auschel, and Carl K. Eicher, "Disguised Unemployment in Agriculture: A Survey," in Carl Eicher and Lawrence Witt, eds., *Agriculture and Economic Development* (McGraw-Hill, 1964), pp. 129–44; Gunnar Myrdal, *Asian Drama: An Inquiry into the Poverty of Nations*, Twentieth Century Fund,

tropical countries of Central and South America[34] lived in rural areas directly dependent on agriculture and forestry (see table 6). Seventy percent of the active rural labor force of 35 million is at the subsistence level with a gross annual output of less than $200 per worker. Seventy to 90 percent of what this group produces is either consumed directly by the family, in the case of agricultural products, or is spent on subsistence-level food and shelter,[35] thus effectively stifling the rural demand for industrial consumer goods. The low level of agricultural technology has the same effect on the demand for manufactured production inputs.

Second, the tropical countries of Latin America all have substantial unexploited natural resources, particularly in the humid lowlands. Thus the low marginal productivity of labor cannot be attributed to a scarcity of natural resources.

Third, all the countries have a clearly defined modern, or "capitalist," sector and a subsistence sector. Within the modern sector there are three types of agricultural enterprise: the traditional hacienda, or large farm, which has low levels of capital use and relatively high labor-output ratios; the estancia, or large ranch, dedicated to extensive livestock production with low labor input; and the commercial plantation, often export oriented, where capital and labor are combined explicitly to maximize profits and where there is apt to be a high level of mechanization and advanced technology. Apart from these typically large-scale operations there is a range of small and medium-sized commercial farms that have one or more of the characteristics listed above. The subsistence sector, which accounts for about 70 percent of the rural population, is characterized by poverty-level single-family operations and restricted market orientation. It reflects a low standard of living and should not be confused with subsistence production, which implies family consumption of 100 percent of the farm output, i.e., zero sales.[36]

Inc. (Random House, 1968), pp. 2050–61; T. W. Schultz, *Transforming Traditional Agriculture* (Yale University Press, 1964); and Stephen Marglin, "Comment" (on Dale W. Jorgenson, "Testing Alternative Theories of the Development of a Dual Economy"), in Irma Adelman and Erik Thorbecke, eds., *The Theory and Design of Economic Development* (Johns Hopkins Press, 1966), pp. 60–66.

[34] Mexico, British Honduras, El Salvador, Honduras, Nicaragua, Costa Rica, Panama, Colombia, Ecuador, Peru, Bolivia, Paraguay, Brazil, French Guiana, Surinam, Guayana, and Venezuela.

[35] A. L. Domike, "Industrial and Agricultural Employment Prospects in Latin America" (paper presented at the Conference on Problems of Urbanization and Employment in Developing Countries, Caribbean Research Institute, St. Thomas, Virgin Islands, November 1967).

[36] For a discussion of the concepts of subsistence production, level of living, and economy, see Clifton Wharton, "Subsistence Agriculture: Concepts and Scope," in *Subsistence Agriculture and Economic Development* (Aldine, 1969), pp. 12–19. See also the interpretation of nonmonetary subsistence versus the monetary sector used by FAO in *Indicative World Plan, Provisional Regional Study No. 3, Africa, South of the Sahara* (Rome, 1968), pp. 6 and 22.

This organization of agriculture results in considerable concentration of land ownership. For Latin America as a whole it is estimated that 40 percent of the land is in the hands of 3 percent of the landowners, while 2 percent of the land is farmed by 40 percent of the producers, most of whom are in the subsistence group. This structure, and particularly the existence of a subsistence sector, has two important implications for the economic and social development of the tropical countries of Latin America: it affects the terms of trade with the rest of the world and the generation of productive employment.

In a technical sense the natural resource base for most tropical export products may be considered virtually unlimited. At the same time there is a large reserve of underemployed labor. Thus the increased costs of production (reflected in higher prices) occasioned by an expansion in export demand will be primarily those associated with the higher unit capital inputs required. The supply of capital has not been seriously limiting. On a worldwide basis and over the long run, therefore, the supply function tends to be highly elastic. This supply situation—combined with limited markets in the developed countries caused by slow population growth, low income elasticity of demand, synthetic substitutes, and low price elasticity of demand for most traditional tropical products—maintains a downward pressure on prices.

In general, tropical agriculture based on exports has little expectation of achieving a major increase in its contribution to development. As long as the marginal productivity of labor is lower than the conventional wage, increases in productivity will do little to improve the lot of the rural worker. Benefits will accrue to the foreign buyer through lower prices, to the government through increased tax revenues, or to the landowner.[37] International commodity agreements may give relief from major price fluctuations but cannot be expected to maintain artificially high prices, i.e., prices unrelated to the costs of production.[38] On the other hand productivity increases in the subsistence sector would benefit rural labor in terms of raising real income and consumption. This suggests that—given employment and income distribution objectives—capital, land, and knowledge over which the government exercises control should be placed at the disposition of subsistence producers and those in the capitalist sector who are producing for domestic consumption. The frequently stated requirement is the reform of credit, tax, land tenure, marketing, and educational institutions. In addition, solutions may be sought through the development of new lands.

---

[37]The benefits to the owners of land and capital will be determined by (1) the absolute amount of these factors they own, and (2) the relative proportion of total output entering the market. The subsistence farmer will benefit little since he scores low on both counts.

[38]J. W. F. Rowe, *Primary Commodities in International Trade* (Cambridge, England: Cambridge University Press, 1965), pp. 209–20.

Table 6. Estimated Rural and Urban Populations and Division of the Work Force Between Subsistence and Modern Sectors in the Principal Tropical Countries of Latin America, 1970

Country	Population (million)			Active work force (million)[a]							Productivity ($/person in active work force)[b]		
				Modern sector			Subsistence sector				Modern sector	Subsistence sector	Total
	Urban	Rural	Total	Urban	Rural	Total	Urban	Rural	Total	Total			
Brazil	44.43 (48%)	48.81 (52%)	93.24 (100%)	12.50 (43%)	5.10 (17%)	17.60 (60%)	2.18 (7%)	9.62 (33%)	11.80 (40%)	29.40 (100%)	1,457 (153%)[c]	204 (21%)[c]	954 (100%)[c]
Colombia	12.78 (58%)	9.38 (42%)	22.16 (100%)	3.07 (44%)	1.08 (16%)	4.15 (60%)	0.64 (9%)	2.12 (31%)	2.76 (40%)	6.91 (100%)	1,519 (152%)	212 (21%)	997 (100%)
Ecuador	2.76 (46%)	3.27 (54%)	6.03 (100%)	0.69 (36%)	0.14 (7%)	0.83 (43%)	0.20 (10%)	0.91 (47%)	1.11 (57%)	1.94 (100%)	1,628 (197%)	235 (28%)	828 (100%)
Peru	6.69 (49%)	6.90 (51%)	13.59 (100%)	1.77 (41%)	0.32 (7%)	2.09 (48%)	0.49 (11%)	1.81 (41%)	2.30 (52%)	4.39 (100%)	2,394 (202%)	180 (15%)	1,185 (100%)

Venezuela	7.74 (72%)	3.02 (28%)	10.76 (100%)	2.13 (66%)	0.45 (14%)	2.58 (80%)	0.17 (5%)	0.50 (15%)	0.67 (20%)	3.25 (100%)	2,769 (124%)	174 (8%)	2,237 (100%)
Mexico	31.59 (62%)	19.13 (38%)	50.72 (100%)	7.18 (46%)	3.04 (19%)	10.22 (65%)	0.88 (5%)	4.65 (30%)	5.53 (35%)	15.75 (100%)	2,909 (149%)	178 (9%)	1,950 (100%)
Central America[d]	5.02 (34%)	10.0 (66%)	15.02 (100%)	1.47 (31%)	0.60 (12%)	2.07 (43%)	0.33 (7%)	2.38 (50%)	2.71 (57%)	4.78 (100%)	1,976 (209%)	157 (17%)	945 (100%)
Others[e]	4.83 (38%)	8.00 (62%)	12.83 (100%)	1.29 (32%)	0.35 (9%)	1.64 (41%)	0.43 (11%)	1.94 (48%)	2.37 (59%)	4.01 (100%)	1,613 (215%)	154 (21%)	751 (100%)
Total	115.84 (52%)	108.50 (48%)	224.34 (100%)	30.10 (42%)	11.08 (16%)	41.18 (58%)	5.32 (8%)	23.92 (34%)	29.24 (42%)	70.42 (100%)	1,988 (160%)	190 (15%)	1,239 (100%)

Sources: CELADE, *Boletín Demográfico*, año 2, vol. 3 (Santiago, Chile, January 1969), pp. 8–9; unpublished manuscript of Raúl Maldonado, División de Investigaciónes del Desarrollo Económico, CEPAL, Santiago, Chile, 1968; and Estaban Lederman, *Hacia una política de los recursos humanos en el desarrollo económico y social de América Latina*, ILPES (Santiago, Chile, April 1969).

[a]Nonspecified employment categories that amounted to 5 percent of the total work force were distributed 50:50 between the two sectors.

In the division between urban and rural, it was assumed that urban included all activities except agriculture.

[b]Production estimates exclude transfer payments.

[c] Average productivity of each sector expressed as a percentage of average productivity for the total work force.

[d]Excluding Panama.

[e]Bolivia, Panama, Paraguay, and Dominican Republic.

The question of employment is central in economic development, and a subsistence sector in tropical Latin America containing about 40 percent of the total population merely serves to reemphasize the importance of this issue. The formation of jobs in the modern sector[39] over the period 1950-62 was at an annual rate of 4.8 percent, the increase in urban subsistence activity was 3.7 percent, and the increase in rural workers (and population) was 1.5 percent. It is crucial to development to know the capacity of the modern sector to create jobs and, given this capacity, what the objective for land development should be, both in terms of supplying food to the expanding urban population and of creating productive employment and effective rural demand for the products and services of the modern sector. It is then necessary to know how the land development and employment objectives would affect the flow of capital into agriculture and forestry for production inputs, the upgrading of human resources and knowledge, and the infrastructure to open up new areas.

Subsistence workers in rural areas are generally able to provide themselves with the minimum level of food, clothing, and shelter from the resources immediately at hand through the intensification of land use. The agglomeration of people in cities, where these elemental resources are harder to obtain, can easily become a welfare problem and a serious source of political unrest, with an appreciable cost to society. Thus there are social, political, and economic reasons for attempting to reduce the rate of migration from rural to urban areas. As already indicated the quest for expanded employment, more equitable income distribution, and improved efficiency in agriculture may follow any or all of three complementary courses: (1) opening up new lands, which is an alternative with seemingly vast potential in most countries of tropical Latin America; (2) changing the agrarian structure, notably land tenure; or (3) deepening the capital investment in lands already exploited through research and extension and the use of irrigation, fertilizers, fencing, pesticides, improved seeds, and so on. If one assumes that agrarian reform would accompany either of the other two courses, the critical question is whether more employment per unit of investment can be generated through new-land development or through the intensification of agriculture. The answer depends on the government's capacity to define and implement a technology policy for both agricultural production and capital formation (infrastructure and land improvement).

Sociopolitical and Institutional Factors

The existence of a subsistence sector adds a degree of urgency to the sociopolitical considerations that guide public policy. These center on social

---

[39]Domike, "Employment Prospects." The modern sector includes mining, manufacturing, construction, basic services (transport, utilities, etc.), commerce, and government.

justice and political stability and, in the case of land, manifest themselves in programs for balanced regional development and agrarian reform. In addition the question of the ambition and incentives of rural labor, managers, and landowners must be taken into account.

Regional Balance

Over the long run the elimination of regional disparities and the redistribution of land may be the course that will create possibilities for a maximum economic growth rate. It is likely, however, that over the short run the objectives of national economic development will conflict with these sociopolitical goals.[40]

Those who make development decisions regarding unexploited land resources of the humid tropics of Latin America are not generally motivated by any impulse to improve the welfare of the indigenous population and thus to correct the disparity between it and the rest of the population. The humid tropics in Latin America are sparsely inhabited, mostly by selva, or jungle, Indians who are outside the political process. One may even argue that development has disutility for these tribes, who often abandon their traditional territory in the face of the "invasion" and retreat deeper into the jungle. The motive for the settlement of new lands in the humid tropics is therefore based on the relief of poverty in other regions, notably in the highlands of Mexico, Central America, and the Andes and in northeast Brazil.

Thus in the area covered by this study the policy of correcting regional disparities operates through the movement of population from depressed regions into adjacent unexploited humid tropical lands or to new irrigation projects along the Pacific coast and in northeast Brazil. The theory behind this policy is that (1) after the population transfer the depressed region will have a higher ratio of resources to population with resultant higher levels of per capita consumption, and that (2) unless the emigration takes place living standards will progressively deteriorate with increasing population. In practice the effect on the depressed region will be governed by the agrarian structure as long as there is an excess of population that forces the marginal productivity of labor to approach zero.

If the agrarian structure in a depressed region from which population has been transferred is such that the majority of the people own or control resources, then it is to be expected that welfare would be increased if each family had more resources (land, water, or forest) to work with. Labor, however, may not have the knowledge, ambition, or access to capital to utilize additional endowments of natural resources. Even if the families do produce an excess over consumption, the marketing structure may be such

[40]Stefan H. Robock, "Strategies for Regional Economic Development," *Papers and Proceedings of the Regional Science Association* (November 1965), pp. 129–41.

that all the surplus accrues to middlemen or consumers who live outside the region. To the extent that wage labor is involved, income will rise only if emigration has been sufficient to cause the marginal productivity of labor to rise above the conventional wage rate and if the higher wages do not attract labor from adjacent depressed areas on a scale sufficient to force wages down to the original conventional equilibrium.[41] When sufficient emigration has occurred throughout all the depressed regions of the country to cause the conventional wage to approximate the marginal productivity of labor, any additional emigration would decrease regional income disparities. In the short run the region probably would be just as depressed after the transfer of population as it was before. To the extent that the new settlers in the selva or on irrigation projects enjoy a higher level of consumption than formerly, the national welfare has been increased, but the regional disparity remains. This disparity may be further aggravated if the labor that migrates is more productive than that which stays put.

With respect to the second part of the theory, living standards may not necessarily decline with rising population if the physical, economic, social, and institutional conditions are conducive to the adoption of improved technology, particularly that which is labor intensive. If such technology is adopted the surplus created will accrue to the owners of land and capital as long as the marginal productivity of labor is less than the conventionally determined wage. But distribution effects aside, subsistence levels for the expanding population can be maintained through technology. If conditions are not conducive to the adoption of technology, the impact of expanding population will initially be determined by the ownership structure of land and capital. If the majority of the resources in the region are exploited and are owned by individual families, increasing population would result in an attempt to maintain consumption levels by intensifying production through increased labor inputs. Eventually population pressure would lead to lowered real income per capita and a *minifundio* system.[42] If on the other hand there is concentration of ownership of land and capital, it is conceivable that the patronal system could absorb the increasing labor force and maintain the prevailing subsistence standards. Thus levels of living need not decline with

---

[41] Effective farm labor unions or state wage orders may increase the conventional rate, but the corollary is an even greater exodus from agriculture if full employment is to be achieved.

[42] The principal characteristic of the *latifundio-minifundio* system is a highly unequal distribution of productive land, which results in the correspondingly unequal distribution of political and economic power between *latifundistas* and *minifundistas. Latifundia* are frequently referred to as *estancias* or *haciendas*, and their owners are referred to as *patróns.* The *minifundistas* constitute the subsistence group and may be employed directly or as sharecroppers on the *latifundia.*

increasing population until the entire surplus from land and capital is distributed to the subsistence labor force.[43]

Agrarian Reform

Changes in the agrarian structure are seen as the means of improving social equity in the short run and of creating the preconditions for efficient agriculture and improved labor and capital mobility, which will reflect on the performance of the whole economy over the long run. In principle the intent is to change the economic, social, and political structure by creating a new socially and economically mobile group from the campesino class that will actively participate in society, thus reducing the political power of a landed oligarchy.

Agrarian reform programs are of four types:

1. The most commonly accepted type is the purchase or expropriation of large holdings and the redistribution of these holdings to landless workers, often the former employees on the property. In such programs the government generally establishes a minimum unit to be granted to the farm worker and a maximum unit to be retained by the original owner. Under this procedure expropriation and subdivision may proceed at random and many large haciendas may be left intact. Subsequently they may be subdivided through inheritance or taxation. Or they may remain as family or corporate farms and eventually become an accepted production unit as the system goes through the cycle: land subdivision, the disappearance of the subsistence sector following capital formation in agriculture and industry, and the eventual reaggregation of land. However, while a heterogeneous mixture of property sizes may survive on land already exploited, if the government is to be consistent in its reform policies it cannot allow new areas (which are generally under state control or ownership) to be subdivided into less than the minimum or more than the maximum size established by the reform program. As a rule the government adopts something approaching the minimum unit as the standard for subdivision in frontier areas.

2. Squatters who are in physical possession of land through invasion of either the public domain (i.e., spontaneous colonization) or private lands (e.g., campesino take-overs in Peru) may be granted legal title. Thus as legal owners they may mortgage the land to obtain credit; and government services such as extension, public health, and police protection may be more readily

---

[43] For a discussion of land intensification and fragmentation under population pressure, see John C. de Wilde, *Experiences with Agricultural Development in Tropical Africa*, vol. 1 (Johns Hopkins Press, 1967), pp. 71–94.

forthcoming. Further, the security of ownership may provide incentive for fuller exploitation of the land.

3. Colonization, when colonists are drawn from the subsistence sector, is a form of wealth redistribution and therefore supports agrarian reform. To the extent that colonization forms the nucleus for the dynamic growth of a region, its importance goes far beyond the reform aspects. In those countries where the land-owning class is still politically strong, colonization of new lands may be promoted as the prime means of alleviating campesino pressure for land redistribution, but not all colonization results in a more equitable distribution of wealth. Colonists are not necessarily always drawn from the subsistence sector—e.g., the military colonies in eastern Peru and along Brazil's northern frontier, the settlements on large units in northern Guatemala, and the Japanese immigrant colonies in the Bolivian tropical lowlands and in Brazil. Spontaneous colonization generally associated with new highway construction may result in the settlement of people from both the modern and subsistence sectors.

4. Development programs designed specifically for agricultural workers and *minifundistas* are considered agrarian reform. These programs include the promotion of labor unions to improve the bargaining position of farm workers; subsidized credit and special extension services to small farmers; the promotion of cooperatives to achieve economies of scale, vertical integration, and marketing leverage; and adult education courses and the development of artisan industry in rural communities. Such programs may be operated independently or in association with any of the other three types of reform programs.

Institutions and Motivation

There are certain limitations on the capacity of the agricultural sector in the tropical countries of Latin America to absorb capital. It would also seem that such limitations can in no way be attributed to restricted land resources. For example the lack of knowledgeable supervisory personnel and skilled labor seems to be more than a temporary phenomenon. The institutional structure restricts the flow of resources to the training of needed managers and skilled workers. The modern sector has a vested interest in maintaining low wage rates and thus has little incentive to use its political and economic influence to promote the transfer of production knowledge and credit to the subsistence sector. Higher productivity in the subsistence sector would be likely to bring an upward pressure on wages.[44]

Three factors appear to be particularly important in determining the response of subsistence farmers to the increased availability of land, capital, and new technology: the value attached to leisure, the extent to which motivation

[44] Lewis, "Economic Development," p. 149.

is dictated by the social system, and the relationship between the agrarian structure and the response to economic incentives. One of the implications of the theory of low marginal productivity of labor is that leisure has little or no value.[45] Under this circumstance it is to be expected that any technique that would offer an additional return for labor input would be adopted immediately. In fact extension services in subsistence communities have not had great success, nor have the farmers universally shown themselves willing to accept credit for such aids as fertilizers and pesticides.

Several explanations, inconsistent with each other in varying degrees, have been offered for this situation. One is that traditional methods persist in subsistence communities because the inhabitants are unresponsive to economic incentives and let traditional social norms guide their decisions.[46] A second is that the decision makers do attach a value to leisure (i.e., the marginal value product of labor is above zero) and therefore reject the new techniques if the additional labor required, either for production operations or investment, is not adequately compensated by the expected reward.[47] Another explanation is that the agrarian structure may be such that any surplus resulting from the new techniques and additional labor will accrue to agricultural suppliers, middlemen, and consumers. Thus the potential economic incentive is negated.[48] Finally, some analysts, such as Schultz, contend that farmers accept new technology on the basis of expected profit alone. In his opinion, whether or not farmers attach a value to leisure, the cost of capital inputs may be excessive when supplied in small quantities to isolated areas without an established distribution system. More important, the farmer may consider the risk and uncertainty associated with an untested technique involving a cash outlay to be unwarranted. Schultz maintains that there is little doubt that subsistence farmers are more conservative than commercial farmers in advanced areas in accepting risk and uncertainty, but that nevertheless they try to maximize their expected profit.[49]

The decision framework of a subsistence family enterprise is critical. It has been argued that until the family is forced by population pressure to abandon the traditional extensive farming methods (forest-fallow), there may be considerable resistance to the adoption of new techniques involving a reduction

[45] N. Georgescu-Roegen, "Economic Theory and Agrarian Economics," *Oxford Economic Papers*, vol. 12, no. 1 (New Series, February 1960), pp. 29–31.

[46] J. H. Boeke, *Economics and Economic Policy of Dual Societies as Exemplified by Indonesia* (New York: Institute of Pacific Relations, 1953), pp. 101–12.

[47] Ester Boserup, *The Conditions of Agricultural Growth: The Economics of Agrarian Change under Population Pressure* (London: Allen and Unwin, 1965), pp. 65–69.

[48] Solon L. Barraclough, "Agricultural Policy and Land Reform" (paper presented at the University of Chicago Conference on Key Problems in Economic Policy in Latin America, November 1966).

[49] Schultz, *Transforming Traditional Agriculture*, pp. 162–68.

in customary leisure.[50] This implies continuous extension of subsistence farming until all of Latin America's tropical territories are settled. An alternative explanation of the conservative attitude of campesinos rests on the historical structural factors that have limited their resources—and therefore their margin for risk-taking—deprived them of education, and made them suspicious of governments, landlords, and commercial interests alike. Where such conservatism is an obstacle to progress, migration to new lands may be expected to have a positive effect on the attitudes of campesinos by affording an opportunity to break with traditional conditions that have dictated behavior.

In Latin America, evidence of noneconomic or cultural motivation and of subsistence farmers attaching an excessive value to leisure is difficult to find. Acceptance of the thesis that campesinos do respond to economic incentives, and that if there is nonresponse it can be attributed only to their high level of aversion to risk and to their expectations of expropriation by other groups of the surplus generated by sacrificing leisure, places the focus on communication and structural change.

It is generally conceded that land distribution alone will do little if anything to increase the market surplus from agriculture in the short run. The provision of credit, extension, and marketing services to small farmers is costly and yields relatively little return. Thus the impact of land reform must be long term; and if economic efficiency is to be achieved, some form of collective action by small producers becomes essential. For this reason, in the sixties much attention was directed to new forms of agricultural enterprise involving group action. Other structural changes, which would provide economic incentives, improved education, and other amenities in rural areas, would affect commercial farmers and those subsistence farmers who enter the commercial group as a result of agrarian reform. The principal argument against improving the incentives without agrarian reform is that, while there would be a production response, income distribution would be further skewed toward the big landlords. The substitution of capital for labor would increase, thus slowing the rate of increase in rural jobs. With a continuing labor surplus, farm wages would remain at low levels, permitting only limited expansion in effective rural demand. The consequence would be accelerated rural-urban migration, which would be compounded in the event of successful union or state efforts to raise minimum wages, thus aggravating an already acute urban unemployment problem.

Summary

A vast agricultural and forestry potential awaits exploitation in the humid tropics of Latin America. The prospects for development of more than a

---

[50] Boserup, *Conditions of Agricultural Growth*, pp. 35–42.

fraction of this potential within the next few decades appear slim, however. The role of these lands in Latin America's development, with the exception of Brazil, has been minor. Before World War II the principal type of exploitation was plantation agriculture oriented to highly unstable export markets. Government policies oriented to settlement were spasmodic, often taking the form of legislation rather than practice, and were generally motivated by a desire to establish territorial sovereignty. The various development policies propounded or practiced from the 1940s to the 1960s—import substitution, industrialization, export promotion, structural reforms to expand domestic consumption, and the establishment of the Latin American Free Trade Association—touched only marginally on tropical lands. Since 1960 more attention has been directed to the humid tropics, in particular as a means of offsetting the external dependency of the region and of creating sources of employment through new growth poles in the interior.

The strategy for agriculture involves action directed to changing the agrarian structure, while simultaneously striking a balance between expansion onto new lands and intensification on present farming areas. The issue is governed by a political decision as to who benefits and who pays. It also depends on economic returns from available alternatives and the capacity of the nonagricultural sectors to generate productive new jobs, which in turn places certain demands on agriculture to satisfy expanding urban food requirements. The actual response of agriculture to programs designed to increase productivity or to move people to the tropical land frontier in an effort to achieve greater total and per capita output is strongly influenced by the institutional structure.

The production and employment generated from land will be a central factor in the development of tropical Latin America until the critical point is reached when the rural population starts to decline in absolute terms. The hypothesis that more capital and employment can be generated through the creation of wholly new resource-based growth poles in the interior than through more intensive development in settled areas remains to be tested. Whatever the mix of strategies adopted, the effective exploitation of Latin America's tropical land resources will depend on a wide range of structural factors affecting input and product prices, services in rural areas, the type of technology adopted, the flow of capital into or out of the agricultural sector, income distribution, employment, and effective demand of the rural population for the goods and services provided by the domestic nonsubsistence sector.[51]

[51]Estevam Strauss, *Metodologia de evaluación de los recursos naturales*, Cuadernos del ILPES, Serie II, no. 4 (Santiago, 1969), pp. 67-70.

TWO THEORIES
OF LAND DEVELOPMENT
IN THE HUMID TROPICS

Why the humid tropical lands of Latin America remain largely underdeveloped[1] and unpopulated 400 years after the arrival of the conquistadors is a subject of much controversy. The lack of development has sometimes been brushed off as a historical accident or as the result of cultural heritage. The inaccessibility of the lands has been blamed in other instances. Still another explanation is that the adverse natural environment in the humid tropics is inimical to the health of settlers and to agricultural productivity. The controversy mounts when it comes to such questions as the productive capacity of the land and forest reserves and proposals for their development.

The most widely held explanation for the lack of development is ecological. As L. R. Holdridge has stated: ". . . the order of agricultural selection of lands as a basis for settlement probably has always followed the same pattern. Men looked first of all for a satisfactory climate, second for fertile soils, and third for favorable topography. Only in these late years of high population pressure has there been any appreciable agricultural movement into the wetter life zones."[2]

Many experts contend that experience with the settlement of the humid tropics leaves little room for pinning hopes of social and economic progress on the exploitation of new lands. They are opposed by those who have marshaled some data and a considerable body of theory to support their faith in the eventual realization of the productive potential of the humid tropics. The lack of any definition of the resource capability and preconditions for development has offered much scope for theorizing and speculation. For example, estimates of the population that could be sustained by the land resources in Brazil alone range from 500 million to 3 billion.[3] The principal

---

[1] Twelve to 15 percent of the total area and 17 to 20 percent of the estimated agricultural potential have been exploited.

[2] L. R. Holdridge, *Life Zone Ecology* (San José, Costa Rica: Tropical Science Center, 1967), p. 16.

[3] K. J. Beek, *Soil Map of South America 1:5,000,000*, FAO/UNESCO Project, World Soil Resources Report no. 34 (Rome: FAO, November 1968), p. 280.

ideas of a wide range of analysts are synthesized and presented below in the form of the cases for and against development of the humid tropics. These negative and positive theories constitute introductory material to the later discussion of current practice and problems in the development of new lands.

The Case against Development

The pessimistic view of efforts to expand the tropical land frontier holds that these efforts make little economic, social, or political sense at the stage of development in which most Latin American countries currently find themselves. The case rests on the following premises:

1. In terms of economic returns, large tracts of the humid tropics do not warrant consideration for development at the present time. Developmental requirements for investments in infrastructure are extremely high, and the indivisibility of most of these creates a tendency to excess capacity in new areas. A developing country can ill afford to have scarce high-priced capital tied up in idle form. Effective flood control in areas subject to heavy seasonal rain, where the upper catchment is steep mountainous country in which dams would have only limited capacity and where the lower catchment is mainly flat and even low lying, would require heavy investment in multiple dams and dyking. Drainage in the gently sloping lowlands is also likely to be expensive. Penetration roads into these areas are costly because of (a) the long distances that must be traveled in order to serve isolated patches of fertile soil and connect them to major markets; (b) the difficult terrain through which they must pass—high mountain ranges, wide rivers, dense jungles, or swamps; and (c) the high rainfall. The combination of these factors results in high construction investment per kilometer and per hectare or per capita served, heavy highway maintenance costs, and expensive vehicle operation per ton-kilometer.

2. Aside from outbound freight rates the competitive margin of items from the interior is still further prejudiced if production inputs must be brought in. As long as yields remain high because of residual soil fertility, forest ashes, and weed-free seed beds, new areas may offer competition. In most tropical zones, however, the exhaustion of soil nutrients and increasing weed infestation and disease dictate bush-fallow, increased imported inputs, or expanded area per family. In the event that yields and prices are insufficient to warrant hired labor or mechanization, the high cost of inputs and the increasing demands on family labor to combat the yield-reducing influences (the "hollow frontier" thesis) may force the colonist to abandon his efforts to maintain production. Tree crops that are less susceptible to these influences in the humid tropics are almost without exception those with the most serious market limitations. There is also considerable risk and uncertainty

associated with the application of technology in individual cases. Unexpected plant and animal diseases may appear, and the side effects from using fertilizers and pesticides are not always well understood.

Under such conditions peasant farmers drawn from a different environment, such as the altiplano, may be unwilling or unable to finance and apply the required level of technology. If farming is permitted to continue without the adoption of the bush-fallow rotation, advanced technology, or labor-intensive and capital-intensive conservation procedures, the soil in many areas could deteriorate to the point where the period required for soil rebuilding would be likely to be well beyond the time span considered by any development planning agency.

3. Many of the products suited to the tropical environment, such as bananas, sugar, coffee, and cacao, have a limited domestic market due to the low levels of purchasing power of the great majority of the population; or growth potential may be constrained by already high levels of per capita consumption. Opportunities for export from Latin America to industrial nations are restricted by tariff policies, African competition for the European market, low coefficients of income elasticity in the demand for tropical products, and the relatively slow rates of population growth in the developed countries.[4]

4. A policy of tropical land development will contribute far less to the achievement of national social and political goals than the alternatives will. One social development objective is more equitable distribution of land and income. Directed colonization of humid tropical lands as a means of achieving this goal is an uncertain and expensive procedure. Apart from the technical and economic uncertainties mentioned above, there is substantial risk with respect to the adaptability of the new settlers to the new environment, their management capability, and their motivation. The massive state outlays required by paternalistically directed colonization for infrastructure, land preparation, housing, social services, family moving expenses, farm operating capital, and project administration effectively limit potential resettlement by this means to an insignificant fraction of the rural population. The basic inequities of the mass of rural families will remain unsolved.[5] The only way such inequities can be corrected on a scale and at a rate sufficient to satisfy political realities within the resource capability of the tropical countries is through major institutional changes affecting taxation, land tenure, educa-

[4] Fernando Rozensweig, "The Economic Problems of Tropical Development" (paper presented at the Conference on the Potentials of the Hot-Humid Tropics in Latin American Rural Development, Cornell University, Ithaca, N.Y., December 1965).

[5] S. L. Barraclough and A. L. Domike, "La estructura agraria en siete países de América Latina," El trimestre económico (Mexico), vol. 32, no. 130 (April–June 1966), pp. 261–63.

tion, public administration, and the development of employment in nonagricultural sectors.

Semidirected or spontaneous colonization may be promoted as a means of maximizing settlement per unit of state investment. This procedure, however, is also restricted by the availability of capital and the ability of the government to control the type of development, protect property rights, and ensure equitable distribution of land.

5. A political objective of the settlement of remote unpopulated tropical areas in the vicinity of national boundaries is the establishment of sovereignty. But cheaper means are available for the achievement of this goal, such as direct defense expenditures or recourse to international arbitration in the event of a border dispute. Within the context of geopolitics, however, this is not to underestimate the importance of reducing the area of largely unoccupied territory.

6. A policy of developing remote humid tropical regions is extremely difficult to implement from the point of view of public administration. The combination of private and public initiative and investment needed for economically viable development in the humid tropics requires a degree of political stability, institutional coordination, technology, pioneer management ability, and investor confidence that is rare in most tropical Latin American countries. The evaluation of the physical development potential, investment requirements, costs of production, markets, social aspects, infrastructure, and social services for proposed projects is seldom systematically carried out and used as a basis for investment and program decisions. Studies often become obsolete before any decisions are made. Once a project is initiated, budget problems, shortage of trained personnel, lack of coordination, or change of government and policy may cause delay in the provision of essential components, such as access, credit, or extension, thus postponing the realization of benefits from the investment.

In the case of spontaneous colonization, which is generally associated with penetration highways, the government may be incapable of effectively regulating the type and conditions of development, or unwilling. The consequences of lack of regulation may be (a) the destruction of forest resources, which should either be harvested in the course of land clearing or left as a basis for forest industry and soil and water conservation in areas unsuited to agriculture; (b) the destruction of wildlife and fishery resources, which otherwise may provide long-run economic returns through controlled harvesting or tourism; (c) the extension of the *latifundio* system through opportunists claiming huge tracts of land and taking the law into their own hands to enforce the claim; (d) the extension of the subsistence *minifundio* system; (e) settlement by colonists who have no conception of how to farm under humid tropical conditions in the lowlands, which may result in disastrous destruction of the soil resources; and (f) injustice to colonists who unknowingly settle on land already owned by an absentee landlord—once the land is developed, the owner may present his legal title and evict the colonist.

The essential negative aspects of humid tropical land development have been summarized by Wright and Bennema:

It is no accident that much of the yet unfarmed land in Latin America lies within the humid tropics, for here are to be found the soils where failure to understand the dynamic nature of the soil system brings swift disaster. The whole history of Man's penetration of these regions has been chequered by high hopes followed by failure, and those who have remained have often chosen to emulate the shifting cultivation system of the indigenous farmers. Few indeed are the examples of successful, efficient and permanent agricultural industry established in the humid tropics, and most of these are concerned with special crops on especially favored soils . . . .

Unfortunately, most farmers in the humid tropics are not in a financial position to wait the five to ten years necessary before any substantial farm returns are available under the slow and gentle method of molding the soil to its new life. . . . The problem of establishing a farm in the humid tropics can thus be formidable, especially where a new agricultural settlement involving wide land clearance is envisaged. Machines and fertilizers in abundance can sometimes achieve the objective; but trained operators, easily taught farmers and readily available supplies of fertilizers are less easily found. . . .

Alluvial soils are probably the most popular soils in the humid tropics for major agricultural industries, but they are liable to occasional flooding and access road construction is often difficult owing to great scarcity of hard rock or gravel for ballasting. . . .

Finally, passing the whole picture of Latin American soil resources in review, it is clear that the greatest increases in agricultural production may be expected from more intensive utilization of the humid temperate zone soils rather than new agricultural endeavour on the soils of the humid tropics; and from more efficient use of the humid temperate zone tropics; and from more efficient use of water for irrigation on the soils of the semi-arid and subhumid regions, rather than from making available new water supplies to desertic regions. . . . Many Latin American countries are now introducing agricultural reforms to resolve their economic, social and demographic problems; it is likely that these will have their greatest effect when they are aimed firmly at the old established farming districts, where the hope of increasing production is far greater than in most newly opened agricultural settlements.[6]

[6] A. C. S. Wright and J. Bennema, *The Soil Resources of Latin America*, FAO/UNESCO Project, World Soil Resources Report no. 18 (Rome: FAO, 1965), pp. 113–15.

The Case for Development

It is evident from the policies, programs, and investments currently in effect in Latin America (see chapter 3) that the pessimistic view is not widely held by decision makers. Or if such views are countenanced, it must be assumed they are more than offset by positive considerations. All countries in the humid tropics have launched campaigns on all fronts to accelerate occupation of the forested lands north of the 23rd parallel. Undoubtedly they have optimistic expectations regarding production, exports, and employment. A major driving force in Brazil is the expectation that through northern and western penetration into Amazonia during the next ten to fifteen years, it will be possible to double or triple the "miracle" of Paraná, São Paulo, Goiás, and Minas Gerais that has been achieved over the past two decades. Thus, in fact, many of the negative aspects listed above are directly refuted. The basic tenets of the developmental approach are:

1. Capital, labor, and entrepreneurs will spontaneously follow the new highway systems to seek and exploit new economic opportunities. These pioneers, whether individual or corporate, will depend on trial and error and accumulated practical knowledge and will bear the costs and risks of discovery and development. Some will fail, but the net result will be the evolution of a profitable farming system adapted to the resource potential. Should the state elect to enter into directed settlement ventures, it will overcome the bottlenecks that have stymied such projects to date. While there may be forest destruction and other damage to the environment, the high discount rate placed on postponing present consumption rules out the conservation approach. In the near future public administration and the institutional structure will permit regulation of the land development procedures in such a way as to assure equitable income distribution and rational use of natural resources.

2. The sun is the elemental source of the energy that supports life; the mechanism by which this energy is converted to human use is photosynthesis. In spite of low soil fertility the temperature and moisture regime in the humid tropics provides one of the most efficient bases for converting energy into vegetation. Evidence suggests that where soil nutrients and water are not limiting the biological potential of pasture in temperate zones is about 20 tons of dry matter per hectare per year compared with over 40 tons in the tropics.[7] The unsatisfactory results obtained from much of the agriculture in this region must be ascribed to a traditional focus on upland cropping systems

[7] J. P. Cooper, "Potential Production and Energy Conversion in Temperate and Tropical Grasses," *Herbage Abstracts*, vol. 40, no. 1 (March 1970), p. 12.

combined with efforts to adapt temperate agricultural technology to tropical conditions. In the past an attempt has been made to overcome the natural environment through the use of heavy machinery; the development of varieties of exotic plants and animals adaptable to tropical conditions; and the application of huge quantities of chemicals in the form of fertilizers, pesticides, herbicides, and so on. What is required is a thorough understanding of the dynamic nature of the ecological system—the interrelationships and balance among such factors as soil, hydrology, vegetation, wildlife, and climate.[8] The new approach, therefore, should be tried within countries where planners are well aware of the biases that may be introduced by scientists who have gained their knowledge and experience in the advanced agriculture of temperate countries.

It is envisaged that this approach would be based on a long-term view of the use and conservation of natural resources, with development starting from the virgin forest state. It would be necessary to support any program of this sort with a substantial research effort. If past failures are to be avoided, ecological studies, land capability classification, and careful land-use planning would be required before development is initiated. At the present time there is insufficient technical and historical data to show where permanent agriculture can be sustained and under what management system. Until this information is available the forest should not be regarded as a "negative" resource that must be destroyed—its value in conserving or building soil fertility for future agricultural use or as a potential source of industrial raw materials should be recognized, and it should be managed and harvested accordingly.

3. Vastly increased technical manpower and capital should be put into the scientific research and field testing underlying truly efficient forestry, agriculture, and associated processing industries.[9] The technology of traditional tropical export crops is fairly well understood. But the technology of domestically consumed products is less well understood, and little is known of the technology of what is believed to be a wide range of potential agricultural, forestry, fishery, and wildlife products. Particular attention should be paid to the management, extraction, and industrialization of wood and foliage from native forests for the production of such items as lumber, plywood, particle board, paper, chemicals, and food for livestock or for human consumption. In addition there is much to be done in the field of the selection and breeding of native plants and animals. Research in agriculture must develop "salable"

<hr/>

[8]L. R. Holdridge, "Ecological Indications of the Need for a New Approach to Tropical Land Use," *Economic Botany*, vol. 13, no. 4 (December 1959), p. 278–80.

[9]NAS-NRC, "Proposal for the Creation of a Tropical Research Foundation" (March 1965, mimeo.); and T. W. Schultz, "Education and Research in Rural Development in Latin America" (paper presented at the Conference on the Potentials of the Hot-Humid Tropics in Latin American Rural Development, Cornell University, Ithaca, N.Y., December 1965).

innovations, i.e., where the ratio between anticipated improvement in income and possible loss from adoption of the innovation is high enough to be acceptable to the farmer at costs within his financial means.[10]

4. Attention must be diverted from preoccupation with the markets for traditional high-volume tropical exports to the many possibilities for small-volume high-value items, such as chicle, pyrethrum, naranjilla, palmito, avocado, spices, processed citrus, and specialty gourmet foods. Coordinated research is required for improved products and management and market promotion for the export of many tropical fruits, foods, fibers, and oil.[11]

5. A huge pasture and livestock potential awaits development on tropical lands that are unsuited to cropping, which would help to supply the almost insatiable world appetite for animal protein. The key is new technology for the selection and breeding of legumes and grasses, rhizobium innoculation, and plant nutrition. J. Griffiths Davies has stated the case as follows:

We believe that there are enormous tracts of land which today cannot be used for growing food for direct human consumption but which can be exploited for growing stock feed—though not necessarily by exploiting existing methods and plants. There are extensive areas of such regions in Asia, Africa and South America. Drought, flood and soil infertility all play their part . . . in preventing the human race from living on them, or in providing only an inadequate and precarious existence for a sparse population. Where the vagaries of climate preclude the growing of crops for direct human consumption, productive pastures can be grown. The ruminant can be interposed between this inhospitable and precarious regime and the human being. . . .[12]

6. Development in the humid tropics should be concentrated and associated with mineral exploitation, major highways, and an integrated complex of forest and agricultural-processing industries.[13] Unless development is concentrated it is impossible to establish the "critical mass" of raw material needed to supply a specialized industrial complex that is able to handle the wide diversity of agricultural and forestry items. In addition, the establishment of processing industries introduces capital, a high level of technology, and a focus for motivation and organization and provides a source of working

[10] Stephen Marglin, "Some Hypotheses about Innovation in Backward Agriculture" (Harvard University, March 1964, mimeo.).

[11] Norwood C. Thornton, "Opportunities for Agricultural Research in the Tropics and Their Relation to Development," *Ceiba*, vol. 12, no. 1 (July 1966), pp. 22–26.

[12] See the preface by J. Griffiths Davies, in *Some Concepts and Methods in Sub-Tropical Pasture Research*, by the staff of the Cunningham Laboratory, CSIRO, Brisbane, Australia, Bulletin no. 47, Commonwealth Bureau of Pastures and Field Crops (Farnham Royal, England: Commonwealth Agricultural Bureaux, 1964), p. xi.

[13] Joseph A. Tosi and Robert F. Voertman, "Some Environmental Factors in the Economic Development of the Tropics," *Economic Geographer*, vol. 40, no. 3 (July 1964), pp. 202–4.

capital and extension services to the small producers.[14] Unlike widely dispersed colonization projects, concentrated development should create many more job opportunities and relatively high population density, with simplified administration, lower infrastructure investments per capita or per unit of output, and a greater probability of achieving labor specialization and a dynamic process of economic growth. Development along these lines will necessitate the concerted efforts of the governments, private enterprise, and the international financing agencies.

Summary

Proponents of the negative theory maintain that immediate investment in tropical land development in Latin America cannot be justified on economic, social, or national security grounds. This lack of justification is based on experience and the existing agrarian structure; the administrative capacity of public agencies; government taxing ability; domestic and export markets; and the technology of agriculture, forestry, and transport.

Those adhering to the positive theory, which rationalizes current land development policies, hold that present consumption is the operative rule and that only through experience can solutions be found to the problems of the humid tropics. Another facet of the positive approach is the adoption of a program of natural resource development directed toward working with the environment rather than against it. This would involve (1) a coordinated research program in ecology, land capability and utilization, and the selection of native flora and fauna; (2) the development of specialized production unaffected by the market limitations of traditional tropical crops; (3) concentrated development based on integrated agricultural and forest industry complexes; and (4) wherever possible, combining development with mineral exploitation that might support the basic infrastructure.

Thus the negative aspects essentially are reinforced by this basically conservationist part of the positive approach that rests on the postponement of resource use. Time is needed for an inventory of tropical lands and forests; research into the technology of primary production, processing, and marketing; and the creation of adequate organizations and administrative procedures. Experience bearing on these negative and positive aspects of land development is examined in the case studies presented in chapters 5, 6, and 7.

[14]George C. Lodge, "Food Processing–Key to Economic Development," *Harvard Business Review*, October 1966, pp. 6-16.

THE DEVELOPMENT OF NEW LANDS: CURRENT PRACTICE AND PROBLEMS

In general the objective for the settlement of new lands is the utilization of idle natural resources to accelerate economic and social development. Inherent in this objective are (1) the optimization of resource use and the rate of economic growth by comparing the costs and returns of available alternatives; and (2) the achievement of other goals, such as more equal income distribution, social justice, or political stability. The case of profit maximization is uniquely exemplified in central Brazil, where a group of entrepreneurs have evolved who, operating individually or in corporations, have become specialists in identifying and exploiting opportunities to profitably till new lands. This group has operated primarily in the south, particularly in São Paulo and Rio Grande do Sul, expanding first through northern Paraná, southern Mato Grosso, Goiás, and southern Minas Gerais and currently moving north, spurred on by the tax remission incentives offered by the Superintendencia do Desenvolvimento da Amazonia (SUDAM).

A frequently cited objective for government programs for the development of tropical lands is the relief of existing personal and regional income disparities. Specifically this implies the creation of employment for underemployed rural labor and an increase in income per family in the disadvantaged campesino class. Another reason for occupying virgin lands that has had powerful political backing is national defense and the establishment of territorial sovereignty.

Many people also view the settlement of virgin humid tropical lands as an inevitable consequence of population pressure. If the objective is to establish commercial family farmers and agricultural and forestry industries in the new areas and eventually in the existing depressed areas, the rural sector undoubtedly would play an important role in economic development. On the other hand if the objective is merely to provide living space at subsistence levels to slow down the urban migration of the ever-pressing rural population, the policy becomes one of minimizing the negative effects of population pressure. Under such conditions, in theory one might expect to find a parallel objective of restricting population growth. In practice this is not the case. Regardless of theory or practice it would require more than a generation to alleviate population pressure through birth control—a time period that has little relevance for political decision makers.[1]

While the preambles to government programs and investments to open up new lands for settlement generally include homage to accelerated economic growth, land for the landless, income distribution, and improvement in the balance of payments, there are many cynics who hold that the real motive is to assuage pressure for land reform. For example Albert Hirschman has said that "colonization may be expected to be amply tried out in a country where landowners are powerful and where virgin, state-owned lands are plentiful ... because [such] schemes appear to offer an escape from the nasty class struggle."[2] If this is the genuine political motivation behind many settlement projects, it may be unnecessary to look further to determine why, as Hirschman puts it, they are "failure-prone."

Direct Government Programs

To achieve their various land development objectives, Latin American governments employ the following principal procedures:

1. Directed or semidirected colonization aimed at bringing about intranational population shifts.
2. Assisted settlement of foreign immigrants.
3. The construction of penetration roads into new areas with the expectation of spontaneous colonization.
4. Promotional policies designed to attract a flow of private investment into virgin areas.
5. State or mixed private-public enterprise to undertake any combination of land development, primary production, or industrialization.
6. The creation of regional development authorities.

These procedures can be combined in a variety of ways.

Colonization

The goal of public policy for and investment in the development of humid tropical lands in Latin America is generally some form of land settlement. Directed colonization is based on the premise that unless the settler is provided with the full range of facilities and services—access roads, infrastructure, cleared land, housing, resettlement expenses, education, health services, pro-

---

[1] Solon L. Barraclough, "Economic Implications of Rural-Urban Migration Trends from the Highland Communities" (paper presented at the Conference on Development of Highland Communities in Latin America, Cornell University, Ithaca, N.Y., March 1966).

[2] Albert O. Hirschman, *Journeys toward Progress—Studies in Economic Policy-Making in Latin America* (New York: The Twentieth Century Fund, 1963), p. 138.

duction credit, and extension—the political, social, or economic objectives of land development will not be fully realized.

The following factors have been identified as crucial to the success of all forms of colonization: selection of the right site; selection of the right colonists; physical preparation of the site before settlement; adequate capital, whether supplied by the settler or the state; organization of central services and project administration; the area per settler; and the conditions of tenure.[3] In a large number of cases the prerequisites to satisfy these criteria have not been met.[4]

In the case of government programs to foster foreign immigrant colonies in tropical Latin America the purpose presumably was to extend development into lands that were not in demand by nationals. A further purpose may have been to generate more interest among nationals in the settlement of humid tropical lands. There is little information available on the extent to which the foreign settlers have had a wider influence on tropical land development through secondary effects, such as their own expansion into virgin areas, the attraction of nationals into adjacent areas, the demonstration of management practices to the local population, or the creation of secondary employment.[5]

In the achievement of regional equalization objectives, the origin of colonists is an important consideration. Evidence in the Huallaga Valley of eastern Peru indicates that where scattered settlement and development of towns has already taken place most of the settlers on new lands come from the local area and not from other depressed regions. In this kind of developing frontier, where there is an extensive system of forest-fallow land use and no apparent population pressure, population could be expected to increase; in fact, there has been a slight loss of population in some of the eastern departments of Peru. The causes of such a situation should have important implications for development policy in the humid tropical areas.

Penetration Roads

The premise for the construction of penetration roads as the principal stimulus to new-land development is entirely different from that of directed colonization. It is hoped that highways connecting major urban markets, export points, and centers of rural population pressure will result in a flow of people and capital into the new area.

There is no doubt that in many areas highways have proved to be a positive force for land development and have created economic opportuni-

[3]W. Arthur Lewis, "Thoughts on Land Settlement," *Journal of Agricultural Economics* (Great Britain), vol. 11, no. 1 (June 1954), pp. 3–11.

[4]José Monje Rada, *Estudio de costos de colonización* (La Paz: AID, September 1963), p. 99.

[5]CIDA, *Land Tenure Considerations and Socio-Economic Development of the Agricultural Sector: Brazil* (Washington: OAS, 1966), pp. 533–49.

ties.[6] A number of observers hold the view that the only essential prerequisite to development of the humid tropics is the establishment of a road network.[7] Two negative aspects have been observed in some cases. First, there may be indiscriminate destruction of natural resources, i.e., the issue is conservation versus depletion. Second, in areas opened up by these highways, exploitation of lands may be on the extensive forest-fallow system. As a consequence, at least in the early stages, the traffic, production, and employment generated may not justify the investment relative to alternative uses of the capital. This is especially true where high-cost construction is necessary under difficult topographic, soil, and climatic conditions if the road is to be usable with reasonable maintenance expenses.

One of the alternatives to highways in solving the access problem in the humid tropics is air transport. Unsubsidized air services have supported commercial, agricultural, and even forestry enterprises over the past fifteen to twenty years in these areas. In southern Peru lumber is flown 75 kilometers from the Madre de Dios river to the roadhead at a cost of 5 cents per board foot. About 8,000 tons of beef per year are flown from the Beni plains of eastern Bolivia to La Paz at 9 cents per kilogram. Whether air transport, with improved technology and two-way payloads, can support large-scale development is questionable. But it does offer the possibility of maintaining specialized production in areas that have no chance of highway access within the near future and of transporting equipment for land clearing and highway construction in remote areas. It has been argued that in mountainous terrain, where the costs of highway construction and maintenance and vehicle operation are high and the distance by road may be 2.5 times the air distance, the total transport bill may well be less if planes are used.[8]

Public and Quasi-Public Enterprise

The government, either through its regular departments or by the creation of a state corporation, can intervene directly in the development of frontier areas at all levels—land preparation, primary production, industrialization, transport, and marketing. Problems frequently associated with government operations have been bureaucratic administrative procedures, the scarcity of

[6] See Barbara R. Bergman, "The Cochabamba-Santa Cruz Highway in Bolivia," in G. W. Wilson and others, *The Impact of Highway Investment on Development* (Brookings Institution, 1966), pp. 17–54.

[7] Raymond E. Crist, *Andean America—Some Aspects of Human Migration and Settlement*, Occasional Paper no. 3 (Graduate Center for Latin American Studies, Vanderbilt University, May 1964).

[8] "El papel de la aviación civil en los proyectos de colonización," Documento no. UP/G.36/17 (paper prepared by the General Secretariat, OAS, and presented at the Second Inter-American Meeting of Experts in Civil Aviation, Pan American Union, Santiago, Chile, July 1964).

capital and of management and technical personnel, and the absence of a marketing organization for exports.

Large-scale state agricultural land development or forestry enterprise has not been undertaken in tropical Latin America. Probably the best-known example of this type of operation in the humid tropics was the groundnut scheme carried out in Tanganyika in 1948–50 by two British public corporations, the Colonial Development Corporation and the Overseas Food Corporation. Their experience illustrates some of the problems. The project was one of enormous dimensions—1.3 million hectares and an investment in excess of $100 million in mechanized land clearing and the production of groundnuts. By definition the venture was of no interest to private capital, and management personnel having the knowledge of tropical agriculture and the administrative ability to cope with such a project were difficult to obtain. The studies of soil resources; climate; and plans for land clearing, planting, and crop husbandry were superficial and guided by theory rather than practice. The project was directed from a distance by people under the illusion of omnipotence—an illusion that often accompanies the administration of huge public resources. Moreover the government was influenced in its decision by an erroneous assessment of the world supply and demand for vegetable oil and its potential effect on rationing in the United Kingdom.[9] The cumulative consequence of these factors was a loss of $85 million in two years.

Projects of this type have not been launched by governments in South and Central America, but elsewhere there are cases of successful state ventures in tropical agriculture on a relatively small scale. An example is a 2,000-hectare banana plantation in Surinam taken over by a public corporation in the early sixties. This corporation has expanded its activities to service small private banana producers and handles export marketing through a contract with the United Fruit Company.[10]

Regional Development Authorities

Autonomous regional agencies have been employed to further development of the humid tropics in Mexico, Guatemala, Colombia, Ecuador, Brazil, and Venezuela. The agencies are usually created to exploit a specific natural resource; e.g., hydroelectric power in the case of the Papaloapan and Grijalva commissions in Mexico and the Cauca Valley Corporation in Colombia, iron ore for the Corporación Venezolana de Guayana, or land in the case of the Empresa Nacional de Fomento y Desarrollo Económico de Petén in Guate-

---

[9] Bernard O. Binns, *Las plantaciónes y demás fincas rústicas de explotación centralizada*, Estudios Agropecuarios no. 28, FAO, Land and Water Division (Rome: FAO, December 1955), pp. 29–32.

[10] H. B. Arthur, J. P. Houck, and G. L. Beckford, *Tropical Agribusiness Structures and Adjustments: Bananas* (Harvard University Press, 1968), p. 62.

mala. Aside from the particular natural resource focus, the authority normally assumes responsibility for the promotion of integrated multisectoral development of the region, with an independent budget for the preparation of a regional plan and special investment projects or programs. In addition it may have the power to coordinate the activities of government agencies in the implementation of the development plan.

A special case among regional agencies is the SUDAM, which together with the Banco da Amazonia is charged with promoting the development of more than 5 million square kilometers of the Brazilian Amazon—an essentially unpopulated region of enormous land, forest, and water resources and unknown mineral wealth. Unlike most other agencies in the humid tropics in Latin America, an important focus here is the promotion of private investment. Procedures include a rebate of up to 50 percent on federal income taxes for investment in approved projects; selective duty-free import of equipment; exemption from federal and state taxes on incomes, sales, or exports for varying periods; and granting to foreign investors the right to repatriate profits and capital.

Reference has already been made to the question of achieving regional balance through the promotion of settlement and investment in the unoccupied humid tropics of Latin America. The approach adopted by regional authorities, and particularly that exemplified by SUDAM, is in no way motivated by the economic status of the few residents of the area. That is, there is no concept of "depression" or of "underprivileged" like that associated with such agencies as the Corporación de Desarrollo de Puno in Peru, which was established to promote the development of the heavily populated Peruvian altiplano, where the majority of people derive a miserable existence from the limited land resources. Thus, leaving national security aside, the motivation to develop such regions derives from the proposition that existing concentrations of economic activity and population will benefit from decentralization. In the practical world of politics the diversion of funds from populated to unpopulated, or from relatively prosperous to relatively depressed, regions is likely to encounter some resistance.[11] Thus if policy makers are to be convinced, it is necessary for decentralization proposals involving the vacant tropical lands to have sound criteria for the selection of areas, an economic and social framework for the evaluation of alternatives, and the definition of a regional development strategy.[12] In the absence of these conditions national security tends to become dominant, and one finds military influence behind many programs for the development of such areas as the Paraguayan Chaco, Amazonia, or Petén in Guatemala.

[11] Lewis, "Thoughts on Land Settlement," p. 6.

[12] Jorge Ahumada, Luis Lander, and Eduardo Neira Alva, "América Latina, un desafio para la teoría regional," *Cuadernos de la Sociedad Venezolana de Planificación,* vol. 1, nos. 3-4 (October–November 1962), pp. 34-47.

Private Initiative and Government Promotion Policies

Land Development Promotion

The underlying premise of promotion policies is that unless some concessions are granted, capital, labor, and management will not be attracted to develop new humid tropical lands—or will not be attracted at a sufficient rate and in the form necessary to meet the government's development objectives. In general these policies are aimed at creating a business environment that will stimulate a flow of private investment in support of penetration roads or other infrastructure projects. Procedures may include granting rights to ownership or use of land on favorable terms; tax relief; subsidized credit, inputs, product prices, or freight rates; import privileges on production equipment; government purchasing contracts; and investment and profit remittance guarantees to foreign investors.

Since the emphasis is on private investment the possibility arises of conflict between private and social goals, specifically in the areas of labor-intensive versus capital-intensive development and small-scale versus large-scale operation. Principally these conflicts can occur in the methods of land clearing and the construction of infrastructure, the system of agricultural production, monopoly in agricultural and forest processing industries, and conservation.

Traditionally, jungle land has been cleared by the slash and burn technique, which is labor-intensive. The only capital involved is the ax and machete. Land cleared in this fashion can be farmed only by hand methods until the stumps rot. On areas that were formerly densely forested, it may be difficult or impossible to use draft animals. The chief advantages of this system are that it is cheap, it can be undertaken on any scale, and land can be converted from jungle to sown crop in less than a month. Further, if clearing is undertaken by colonists whose alternative opportunity costs approach zero, there is the creation of productive capital in agriculture at very little cash outlay.

Capital-intensive methods involve either chemical defoliation or the use of a wide variety of heavy machinery. At its present stage of development chemical defoliation is prohibitively expensive. Aside from high cash costs the principal disadvantages of mechanical clearing are the loss of organic matter and structural damage to top soil. Any large-scale operation, however, particularly those associated with processing plants, is likely to use mechanical methods for land clearing, cultivation, and harvesting. This is done primarily because of the limitations of the labor supply or because of management difficulties with large numbers of workers. An additional factor is the relatively high cost of labor in frontier areas. The wage rate tends to be set by the alternative opportunity of taking up 30 to 40 hectares of land and farming by the forest-fallow system, or by a more intensive system if capital is available.

Thus, regardless of management and labor supply problems, it may pay the individual operator to adopt labor-saving technology.

When agricultural processing plants are established in new areas, it is a general practice to have an integrated farming enterprise sufficient to ensure a supply of raw materials that will allow a break-even level of operation for the first phase of the plant. This type of operation is reflected in plans for two integrated plants in the Huallaga Valley of eastern Peru. One is a state enterprise and the other is private. For the state enterprise an investment of $5 million is contemplated for a plant for processing palm oil at Tocache plus $350,000 for the establishment of a basic palm plantation of 3,000 hectares. The private project involves the clearing of 2,000 hectares of forest for a rice-pasture rotation and the installation of a $1.5 million rice mill with a capacity of 16,000 tons a year.[13]

Processing plants like these, whether state, private corporate, or cooperative enterprise, can be strong positive factors in creating a viable agriculture in new areas. A fundamental problem is the assurance of a supply of raw material. This problem is compounded as the process becomes more complicated and there are significant economies of scale in both production and marketing, e.g., sugar, bananas, palm oil, and tea. Colonists on small farms may lack the knowledge, confidence, and discipline required for contract production until they have an opportunity to observe the system in operation. It is not difficult to visualize how national agrarian reform policies may run counter to land development promotion policies and the interests of processing companies that seek to control their source of raw materials during the early stages of establishment.

There are other forms of promoting investment in tropical areas. Concessions are granted to land development companies that put in infrastructure, clear the land, and subdivide. Much of the development in the states of São Paulo and Paraná was carried out under this system. In other cases there are special programs of credit, extension, or government-supported research and marketing to promote livestock or highly specialized production—herbs, chicle, papain, sugar, or rubber. An example is the coffee diversification program of the Instituto Mexicano de Café designed to raise coffee yields, reduce the coffee area, and promote the production of avocados, citrus, livestock, and rubber.[14]

In most humid tropical areas, forest industry is a potential source of income and employment. Forest production may be considered as directly competitive with agriculture as a use for land in certain areas, as noncompetitive in areas unsuited to agriculture, as an associated activity in clearing native

[13]Marion Baldwin, "$3 Million Rice Project for Yurimaguas," *Peruvian Times* (Lima), May 12, 1967.

[14]Instituto Mexicano de Café, *Tecnificación de la caficultura y diversificación de cultivos* (Mexico, July 1965).

forest for agriculture, or as an additional crop in the rotation. Reference has been made to the problems of forest exploitation. There are many small- and medium-scale lumber and plywood mills operating on the fringes of the tropical forests and along the major navigable rivers. The physical potential has hardly been touched, but further expansion depends on markets, and the establishment of markets depends on reasonable freight rates, technology for the development of marketable products, and favorable unit costs of production. In many cases the requirement for development is that it will attract a large-scale highly integrated enterprise.

Historically, investments in the humid tropical lands often have been made by foreign corporations, such as the United Fruit Company, that have highly specialized knowledge of production and processing and an extensive marketing organization. In many countries this type of investment involving ownership (whether national or foreign) of large areas of land is likely to be viewed with disfavor because of reform policies oriented to land and income distribution. Moreover there are compelling arguments in favor of colonist participation in such ventures. Under these circumstances, and if private capital and enterprise are to be involved, alternative types of organization must be sought in order to accelerate the development of frontier lands in the humid tropics.

Plantations

Within the context of tropical land development, plantations have special characteristics and therefore should be considered separately from other forms of private organization. In the first place the plantation system is not indigenous to Latin America. It was developed by European entrepreneurs to produce specialized tropical products for their own domestic market. The areas opened up were invariably unpopulated; thus it was necessary to import labor, frequently as slaves, as well as capital and enterprise. For this reason plantations became associated with a resident labor force and the provision of a number of services—health care, housing, and utilities—hitherto unknown in the region. The organization is usually corporate with all that this entails in any industry—separation of ownership and control, salaried management, disassociation of owners from the land and from labor, free access to the world's capital markets, and management for the exclusive purpose of achieving maximum operating profits and increasing the asset value or share values.

As a result of ready access to capital the rate of expansion is not subject to a limitation imposed on individual owners—that a large part of new investment must come from savings out of current operations. Production is specialized; advanced technology is employed to produce a single commodity for export. The commodity usually requires a relatively long growing period (more than two or three years to reach full production), e.g., rubber, cocoa, bananas, or tea. The isolated and unique conditions connected with the operation dictate that plantation operators conduct research and develop their own production procedures. The principal advantage rests on economies of scale. Such economies may be reflected in production; in connection with vertical integration into processing, transport, and marketing; or in some cases through horizontal integration permitting geographic dispersion.[15]

The Caribbean banana industry illustrates many of the factors that have made the plantation system competitive in exploiting specialty crops in the humid tropics. Owing to the perishable nature of the fruit, production must be scheduled to assure a steady flow. Coordination of cutting and shipping is essential, as are transport to market under controlled conditions in special ships and storage in special ripening chambers. In this situation the benefits of vertical integration and large-scale operation are obvious. Because of the incidence of localized hurricanes, an organization that operates scattered plantations under unified control has a decided advantage. An individual grower can be put out of business by a hurricane. The incidence of Panama and sigatoka diseases has had just such an effect in many areas. When Panama disease occurred it was necessary to move plantations to new areas. Only a company can do this; the small planter is relatively immobile and must seek an alternative crop. In the case of sigatoka many of the small growers were forced to eliminate their bananas since they were unfamiliar with control techniques or unable to finance spraying equipment.[16]

Without doubt the plantation form of organization has shown itself capable of mobilizing capital, labor, management, and technology to effectively overcome the difficulties associated with agricultural and forestry operations in the humid tropics. In the words of Ida Greaves: "The plantation has changed the face and the economy of every area in which it has been established, and in many instances it has laid the basis of modern economic development in primitive and unused lands . . . , brought hitherto deserted and isolated regions . . . into the orbit of international trade, and played an important part in some of the historical movements that shaped the economy of the modern world."[17]

In view of the apparent success of the plantations, how might the system be mobilized or adapted to open new tropical lands in the future? In Latin America, plantations of the type referred to here have become identified with economic imperialism. The attributes listed by Dr. Greaves are the antithesis of those that might be sought by the external dependency school. The plantation may be construed as a perpetuation or extension of the dualistic

[15] While one could debate the definition of plantation, it is believed that the description given conforms with the common usage in Latin America, especially when applied to such organizations as the United Fruit Company.

[16] IBRD, Economics Department, "The Banana Industry of the Caribbean Area" (1948, mimeo.).

[17] Ida C. Greaves, "Plantations in the World Economy," in *Plantation Systems of the New World*, Social Science Monograph no. 7 (Washington: Pan American Union, 1959), p. 18.

economy.[18] Because the plantation may preempt the best new lands or appropriate the better lands now in food crops, causing the transference of subsistence producers to marginal lands unsuited to cropping, it may also be regarded as a threat to the landless campesino.[19] With respect to export crops there appears to be little latitude to change from a large-scale vertically integrated structure, although changes may be made in the type of ownership and in the relationships between owners and managers.

Wherever there are sound reasons to expect economies of scale, the alternative to private corporate agriculture rests with public enterprise, quasi-public corporations, or cooperatives. The cooperative form of organization in Latin America is as controversial as humid tropical land development itself. Dr. Greaves, a nonbeliever, has said: "Cooperative is a hypnotic word to people imbued with political doctrines of nineteenth century Europe, but the social and economic environment in the tropics differs from that in which the word acquired its European significance, and cooperation here can mean anything from coercion to chaos."[20] As the political situation has changed over the past two decades, a number of modifications have been made in the traditional plantation structure. Corporations have divested themselves of primary production in favor of individual contract growers, cooperatives, or state enterprise.[21]

Summary

The objectives of government programs to develop tropical lands are vaguely formulated at best. The real motives—an alternative to agrarian reform, or territorial sovereignty, or employment, or the exploitation of idle resources to accelerate economic growth—are difficult to discern. The particular measures that have been adopted by governments to achieve explicit or implicit objectives take the form of colonization, penetration highways, regional development agencies, state enterprise, and concessions to promote private investment in land subdivision or plantations. A number of efforts in the planned transfer of population to new tropical lands have resulted in total failure or stagnation. What attracts and what repels migrants is very imperfectly understood. For instance in parts of the tropical frontier regions of Peru there has been a population decline; in contrast, population in areas opened up by the Belém-Brazília highway increased 8 percent annually from 1.3 million to 2 million over five years, 1960-65.

[18] Raymond E. Crist, "Comments" (on "Plantations in the World Economy"), *Plantation Systems of the New World*, p. 25.

[19] L. R. Holdridge, *Life Zone Ecology* (San José, Costa Rica: Tropical Science Center, 1967), p. 118.

[20] Greaves, "Plantations in the World Economy," p. 21.

[21] For a discussion of alternative arrangements, see Arthur, Houck, and Beckford, *Tropical Agribusiness*, pp. 51-64.

There can be little doubt of the risk and uncertainty associated with tropical land development stemming from market instability or saturation, lack of production technology, or the requirement of new forms of social organization. Thus governments should move with caution where they are directly involved. In the case of indirect action through private entities—which, if given adequate concessions or guarantees, may be better able to overcome a number of the problems and reduce uncertainties—there is a tendency toward conflict between private and social goals. This is particularly true when agrarian reform is seen as a primary vehicle for income distribution and external dependency is of major concern.

IV PROJECT EVALUATION

In attempts to develop Latin America's tropical lands the policy issues have been clouded by confused objectives; insufficient data on the physical, human, and institutional aspects involved; emotive discussion of erosion and natural resource destruction; and vague suggestions of an El Dorado. The balance of this study is directed toward the clarification of some of these issues through ex post evaluation of tropical land development projects. The question of interdependence among projects and spillover effects is discussed below.

Goals and Performance Criteria

To try to define the goals of tropical land development in Latin America is to court debate and dissent on the part of philosophers, sociologists, political scientists, and the like. As Castle and Youmans have stated:

Society undoubtedly has many and varied objectives when national programs are undertaken in education, highways and natural resource investment. The economist can never be sure just what these objectives are. Presumably they are sometimes stated by decision-makers. Yet surface statements need to be taken with a grain of salt. In order to ascertain objectives with precision, one would have to examine motivation of participants in the decision process. Even then one would be faced with the problem of either assigning relative weights to the preferences of the participants or taking the result of the political process as given.[1]

The objectives of public policy for new-land development are generally expressed in the following terms:

1. A net increase in total agricultural and forestry output or gross regional product.

[1] E. N. Castle and R. C. Youmans, "Economics in Regional Water Research and Policy," *American Journal of Agricultural Economics*, vol. 50, no. 5 (December 1968), p. 1664.

2. An economic return on public investment or on combined public and private investment.
3. Classification of the total number of beneficiaries, distinguishing between present residents and new immigrants.
4. Market orientation of agriculture, specified as a minimum percentage of total farm output sold on reaching full development.
5. A minimum acceptable income measured by average income and the percentage increase over existing incomes of the potential beneficiaries.
6. A net increase in employment.
7. Beneficiary participation expressed in terms of a minimum percentage of project or production decisions made or influenced by the settlers.
8. A net saving in foreign exchange.
9. External effects, such as the training of technicians in project administration, tropical agriculture, and regional development; the accumulation of experience that can be applied outside the project area; the building of strong government institutions equipped to effectively undertake complex projects; and self-sustaining development of the forest frontier.

The Tingo María colonization project in Peru[2] provides a practical example of some specific objectives for a planned public expenditure of about $30 million. The direct achievements were to be (1) the incorporation of 55,000 hectares (ha) of new land; (2) the rationalization of tenure and the resettlement of 2,150 existing subsistence settlers on 30,000 ha; (3) the settlement of 3,100 additional colonists, who were expected to come from the depressed and overpopulated sierra region; and (4) the creation of a commercial agriculture that would increase the supply of agricultural products on the domestic market (with the presumption of lowered consumer prices) and save foreign exchange through import substitution.

The indirect and external effects expected from the project were (1) the promotion of sustained expansion of national economic frontiers; (2) the incorporation of larger numbers of the rural population into the economy through improved utilization of natural and human resources in the agricultural sector; (3) the cultivation of new lands to alleviate social pressures, regional and sector income disparities, and massive migrations from the hinterland to major cities and to provide a source of employment for rural families displaced by reorganization in the sierra under the agrarian reform law; (4) the regeneration of the stagnant agricultural sector whose restricted output poses a serious obstacle to industrial expansion due to low levels of rural purchases, high urban food prices, and the need to use scarce foreign currency to import food; and (5) the improvement of the administrative and

---

[2] See chap. 5 for a detailed discussion of the Tingo María project.

technical capacity of the two government agencies responsible for execution of the project.

It is readily apparent that a number of these goals represent extra-market goods that cannot be monetized or quantified in other terms. Further, several have been expressed in such general terms that even some form of qualification of their particular impact appears to be out of the question. This situation presents obvious problems in the application of any meaningful achievement test. An additional complication arises as a result of the noncomplementary nature of some of the objectives. For instance, economic objectives may dictate that mechanization and high-technology agriculture be applied at the expense of beneficiary participation, income distribution, and employment generation objectives. Economies of scale in integrated plantations or cattle development involve a similar conflict. The need to attract entrepreneurial ability and private capital may dictate subdivision into blocks larger than the 10–15 ha generally established, thus sacrificing some of the income distribution objective. The relative importance attached to the proliferation of subsistence agriculture versus the degree of market orientation or foreign exchange saving will also influence both employment and income distribution goals. Theoretically, if criteria other than aggregate economic efficiency are to be introduced into a comprehensive evaluation of performance, they should be weighted.

Aside from these apparently insuperable difficulties, there is the possibility mentioned earlier that stated objectives may not reflect the real motive for a project. It was suggested in chapter 3 that in certain cases colonization may be prompted by a desire to alleviate pressure for land reform. With such multifarious and conflicting goals and potentially devious underlying motivations, can useful indices of success and failure be identified? In the final analysis success can be gauged only within the context of a national development strategy. None of the seven countries examined in this study had specified development goals and a strategy for their achievement with sufficient precision to permit such an evaluation. Therefore individual projects are evaluated in terms of their relative efficiency in contributing to stated national objectives.

Benefit-Cost Analysis

An ample literature exists on techniques and systems for the evaluation of public policy for natural resource development.[3] The purpose here is to examine the application of these techniques to the problem of developing

---

[3]The following authors are among those who have synthesized the main issues: Roland N. McKean, *Efficiency in Government through Systems Analysis* (John Wiley, 1958), pp. 103–89; Otto Eckstein, *Water Resource Development: The Economics of Project Evaluation* (Harvard University Press, 1958); S. V. Ciriacy-Wantrup, "Benefit-Cost Analysis and Public Resource Development," in S. C. Smith and E. N. Castle, eds.,

new lands in the humid tropics under the institutional conditions prevailing in Latin America. The discussion covers the use and limitations of benefit-cost analysis; the financial implications of government programs—notably the question of who pays; welfare considerations, particularly as they affect employment, income distribution, and resource conservation; and the identification and measurement of external economies as justification for governmental action to accelerate the settlement of new lands.

Theoretically it is possible to encompass all the aspects mentioned in the previous paragraph within a benefit-cost (B/C) framework. The degree of sophistication that usefully may be introduced into the evaluation of a project depends on how precisely the goals are specified, on data availability, and on whether the problem is to indicate immediate feasibility or infeasibility of a single one-stage project without budget constraints or is to establish the sequence from an array of projects (or a multistage project) in the presence of budget constraints.

If objectives are unquantifiable, they are not subject to manipulation through B/C analysis. If they are conflicting, a system of weighting must be introduced. On the assumption that policy should be guided where possible by systematic procedures, it is to be expected that project analysts will strive for improved quantification of goals and weighting factors. As indicated above the state of the art as it has been applied to tropical land development has not progressed far along these lines. Almost without exception, projects have been appraised for their immediate feasibility in a static framework, i.e., no change in demand (prices and interest) over time and without regard to sequence or budget limitation.

In the final analysis, it appears that the fundamental prerequisite for approving a project has been a B/C ratio of 1:1 at discount rates such as the 6 percent charged on international loans, 8 percent on government bonds, or, say, 15 percent as an estimate of the market rate of interest (opportunity cost). Benefits are measured as the net addition to aggregate consumption expressed in consumer prices;[4] that is, the ratio reflects a pure economic efficiency criterion without regard to the recipients of benefits or the bearers of costs. The B/C ratio is always supported by extensive qualifying remarks

---

Economics and Public Policy in Water Resource Development (Iowa State University Press, 1964), pp. 9–21; Earl M. Kulp, *Rural Development Planning, Systems Analysis and Working Method* (Praeger, 1970); J. A. King, *Economic Development Projects and Their Appraisal* (Johns Hopkins Press, 1967); A. O. Hirschman, *Development Projects Observed* (Brookings Institution, 1967) pp. 160–88; Joseph L. Tryon and F. E. Cookson, "A Critical Survey of Project Planning" (National Planning Association, July 1965, mimeo.); and Stephen A. Marglin, *Approaches to Dynamic Investment Planning* (Amsterdam: North-Holland Publishing Co., 1963).

[4] Net additions to aggregate consumption resulting from a project are taken to be the gross regional product less the opportunity cost of the factors employed in the geographic area of the project. The components of this benefit measure are shown in equation (2).

extolling the externalities and noneconomic benefits to be derived from the project. In some cases the ratio may be accompanied by a financial analysis and cost-effectiveness estimates, i.e., public expenditures per unit of the factors to be maximized, such as new employment generation, total number of beneficiaries, net foreign exchange saving, private capital mobilized, or productive capital mobilized through utilization of underemployed human and natural resources.

In chapter 5 the ex post project evaluations are based primarily on these traditional procedures so that they can be compared with the ex ante projections. The question of improvements in the appraisal and design of tropical land development projects, in view of experience plus recent additions to the theory of evaluation that formally incorporate dynamic aspects, income distribution, and "merit wants," is taken up in chapter 9.

In the traditional B/C analysis discussed above, guided by economic efficiency expressed in terms of net increments to aggregate consumption, the ratio R is given by $R_1 = (B - C_a)/C_p$ where it is desired to compare projects on the basis of the relative efficiency of government investment;[5] or $R_2 = B/(C_p + C_a)$ if the concern is efficiency in total resource use where

B = increment in aggregate consumption,

C_p = public costs associated with the project,

C_a = autonomous private investment stemming from new opportunities opened up by the project.

Throughout chapter 5, R_2 is used as the measure of project efficiency, and the specific procedure applied is the net present value (NPV) of investment, which is calculated as follows:

$$NPV = \sum_{t=0}^{n} \frac{B_t}{(1 + i)^t} - \sum_{t=0}^{n} \frac{C_{pt} + C_{at}}{(1 + i)^t} \tag{1}$$

where B_t and $(C_{pt} + C_{at})$ represent the streams of contributions to aggregate consumption and costs respectively; n is the economic life of the project, which more appropriately should be infinity when agriculture is the principal activity; and i is the discount rate. If the expression above is equated to zero and solved for i, the result is the internal rate of return (IRR).[6]

---

[5] In this case all benefits (after allowing for the opportunity cost of private capital and labor) are attributed to the public investment.

[6] While the NPV and IRR procedures do not automatically yield the same results in that the IRR sometimes may have more than one value, the IRR is used in chapter 5 since the structure of the cash flows in the projects studied is such that when $NPV = 0$,

It is generally accepted that prevailing market prices for labor, foreign exchange, savings, and capital do not provide a sound basis for project evaluation. While direct expenditures and earnings (at market prices) associated with a tropical land development project may be readily identified, the real issues, as implied above, are the net addition to aggregate consumption throughout the economy, the distribution of this consumption, improvement in the balance of payments, the increase in the rate of saving, and the reduction in unemployment. An attempt to quantify the macro-economic objectives of a new-land development project would depend on an equilibrium model of the economy. This would require estimates of the alternative opportunities of the factors employed; backward and forward linkages; the effect on aggregate demand and the ability of the economy to satisfy such demand; the substitution of project agricultural and forest output for that of other areas or imports; the import component of investments, inputs, and consumption expenditures resulting from the project and the export component of production; tax generation and how the government will spend such taxes; and the monetary and fiscal policy of the government.

The quantification or monetization required even for traditional B/C analysis is unquestionably open to attack. The use of shadow prices is said to be merely the economist's technique for injecting his own value judgments into the decision-making process in the guise of pseudo-objectivity. Projections of production, prices, costs, and rates of development are subject to enormous margins of error. Even in ex post situations, the analyst is dependent on highly questionable index numbers to adjust for inflation and is wholly ignorant of what might have happened in the project area in the absence of the particular public investment under consideration.

Some of the problems can be illustrated from the cases examined. On the Caranavi project in Bolivia, domestic price indexes showed a compound annual inflation rate of 28 percent over the twenty-five-year period evaluated (index increasing 375 times), while inflation in terms of foreign exchange was 25 percent (index increasing 230 times). In the case of the lower La Lana–La Trinidad basin in Mexico the government put $2.7 million into land settlement and highways between 1954 and 1967. Private investments amounted to about $3 million. Since these investments were made on the periphery of a region (the state of Veracruz) where 600,000 ha of new tropical lands were brought into production over the decade 1950–60, how much of the development and private investment in the basin could be attributed to specific government programs?

$i = IRR$. One advantage of the IRR in this instance is avoidance of discussion of the value of i, which represents the social opportunity cost of capital. For a discussion of formulas for measuring investment efficiency, see Jack Hirshleifer, James C. DeHaven, and J. W. Milliman, *Water Supply Economics, Technology and Policy* (University of Chicago Press, 1960), pp. 152–74.

On the Santo Domingo de los Colorados project in Ecuador, which called for a public expenditure and credit program of $4 million in three years, measurement of the impact of this specific investment in terms of attributable benefits is rendered impossible by the complex of programs that have been undertaken since 1950, all of which have contributed to the dynamic state of development evident on the project area. In 1957 the Pilot Plan for Directed Colonization was initiated in the same area with a budget of $3.83 million, of which $2.27 million were disbursed before the program was abandoned. Although this effort was regarded as an expensive failure with only about fifty families remaining in the project area, it provided valuable experience for structuring the second project.[7] After 1955 an extensive highway construction program was undertaken in the Guayas River basin. Between 1957 and 1966, $57 million worth of highway construction was authorized, all of which was to the benefit of the project region. In addition a $20 million five-year national highway maintenance program was initiated in 1964. As a consequence of these investments the project area now lies on either side of the paved highway that connects the capital city with Guayaquil, Ecuador's principal port. In addition the project area is an important junction between the highlands and the port of Esmeraldas on the north coast. The effect of this strategic position, apart from natural resource endowment, can hardly be overestimated; the town of Santo Domingo de los Colorados, which had no more than a few hundred inhabitants in the early fifties, had a population of 6,000 in 1962 and 12,000 in 1967 and is projected to reach 36,000 by 1985.[8]

In the Upano Valley in Ecuador the mere discussion of a $5 million project plus a $0.3 million investment in two airports in 1963-64 appears to have been sufficient to launch an immediate wave of spontaneous settlement and private investment based purely on expectations—since specific project investments were not started till 1966. A similar situation occurred in Tingo María following the project proposal in 1962, four years before the first disbursement of public funds. Clearly a crucial question is: What will be regarded as the starting date of a project in such cases? The rule is that the supply price of previous investments be taken as zero. If the start of a project is taken as the date of the first suggestion or some token public expenditure, and if either of these measures is sufficient to set in motion a stream of private investments, the NPV of the bulk of the public investment clearly will be improved by delay.[9] Regardless of whether the delay is intentional or due

[7]CIDA, *Tenencia de la tierra y desarrollo socio-económico del sector agrícola, Ecuador* (Washington: Pan American Union, 1965), pp. 342–45.

[8]Unpublished data, Junta de Planificación, Quito, Ecuador, 1968.

[9]It is evident that if such a procedure becomes the rule, private investors will revise their expectations accordingly. In addition, the delay would be finite since investors or colonists would eventually scale down their expectations and possibly abandon the area.

to bureaucratic hitches, assuming development in the interim, the NPV is greatly favored by adoption of the earlier starting date.

In spite of the drawbacks, B/C analysis does allow identification of a number of the crucial factors and their interrelationships that influence the design of land development projects. To begin the analysis of some of these relationships, the following terms are defined:

$n =$ project life,

$i =$ discount rate,

$P_{a1} =$ gross sales of primary products (agricultural) in the project area,

$P_{a2} =$ gross sales of primary products elsewhere in the country,

$P_{a3} =$ gross sales of primary products for export from the country,

$A_a =$ imputed value of home consumption of primary products,

$V_s =$ gross sales of nonprimary products (induced by the project) less purchases from the primary sector in the project ($V_s = S_s v_s$),

$S_s =$ number of families in nonprimary activities in the project area,

$v_s =$ gross per family production in nonprimary activities less purchases from the primary sector in the area,

$I_a =$ value of production inputs imported to the project area for primary activities,

$I_s =$ value of production inputs imported to the project area for nonprimary activities,

$L_a =$ the opportunity cost of labor in primary activities,

$L_s =$ the opportunity cost of labor in nonprimary activities,

$K_{x1} =$ fixed public investment in the project effectively unrelated to the number of settlers,

$K_{x2} =$ public investment in the project that is proportional to the number of families,

$K_{p1} =$ private investment in primary activities,

$K_{p2} =$ private investment in nonprimary activities,

$I_x =$ annual public expenditures in maintenance of infrastructure and services in the project area.

It is convenient to have summary expressions of the gross value of primary production; hence, the following are defined:

$$G = P_{a1} + P_{a2} + P_{a3} + A_a = S_a g_a$$

where

S_a = number of families in primary activities in the project area,

g_a = gross per family production in primary activities.

With these variables an expanded version of the NPV expression (equation 1) can be written as follows:

$$NPV = \sum_{t=0}^{n} \frac{(P_{a1} + P_{a2} + P_{a3} + A_a + V_s) - (I_a + I_s + L_a + L_s)_t}{(1 + i)^t}$$

(2)

$$- \sum_{t=0}^{n} \frac{(K_{x1} + K_{x2} + K_{p1} + K_{p2} + I_x)_t}{(1 + i)^t}$$

While maximizing the NPV may be an objective of project design, budgetary limitations and employment objectives require consideration of trade-offs. Where employment generation is important the ratios $K_{x1} + K_{x2}/S_a + S_s$ and $I_x/S_a + S_s$ become significant. Where reduction in immigration to existing urban centers is weighed heavily, projects may be designed to achieve high S_s/S_a ratios, especially if linkage effects from primary production are weak elsewhere in the economy. It has been postulated that P_{a2} and P_{a3} are constrained by markets. In this case the opportunities for expansion of settlement depend largely on maximizing $(P_{a1} + A_a)$. Since P_{a1} is a function of S_s, the employment multiplier S_s/S_a becomes an important element as long as the per capita consumption of new population in the project area is higher than formerly.

If the terms above are used, gross regional product (GRP) can be calculated in the following manner:

$$GRP = (G + V_s) - (I_a + I_s) .$$

(3)

Labor and natural resources are the two factors entering the estimation of benefit (net increment in aggregate consumption), which in turn is the numerator for the IRR calculation. Since natural resources are assumed to have a zero opportunity cost in the case of new-land development, the benefit may be summarized as

$$B = GRP - (L_a + L_s) .$$

(4)

With this measure of benefits from land settlement the NPV tends to be sensitive to L_a and C_a in cases where S_a is high relative to $K_{x1} + I_x$ since K_p

and I_a as a general rule are minor items. Thus the project analyst is inexorably drawn into the web of estimating the opportunity cost of labor.[10]

For the evaluations in this study no attempt has been made to produce empirical proof of the range of labor values used. Nevertheless, if the concept of social accounting has any validity as a guide to policy and project selection and design with respect to the development of new lands in the humid tropics of Latin America, quantification of this variable is of considerable importance. The relevance of labor in the equation stems from the following conditions peculiar to tropical land settlement: (1) the basic orientation has been, and is likely to remain, the unpaid family labor input; and (2) since natural resources are valued at zero and arguments have been advanced to minimize unit capital investment, labor cost assumes a proportionately more important role than in many public investment projects.

Reference was made to criticism of the zero marginal productivity theory in chapter 2. Myrdal has raised a number of questions regarding the applicability of the concept in practical policy formulation.[11] At the other end of the scale the opportunity cost may be taken as the conventional wage for full-time employment paid to unskilled campesinos—a figure that may range from $500 to $1,000 annually per family in the tropical countries of Latin America. Using such figures would provide an excessively conservative basis for selecting economically viable projects.

Financial Aspects

Financial considerations center solely on the flow of public expenditures and revenues as a result of a specific tropical land development project. This factor is of importance in land development policy and project selection to the extent that the revenue-earning capacity of the government is weighted as a criterion for such decisions. It also has welfare or income distribution implications in that the costs of the project are expected to be recovered from the direct beneficiaries (colonists or other residents in the project area). In general, tropical land development involving public expenditures in infrastructure, services, and subsidized credit implies a transference of wealth (or income-earning capacity) to the residents of the project area in that no attempt is made to recoup the full costs. Clearly there is no reason why the residents of the project area should be expected to pay all the public costs involved when benefits may accrue to many others outside the region, such as construction contractors, importers, processors, fertilizer manufacturers, highway users, subsequent settlers in adjacent areas, and so on.

[10] It is assumed throughout that the opportunity cost of the virgin soil and forest resources made available through these projects is zero. In the case of fiscal lands acquired by private developers it is evident that purchase price enters the financial, but not the economic, analysis.

[11] Gunnar Myrdal, *Asian Drama: An Inquiry into the Poverty of Nations*, Twentieth Century Fund (Random House, 1968), pp. 2050–54.

Where financial performance is seriously considered in project selection it is to be expected that the government will wish to maximize the percentage of costs recovered. Taxation on lands, income, sales, exports, purchases, and the like presumably will apply to the residents of the project area at the same rate as elsewhere in the country. Thus the maximizing procedure must be directed to extracting payments from those who have obtained direct access to the use of land and forest resources as a result of the project. Revenues from this source will be governed by the ability to pay and income distribution objectives.

When these two factors are taken into account, plus the tax-revenue expectation, the direct cost recuperation percentage can be calculated and included for decision-making purposes. In the absence of an interindustry matrix there is little point in including an assumed multiplier for revenues from second-stage and subsequent transactions, since the percentage increase is likely to be similar for all projects or policies.

Welfare Aspects

Since redistribution of wealth looms large in virtually all cases of public intervention to accelerate or control new-land settlement, brief mention is made here of the welfare implications in the evaluation of such government policies. The concept of increasing general welfare encompasses a variety of extra-market goods, such as the dignity associated with land ownership, reduction of class barriers, education, health, improved mobility, an increased range of individual choice and decision, and greater participation in society resulting from the higher economic status of the beneficiaries.

Public intervention to redirect resources into tropical land development and improve the level of income (or other welfare aspects) of those associated with the activity clearly involves costs. Krutilla has discussed the question of whether any useful measures of welfare benefits derived from these costs can be helpful in guiding public decisions. He pointed out that a normative and value-loaded framework is unavoidable unless the status quo welfare status (distribution pattern) is accepted, and he concluded that while "the application of criteria for improving welfare . . . cannot be a mechanical or a compellingly logical activity," analysis should be directed to systematic consideration of those conditions "likely to produce consequences superior to those that would result from purely random behavior."[12]

Discussion of welfare objectives often centers on the trade-offs with economic efficiency. It is argued that before one becomes too concerned with redistribution one should have some products to distribute. The issue in this case is whether the increased consumption of one group is in conflict with another group's savings and investment requirements to accelerate production

[12] John V. Krutilla, "Welfare Aspects of Benefit: Cost Analysis," *Journal of Political Economy*, vol. 69, no. 3 (June 1961), pp. 226–35.

and investment. There are several critical factors. To what extent do the investments made in tropical land development involve resources with a low alternative opportunity cost, such as labor or virgin land, and result in production that allows increased consumption of both homegrown and purchased items? If there is a high proportion of low-value resources involved, the resultant redistribution of consumption may well have a positive rather than negative effect on overall development through market expansion. Also, to what extent are extra-market goods or social services connected with the redistribution? Where such aspects are goals of new-land settlement, the cost may be viewed as long-term investment in human resource development, i.e., the additional consumption should not be regarded as a diversion of savings.

In the discussion of the B/C formula, employment was evaluated in terms of jobs created per unit of public investment. No mention was made of the systematic treatment of income distribution objectives, however. In most public programs aimed at expanding agriculture and forestry in humid tropical regions, it is usually implicit or explicit that the direct beneficiaries primarily will be drawn from low-income groups in society. If such a situation were assumed, then employment generation would simultaneously provide an index of the income distribution effect. This position is taken in the project evaluations presented in chapters 5 and 6. No attempt has been made to formally introduce distribution objectives into the B/C calculation through placing a premium (shadow value) on income received by specific groups.

External Effects

Reference has already been made to the stress laid on external economies in justifying public investments related to the opening up of jungle land. To avoid confusion, the types of benefits that may derive from public investments in tropical land development will be briefly reviewed. Direct or primary benefits include the value added in the area directly affected by the project. Value added is taken as the gross value of the agricultural and forestry production of the direct beneficiaries less production inputs imported to the zone and the opportunity cost of labor and private capital. Indirect or secondary benefits are the value added in producer and consumer services provided in the zone that may be wholly or partly attributed to the project, with the same adjustment for imported inputs and opportunity cost of factors as in the direct benefits.

Secondary benefits may be amplified to encompass the value added throughout the whole economy stemming from or induced by the provision of producer and consumer services to the direct beneficiaries in the project zone. The critical issue is the extent to which the resources used in providing these services would have been unemployed in the absence of the project. The determination hinges on (1) correct assessment of the opportunity cost of the labor and private capital involved throughout the life of the project, and (2) on an estimate of the employment of resources generated by alternative uses of the same public funds.[13] Although there undoubtedly is considerable underemployment of labor in the tropical countries of Latin America, the conditions above essentially preclude any useful measure of secondary benefits.

External or spillover effects are those arising from the influence of activities in the project area on the costs or incomes of producers or on the satisfaction of consumers in other areas.[14] Pecuniary external effects will be ignored in the discussion since they reflect shifts in price or asset values that merely lead to transfers of rent without a net increase or decrease in economic efficiency.[15] Technological external effects are those that influence the physical input and output of producers other than the direct project beneficiaries. The special case of externalities that occur when there are underemployed resources has been discussed above as a secondary benefit. In the case of humid tropical land development, the technological external economies and diseconomies center on such aspects as the potential adverse downstream effects and the depletion of soil, forest, wildlife, and scenic resources as a result of forest clearing; the enhanced quality, quantity, and timing of water flows; preservation of the biota for research purposes or as genetic banks for endangered life forms,[16] and the dynamic effect on the development of land and forest resources as a result of the experience gained and technology developed in the project zone. The latter point is the principal hypothesis underlying many government programs for colonization and road-building in the tropical rain forests of Latin America. The specific external economies sought are an autonomous flow of private capital, technology, and entrepreneurial talent into frontier regions in response to "free" production goods made available through the project (access, research, experience, trained manpower); and, because of these factors, the mobilization of underemployed human and natural resources whose opportunity costs may approach zero.

Summary

Evaluation of tropical land development at the present time is effectively restricted to the estimation of the direct project impact in a region of influ-

---

[13]McKean, *Efficiency in Government*, pp. 151–63.

[14]Ibid., pp. 134–50. While external effects may encompass secondary benefits, the obverse does not hold. This is because (1) secondary benefits stem only from attributable value added in the provision of goods and services to the direct beneficiaries of the project, whereas external effects may also include value added that is unrelated to the production and consumption of the direct beneficiaries; and (2) secondary benefits by definition are positive; external effects are frequently negative.

[15]See Julius Margolis, "Secondary Benefits, External Economies and the Justification of Public Investment," *Review of Economics and Statistics*, vol. 39, no. 3 (August 1957), pp. 284–91.

[16]John V. Krutilla, "Conservation Reconsidered," *American Economic Review* (September 1967), pp. 777–86 (Resources for the Future Reprint 67).

ence with the application of static concepts in B/C analysis in the absence of budget limitations. The principal restrictions are:

1. A lack of basic information and analysis that would permit the projection of changing demand for inputs and production and the introduction of dynamic programming.
2. The failure to conceive of a range of competitive or complementary projects that would allow the introduction of budgetary constraints and the problem of project sequence priority.
3. A lack of interindustry matrices that would permit the estimation of external or secondary effects and the impact on aggregate consumption and savings.
4. The lack of a precise definition of development objectives that would allow the use of weights in examining such questions as the distribution of aggregate consumption or savings in foreign exchange.[17]
5. Inadequate data on past experience of the type that might permit the calculation of probabilities of various outcomes.

While few, if any, would claim that a favorable B/C ratio of the type described should be the only criterion for project approval, there is little doubt it is a prerequisite. It would be a gallant loan committee that would approve a highway or colonization project with a negative NPV.

Aside from economic considerations a perusal of project feasibility statements indicates that the authors (government departments) implicitly do not agree that the financial justification rests on the flow of taxes and direct payments from the residents of the project area. Further, any systematic use of welfare or external effects in project selection is ruled out by the lack of a macro framework like that outlined above. In spite of all the drawbacks the B/C technique offers one of the best points of entry for an examination of the tropical land development issue. The critical factors can be identified, and an indication of the sensitivity of performance to changes in these factors can be obtained.

---

[17]The measurement of trade-offs between economic efficiency and income distribution has little significance unless a social welfare function is available. See Castle and Youmans, "Economics in Regional Water Research," pp. 1662–65.

A SURVEY OF
V TWENTY-FOUR
DEVELOPMENT PROJECTS

The principal development measures for humid tropical lands that have been employed or permitted to operate by Latin American governments were reviewed in chapter 3. Here the performance of twenty-four projects (see map 3) is examined. The primary focus of all the projects is the exploitation of new land to generate production, employment, and a population shift toward tropical frontier areas, and all involve forest resources in terms of either systematic harvesting or disorganized destruction. The projects were selected as being representative of the principal procedures applied in new-land development since 1950, a range of ecological and locational situations, and a variety of institutional conditions. Each project is evaluated for the salient features that appear to have influenced its performance.

The development measures are classified under the following headings: directed and semidirected colonization, highways associated with spontaneous settlement, foreign colonization, and private land subdivision and settlement schemes. In order to complement the analysis of colonization, Bolivian experience is drawn upon to illustrate the promotion of livestock development on relatively large-scale units and state enterprise in agricultural processing industries. Many of these activities overlap and can run concurrently in the same region; thus the projects do not fit neatly into the classification, but the categories nonetheless provide a basis for evaluating public policy. In directed or semidirected colonization and in state enterprise the government becomes the prime mover for development. The state plays an indirect role through the provision of infrastructure and services that constitute incentives for individual settlers or corporate interests to take the initiative in exploiting new resources. The government is even more remotely connected with private land subdivision and settlement, foreign colonization, and integrated primary production and processing or forest industries, all of which supply their own infrastructure and services and require only tacit state approval. The combination selected will determine the degree of state involvement in the development process. Another criterion used in examining the projects is the stage of development—pioneer, consolidation, or growth—in the region where the various development measures are applied.

Map 3. New-land development projects in the humid tropics of Latin America.

1 La Joya*
2 Nuevo Ixcatlán*
3 Cihualtepec*
4 La Chontalpa*
5 Petén
6 Bajo Aguan
7 Rigoberto Cabezas
8 Cariari
9 Bataan*
10 Coto Brus
11 Caquetá*
12 Santo Domingo de los Colorados*
13 Puyo-Tena*
14 Valle del Upano*
15 Alto Marañón
16 Huallaga Central
17 Tingo María – Tocache*
18 Caranavi

19 Alto Beni I*
20 Alto Beni II*
21 Chapare*
22 Chimoré*
23 Yapacani*
24 San Juan*
25 Okinawa*
26 Guabirá*
27 Filadelfia*
28 Puerto Presidente Stroessner*
29 Ivinheima*
30 Paraná*
31 Alexandre de Gusmão
32 Gleba Arinos*
33 Alto Turiaçu
34 Guamá
35 Tomé Açu
36 Clevelandia
37 Tournavista (Iparía)*

* Projects analysed

The choice of these criteria implies certain underlying hypotheses about the development process in tropical frontier areas:

1. Public investment and programs for infrastructure and land and for forest development will have significantly different results, depending on the stage of development of the region in question.
2. The increasing role of government in the development of remote jungle frontiers will have an appreciable influence on performance.
3. The measures selected by the government for its intervention will materially affect the outcome.

The three successive stages of development (pioneer, consolidation, or growth) of a tropical land frontier are somewhat arbitrary in the sense that they represent a continuous gradation, and all three may occur simultaneously on a specific project, e.g., Ivinheima in Brazil.

Pioneer zones are primarily subsistence economies in which there is no labor market and a high level of unemployment. No urban development, utilities, or services exist. These zones are further characterized by recent and continuing settlement; limited lands cleared from forest; poor housing, infrastructure, and access; unstable settlement; the absence of a mechanism to establish legal titles; low capitalization in agriculture; little colonist or political organization; and little settler knowledge of soil capability, climate, crops, or management practices. In all the cases studied the pioneer phase was associated only with directed government or private land settlement, although in practice the principal areas of such settlement in Latin America are spontaneous.

The consolidation stage may follow five to ten years after initial pioneer settlement. There is a general upgrading of all aspects of development. Land tenure may be established, and settlement is more stable. Settlers have less contact with their original home areas, and there is less abandonment of land parcels. Some consolidation of holdings occurs, larger crop areas per man are achieved, and market orientation of production increases. The colonists' knowledge of agriculture suited to the zone improves as does their capacity to effectively use credit. Development of urban nuclei with commercial and government services occurs. Increased capitalization in agriculture appears in the form of plantation crops and livestock, a labor market forms, and permanent housing and infrastructure are built. Small-scale processing of agricultural products and saw milling is initiated, with some development of colonist organization or even municipal government.

The growth phase may follow five to ten years after consolidation. It is marked by the development of an urban center and a major flow of private capital into industrial and commercial activity. The urban population provides a significant market for agriculture in the region. Settlers actively participate in a firmly established municipal government. Many central government services are transferred to municipal or private organizations. There is an improved agricultural technology, an accelerating demand for credit, and an increasing capital-labor ratio.

Directed Colonization

Directed colonization is usually characterized by a high degree of government control over colonists with respect to the size and location of farms, land clearing, the resale of land, the crop pattern, management practices, credit availability, eligibility for land, cooperative organization, and the settlers' contribution of time to community activities. The project is automatically defined in terms of its geographic extent, the precise government investments and services provided, and the private investments expected. In effect, directed colonization is only applied on virgin lands, i.e., those in the pioneer stage of development. Throughout Latin America more than 100 such projects have been undertaken to open up tropical forests over the past thirty years. Virtually every tropical country has experimented with this particular approach to land development.

Colonization sponsored by the government, whether directed or semidirected, is the land settlement procedure that has received the severest criticism. In some circles it is equated with public policy for expanding the agricultural frontier in the humid tropics. Seven cases of directed colonization were examined where the principal aim was the development of virgin lands in totally unoccupied regions. In addition La Chontalpa and Bataan, which are complex resettlement projects, were classified as directed because of the extremely high level of government involvement.

Nuevo Ixcatlán and Cihualtepec (Lower La Lana–La Trinidad Basin)

The region comprises about 200,000 hectares (ha) on the southeastern edge of the Papaloapan basin in Mexico (see map 4). Although the basin was opened up by the railroads in the 1870s, development southwest of the southern branch line was confined to a radius of 5 or 10 kilometers (km). In 1950 less than 1 percent of the properties accounted for 90 percent of the land in holdings with an average size of over 15,000 ha.[1] Virtually the only settlement was in ejidos (lands granted under the reform program) and colonies on scattered alluvial flats along the rivers. The rivers remained the only form of access to the region until 1953, when about 500–700 families lived there.

[1] Districts of Mixes and Choapan, Oaxaca. Secretaría de Industria y Comercio, Dirección General de Estadística, *III Censo Agrícola-Ganadero y Ejidal, 1950* (Mexico, D.F., 1954).

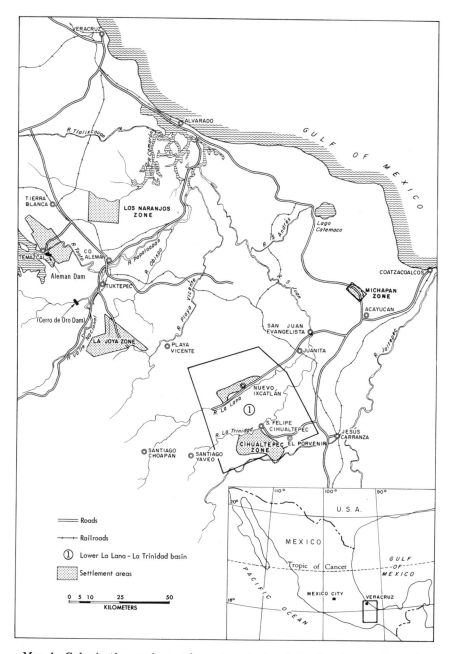

Map 4. Colonization and resettlement projects of the Papaloapan Commission in the states of Veracruz and Oaxaca, Mexico, 1953–1961.

In 1954 the Papaloapan Commission initiated construction of 77 km of penetration roads into the region as the first stage of a resettlement program for families displaced by the Aleman Dam. By 1967, 1,180 families had been established on 30,000 ha in the Nuevo Ixcatlán and Cihualtepec projects. The total government investment, excluding transfer payments, amounted to $2.17 million (see table 7). During this fifteen-year period the ejidos, colonies, small property holders, and timber concerns built approximately 120 km of road on their own account; land in exploitation was expanded from about 25,000 ha to 150,000 ha; and population increased from about 3,000 to 18,000. Private investment in the region was about $3 million, of which 50 percent is accounted for by cattle brought into areas outside the two projects.

Over the fifteen-year period 1953–67 gross annual agricultural production was estimated to have increased from $0.5 million to $2.8 million. Gross regional product (GRP), including forestry and services, was estimated at $3 million in 1967 (see table 8). Subtracting the value added in services and an opportunity cost of $240 per family employed in agriculture and forestry from the flow of GRP, the internal rate of return (IRR) on all investments in

Table 7.   Investment by the Papaloapan Commission and
Instituto Nacional Indigenista in the Nuevo Ixcatlán,
Cihualtepec, and La Joya Projects, 1954–1967

(*$ thousand*)

Category	Investments and Costs			
	Nuevo Ixcatlán	Cihualtepec	La Joya	Total
Planning, administration, and overhead	98	69	47	214
Roads	344	268	244	856
Water supply, schools, and clinics	40	41	43	124
Housing	176	47	85	308
Moving and settlement[a]	336	112	159	607
Indemnity payments[b]	288	219	46	553
Purchase of land[b]	24	0	0	24
Property survey and subdivision	112	80	85	277
Credit[b]	88	0	2	90
Operation and maintenance				
Roads and water supply	104	85 }	99	542
Other services[c]	158	96 }		
Total	1,768	1,017	810	3,595

Sources: Papaloapan Commission and INI.

[a] Includes all INI expenses in operation of settlement projects.

[b] Transfer payments.

[c] Health, education, and police. This figure includes an estimate of costs incurred by the municipalities in providing police services.

Table 8. Estimated Production in the Lower La Lana–La Trinidad Basin
and La Joya, 1966–1967

($ million)

	Value of Production[a]					
	La Lana–La Trinidad Basin				La Joya	
	Nuevo Ixcatlán	Cihual- tepec	Other areas	Total	Project	Region
Agriculture and livestock						
1. Consumed on the farm or sold for consumption in the region[b]	0.12	0.09	0.40	0.61	0.06	0.19
2. Exported from the region[b]	0.25	0.10	1.85	2.20	0.02	0.20
3. Total (1 + 2)	0.37	0.18	2.25	2.80	0.08	0.39
4. Value of imported inputs[c]	0.02	0.01	0.13	0.16	–	0.02
5. Value added (3 – 4)	0.34	0.18	2.12	2.64	0.08	0.37
Forestry and barbasco						
6. Exports from the region[d]	0.02	0.02	0.05	0.09	–	0.04
7. Value of imported inputs[e]	–	–	–	–	–	0.02
8. Value added (6 – 7)	0.02	0.02	0.05	0.09	–	0.02
Services in the region						
9. Value added in distribution of primary and secondary products[e]	0.02	0.01	0.06	0.09[f]	–	0.02
10. Value added in distribution of production inputs and consumer goods[e]	0.05	0.02	0.11	0.18	–	0.04
11. Total value added (9 + 10)	0.07	0.03	0.17	0.27	–	0.06
Gross regional project (5 + 8 + 11)	0.43	0.23	2.34	3.00	0.08	0.45

Sources: Municipalidad de Tuxtepec and field estimates.
Note: Dashes indicate "negligible."

[a]Calculated on the basis of estimates of per capita consumption, total sales, and shipments out of the region.

[b]At prices received by the producer at the farm or plant.

[c]At the cost to the producer at the farm or plant less the value added in distribution by agents within the region. In La Joya, chiefly consists of raw barbasco shipped down the Cajones River for processing at the plant in Macedonio Alcalá.

[d]Includes the value of processed products; where processing is involved the value of raw materials from the region is excluded.

[e]Value added through transport, storage, wholesaling, and retailing. For La Joya, estimate is based on the assumption that value added by factors in the region is $5.60 per ton on estimated total exports of 2,800 tons from the region.

[f]Estimated on the basis of 50 percent of a total value added equivalent to $12.50 per ton of produce shipped out of the region and $1.70 per head of livestock shipped.

the zone is about 15 percent for the fifteen years. Thus if all benefits are attributed to the sum of private and public investments, it appears that the commission's investments were amply justified without any further projection of costs and returns. If benefits are measured solely in terms of the increased production from the 30,000 ha incorporated by the two projects, however, the IRR on the public investment plus that of the 1,180 colonists, calculated on the same basis as above, becomes zero. Extrapolation of 1967 costs and returns as a constant to 1976 (a twenty-five-year project life) raises the figure to 8 percent. This leads to the conclusion that the project investments themselves were, or will prove to be, uneconomic when considered in isolation, but taken in combination with development in the region served by the project infrastructure they appear to be justified in economic terms. Indications are that the roads, which took 30 percent of the colonization outlay, were largely responsible for stimulating private investment in agriculture that paid handsome dividends.

The pattern of development in the region has weak backward and forward linkage effects that could induce secondary employment. Purchased inputs amount to about 5 percent of gross production and are chiefly in the form of livestock, whose development requires a low labor component. The production exported from the region requires little processing before final consumption, and within the region the ratio of service to primary employment is about 1:20.

With respect to income distribution, evidence from Nuevo Ixcatlán indicates that the traders, who account for 5 percent of the population, earn 50 percent of the total income, i.e., a per capita income twenty times that of the colonists. This inequality may be explained by the severe shortage of credit from the regular commercial banks or the state; the lack of organization on the part of the settlers; and the absence of any effective government policy or mechanism to regulate the commercial sector, promote competition, or educate and assist the settlers to organize.

La Joya

The region encompasses 60,000 ha in Mexico between the Valle Nacional and the Playa Vicente rivers, both tributaries of the Papaloapan River on the western margin of the basin (see map 4). It is the area served by a 40-km road built by the Papaloapan Commission in 1955–56 to give access to the La Joya project for resettlement made necessary by the construction of the Aleman Dam.

Unlike the lower La Lana–La Trinidad basin, there was considerable development in this region prior to the construction of the road. In 1940 there were 700 families on 14,000 ha. By 1953 when the commission examined the settlement potential, the area had been thoroughly explored by potential colonists, and over 1,000 families were occupying lands in the region. The preliminary reconnaissance, however, established the availability of 8,000 ha (50 percent cultivable) that could be subdivided into 450 parcels of 10 to 30 ha each. Between 1956 and 1958, 360 families were located on the project. But when the land was cleared it was found to be less fertile than expected, and the cultivable lands were less extensive than estimated. It transpired that the cultivable area had been overestimated by about 50 percent, leading to the abandonment of about 30 percent of the properties between 1959 and 1960. As a result of this, plus abrasive encounters with colonists over rights to timber and lands, colonist disinterest in extension services, and internal problems among the ejidos, the commission relegated the area to a low priority in the overall Papaloapan program.

All maintenance operations on the last 20 km of road were suspended in 1960, and plans were dropped for the construction of bridges that had been included in the original specification. Since the two principal crops, rice and sesame, are harvested in the wet season, both the merchants and settlers attempted to maintain transport through the use of tractors, which ruined the roadbed after two years. Most of the government services were withdrawn by 1964. The cumulative effect of these circumstances in the first eight years of settlement was a 30 percent decline from the peak area that could be maintained in crops, a 30-50 percent decline in yields, a 200 percent increase in freight rates because of the loss of road access, and the elimination of all expectations of dynamic development in the project area.

The public investment in the region directly related to the La Joya resettlement project amounted to $0.8 million over the period 1954-67 (see table 7). If transfer payments and regular service expenditures[2] are excluded, the direct public outlay chargeable to new-land development is $0.6 million. If GRP is used as the measure of benefits (excluding services and applying an opportunity cost of $240 per family in agriculture and forestry), the net present value (NPV) of the cash flow is minus $475,000 at a 15 percent rate of interest over the fourteen years 1954-67. If the project is considered in isolation, the NPV is minus $650,000.

While the La Joya project was clearly uneconomic it can be shown that certain elements of the public and private investment in the region were viable. The dynamic elements in the development of the region since 1954—the spontaneous settlement of 200 families, the forest industry, and the sugar and rubber programs—stem from the road or other programs unrelated to the La Joya settlement. If all expenditures and returns directly associated with the La Joya project (excluding roads and forestry) are subtracted from the GRP, the IRR becomes 25 percent. The evaluation is highly

[2] Land purchase and indemnity to settlers may be considered transfer payments chargeable to the Aleman Dam. Operation and maintenance of water supply, education, extension, and police services may be regarded as expenses associated with population regardless of location.

sensitive to the forestry activity—elimination of the costs and returns from the Pueblo Viejo mill in the 1956–58 period reduces the rate from 25 percent to 7 percent. Since natural resources were assumed to have a zero opportunity cost, the exploitation of precious red cedar and significant quantities of commercial timber species yielded a high value added. The most significant aspect, however, is that this return was obtained in the critical early years of the project. At discount rates of 15–20 percent, the same increment earned fifteen years later would have little impact on the benefit-cost (B/C) ratio.

The continuing development sequence associated with promotion programs in sugar and rubber in the region may be attributable in part to the commission's original investments. While there are many uncertainties about the market and the ability of the soils to sustain continued cropping without excessive chemical inputs, the rubber and sugar programs may radically change the economy of the La Joya region. The inflow of capital and the influence of field supervisors may mean that 50–70 percent of the cultivable area, which now must be left in bush-fallow, could be largely transformed into permanent agriculture with increasing employment. If price relationships are maintained at the 1967–68 level, however, the value of production from plantings made at that time on less than 5 percent of the cultivable area should amount to $0.2 million[3] by 1978—the equivalent of the total gross value of agricultural exports from the region in 1966–67. In the case of sugar the gross value of cane sales from plantations existing in 1967 could amount to $0.22 million by 1970.[4]

La Chontalpa

The La Chontalpa project on the coastal plains of Tabasco, Mexico, is one of the most ambitious and comprehensive schemes for humid tropical land development yet undertaken in Latin America. (See map 3.) The overall plan being executed by the Grijalva Commission[5] includes construction of the Malpaso Dam on the Grijalva River with a reservoir of 39,000 square km and a storage capacity of 13 million cubic meters; installation of a 360,000-kilowatt hydroelectric plant; flood control levees; and the phased development of 270,000 ha that received flood protection from the dam.

Phase I covers 140,000 ha, and the initial plan called for a pilot project, El Limón, on a gross area of 52,000 ha, where 3,265 families were in residence prior to the project. Drainage and irrigation were planned for the development of intensive agriculture on 42,000 ha to be farmed by 3,300 families with the employment of 1,000 additional workers at full production. The

---

[3] A yield of 1 ton of centrifuged latex per hectare from trees more than fifteen years old at a price of $1,360 per ton.

[4] A yield of 50 tons of cane per hectare at a price to the producer of $4 per ton.

[5] The Grijalva Commission is a semiautonomous agency under the jurisdiction of the Secretaría de Recursos Hidráulicos.

gross output from the area would be increased twentyfold over a fourteen-year period. The total budget for a five-year development period was $62.5 million, with civil works accounting for $46 million, or $1,070 per hectare, divided as follows:

Dykes, drainage, and land leveling	$ 540
Feeder roads	$ 255
Forest clearing	$ 125
Irrigation	$ 150
Total	$1,070

Urban facilities and services were to cost $10.2 million ($3,100 per family) with the balance of $8.3 million in indemnities, agricultural equipment, and installations. The total public investment for the program was $1,500 per hectare, or $18,950 per family farm.

This plan was subsequently modified to postpone irrigation, lower the standard of urban facilities, expand the gross area to 83,000 ha (72,000 ha in intensive agriculture), and settle 6,200 families. The expanded project was renamed La Chontalpa. The budget remained unchanged, and agricultural credit requirements were set at $23 million. Land development costs were estimated at $600 per hectare–$220 in drainage and dykes, $340 in feeder roads, and $40 in clearing. Investment in urban facilities and community services was reduced to $1,200 per family. The overall unit costs of the project under the revised plan were lowered to $870 per hectare and $10,000 per family.

Before the project the area was occupied by 4,700 families, who farmed about 36,000 ha in subsistence shifting agriculture. The gross value of production was about $540 per family. Throughout much of the region, annual flooding extending over a period of three to four months precluded intensive development on the rich alluvial soils. The gross output in 1965 was estimated at $3.5 million. When fully developed, La Chontalpa was expected to yield $24 million in annual production, which could be increased about 60 percent with supplementary irrigation.

Development was started in 1966. The principal elements of the plan were (1) the habilitation of all lands through drainage and forest clearing; (2) the provision of all-weather access roads; (3) the dissolution and restructuring of existing ejidos to conform to a rectangular block pattern of twenty-five new ejidos, each of which includes parts of several old ejidos; (4) the relocation of all the families from the diverse ejidos on each block into an urban center; (5) giving each ejidatario within each block rights to a rectangular parcel of 10 ha plus 2 ha of communal pasture; and (6) the provision of credit, technical assistance, and mechanization in order to assure intensive production.

Production management is similar to that of a large corporation. Central management decisions related to crop areas, sowing dates, fertilizer use, and so on, are made by a division of the commission that is staffed through a contract with the Instituto Nacional de Investigaciones Agrícolas (INIA). Implementation of the decisions depends on the agronomist in charge of each section of 2,000–3,000 ha. If they work on their own parcels the ejidatarios receive credit from the Banco Agrícola, and the owner of the parcel is automatically debited in the form of an expanded loan. Work carried out by ejidatarios is certified by the field supervisors before payment. The same procedure is applied with respect to production inputs. The decision rests with the agronomist, and the materials and hired labor are debited to the owner of each parcel. All work is voluntary. The incentive for the ejidatario to work on his own parcel is the expectation that with special care his harvest will be greater. The only obligation he has is to be present at the time of harvesting to approve the distribution of the crop.

The 2,000-ha banana operation is run as a corporate entity in which the ejidatarios with land in the plantation are shareholders receiving dividends at the end of each season after all operating costs, management fees, reserves, and new investment requirements have been subtracted from gross earnings. Shareholders have first claim to employment; they work for wages in any part of the operation, and no attempt is made (as it is in other crop programs) to maintain an accounting for each parcel covering the owner's time, other wage-labor, material inputs, machine time, or production.

Cattle constitute a third variation with respect to ownership and management. The pasture and corrals are held in common by the 200–300 families on the section. Each ejidatario has the right to run a certain number of cattle. The cattle are individually owned except for the bulls, which are purchased under the direction of the commission and debited to the cattle operation. All operating decisions are made by the section agronomist. As the project proceeds it is hoped that the banana and cattle operations can be used as the basis for setting up intensive and integrated operations, such as large-scale hog production, fish culture, and fruit processing, all of which may require more than one section.

In 1967 the Mexican government became concerned about marketing problems inherent in the production plan. Accordingly the area in pasture was increased from 16,000 ha to 42,000 ha on the assumption that beef would have an assured demand. As a result of this change the average area allocated to each ejidatario was increased from 12 to 15 ha, and the number of beneficiaries from the project was reduced from 6,200 to 4,800. The replacement of 18,000 ha of intensive crops by pasture is expected to reduce the gross output of the project at full production by 10–35 percent, depending on which crops are substituted.[6]

---

[6]Gross production from pasture is estimated at $80 per hectare relative to a $255 weighted average for annual crops and $500 for tree crops in full production.

La Chontalpa is distinct from most colonization projects in that two of the major unknowns affecting production and net benefits—the individual preferences, motivation, and capacity of the colonists and the ability of institutions to provide supporting services—have virtually been removed from the equation through the organization of production outlined above. The viability of La Chontalpa, however, is more vulnerable to markets than that of many projects because of the high cash component and the elimination of the unpaid unskilled labor component. The fortunes of the project could well be made or lost on the basis of an export banana industry. The original plan called for about 10,000 ha in bananas, but the commission was able to gain only a concession to supply Germany that justified planting 2,000 ha.

Aside from its unique technical and economic aspects the project is an extreme case of abrupt social change. On most colonization projects the colonist is free to live where he chooses and to produce any crop within the limits imposed by credit. If he does not like the conditions in a new frontier area he is always free to return to his place of origin. In contrast, on La Chontalpa the campesino must accept relocation to an urban center, the automatic granting of production credit, and at least temporary abdication of his right of decision over products and management practices. His alternative is to accept 100 percent indemnity and leave the district.

These impositions on the campesino are dictated by both economic efficiency and welfare criteria. Since $55 million are to be spent in productive infrastructure, this cannot be left idle or in the hands of incompetent or unmotivated farm managers for long if the project is to show a positive B/C ratio. For this reason little time can be wasted in persuading the campesinos of the advantages of the proposed changes. Further, there may be little point in trying to educate campesinos in a theoretical concept of housing, social services, farm management, and consumption for which they have no reference point. Production efficiency requires that qualified technicians make and implement the management decisions; that mechanization and other advanced technology be used to assure high yields and bring the land into full production as fast as possible after completion of the infrastructure; and that campesinos not live on their lots, since this would interfere with the operation of machinery. Welfare efficiency requires that the campesinos live in urban centers where they can be offered a level of housing, community facilities, extension, health services, utilities, and education far beyond anything that could be provided if they remained on their farms.

The engineering requirements for construction efficiency have forced a pace of land clearing and resettlement that allows no time for testing management practices or methods of assisting campesinos to adjust to their new situation. The importance of lead time and a slower rate of development, if feasible, is illustrated by this experience. If experimentation had been started earlier it would have been possible to avoid the risks inherent in gaining knowledge under commercial-scale conditions. For example, in 1967 poor yields on large areas of rice and sorghum were attributed to wrong planting dates. Accordingly, planting on 500 ha in 1968 was advanced two months for sorghum and set back one month for rice. Under pressure to clear land, in 1968 the commission planned to experiment with off-season clearing of 1,700 ha. The risks were possible damage to the soil structure from working tractors on wet ground and the inability to burn felled trees, which could lead to weed infestation and substantial problems in eventually clearing the area. In fact, the soil suffered no serious damage, but severe delays and increased costs were experienced during the land clearing (see chapter 6). With sufficient time such experiments could be undertaken on pilot plots.

The IRR based on projections for the original project is on the order of 8 percent, assuming the opportunity cost of labor is $240 per family. In the modified plan the theoretical return is slightly lower. In spite of the 75 percent expansion in productive area, the total projected output was reduced about 10 percent because of the elimination of irrigation and an increase in pasture from 22 percent to 60 percent of the project area. The execution of the project to date, considering the enormous complexity in engineering and human terms, is its most outstanding feature. By 1968 approximately 30 percent of the forest clearing had been completed, and about 25 percent of the project area was in cultivation. While the probabilities are good that the production schedule will be met, project performance depends on whether costs have been underestimated and whether an IRR of 5-10 percent is acceptable.

Centralized management by the state, with forced urbanization as a basis for new-land development, must be regarded as experimental, although one may well ask whether it is necessary to experiment on a $60 million scale. There are many positive features—production efficiency and the undeniable advantages of urbanization in terms of economies in providing health, education, recreation, utilities, and other community services. There are also problems. What level of coercion must be considered unacceptable? How should the campesinos be helped to rebuild a new ejido and municipal organization? How can the ejidatarios be educated to work and to organize and manage their lands so as to maintain or improve the high levels of production set under the INIA administration?

Bataan

The 10,500-ha property that comprises the Bataan settlement project[7] lies on the Caribbean coast of Costa Rica. (See map 3.) It was formerly owned by

[7]This section on Bataan is based on materials prepared by, and discussions with, Claudio Meira, who undertook an evaluation of this project for the IDB in 1968; and Fausto Jordan and Gamaliel Carrasco, "Evaluación Administrativa, Financiera y Técnica del Instituto de Tierras y Colonización" (Misión FAO/BID, July 1968, mimeo.).

the United Fruit Company, which abandoned its plantation in 1930 because of sigatoka disease. The area remained idle until the early 1940s when the company established abaca under contract to the U.S. government. These operations were suspended in 1959 and about 1,000 employees were laid off. The Costa Rican government subsequently purchased the block with the intention of relieving unemployment through subdivision and intensive development. The project, formulated in 1963, called for the settlement of 600 families on 8-ha lots and the participation of the families in the cooperative development of 810 ha of bananas, 550 ha of cacao, and 3,000 ha of pasture with 1,500 head of cattle. The financing of the project required $1.5 million for land development, machinery, and building plus $0.5 million in production credit.[8]

During the four-year period between the suspension of the United Fruit Company's operation and the initiation of the government project, about 300 families (apart from 1,000 ex-company employees) occupied land in the area. For the most part these people refused to join the project under the prescribed conditions. It also transpired that the ex-employees were not really interested in farming. Consequently most of the colonists under the program were recruited in the central highlands. The planners envisaged the use of the company housing and urban infrastructure for the colonists. Since the former employees were already in occupation, however, and the new settlers preferred to live on their own lands, this proved impractical. Preference granted to the new colonists in the banana cooperative has further aggravated the employment problems in the zone. The combination of these factors and the government's refusal either to recognize the 300 spontaneous squatters or to grant titles to the 270 official settlers has resulted in social conflict and instability.

Under the original plan the IRR is between 20 and 40 percent, depending on whether the opportunity cost of labor is taken as $430 per family or zero. Based on a twenty-five-year project life, assuming no further government investment beyond 1968, and with official settlement reaching 50 percent of the projected level, revised estimates of the cash flow yield a performance ranging from an NPV of minus $900,000 at a 15 percent discount rate to an IRR of 10 percent.[9] The wide difference between the original plan and the revised projections may be attributed to a series of miscalculations in the former; e.g., expected rice yields 300 percent above the national average, cacao 150 percent above, and corn 220 percent above. In fact not even the

[8]Instituto de Tierras y Colonización, *Proyecto de colonización de Bataan* (San José, Costa Rica, 1963).

[9]The difference in these results indicates the sensitivity of performance to a high opportunity cost of labor in a situation where both investment and returns are relatively modest. With labor valued at $430 per family, expressed as present worth, it accounts for 52 percent of total costs ($n = 25$ and $r = 15$).

national averages have been realized. Plans or a budget to rehabilitate the partially destroyed drainage system, estimated at an investment of $0.5 million were omitted. The zone for cattle proved unsuitable—the program has cost double the stipulated amount per head, and only about 25 percent of the original area scheduled for pasture was deemed credit worthy by the Banco de Costa Rica. Finally, the planned value added by the cooperative of $400,000 annually at full production was overly optimistic—in 1968 the cooperative lost about $160,000.

Bolivian Piedmont Projects

In the late 1950s the Alto Beni region became a focus for tropical land development in Bolivia (see maps 5 and 6). Under an ambitious plan, staged colonization of about 1.6 million ha was envisaged. Area I was to be settled by 640 families on 9,000 ha, Area II by 1,250 families on 36,000 ha, and Area III by 250 families on 7,000 ha. Area IV, comprising 50,000 ha, and Area V, comprising 1.5 million ha, were to absorb 15,000–20,000 families. The objectives were as follows:

1. To connect the Beni plains with the markets on the altiplano through a trunk road and feeder roads that would incorporate neighboring areas into agricultural and forestry production, thus paving the way for accelerated spontaneous colonization.
2. To promote the integrated development of the Alto Beni region for agricultural production destined for the altiplano and export and thus to improve the balance of payments.
3. To transfer families from the valleys and altiplano who lack employment opportunities and have little or no land in order to improve living standards, reduce social and economic pressures, and integrate the Indian population into the national economy.[10]

This led to one of the most extensive programs of directed colonization in Latin America, conceived as the catalyst for a spontaneous transfer of 100,000 families from the altiplano to the tropical lowlands in the decade 1961–70. During the first stage, initiated in 1960, a 74-km access road from Caranavi was constructed and 640 families were settled on Area I in the Alto Beni region.

This was followed by the signing of a $9.1 million loan agreement with the Inter-American Development Bank (IDB) in 1963 for colonization in Areas II and III, subsequently named Alto Beni II, plus projects in Chimoré and Yapacani (see tables 9 and 10). The initial plan submitted to the IDB was to

[10] Hernan Zeballos, *Sintesis informativa sobre el proyecto de desarrollo del Alto Beni al 31 Diciembre, 1962* (La Paz, Bolivia: CBF, January 1963), p. 4.

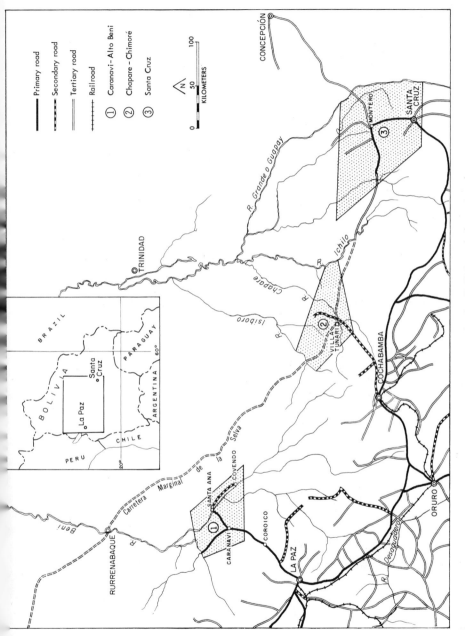

Map 5. Colonization zones in the Bolivian piedmont region.

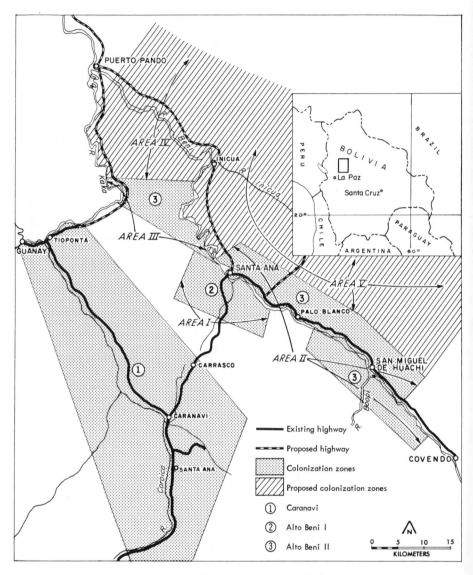

Map 6. The Caranavi–Alto Beni colonization zone, Bolivia.

settle 14,400 families on the three projects by the end of 1965. This figure was subsequently modified to 4,000, but the final program called for the transfer of 8,000 families from the altiplano in a period of two and a half years—1,500 to Alto Beni II, 4,000 to Chimoré, and 2,500 to Yapacani. The World Food Programme agreed to support this colonization effort to the extent of $2.54 million. Rations under the scheme were calculated on the basis of the initial plan for 14,400 families with an average family size of five, i.e., a total population of 72,000. When the program was amended later to cover only 8,000 families the total quantity of food to be distributed remained unchanged. Most of the associated highway construction was financed by AID. The total resources available for the four directed settlements of 8,640 families (including 640 families on Alto Beni I) amounted to $27 million.

Alto Beni I. Under the original plan for Alto Beni I, settlement was to have been completed by 1962 and the forestry potential was to have been

Table 9.   Resources Available for the Alto Beni I, Alto Beni II, Chimoré, and Yapacani Colonization Projects, 1959–1969

($ thousand)

		Funds	
Source of financing		Authorized	Estimated expenditures to December 1969
IDB:	Colonization and production credit (Alto Beni II, Chimoré, and Yapacani)	9,100	6,700
AID:	Yapacani-Puerto Grether road[a] (Yapacani)	5,500	5,000
	Villa Tunari-Puerto Villarroel road (Chimoré)	5,200[b]	5,000
	Santa Ana-Covendo road (Alto Beni II)	333	300
	Caranavi-Santa Ana road (Alto Beni I)	1,830	1,830
	Colonization (Alto Beni I)	1,407	1,400
	Community centers (Alto Beni II, Chimoré and Yapacani)	300	200
WFP		2,537	900
Bolivian Government: Project administration		850	850
	Total	27,057	22,180

Sources: CBF, INC, IDB, AID, and WFP.

[a] Including the Yapacani bridge plus $1.6 million for an additional four spans and river control works as a result of 1966 floods.
[b] Prorated according to percentage of highway traversing the project area.

Table 10.   Estimated Public Expenditures to Complete Directed
Colonization in the Bolivian Piedmont Region, 1959-1970

($ thousand)

Project	Budgeted public expenditures			
	Settlement activities	Trunk highway	Credit[a]	Total
Alto Beni I				
Total	1,407[b]	1,830	0	3,237
Per ha[c]	352	458	0	810
Per family[d]	2,701	3,520	0	6,221
Alto Beni II				
Total	2,552	282[e]	400	3,234
Per ha	142	16	22	180
Per family	1,700	188	266	2,154
Chimoré				
Total	2,037	5,200[e]	198	7,435
Per ha	102	260	10	372
Per family	2,037	5,200	198	7,435
Yapacani				
Total	3,041	5,500[e]	335	8,876
Per ha	43	79	5	127
Per family	1,323	2,391	146	3,860
Total	9,037	12,812	933	22,782
Per ha	84	119	9	212
Per family	1,690	2,408	174	4,272

Sources: INC, CBF, IDB, AID.

[a] Includes only production credit. All other items such as food, housing, tools, and other charges on colonists are included under settlement activities.
[b] Includes credit.
[c] Area planned for agricultural production according to 1969 estimates: Alto Beni I, 4,000 ha; Alto Beni II, 18,000 ha; Chimoré, 20,000 ha; and Yapacani, 70,000 ha.
[d] Colonists planned for settlement according to 1969 estimates: Alto Beni I, 520 families; Alto Beni II, 1,500; Chimoré, 1,000; and Yapacani, 2,300.
[e] Costs prorated on the basis of percentage of trunk highway located in the project area.

fully exploited. The IRR on total investments, including $1.7 million in the access highway, was 48 percent and 56 percent, using an opportunity cost of $150 and zero, respectively, for family labor. Excluding the extravagant projection of forestry benefits, these figures were reduced to 12 percent and 15 percent.

In practice, forestry production has been 1-2 percent of the expected potential. While the settlement was essentially completed in the fourth year, agricultural output in 1968 was only 40 percent of the level planned for that year. Under the revised agricultural plan of the Instituto Nacional de Colonización (INC) for 1969-84 the project will reach a full production 42 percent below the originally projected level, with a lag of one year in its realization.[11] These reductions in agriculture and forestry lower the IRR from 48 percent to 8 percent.

Aside from the disparity between theory and practice measured in economic terms, the policy on colonist debt obligations, while calculated to make the project financially viable, was unrealistic. Accumulated debts were well beyond the repayment capacity of the colonists, which led to an impasse on titles since a prerequisite was the repayment of all charges allocated.

The questions of output, saving, capitalization, and repayment capacity are crucial to the financial analysis. A survey made by the INC in 1968 showed the colonists' length of residence to be four to five years. In this time each colonist had cleared an average of 3.4 ha, of which 0.5 ha was in bush-fallow, and the remainder was in crops. The gross value of output per family was $510 with a value added of about $480 and a net saving of $80 (see table 11). If these figures are used as the basis for estimating full production for a usable area of 6–7 ha, net savings may reach $200–$300 after ten years. Assuming that half the savings are available for servicing a twenty-year loan with a five-year grace period at 6 percent interest, supportable indebtedness would amount to $900, or 15 percent of the public investment.[12]

Deficient performance on Alto Beni I has been attributed to administration in both planning and execution. International advisors were naive. Land was poorly selected and crop programs were unrealistic. Centralized administration in La Paz was unresponsive to the requirements of colonists and field staff, which resulted in inappropriate programs, inefficient control, and inability to learn from experience.[13]

Alto Beni II. The Alto Beni II project was initiated by the Corporación Boliviana de Fomento in 1963 and transferred to the INC in 1965. The original plan was to settle 300 directed and 1,000 semispontaneous colonists on 36,000 ha, of which 18,000 ha were considered suitable for agriculture. The directed colonists were to receive nine times as much assistance as the semispontaneous settlers in the form of housing, land clearing, fencing, water supply, and plantations. The intention was that these farms would serve as demonstrations for the other settlers. This idea was subsequently found to be unworkable because of social tensions caused by the creation of an elite group that accounted for 23 percent of the project population.

The ex ante IRR's for the project were 30 percent and 55 percent, depending on the opportunity cost of labor used in the calculation. Settlement

[11]Since 1965 two revised production plans have been prepared, one of which would give twice the gross output of the other.

[12]Theoretically, it should be possible to achieve much higher recovery levels by reducing colonist consumption. See the section on credit and capitalization of agriculture in chapter 8 for a discussion on the calculation of indebtedness.

[13]Unpublished data, AID, La Paz, Bolivia.

Table 11. Production and Income of Settlers on Four Directed Colonization Projects in the Bolivian and Peruvian Piedmont Regions, 1968

	Alto Beni I		Alto Beni II		Chimoré		Yapaceni		Tingo María[a]	
	Per family	Per ha cleared	Per family	Per ha cleared	Per family	Per ha cleared	Per family	Per ha cleared	Per family	Per ha cleared
	Years									
1. Average residence	4.7		2.5		2.9		4.1		8.1	
	Hectares									
2. Usable area	6.5	110	10.0	110	17.0		25.0		17.0	
3. Area cleared: Total	3.4	40	2.6	70	4.6		12.4		8.4	
4. Per year of residence	0.7	–	1.0	180	1.6		3.0		1.0	
5. Area in production	2.9	10	2.5	–	3.8		6.1		5.4	
6. Area in permanent crops	2.0	10	1.4	10	2.4		1.6		4.3	
	Man-days									
7. Annual labor requirement	640	190	900	350	1,000	220	1,400	110	830	100
	Dollars									
8. Cash sales	380	110	290	110	190	40	480	40	760	90
9. Home consumption	130	40	170	70	230	50	280	20	320	40
10. Gross production (7 + 8)	510	150	460	180	420	90	760	60	1,080	130
11. Purchased inputs: Hired labor	–	–	–	–	50	10	250	20	240	30
12. Other[b]	30	10	30	10	40	10	80	10	310	40
13. Total (11 + 12)	30	10	40	10	90	20	330	30	550	70
14. Amortization payments[c]	(20)	–	(30)	–	(50)	–	(110)	–	90	10
15. Value added in project zone (10 – 12)	480	140	430	170	380	80	680	50	530	60
16. Net cash income (8 – 13)	350	100	250	100	100	20	150	10	210	20
17. Consumption expenditures	270	80	250	100	320	70	420	30	500	60
18. Net saving (16 – 17)	80	20	0	0	–220	–50	–270	–20	–290	–40

Sources: Field survey of 120 colonists, INC, La Paz, Bolivia, 1968; and survey of 50 colonists, ONRA, Aucayacú, Peru, 1968.

Note: Dashes indicate "negligible."

[a] Pueblo Viejo, Aucayacú, and La Morada.

[b] Other inputs are assumed to be imported into the project zone.

[c] Theoretical annual amortization payment calculation on the basis of outstanding loans in 1968.

was completed three years behind schedule, forestry benefits have been negligible, and agricultural production in 1968 was 25 percent of the programmed level. The INC revised plan established a level of full production 25 percent below the original, which resulted in adjusted IRR's of 24 percent and 30 percent. With such high rates the full public investment theoretically should be recoverable from the direct beneficiaries; calculating repayment capacity under the same assumptions as those for Alto Beni I, about 50 percent could be recouped.

In spite of the mistakes on Alto Beni I the execution of Alto Beni II left much to be desired. Poor scheduling led to the preparation of lands for settlement at the wrong time of year, and many colonists who entered at the beginning of the rainy season became disheartened and left. Traditional campesino unions were banned, while cooperatives were imposed and specifically prohibited from taking on any political overtones. Suspicion and poor management made the system essentially inoperative from the outset. In many cases the campesinos were given an exaggerated picture of the benefits. Those disillusioned settlers who returned to the altiplano defaulted on their debts and discouraged potential candidates. Furthermore, colonists who took over abandoned lots were expected to assume not only the defaulted debts of the former occupants for land improvements, but also loans for food and drugs that had been charged at full market price plus transport.

Chimoré. The Chimoré project, initiated in Bolivia in 1963, is an extension of the spontaneously colonized Chapare region. It encompasses 120,000 ha, of which 47,000 ha were estimated to be suitable for settlement along a 50-km section of the Carretera Marginal de la Selva (see maps 5 and 7). The plan was to settle 4,000 families by 1965. The ex ante IRR's were calculated at 23 percent and 27 percent.[14] By 1968 the project had achieved only 20 percent of its settlement goal and 10 percent of its programmed gross production target for that year. A series of administrative problems similar to those experienced in the Alto Beni—difficulty in coordinating the highway construction program, deficiencies in the technical evaluation of the agricultural potential of the area, and unrealistic projections of the marketability of products—made a radical adjustment necessary. Under a revised INC plan the total number of colonists was reduced by 75 percent, and gross output at full production was lowered by 80 percent with a six-year delay in its realization.

With these adjustments the IRR's became 14 percent and 18 percent. Confidence in the completion of the revised program has been somewhat shaken by the appearance of such discrepancies in both project goals and performance over the first five years of operation. In addition a 1968 survey showed that family cash consumption expenditures exceeded cash income by about $200 (see table 11). This artificial situation indicates that withdrawal

[14] No forestry benefits were assigned to the project.

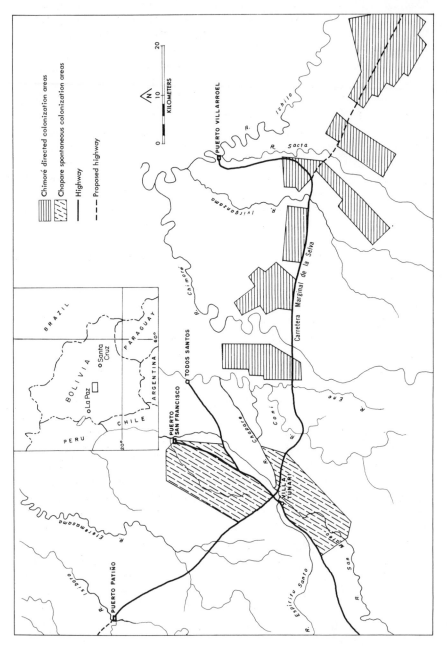

Map 7. Chapare-Chimoré colonization zone, Bolivia.

of special support in the region could result in massive abandonment and that chances of recovering part of the government investment ($2,000 per family excluding the trunk highway) are remote.

Yapacani. The Yapacani area lies 130 km east of Santa Cruz (see map 8). Of the four projects in the Bolivian piedmont region, Yapacani was generally considered to have the best chance of success because of paved highway access, the possibility of ready integration in the dynamic Santa Cruz economy, flat lands, and a more healthy and manageable climate. The plan called for the settlement of 2,500 families by 1965 on 90,000 ha, of which 75,000 ha were classified as suitable for agriculture. The projected IRR's were 18 percent and 25 percent (exclusive of forestry costs and benefits).

Once the project was launched it was found that estimates of the soil capability were in error. Large areas thought suitable for growing bananas and intensive crops on lots of 10-15 ha were found adequate only for cattle on 50-ha lots. Also, an extensive zone to the west was discovered to be susceptible to annual flooding, making settlement impossible. Accordingly the trunk road was reduced from 63 km to 22 km. In addition, failure to take adequate account of the instability of the piedmont river systems resulted in the washing out of the eastern approaches to the Yapacani bridge within a few months of its completion, requiring $1.6 million for river control works and four additional spans.[15] As a consequence the settlement target for the original area was reduced from 2,500 families to 1,200 families, 360 of whom were residents before the project. The INC response to these setbacks was the incorporation of an additional 64,000 ha along the Moile river (see map 8) where 750 spontaneous colonists were already located. In this manner, by 1970 the total project beneficiaries numbered 2,500, of whom 1,300 could be classified as new colonists.

Although the project has been wholly restructured, the IRR's under the new plan are virtually the same as the original ex ante estimates. While the project appears to be viable, certain of its components obviously are considerably more viable than others. The incorporation of the Moile area involved a small marginal investment and reduced the average cost for settlers west of the Yapacani River by 30 percent. The inclusion of the spontaneous Buen Retiro area (map 8) east of the river—an area that accounts for 30 percent of the total settlement—greatly improves the project's cash flow. None of the $5.5 million in the bridge and the trunk road, nor the greater part of the $3 million expended in general settlement operations, are assignable to this area, while a third of the value added may be attributable to it.

---

[15] For a discussion of highway projects in the Bolivian tropics, see *U.S. Economic Assistance to Transportation in Latin America*, Twenty-seventh Report by the Committee on Government Operations, H. Rept. 91-1229, 91 Cong. 2 sess. (June 25, 1970), pp. 22–25.

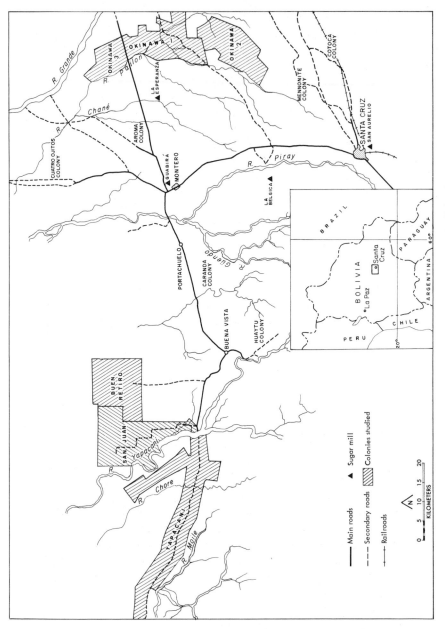

Map 8.   Santa Cruz colonization zone, Bolivia.

Semidirected Settlement

Colonization of the semidirected type involves specific government invest-ments and programs of assistance to spontaneous colonists in a region that is in the consolidation stage of development. The specific objective is to up-grade production and promote spontaneous colonization in the peripheral areas. In many instances a prime objective may be the elimination of *mini-fundia* or the rationalization of the subdivision and tenure system, e.g., Tingo María and La Chontalpa. The exact area and number of settlers to whom the programs will apply are stated. The programs have a finite budget and time limit, and the objectives are normally specified in terms of the number of new settlers, the area to be developed, and the expected increase in production.

If it is accepted that semidirected settlements are special programs aimed at the consolidation and expansion of spontaneous colonization, there is an immediate problem for economic evaluation in isolating and measuring the impact of such programs. The distinction between directed and semidirected is somewhat arbitrary—very few projects are undertaken in areas that are completely uninhabited.

Santo Domingo de los Colorados

The Santo Domingo de los Colorados project area covers 270,000 ha in the Guayas basin, 100 km west of Quito, Ecuador (map 9). The Instituto Ecuato-riano de Reforma Agraria y Colonización (IERAC) initiated a $4 million program of consolidation and expansion of colonization in this zone in 1964. The purpose was to develop 170,000 ha, of which 75,000 ha were already occupied by 1,600 families. Activities were to include the construction of 180 km of feeder roads; the provision of a social infrastructure and credit for housing; agricultural development supported by cooperative promotion, titling, extension, and research; and the subdivision and distribution of unoc-cupied lands.

Settlement of the area dates from the early forties, and net immigration is estimated to have been between 400 and 600 people annually until 1957. The combination of the highway program and propaganda associated with the Pilot Plan[16] accelerated the annual immigration to about 3,000 over the period 1958–62, a rate that was sustained during 1963–68 with the comple-tion of the paved highway to Quito in 1963 and subsequent western and southern connections. Rural settlement on the project area grew from 1,000 families in the 1950–55 period to 12,000 in 1968. The introduction of a $4 million project into the middle of such an ongoing stream of investments and associated agricultural and urban development clearly leaves little room for a meaningful measure of the economic return on the investment.

[16] A $3.83 million pilot colonization scheme initiated in 1957. See discussion of benefit-cost analysis in chapter 4.

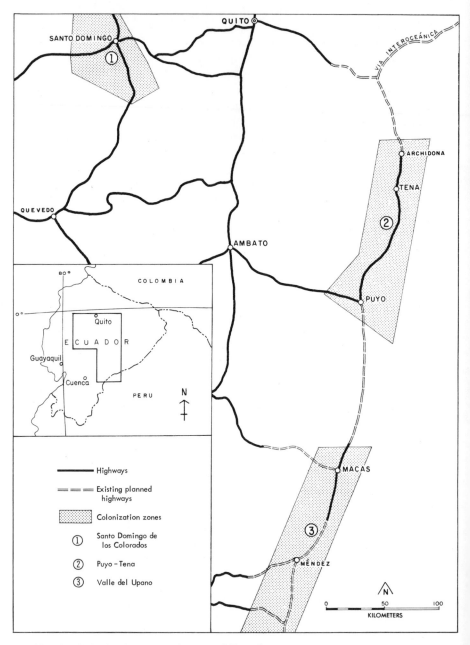

Map 9. Colonization zones in central Ecuador.

There can be little doubt that the various measures applied in this favorable location have had a positive effect on development and have stimulated private investment. An outstanding characteristic of the project is the flexibility shown in implementation under conditions of extreme political and administrative instability. Between 1964 and 1968 Ecuador experienced four changes of government; there were eight ministers of agriculture and five project directors. Moreover the IERAC budget was drastically cut from 1966 onward.

In spite of these apparent negative elements there have been no disastrous setbacks in the progress of the project. Since emphasis was on assistance to spontaneous settlement, changes in policy and the level of government assistance—which may have had serious effects under directed pioneer colonization—were absorbed in the ongoing programs of several thousand individual producers. The axis of the program's feeder roads, titling, supervised credit, and cooperative promotion was pressed forward as funds and staff permitted. Between 1964 and 1968, 270 km of roads were built and 300,000 ha were surveyed for subdivision; 5,400 families received services under the program, 2,800 titles were issued, $2.4 million was granted in credit, the Consorcio de Cooperativas was formed with seventy affiliated cooperatives and a total membership of 5,000, and the area in crops was expanded by 50,000 ha and in pastures by 23,000 ha.

It would appear that a high level of settlement stability has been achieved. Ninety percent of the colonists work exclusively in agriculture on their own farms or in association with neighbors. Only 2 percent of the colonists do not live full time in the project area. The average income of the settlers is about $800 per family (50-60 percent in cash sales). In a survey carried out in 1968 it was estimated that families with more than six years' residence have incomes approaching $1,500; the incomes of those who have received credit (average $2,200) reach $1,700.[17]

There is evidence of significant capital accumulation among the colonists. A study conducted in one cooperative showed the land-clearing sequence as an average of 1.75 ha in the first year and about 1 ha annually from the second to seventh years. Thereafter it appears that savings were sufficient to raise the rate to about 2 ha and to maintain about 90 percent of cleared lands in production. The average increase in the net worth (land improvements and increased livestock inventory) of these farmers during 1967 was estimated at $300 to $400.[18]

Future development of the area is related to (1) the functioning of cooperatives in the fields of credit, marketing, and production as a means of

[17]Survey by IERAC, 1968.

[18]Case study of the twenty-three members of the Cooperative Riobambeños del Rio Chilimpe, conducted by Peter M. Gladhart, Cornell University, 1968.

achieving the economies of scale in crops such as abaca, rubber, and African oil palm; (2) the future of the export banana trade, particularly Taiwan competition for the Japanese market; and (3) the availability of capital, management, and cattle to permit the transition of much of the area into pasture for cattle fattening.

Valle del Upano

Located 200 km east of Cuenca, Ecuador (see map 9), the region comprises 270,000 ha, of which 170,000 ha are suitable for agriculture. It has been settled since the early days of the Spanish occupation, and in 1964 when the project was initiated there were 1,430 colonists plus 400 Jíbaro Indians living on 43,000 ha. The plan was to settle an additional 1,150 families on 35,000 ha on lots of 30 to 50 ha each in the first phase and to settle 3,000 families on 92,000 ha in the second phase.[19] The budget for the first phase was $5.66 million—$2.81 million for a 141-km penetration road, $0.78 million for 174 km of feeder roads, $0.33 million for airport improvement, $1.23 million for credit, and $0.51 million for titling and project administration. The ex ante IRR's were 55 percent and 60 percent, assuming opportunity costs of labor at $250 per family per year and zero, respectively.

This phenomenal projected performance was based on the following assumptions in the original feasibility studies:

1. That the gross value of agricultural production of the new colonists in their first year of occupancy would be double that of the existing settlers in the region ($180 per family).[20]
2. That in the tenth year these new settlers would increase their first year's output by seven times, i.e., with a total private investment of $3,700 over a nine-year period, the colonists were expected to realize a gross annual production of $3,000 after the ninth year and a net return on capital and family labor of $2,750. If labor is valued at $250 per family, this represents a 60-70 percent return on private capital invested.

The basic questions are: How realistic were the cost and production estimates? Was gross agricultural production per family in 1964 only $180 per year?

News of the proposed project, two airfields built by IERAC, and the initiation of air cargo services appear to have spurred both immigration and production since 1964. CREA has estimated that net annual immigration into

[19]CREA, *Proyecto de colonización del Valle del Rio Upano* (Cuenca, Ecuador, 1964), pp. 5-10.

[20]Ibid., pp. 127 and 174.

the zone between 1964 and 1968 was about 180 families, i.e., a total of 900 families, an increase of 50 percent in total population over the five-year period. If so, approximately 75 percent of the programmed new settlement had already occurred by 1968.

In a survey made in 1968 by the University of Cuenca, residents who arrived within the five-year period 1964-68 accounted for 30 percent of the total population; 20 percent had arrived between 1959 and 1963 and 22 percent between 1954 and 1958. This indicates that the rate of immigration accelerated after 1964 and further substantiates the total increase in population in 1964-68 as being on the order of 40-50 percent.

Based on the rate of immigration above and on production estimates for 1967, the gross value of agricultural output per family was $550.[21] The University of Cuenca survey shows the settlers' source of income to be diverse—45 percent from cattle, 10 percent from crops, 10 percent from commercial activities, 15 percent from professional services, 7 percent from artisan or industrial employment, and 13 percent from miscellaneous activities. Seventy percent of the settlers are engaged in agriculture, but only 20 percent to the exclusion of other activities. On the basis of these figures, the gross value of annual agricultural production in 1967-68 was estimated at $750 per family in agriculture, and the average gross income from all sources for all settlers was $1,000.[22]

If these estimates of migration and income are accepted, plus the figure of $180 for the average annual gross production per family in 1964, development over the four-to-five-year period was indeed impressive—a 300-400 percent increase in average output per family and a 50 percent increase in the number of families, or a 450-600 percent increase in total gross output. There is no reason not to attribute this increase to the project. Undoubtedly some of the impact must stem from the expectation of advantages from road access. However, since the road up to 1968 was of no direct benefit to producers (except as access to airports), the critical factors seem to be (1) the airport and associated services; (2) access roads to the airports; (3) greater spending in the zone due to project activities; and (4) confidence inspired by the land-titling scheme, roads, credit, extension, and other social services.

Under such favorable circumstances economic justification seems assured. An IRR of 16 percent over a twenty-five-year economic life would be given if the value added in agriculture only reaches 50 percent of the projected tenth-year level, assuming that there are 2,600 families in residence by 1972, an additional $1 million invested in highways, and $250 per family as the opportunity cost of labor.

[21] Tudor Engineering Company, *Estudio comparativo y* analítico *de las dos rutas propuestas de acceso al Valle del Río Upano* (San Francisco, 1967), p. B-7.

[22] Survey of ninety-two farmers carried out by the economics faculty of the University of Cuenca under the direction of Claudio Cordero in 1968.

Tingo María-Tocache

The project area is 630 km by road from Lima and stretches along the Huallaga River for about 200 km in the selva region of eastern Peru. (See map 3.) Spontaneous settlement started about 1932, but the first real impetus for development was the Huánuco-Pucallpa highway, which was constructed during the period 1938-40. In 1938 a law was passed reserving for colonization a strip of 10-20 km on either side of this highway (800,000 ha), and $400,000 was allocated to support settlement. From 1939 to 1945, 65,000 ha were distributed in 325 lots of 15 ha each, 383 of 30-100 ha, and 35 of 100-300 ha, resulting in about 700 settlers with 2,900 ha under cultivation.

From 1946 to 1954 the basis of the Tingo María economy was bananas, and significant portions of the land were in coca and tea. By 1956 sigatoka and Panama disease had virtually wiped out the banana plantations, and many settlers abandoned their lands.[23]

In 1949 an Italian company[24] launched a land development scheme designed to settle about eighty Italian immigrant families on a concession of 48,000 ha. A total of forty families arrived, but only two remained in 1968. Over a twenty-year period the company invested an estimated $2 million in housing, a sawmill, access roads, a 9-km railroad, plantations, and clearing about 1,000 ha. In 1968 there were seventy-six men on the payroll.

The only other organized settlement resulted from an attempt to set a precedent for the transfer of people from the *barriadas* (slums) of Lima to the selva region. In 1964 eighty families were given substantial assistance to establish themselves at La Morada on the Huallaga River, 95 km south of Tingo María. In 1965-66, $430,000 in supervised credit was disbursed to the colonists. Only forty colonists remained in 1968, and repayment of the loan obligations has been on the order of 10 percent.

The official Tingo María-Tocache project originated with a study of natural resources on 290,000 ha in 1961-62.[25] It was found that available timber amounted to 2,400 million board feet in standing trees, of which 50 percent could be exploited economically. Sustained-yield management of these forests would yield 40 million board feet of sawn lumber annually with a gross value of about $2 million. The total value of potential lumber production over the twenty-year period 1962-81 was estimated at $100 million. Some 96,000 ha were established as suitable for agriculture; of these, 10,500 ha

[23] Plantations were primarily of the Gros Michel variety of bananas, which were the most susceptible to sigatoka and Panama disease. See Chira C. Magdaleno, Monografía *de la Provincia de Leoncio Prado* (Lima, Peru: Compañía de Impresiónes y Publicidad, May 1959), p. 191.

[24] Sociedad Anónima Italo-Peruana Agrícola Industrial.

[25] SCIF, Ministerio de Fomento y Obras Publicas, Programa de Evaluacion de Recursos Naturales, *Evaluación del potencial económico y social de la zona Tingo María-Tocache, Huallaga Central* (Lima, Peru, May 1962).

were in cultivation supporting a rural population of 19,000 (urban population, 9,500). It was estimated that there were about 4,800 colonists in the project area, 220 with firm titles, 1,410 with applications pending on fiscal lands, and 2,150 settlers without rights. The total area claimed amounted to 170,000 ha. The study also indicated that full development of the area over twenty years (1962–81) would result in a rural population of 118,000—including local population growth and more than 10,000 immigrant families.

On the basis of this study the Oficina Nacional de Reforma Agraria (ONRA) prepared a twenty-year plan to reorganize tenancy on 30,000 ha occupied by 2,150 families and bring 66,000 ha of forest land into production; in the first six years 4,550 families were to be resettled or colonized. These families were to receive special technical assistance and credit over a sixteen-year period at a total cost of $25 million.[26] This plan was subsequently modified and the objectives of the final project, implemented in 1966, were the reorganization of tenancy on 30,000 ha, bringing 55,000 ha of additional land into production, and granting technical assistance and credit to the 2,150 families considered to be residents plus 3,100 new colonists who were to be established in four years. The budget, including credit, for these four years was $30.3 million. The project formed part of the complex of agricultural development associated with the proposed 2,445-km Peruvian section of the Carretera Marginal de la Selva, since the colonization area lies along a 175-km section of this highway.

Development in the region over a thirty-year period has resulted in sharp disparities in the structure and amount of family income between the older and newer areas. While average consumption is $1,570 per family, the range is $190 to $22,000. In the Naranjillo region where average residence is eighteen years, settlers have been able to develop nonagricultural activities that generate over $1,000 gross per year (see tables 12 and 13), representing sizable interests and employment in forestry, services, and commerce.

The ex ante IRR's, based on a twenty-five-year project life starting in 1962, were 21 percent and 23 percent (opportunity cost of labor assumed at $150 and $200 per family, respectively). In fact, however, 1962 was not the base year for the project, and in the five-year interim (1962–65) before major public investments were made the situation in the region changed markedly. The news of the proposed colonization in the area and the provision for granting titles, credit, and technical assistance gave impetus to a movement of spontaneous colonists, particularly from neighboring areas. It is estimated that between 1962 and 1966 about 600 families occupied lands in the project area without any official action. The project was to have started with 2,150 previously established settlers in accordance with the original 1962 estimate; instead, the number was placed at 5,400 in 1966—the result of a more thor-

[26] ONRA, *Colonización Hallaga, Tingo María-Tocache* (Lima, Peru, 1965).

Table 12.   Family Income in the Four Southern Areas of the
Tingo María–Tocache Project, 1967

Residence, development, and income	Area				Total and average
	Naranjillo	Pueblo Nuevo	Aucayacú	La Morada	
Number of farms in sample	22	35	38	41	136
Average residence (years)	18	7	6	6	8
Area in cultivation per farm (*ha*)	22	9	8	7	10
Area in cultivation per year of residence (*ha*)	1.2	1.3	1.3	1.2	1.3
Family income					
Gross agricultural production ($)	6,260	1,640	1,080	1,160	2,050
Nonagricultural income ($)	1,190	70	40	70	260
Total gross production ($)	8,450	1,710	1,120	1,230	2,310
Purchased inputs, including labor ($)	2,350	600	370	300	750
Consumption and savings ($)	6,100	1,110	750	930	1,560

Sources: ONRA, and the FAO-IDB study group on financing agrarian reform, Lima, Peru, 1967.

ough survey and of migration. Thus before the project got underway the final target for new colonists was scaled down from 3,100, since the number of families in residence in 1966 already exceeded the number specified in the original plan. It was not until 1967 that ONRA put an end to unauthorized settlement of new lands. Taking 1966 as the base year and a twenty-five-year life, the IRR's were 17 percent and 19 percent.[27]

A survey of eighty-five colonists showed a 30 percent increase in consumption and savings per family and the incorporation of an additional 3 ha per farm between 1965 and 1967.[28] In assessing achievement at the farm level, there are two critical questions: How much of the improvement is directly attributable to the project? What have the various components—legal tenure, credit, technical assistance, roads, and social services contributed to the total achievement?

[27]If 1962 is taken as the base year, i.e., if the increased value added in the region over the period 1963–67 is attributed to a public investment program that did not start in earnest until 1967, the IRR's are 25 percent and 40 percent.

[28]From the survey by ONRA and the FAO-IDB study group on financing agrarian reform, Lima, Peru, 1967.

Table 13. Income Distribution on the Tingo María-Tocache
Colonization Project, 1967

Income per year	Area				Total and average
	Naranjillo	Pueblo Nuevo	Aucayacú	La Morada	
	Percentage distribution				
$150– $400	0	15	25	20	17
$400– $900	10	25	45	50	35
$900–$1,800	15	50	20	20	26
$1,800–$3,750	25	10	10	10	12
Over $3,750	50	0	0	0	10
Total	100	100	100	100	100
	Average income ($ per family)				
$150– $400	0	260	220	220	220
$400– $900	600	600	600	630	600
$900–$1,800	1,270	1,230	1,310	1,190	1,230
$1,800–$3,750	2,910	2,200	2,010	2,500	2,500
Over $3,750	8,200	0	0	0	8,200
Average	6,100	1,110	750	930	1,570

Sources: ONRA, and the FAO-IBD study group on financing agrarian reform, Lima, Peru, 1967.

Of the 5,400 residents in the zone in 1966, less than 10 percent received titles during the period in question; thus the impact attributable to this aspect appears to be minor, although the expectation of improved security of tenure presumably contributed to the progress of the settlers. The $100,000 disbursed in credit probably had little direct effect on settler incomes—40 percent was allocated to housing and 30 percent to cattle purchases that would not show a return for two or three years. Social services may be expected to have their major impact on the number and type of new settlers attracted to the project and on the general stability of the settlement. It is unlikely that this element would have had any significant effect on the productivity of colonists who have been in the region five to eight years,[29] and it is probable that some of the production increase would have occurred without the project. Thus it appears that the major factor in development in these early years was the impact of roads and rising expectations.

Is the assumption that the project can benefit 5,250 families over a twenty-year period and earn 10 percent on the investment sufficient reason to invest public funds to the tune of $30 million? In the statement of project goals it is implicit that these benefits are insufficient to justify the project. In

[29]The hypothesis may be advanced that short-term gains in labor productivity can be obtained through improved levels of health. If labor is scarce and farming operations cannot be maintained when one or more of the farm family is ill, the element may have an important effect indeed.

order to assemble adequate support for the investment, therefore, additional benefits are cited: opening new lands for spontaneous colonization, exploitation of forest resources, and the provision of a demonstration project that would have a major effect on employment and future development throughout the selva.

But it is unlikely that significant lands will be available for massive spontaneous colonization within the project area. The principal possibility lies in opening lands to the north along the Huallaga River, which would require additional investment in the Puerto Pizana–Campana stretch of the Carretera Marginal de la Selva and in penetration roads.

It is more difficult to be specific about the proposal to set in motion a dynamic development process in the selva region that will cause major population shifts from the sierra over a relevant planning period of one or two generations. Recent history is not particularly encouraging on this score. Of the population that settled in the Tingo María–Tocache region prior to 1962, it is estimated that 25 percent came from the coast, 40 percent from the sierra, and 35 percent from the selva. The migratory tendency in recent years appears to be more toward resettlement within the selva. Most of the influx of population into the project area between 1960 and 1967 is believed to have come from neighboring tropical areas. The 1967 survey of project beneficiaries shows that 10 percent came from the coast, 40 percent from the sierra, and 50 percent from the selva.[30] In the project zone, the net increase in population over the period 1964–68 that can be attributed to the project was 8,000–10,000.

The demand for labor has raised wages in the area substantially. In 1966–67 the average daily rate without food was 90 cents per day and in 1968, $1.15. In spite of this rise and a marked differential between the rate for the project and that prevailing in the sierra, there has been no significant inflow of people from the highlands in search of work. The causes of this immobility might provide important guides to future policy for colonization in the selva. It appears that, although ONRA's responsibilities include improving the lot of underprivileged campesinos from the sierra, the agency is nevertheless sensitive to political realities requiring tangible evidence of settlement, production, and improved income levels in a relatively short time in order to justify the costs, infrastructure, and services provided. Consequently the project has been promoted in tropical areas farther down the Huallaga River with the expectation of recruiting better colonist material than that available in the sierra.

Another facet of the same problem is production objectives that dictate capital-intensive practices and have given rise to demands on the part of both ONRA and the colonists for mechanization and cattle. The project adminis-

[30] Survey by ONRA and FAO-IDB study group.

tration elected to airlift bulldozers from Lima to clear forest for the African oil palm plantations at Tocache. Cattle development poses a further dilemma because of high credit requirements. By definition any ONRA program must cater to small farmers or landless campesinos, thus automatically excluding any significant flow of private capital. Even with the relatively modest goal of developing herds of 100 cattle over a fifteen-year period, at $6,000 per colonist, credit can be granted to only a few. Under these circumstances the minimum income criterion[31] becomes critical, since the inverse relationship between capital per capita and the total number of beneficiaries is self-evident if private capital is excluded from the equation.

While there may be some question about achieving the goal of shifting population from the sierra to the selva, about income distribution within the project, and about expectations of external effects, there is clear evidence of development to the benefit of low-income campesinos and of rapidly rising production. A goal of $2,300 per family in 1980 may well be overstated. If the full production level were two-thirds the projected level and its attainment were delayed until 1985, the IRR would be reduced from 17–19 percent to 4–10 percent. Since forestry benefits were not included in the calculation, however, and since a strong case can be made for excluding much of the trunk highway investment from project costs, the probability of a satisfactory performance appears good, with an IRR of 10–15 percent.

Puerto Presidente Stroessner

The Eje Este, a 400-km paved highway from Asunción, Paraguay, to Foz do Iguaçu on the Brazilian border, was built in the late fifties and opened up a large virgin forest area in southeastern Paraguay for agricultural settlement. In 1961 the Comisión de Administración de Puerto Presidente Stroessner (CAPPS) was charged with the colonization of 45,000 ha lying 18 km west of the Brazilian frontier. (See map 3.) Four hundred spontaneous colonists were already in residence—the program planners had estimated a total of 700. Subsequently the area was enlarged to incorporate a 10,000-ha forestry program with financing from the United Nations Development Program and the Agency for International Development. The objective for the number of settlers was raised to 900, then to 1,200.

The project was initiated primarily on the basis of agriculture; timber milling was added, plus long-term plans for a pulp industry. CAPPS later reached an agreement with foreign interests to install cold storage units and a feed plant in support of a pork industry. The total public budget is $3.87 million for feeder roads, plantations, mill improvement, forest nurseries, and farm storage facilities. Agricultural development is based on a flow of spontaneous colonists to peripheral areas and on consolidation of existing settlers.

[31]Minimum income is taken up in chapter 6.

Parcels vary in size from 20 to 100 ha, with the majority in the range of 25-30 ha. Colonists receive title when they pay 20 percent of the government price at the time of occupancy; the balance is due over a ten-year period.

Although the project was not conceived as an integrated program, it is an example of consolidation and expansion of spontaneous settlement in an area with favorable locational and natural resource characteristics. A sequence of projects has evolved in response to colonist demands and perceived opportunities. The relatively modest public outlay of $4 million appears to have generated a flow of human and capital resources to the region that is leading to integrated development and the creation of an important labor market outside agriculture.

Highways and Spontaneous Colonization

The chief problems in defining a program of support for spontaneous settlement are the specifications of the geographic boundary and of the government activities to be correlated with development in the area. Since spontaneous development is more often than not attributed to a road, the limits of the project may be prescribed by the zone of influence—usually set by physical characteristics such as river basins, mountain ranges, or distance. Government services—health, credit, and extension—are provided in response to the demand of the settlers. This is in contrast to directed and semidirected projects where services are provided principally in order to create a demand for new lands. Thus aside from a penetration road that may be oriented to the pioneer stage of development, e.g., the Brasília-Acre highway, the subsequent provision of services is applied to the consolidation phase. In summary, a spontaneous project will include the complex of government programs in highways and other services dating back to the earliest settlers.

A widely held image of spontaneous colonization is that it is the most miserable form of subsistence agriculture; for this reason, its extension must be regarded as one of the worst forms of social evil, all the more so when the useless destruction of soil and forest resources is taken into account. In some quarters, therefore, it is advocated that access, infrastructure, and services should be withheld, because the lack of such assistance will force abandonment of the lands. Three of the four spontaneous areas examined here, however, demonstrate the establishment of viable agricultural and urban centers within a relatively dynamic regional economy. The settlers, together with the commercial interests that buy and sell their products, have achieved a degree of stability as well as sufficient political leverage to induce the central government to provide needed services.

Caranavi

The area of spontaneous colonization in the humid subtropical zone of Caranavi lies 100 km northeast of La Paz, Bolivia (maps 5 and 6). About

65,000 ha are occupied by 207 settlements, and the total population was estimated to be 36,000 in 1967. Settlement occurs up to 30 km from the road; taking this as the maximum range of influence of the existing highway network, the potential area may be estimated at about 500,000 ha.

The first colonists in the lower valley established themselves in 1945 at Santa Ana, 70 km below Coroico. In the same year construction of the 75-km road from Coroico to Caranavi was initiated with the objective of providing access to the plains of the Beni for reasons of economic development and national security; no specific consideration was given to the development potential of the lower Coroico valley. At that time there were few settlers in the lower valley. With road construction underway the rate of colonization accelerated. The road reached Caranavi in 1953, and by that time the number of colonists had risen to about 500, expanding to an estimated 2,000 by 1958.

In the following ten years the rate of colonization averaged 600 settlers per year, and there were 8,200 colonists by 1967. Reconstructing the cash flow from these colonists and from forest enterprise over the twenty-four-year period 1945–68, and taking into account a public expenditure of $7 million for 170 km of trunk road, 115 km of feeder road, and other services, yields IRR's of 13 percent and 20 percent, with the opportunity cost of labor assumed to be $150 per family and zero.[32] Allocation of any part of the highway expenditures, which account for over 90 percent of public and 50 percent of total costs, to other programs greatly improves these rates. The question of potential external economies and diseconomies is discussed in chapter 9.

Chapare

The colonization zone of Chapare was defined by law in 1905 as an area of 1.8 million ha at the base of the cordillera 150 km east of Cochabamba, Bolivia.[33] (See maps 5 and 7.) The first settlement in the region in 1920 was directed by the army at Todos Santos. The Chaco War provided stimulus to occupy eastern Bolivia, and the 210-km road from Cochabamba to Todos Santos was built between 1937 and 1939. During the period 1937–46 there was significant spontaneous immigration from the highlands, mainly to the vicinity of Villa Tunari. In 1946 floods wiped out part of the road and isolated Todos Santos. The road was not rebuilt. Isolation, plus a series of floods that damaged properties, discouraged further settlement, and in the late forties there was considerable relocation within the region. The rural

---

[32] The hazards of this type of estimate are legion—values must be placed on private investment in farms and forest industries, not to mention public expenditures; internal inflation averaged 27 percent annually from 1945 to 1960; and foreign exchange rates bear little relation to internal purchasing power.

[33] Ministerio de Agricultura, *La colonización e inmigración en Bolivia, leyes-decretos supremos y otras disposiciónes legales* (La Paz, Bolivia, 1965).

population in the vicinity of Todos Santos declined from 3,000 to 300. From 1952 to 1956 there was another influx of settlers; population then remained stagnant until 1964.[34] The net immigration rate from 1964 to 1967 averaged 100 families per year.[35] By that time there were 49,000 ha occupied by 5,500 families.

Property sizes vary between 6 and 24 ha, with an average of 9 ha. The area that a family can manage appears to be stable at 4-5 ha. It is estimated that about 50 percent of the area owned is still in virgin forest where the average length of residence exceeds ten years.[36] Of the area exploited, only 2-3 ha per family are in production—75 percent in permanent crops such as bananas, citrus, and coca. This low level of development is symptomatic of the constraints imposed by ecology, transport, and marketing. The high rainfall (4,000 millimeters) causes severe weed invasion and crop losses. In some areas two-thirds of the bananas remain unharvested because of the lack of all-weather highway access. It is estimated that on the average a third of the region's coca crop is lost due to weather. Further, there is a limit on the demand in Cochabamba and other interior points, especially where farm-to-market freight rates range from $25 to $40 per ton and marketing margins on a crop such as rice amount to 20 percent.[37]

Total investments[38] in the Chapare region from 1937 to 1967 are estimated at $16.8 million.[39] If all these investments are balanced against the gross regional product of Chapare, the IRR for the thirty-year period is on the order of 1 percent. Aside from agricultural and forestry development in the region, it is difficult to imagine what other economic, social, or political activity would be stimulated by the highway investment. In this case the investment was clearly uneconomic.

Caquetá

The Caquetá region[40] covers 1-1.5 million ha that stretch about 250 km through the Andean piedmont area of southeastern Colombia (see map 5). As

[34] John S. Marus y José Monje Rada, *Estudio de colonización en Bolivia, análisis de las características socio-económicas de las colonias*, Ministerio de Asuntos Campesinos and AID (La Paz, Bolivia, December 1962), pp. 144–51.

[35] Unpublished data, September 1967, from INC, Jefe de Colonias Espontáneas del Chapare, Villa Tunari, Bolivia.

[36] E. Garcia Agrega, *Datos agroeconómicos de la zona noreste del Chapare*, Servicio Agrícola Interamericano, Ministerio de Agricultura (La Paz, Bolivia, 1960).

[37] Lionel Terrazas Fossati, *Costos de producción de arroz, papa, maíz, trigo, maní y ají*, División de Comercialización (La Paz, Bolivia: SAI, 1963), pp. 124–25.

[38] Including annual public expenses in maintenance and operation of infrastructure and services.

[39] Including $12 million in the Cochabamba–Todos Santos highway.

[40] This section is based on discussion with, and data prepared by, Harold Jorgenson, who carried out an evaluation of the Caquetá project for the IDB in 1968.

an example of humid tropical land development, the zone is of interest because of its relatively long history of colonization, the magnitude of settlement (the population was estimated at 175,000 to 200,000 in 1968), and the variety of activities that have resulted—directed colonization, cooperatives, supervised credit, road building, and above all, massive spontaneous migration.

In the early years of the twentieth century when colonization began, the Caquetá region was known for its rubber. Florencia, now the principal town in the region, was founded in 1902 and was an important rubber marketing center until 1920, when the boom in this product subsided. During the rubber era the government made a number of sporadic attempts to establish colonies in the region with little success.[41] In 1917 the Shell Oil Company initiated exploration in the area, giving some impetus to settlement. While there was much legislation in the decade that followed—calling for settlement of the eastern jungles and defining property rights, credit, and other immigration promotion procedures—little effort was made to implement the laws.

In 1932 a border dispute with Peru resulted in renewed interest in the area. A road was constructed from the highlands to Florencia, which became the military center for the southeastern region. Discharged soldiers were given incentives to settle in the zone. In the late 1930s many haciendas were established and cattle became the basic industry. Spontaneous migration from the highlands began on a significant scale. By 1938 the population of the region had reached 20,000. By 1950 it had reached 41,000, with about 10,000 urban residents and 5,000-6,000 farm families. The rate of immigration accelerated after 1955, largely as a result of the buildup in political violence in the highlands during the 1948-60 period, when many people abandoned their original communities. Immigration averaged about 2,000 families per year from 1962 to 1968. By 1968 there were about 22,000 farm families and an urban population of 60,000-70,000. Eleven percent were natives of Caquetá, 10 percent had come from western departments, and 79 percent were from the highlands.

A major effort in directed colonization in Caquetá was launched by the Caja de Crédito Agrario in 1959 with the prime purpose of resettling families affected by the violence in the highlands. A reserve of 698,000 ha was set aside, and 745 parcels were surveyed in three virgin forest zones. The program was designed for minimum state expenditures. An established credit limit of $330 per family was used primarily for moving expenses, housing, and subsistence during the first year. Little was available for establishing an economic base for the colonist. After the first year of the scheme it was recognized that the result would inevitably be subsistence agriculture. Accordingly the credit

[41] Victor Daniel Bonilla, *Caquetá 1—el despertar de la selva* (Bogotá, Colombia: Ediciónes Tercer Mundo, 1966), p. 15.

limit was raised to $1,000 but with insufficient supervision to assure that it was not used in consumption. The project suffered from inadequate planning—trails rather than roads provided access to the settlements, little attention was paid to marketing, and there was no systematic analysis of credit requirements. In 1962 the program was discontinued. Of the 1,040 families that had been settled, only 570 remained. Expenditure for infrastructure, services, and administration had amounted to $650,000,[42] and $570,000 in credit had been granted to 620 farmers, representing a total of $2,140 per family settled.

In 1962 responsibility for promoting and administering settlement and agricultural development in Caquetá was transferred to the Instituto Colombiana de la Reforma Agraria (INCORA). As a result of the poor experience of the directed colonization, INCORA reoriented the program toward providing assistance to spontaneous settlement. This aid took the form of highway construction and social infrastructure, supervised credit for development rather than consumption, land titling, and the promotion of cooperatives. Of the 10,000 farmers in the region in 1962, 22 percent had title, 43 percent had a bill of sale, and 35 percent were without any legal document. By 1968 titles had been issued to 4,900 settlers occupying 250,000 ha, and 700,000 ha claimed remained to be adjudicated. Table 14 gives an indication of land use at that time.

Settlement in the region provides a basis for comparison between directed and spontaneous colonists. The principal differences are (1) the apparent higher production efficiency of the spontaneous colonists, (2) a much higher percentage of former farm owners and those with experience in tropical agriculture among spontaneous colonists, and (3) the spontaneous group's substantially lower level of education. The fact that 70 percent of the spontaneous group were farm owners elsewhere suggests that they had resources of their own to invest in new-land development. Furthermore, since there is an inverse relationship between education and efficiency, it might be inferred that education is not a highly significant element in settlement (see table 15).

Total public and private expenditures in the Caquetá region from 1930 to 1968 are estimated to have been about $50 million. Reconstruction of the flow of production over this period, based on the pattern of population growth and 1968 estimates of gross production ($18 million),[43] gives an IRR of about 10–15 percent for the thirty-eight years. This figure is clearly subject to a considerable margin of error. Nevertheless, taking into account the cattle inventory, which is not included as a benefit, there are good grounds for asserting that the development has been economically viable.[44]

[42] Fifty-two percent in administration and overhead, 23 percent in infrastructure, and 25 percent in equipment and services.

[43] INCORA.

[44] Taking the period 1930–58, thus excluding the major investment of INCORA and the Caja de Crédito Agrario, the rate of return becomes 10 percent. It is to be expected

Table 14. Land Use and Farm Income on Farms in the Credit Program Supervised by the
Instituto Colombiana de la Reforma Agraria, Caquetá, 1968

| Zone | Average farm area (ha) | Cultivated area (ha) | Pasture (ha) | Percentage of farm | | | Number of cattle | Pasture carrying capacity (head/ha) | Number of hogs | Income ($) | |
				In crops	In pasture	Exploited				Gross	Net
Florencia	57	5	29	8	51	59	24	0.9	4	3,900	2,000
Morelia	73	10	31	14	43	57	17	0.5	3	800	400
Paujil	75	11	27	14	36	50	24	0.8	3	700	400
La Mora	54	8	20	14	37	51	17	0.8	5	1,000	700
Maguaré	64	10	28	15	43	58	22	0.8	3	1,600	1,100
Puerto Rico	94	18	25	20	27	47	22	0.7	7	1,100	400
Valparaíso[a]	108	11	28	10	26	36	26	1.0	5	600	400
San Vicente[a]	188	9	59	5	31	36	54	0.9	23	2,100	1,000

Source: INCORA survey of 1,990 farms, August 1968.

[a] Areas without highway access.

Table 15. Comparison of Experience and Land Use of Directed
and Spontaneous Colonists in the Caquetá Region, 1963

		Settlers	
Experience and land use		Directed	Spontaneous
Experience			
Former occupation:	Farm owner (%)	28	70
	Renter or share-		
	cropper (%)	22	5
	Farm laborer (%)	35	23
	Nonfarm (%)	14	2
Native to Caqueta (%)		2	15
Average schooling (*years*)		2.2	1.1
Literate (%)		73	48
Land Use			
Size of holding (*ha*)		60	75
Crop area (*ha*)		2	5
Pasture area (*ha*)		9	9
Number of cattle		3	9
Carrying capacity of pasture (*head/ha*)		0.3	1.0

Source: Ronald L. Tinnermeir, *New Land Settlement in the Eastern Lowlands of Colombia,* Research Paper no. 13 (Land Tenure Center, University of Wisconsin, December 1964).

Puyo-Tena

The Puyo-Tena zone lies at the base of the Ecuadorian Andes in the upper reaches of the Pastaza and Napo rivers, both major tributaries of the Amazon. It encompasses about 400,000 ha served by 125 km of roads and a 108-km access highway from Ambato in the highlands (see map 9).

The access road to Puyo was built by the Shell Oil Company to facilitate petroleum exploration in the eastern plains. Construction was completed between 1950 and 1963. Settlement followed immediately and expanded throughout the period. In the early sixties accelerated road construction toward Tena, plus the establishment of two large tea plantations, led to increased migration from the highlands. By 1968 the total population had reached 35,000–40,000, of which about 7,000 were urban, with 500 families employed by the tea companies. There were twenty small sawmills, and four distilleries produced alcohol from sugar cane. The total area occupied by 4,300 spontaneous colonists was about 280,000 ha, of which 15,000 ha were in crops and 80,000 ha were in pasture. Cattle numbered about 20,000 head.

that the major benefits of the $40 million invested by these agencies between 1959 and 1968 will accrue over the decades of the seventies and eighties. Assuming that the 1968 level of production will be maintained to 1988 and counting only operating and maintenance expenses for this period, the rate of return for the 21 years 1959–80 would be on the order of 40 percent.

Total government expenditures in the region probably do not exceed $5 million.[45] While no figures are available for Shell's outlay in the access road nor for the private investment of the tea companies, commercial interests, and the colonists themselves, it appears that viable economic activity has been generated in the region.[46]

The Puyo-Tena region is in the consolidation stage of settlement, with pioneer settlement continuing on the fringes. A degree of subsistence agriculture persists. Judged by other tropical settlement areas, however, the distribution of land appears to have been satisfactory; 70 percent of the holdings are between 25-50 ha in size and 20 percent are 10-25 ha. No units are less than 5 ha, and 5 percent are more than 200 ha.[47]

On the basis of state investments the region represents a successful tropical colonization venture. This has been brought about by (1) taking advantage of an existing privately constructed access road; (2) providing key services as the demand grew, notably, credit after 1954; (3) extension services; (4) extension of the trunk road north of Puyo, plus 35 km of feeder roads; and (5) the granting of titles, particularly after 1960. Some 2,600 titles were issued by 1968.

The two tea companies, Sociedad Ecuatoriana de Desarrollo Industria Agopecuaria (SEDIA) and Compañía Ecuatoriana de Té, have also played an important role in development since 1960. The provision of wage employment for 500 families has attracted many who subsequently took up land in the expanding forest frontier to the north or occupied lands along the penetration roads built by the companies. About 400 colonists have occupied lands around the plantations. When company operations are fully developed it is estimated that 1,200 workers will be permanently employed. In addition SEDIA and the Banco Nacional de Fomento (BNF) have undertaken an experiment in development that may have interesting implications for future small-holder settlement on new lands in the humid tropics. SEDIA has established a nursery to provide plants for 1,000 ha of tea. The company will supply the plants to 200-300 small producers; will provide technical services in planting, management, and harvesting; and has agreed to buy the total output. In support of the project the BNF committed $500,000 to be granted as credit to colonists over a three-year period.

[45] Based on estimates of annual expenditures for 1960-66 in the Municipios of Napo and Pastaza provided by the Junta Nacional de Planificación, plus an allowance of $3 million for highway construction.

[46] Assuming a total investment of $10 million distributed in equal quotas over the twenty-nine-year period 1940-68, lineal expansion in production during this time, and a 15 percent discount rate, value added in 1968 would have had to reach $1.3 million to justify the expenditures. At $200 per family, this appears to be well within the probable output.

[47] Based on 40,000 ha titled by IERAC to 1968.

Foreign Colonization

Foreign colonization (and private land subdivision and settlement as well) may be regarded as private directed projects. Generally, controls are confined to subdivision and certain eligibility prerequisites or conditions for purchase, such as the down payment, residence on the property, land accumulation, and the rate of development. Land development and industrial corporations, whether private or public, present no problems with respect to project definition.

As far as public policy for new-land development is concerned, foreign colonization is unlikely to be a significant factor in opening up the humid tropics of Latin America over the next few decades. Most countries now have the primary concern of utilizing their resources for the benefit of their own citizens, particularly the inhabitants of depressed rural areas. Moreover migration from Europe and Japan, formerly the principal sources of foreign colonists, has declined to insignificant proportions since 1960. A few religious groups from North America and Europe established settlements during the sixties, but at most these groups may be expected to form colonies of only 100 or 200 families—too small to be of consequence to policy makers. Three projects are examined here, the two Japanese settlements in the Santa Cruz region of Bolivia and the Mennonite settlements in the Paraguayan Chaco.

San Juan and Okinawa

The principal justification for the settlement of Japanese immigrants in the period 1955-60 in the Santa Cruz region of eastern Bolivia (map 8) was to substitute domestic production of rice for imports. It was argued that the demonstration effect of these colonists, plus the newly constructed Cochabamba-Santa Cruz highway, would lead to a greater output of rice. But to isolate the demonstration effect of the Japanese from the whole complex of forces that generate increased production would be extremely difficult. In any event, domestic production had completely displaced rice imports within seven years, and by 1964 excess supplies became an embarrassment to the government, especially since the disorganized credit, transport, storage, and marketing of rice resulted in wide seasonal and annual price fluctuations. Attempts at government price control have been ineffective. In 1965 the Japanese colonists produced 6,700 tons of rice out of a total of 37,000 tons (about 90 percent of national production) from the Santa Cruz region. Of the total, 30,000 tons came from the zone north of Montero where the Japanese colonies were expected to have their major impact.[48]

---

[48]Unpublished statistics from the Secretaría Nacional de Planificación y Ministerio de Agricultura, La Paz, Bolivia; Servicio de Emigración del Japón en Bolivia; and Ministerio de Economía, *Informe del comité de racionalización de transporte automotor* (La Paz, Bolivia, 1966), annex 4.

The San Juan colony was established in 1955 on a concession of 35,000 ha on the south bank of the Yapacani River. In 1969 there were 365 farm units of 50 ha each. In spite of the relatively high capitalization of these farms (see table 16) the poor soils have required extensive bush-fallow, with only 30 percent of the cleared area in production in 1967.

Okinawa includes three concessions totaling 55,000 ha on the south bank of the Rio Grande. Settlement was initiated in 1954 and reached a peak of 550 families in 1964. Between 1965 and 1969, 150 families left the area because of unsatisfactory prices for rice (the staple crop), insecurity in marketing or processing under diversification plans for cotton and soya, and severe floods in 1967. The soils are somewhat better than those in San Juan, and because of the more extensive use of purchased inputs, the area in bush-fallow has been restricted. The history of the area shows no bush-fallow until the fifth year of development; by the ninth year 35 percent of the cleared area was in fallow and 30 percent by the twelfth year (1967).

Although the two colonies continue to depend on rice and corn as the basic products of their economies, they have exhibited a number of pioneer

Table 16. Population, Land Use, and Income on the
San Juan and Okinawa Colonies, Santa Cruz, Bolivia, 1967

Population, land use, and income	Colony					Total, both colonies
	San Juan	Okinawa				
		Area 1	Area 2	Area 3	Total	
Families (individual farmers)	280	241	166	57	464	744
Population	1,580	1,557	995	396	2,948	4,528
Average residence (*years*)	7.1	8.3	7.3	5.0	7.9	7.4
Land use per farm (*ha*)						
Crops	8	19	16	12	17	14
Pasture	2	8	7	3	7	6
Bush-fallow	25	12	5	2	8	10
Forest	15	11	22	33	18	20
Total	50	50	50	50	50	50
Average income per family (*$*)						
Agricultural	1,580	2,920	1,920	1,670	2,410	2,220
Nonfarm	330	660	500	250	550	500
Total	1,910	3,580	2,420	1,920	2,960	2,720
Production expenses	930	2,000	1,170	750	1,550	1,420
Net income	980	1,580	1,250	1,170	1,410	1,300
Subsistence living expenses	660	930	660	660	800	750
Net surplus	320	650	590	510	610	550

Source: Survey by the Servicio de Emigración del Japón en Bolivia, Santa Cruz, 1967.

leadership attributes that were expected of them under the original programs. Systematic testing of different crops and varieties has been carried out. Tropical wheat was produced on a commercial scale on Okinawa in 1969; soya has also been introduced on a relatively large scale. The colonies have made major efforts to diversify in the direction of citrus and bananas (230 trees per farm on San Juan), hogs (an average of 9 per farm on Okinawa 1), poultry (215 birds per farm on San Juan), and cattle (6 head per farm on Okinawa 2). In addition, on 1,400 ha on Okinawa 2, colonists have undertaken cooperative mechanized forest clearing and mechanized farming.

The outlay by the Japanese and U.S. governments for the projects, including $1.5 million in credit, amounted to $4.8 million over the fifteen-year period 1954-68 (see table 17). No data are available on reinvestment by the colonists in the projects; the 1967 survey showed an average surplus above subsistence of about $550 per family. For the purpose of computing an economic return on the project, it has been assumed that the 850 families in the first year initially invested $500 each, and that an additional $100 per year was reinvested on each farm with long-term credit included as a development cost (table 17). On this basis the IRR over fourteen years in San Juan is 20-30 percent and in Okinawa, 60-80 percent.

From an economic accounting standpoint the projects appear viable. Bolivia's principal concerns, however, are the multiplier effects—the absorption of labor or other resources, which otherwise would have been unemployed, in direct farm work, transport, processing, or supply of inputs—and external economies, such as the real demonstration effect influencing the training of potential farmers, the rate of settlement, and production efficiency in the Santa Cruz region or elsewhere. Since the total investment in development has been from foreign sources, the creation of employment and consumption of national goods and services must be regarded as a positive contribution to an economy with vast unexploited land reserves and underemployed labor. The colonists employ the equivalent of 800 permanent workers with an annual payroll of $210,000. Apart from hired labor, purchases of production and consumption goods may be estimated at $1.5 million.

The efficiency of the Japanese and their ability to organize, innovate, and cooperate is widely recognized in Santa Cruz, although their contact with local producers is minimal. To some extent they are regarded as a threat by local producers who fear the Japanese may flood an already weak rice market or compete for lucrative sugar contracts. They also are held suspect by entrepreneurs who wish to retain monopolistic control over agricultural processing. While the situation is unquestionably aggravated by cultural differences, it is likely that a carefully selected national group, given major state assistance in order to assure success, would also generate a degree of resentment among less favored local settlers. Nor is there anything in the history or structure of

Table 17. Development Costs of the San Juan and Okinawa Colonies,
Santa Cruz, Bolivia, 1954-1968

(dollars)

| Item | Expenditures | | | | Total, both colonies | Total per farm[a] |
| | San Juan | | Okinawa | | | |
	Total	Per farm[a]	Total	Per farm[a]		
Foreign government[b]						
Project administration	620,000	1,700	140,000	240	760,000	810
Highway construction	450,000	1,240	570,000	1,000	1,020,000	1,080
Machinery and buildings	670,000	1,840	410,000	710	1,080,000	1,010
Social services	240,000	660	170,000	300	410,000	430
Total	1,980,000	5,440	1,290,000	2,250	3,270,000	3,330
Credit						
Short-term production	340,000	940	470,000	820	810,000	860
Long-term development	150,000	410	540,000	940	690,000	730
Total	490,000	1,350	1,010,000	1,760	1,500,000	1,590
Colonists' personal resources[c]	400,000	1,100	740,000	1,290	1,140,000	1,210
Total[d]	2,530,000	6,950	2,570,000	4,480	5,100,000	5,270

Source: Servicio de Emigración del Japón en Bolivia, Santa Cruz, 1969.

[a]Estimated on the basis of the number of farms, 1968–69 (365 on San Juan and 574 on Okinawa).

[b]San Juan was financed primarily by Japan and Okinawa by the United States. Figures exclude direct cash grants at time of emigration and credit for fares.

[c]Estimated on the assumption of $500 per immigrant family invested in the first year (295 families on San Juan and 555 on Okinawa). It is also assumed that for each farm in 1968–69 average reinvestment amounted to $100 annually for an average residence of seven years on San Juan and eight years on Okinawa.

[d]Excludes short-term production credit, which is repaid annually and may be considered an operating expense rather than a development investment.

Santa Cruz development since the completion of the Cochabamba highway that would readily allow one to attribute a given percentage of Santa Cruz production (outside the colonies) to the presence of Japanese immigrants.

Filadelfia

The Mennonite colonization of the central Paraguayan Chaco is an extreme example of the development of low-quality, poorly located tropical land resources. Filadelfia (see map 3) is the largest town in the area and is used here to represent the total Mennonite migration to three separate but adjacent projects founded between 1927 and 1943 by 6,700 migrants from Canada and Germany. Access to the colonies was gained by traveling for 500 km on the Paraguay River from Asunción and thence overland for 250 km. Until the early 1960s this journey by riverboat, truck, and rail required seven or eight days. The first plans for a penetration road through the region were prepared in 1936 after the Chaco War. Construction began in 1957, and the 460 km to Filadelfia were completed in 1964.

Over the forty-year period 1928–68 these colonists acquired more than 0.5 million ha of land. They have 1,300 farms, 40,000 ha in crops, 110,000 ha in pasture, and 72,000 head of cattle.[49] The Mennonite population reached 9,000. In addition about 500 colonists occupied lands on the periphery of the colony after the completion of the Trans-Chaco highway, and about 600 formerly nomadic Guaraní Indian families have been settled on 5-ha parcels by the Mennonites. An additional 900 Indian families earn a living as laborers for the colonists. The total population of the region was about 20,000 in 1968.

No data are available on the total investment made by the colonists, nor would it be an easy matter to assess the social cost of the hardships endured by a generation to develop an inhospitable wilderness. It is hard to imagine such sacrifices by any future generation. These are now sunk costs, however, and the colonies enjoy a physical and institutional infrastructure that appears to be in a strong position to yield high returns on marginal investments. Gross sales tripled in the four years following the completion of the Trans-Chaco highway.[50]

In spite of the high degree of organization, however, this group evidently was unable to achieve any significant breakthrough in development on the basis of local consumption. The colonists' major concern for many years has been to find ways and means of marketing their products in Asunción, and future projections depend exclusively on whether or not the Trans-Chaco is paved.

Private Land Settlement Schemes

Consideration of the possibility of private corporate enterprise playing a significant role in new-land development in the humid tropics may seem anomalous at a time when virtually all the countries of Latin America—plus international agencies—are stressing the need for changes in the agrarian structure that emphasize redistribution of land to give property rights to a majority of rural families in either individual or communal farms. It may well be

[49] Mennonite Social and Economic Committee, Asunción, Paraguay, 1968.

[50] Mennonite Social and Economic Committee; and *Estudio de factibilidad para la ruta Trans-Chaco* (Ottawa, Canada: de Leuw, Cather and Co. of Canada, March 1969), p. 72.

claimed that, along with plantations and foreign colonization, subdivision and the promotion of land development under private auspices is not relevant to government planning for the humid tropics of Latin America. Regardless of the political feasibility of such activities in the future, four cases are reviewed here on the assumption that some of the experience may prove useful in the formulation of public policy.

Companhía Melhoramentos Norte do Paraná

Land development and colonization undertaken by the Companhía Melhoramentos Norte do Paraná (CMNP) in Brazil is in all probability the most extensive and economically successful in the humid tropics of Latin America. It may be argued that this experience exhibits unique conditions that cannot be duplicated readily, because of changes in markets, technology, communications, and the political power structure. Nevertheless the success elements in the project do offer insights for the design and implementation of land settlement in the humid tropics and subtropics.

Between 1922 and 1925 a land company constructed a 350-km railroad from São Paulo to Ourinhos on the Paraná border. During the same period the Paraná Land Company acquired 1.25 million ha of virgin forest on the now famous *terra roxa* (red earth), 200 km west of Ourinhos, and went to great lengths to assure clear title, in some cases "purchasing" the same area two or three times.[51] In 1932 the company completed the 150-km rail extension from Ourinhos to the eastern boundary of its holdings. Subdivision of these lands was initiated in 1930, and the town of Londrina was founded two years later (see map 10).

During World War II the Paraná Land Company sold out to the CMNP, which retained the original land settlement program. The basic policy was to encourage ownership of relatively small parcels—the theory being that this would lead to integrated regional development that would not occur under a *latifundio* system. The individual owners would form the basis of demand for the services of urban centers. Accordingly stress was laid on the planning of towns, the promotion of services and industries, and the establishment of intermediate *chacras* (small farms) of 1–5 ha on the fringes of the urban centers.[52] The main urban centers were located 100 km apart on the trunk road west from Londrina. Londrina itself was planned at the outset for a population of 20,000; in thirty-five years it had reached 120,000. Maringá was founded in 1947 for 150,000 inhabitants; by 1955 all urban lots were sold, and the population in 1968 was estimated at over 100,000. Between the major towns, village centers were established every 15 km.

---

[51] *O estado de São Paulo*, January 15, 1965.

[52] Craig L. Dozier, "Northern Paraná, Brazil: An Example of Organized Regional Development," *Geographic Review*, July 1956, pp. 318–33.

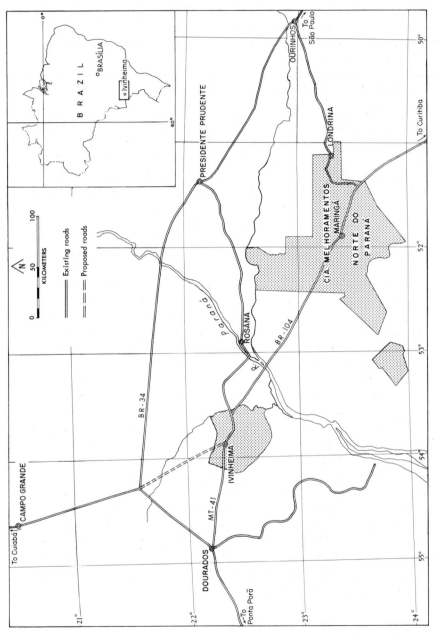

Map 10. Private land settlement schemes in Paraná and southern Mato Grosso, Brazil.

Although the company undoubtedly profited on lands it purchased from the state at $1.25 per hectare and sold in subdivisions with infrastructure in place at $6 plus per hectare, the principal gains came over the long run through ownership retained in key urban parcels. In view of the interest in improved land values there were obvious advantages to the company in reinvesting in the region. Enterprises financed by the company include power generation; sugar refining; insurance; and the manufacture of railroad equipment, cement, and galvanized pipe.

Every effort was made to create conditions that would generate demand for land by small and medium producers, i.e., (1) the identification of good land, (2) good access roads, (3) secure title, (4) stable development policies, (5) availability of urban services, and (6) the development of local markets through the establishment of industries and an expanding group of urban consumers. Of the 1.3 million ha handled by the two companies in the thirty-five years 1932-67, only about 40,000 ha remained to be subdivided; 39,000 farms had been created, and in the first twenty years over 1 million ha had been sold. Five thousand kilometers of access roads had been built. In 1932 the area was essentially in virgin tropical forest. By 1968 the population was estimated at about 1.7 million, of which 40-50 percent was urban.

Ivinheima

The Ivinheima project in Brazil is operated by the Sociedade de Melhoramentos e Colonização (SOMECO). Between 1958 and 1962 this company purchased about 400,000 ha in southern Mato Grosso 725 km west of São Paulo, a westward extension of the coffee lands of northern Paraná (map 10). The company assembled a large consolidated block of land with clear title, gaining control of 70-80 percent of the area, which was subsequently incorporated as the *municipio* (municipality) of Ivinheima. Aside from the quality of the soils, the concentration of suitable soils, and the possibility of assembling a large block of land, the company found market access and potential transport services of equal importance in making its selection. The railhead at Rosana is 30 km east on the Paraná River. If plans could be carried out to extend the railroad to Ponta Porã on the Paraguayan border, the line would bisect Ivinheima. Highway MT-41, designed to provide the principal link between northern Paraná and Ponta Porã (through southern Mato Grosso), would pass through the center of the property; BR-104, the most direct route from Curitiba to Campo Grande, would cross MT-41 at the site selected for the principal town and the SOMECO administrative headquarters.

Anything that SOMECO could do to accelerate the realization of these highway plans would be of enormous benefit to the settlement and above all to the creation of a demand for urban centers. Accordingly the company built a 170-meter bridge over the Ivinheima River in 1963 and opened up a

100-km road across the property. In 1967 this road was accepted by the state of Mato Grosso and established as MT–41. In 1968 there were eight through buses daily on this road. In addition to the trunk highway the company has constructed 1,200 km of farm access roads.

With the completion of aerial photography and the identification of priority areas for settlement, the first-stage plan called for eight urban centers on 45,000 ha, each serving *glebas*[53] of 4,000–8,000 ha containing 250–300 parcels each. The Piraveve *gleba*, consisting of 8,800 ha and including the principal town site, Ivinheima, was selected as the best agricultural area and therefore appropriate as the focus of an attempt to establish successful settlement that would serve as a demonstration and basis for promoting development of the other seven *glebas* in the first stage. Five of these *glebas* were initiated between 1963 and 1968 (see table 18). Topographic surveys of Piraveve were completed in 1961, and 183 lots were sold in 1962. In the following year the company's operation was moved to the Ivinheima site, and plans were drawn up for a town of 60,000.

From 1963 to 1967 SOMECO made every effort to develop an urban center that would offer necessary services to settlers and increase the demand for both farm and urban properties. In order to stimulate rural demand for local urban services the maximum size of a farm was set at 50 ha, and the average was 18 ha. The company initiated a wide range of subsidiary operations—sawmill, brick factory, furniture factory, diesel electric generating plant, water supply, machine shop, hotel, housing for forty-five families in transit to their lots, trucking, road construction and maintenance, warehouse, seed-drying plant, experimental farm, and a marketing agency for the purchase of the settlers' production and for the sale of production inputs. In addition the company built and operated schools, a hospital, and extension services. Since the primary focus of SOMECO is land development, these activities are regarded as transitional and promotional. The company therefore plans to divest itself of industries and services either to state agencies or private interests. In order to increase the autonomy and political leverage of the area the company successfully promoted the formation of a *municipio* in 1966. In 1968 the population of the town of Ivinheima was about 5,000 and of the *municipio*, 28,000. A total of 1,650 lots had been taken up (see table 18).

The interest in creating an active demand for land led to subdivision in relatively small units to attract settlers with limited funds. Colonists nevertheless are required to have considerably more resources than for most government schemes throughout the Latin American tropics. In 1968 a settler acquiring 20 ha would have had to pay $600 in cash with a balance of $900 due in equal annual installments over three years. Emphasis is placed on

---

[53] Large blocks of land, or concessions, for subdivision.

Table 18. Land Settlement on Ivinheima, 1962–1968

Areas	Gleba						
	Piraveve	Cristalin	Itapoa	Ubirata	Jaborandi	Victoria	Total
Rural parcels							
Sold	202	102	239	395	199	191	1,328
Reserved by							
SOMECO	0	0	0	0	24	12	36
Available	91	28	25	97	71	130	442
Total	293	130	264	492	294	333	1,806
Average size (*ha*)	19	20	19	18	17	16	18
Total area (*ha*)	5,500	2,560	5,130	8,745	5,120	5,220	32,275
Chacras[a]							
Sold	231	0	41	58	0	1	331
Reserved by							
SOMECO	240	0	0	0	0	41	281
Available	84	0	48	6	0	0	138
Total	555	0	89	64	0	42	750
Average size (*ha*)	2.7	0	2.4	2.4	0	4.6	2.8
Total area (*ha*)	1,515	0	210	156	0	200	2,081

Source: SOMECO.

[a]Small farms, usually 1–5 ha.

occupying the best lands first, and in order to maximize the demonstration effect the company attempts to impose certain conditions through the sales contract, such as a minimum rate of land clearing (2 ha in the first year) and minimum housing standards. The company delivers lumber and roofing tiles to the property, essentially at cost prices, and advances full credit on these items to promote attractive housing.

The ongoing development activity that has been set in motion in the Ivinheima region, primarily through a SOMECO investment of about $1 million (excluding land purchase) has created employment for 5,000–6,000 families. Although the investments were made over a ten-year period, actual settlement was not initiated until 1963. The rate of urban and rural development that took place over the following five years, if continued, would probably result in a dynamic regional economy approaching that achieved by the CMNP.

Any attempt to evaluate the performance of Ivinheima in economic terms would be of limited value in view of the rapid evolution of the zone that was underway in 1968. On the properties sold by 1967 (approximately half were not occupied full time) the average area developed was 6 ha. On the Piraveve *gleba*, which had been in the process of settlement for four years, the average area cleared was 9 ha per farm, which, taking into account the flow of settlers, represents a clearing rate of about 4 ha annually. The estimated value added by colonists in 1968 was $1.1 million.[54]

If it is accepted that the region in 1968 had virtually reached the stage where active private investment would follow in the development of land, industry, and services, one would expect an accelerating transfer of SOMECO services to municipal or other government agencies and the sale of SOMECO industries. Leaving aside costs and returns associated with these activities and assuming (1) the occupancy of 2,600 parcels programmed in the first stage by 1973, (2) SOMECO budget figures for an average value added of $1,900 per farm at full development, and (3) an economic life of twenty-five years (1959–83) for the first stage, then an IRR of 15 percent would permit an individual colonist investment of about $500 per ha, a figure that appears to be well beyond the requirements for development.[55] In this event, probabilities of the project's economic viability are excellent.

Gleba Arinos

The Gleba Arinos project is one of the most isolated colonization ventures in the Latin American tropics (see map 3). The 200,000-hectare property is located 900 km south of Manaus, Brazil, along 60 km bordering the Arinos River, a southern tributary of the Amazon. Access in 1968 was by a 690-km road from Cuiabá; about 200 km were usable only seven months of the year. The journey by truck required three days.

The land was purchased in 1954 by the Colonizadora Noroeste Mato-grossense S.A. (CONOMALI), and forest clearing was initiated the following year. The first colonists entered in 1956. During the following twelve years a total of 280 families took up lands; 120 remained in 1968 on about 20,000 ha. In addition 20,000 ha were sold to five companies interested in large-scale development of rubber plantations. CONOMALI itself has planted rubber and together with the companies that purchased lands operates its plantations on the basis of subdivision and the sale of 10–15 ha lots. The condition that the company would clear the land and plant and maintain the rubber plantation till the tenth year was included in the sales contract. After the tenth year the buyer may take up residence or sign a management contract with the company. The total area developed in fourteen years amounted to 6,900 ha in rubber and 4,000 ha in other crops and pasture. On the basis of projected production the shipments of rubber from existing plantations should reach 10,000 tons by 1982, with a gross value of $4.1 million.

[54] This figure is based on a survey and farm budgets developed by SOMECO.

[55] The assumptions are that SOMECO and government costs will stabilize at 33 percent of the 1968 level from 1969–83 and that colonists will make their development investments over six years, 50 percent in the first year and the balance distributed equally over the following five years.

The settlement of families without resources of their own in such a remote area appears to be unsatisfactory. CONOMALI experimented with the settlement of fifty families in this category. Since there are neither government services nor other enterprises in the area, the company became responsible for advancing credit plus any other essential services. Thus it was drawn into activities in which it had little experience, and capital was diverted from the principal goals of rubber development, infrastructure, subdivision, and the sale of lands to absentee owners. Further, the low level of living of these people was seen as bad for public relations.

Because of freight rates of $30-$40 per ton to Cuiabá, the market possibilities for the colonists are limited to the immediate area. The chief source of local purchasing power is the capital brought in for the rubber plantations and by the new colonists. As long as development capital continues to flow to the region, cattle may find a market among settlers building up their herds, and expanding wage employment will sustain the demand for yucca, corn, rice, and pork. The principal capital accumulation is in cattle inventories,[56] pasture, and plantations. The plan is to sell the eventual production of the plantations outside the region. After fourteen years of development, agricultural or forestry exports from the project were insignificant.

The population of the region in 1968 was about 2,000. Three hundred families work directly for CONOMALI or other large landholders. In addition about 200 migrant laborers find seasonal work in the rubber plantations or are employed by the company in harvesting native Brazil nuts, rubber, or pelts from the forests along the major rivers. The project is in essence a vehicle for mobilizing private capital to open up new lands for corporate plantation agriculture. Largely because of the project's isolation few family farms have been created. The relevance of the project to tropical land development policy hinges first on the level of complementary agricultural processing and service activity that may be generated. Second, it depends on the steps the government might take to assist a private company to maximize the multiplier effects stemming from a single basic export item; e.g., the provision of part-time wage employment for colonists in the process of becoming established or the full-time employment of people who save, gain experience, and subsequently become farmers on lands adjacent to, or interspersed with, the plantations, whose production is geared to regional consumption requirements. The primary concern of a project design becomes the use of the rubber export component to maximize local consumption.

A project along these lines, the Plano Aliança, was proposed in 1967 by the company in collaboration with the Instituto Nacional de Desenvolvimento Agrario. The plan called for an expenditure of $6.4 million to settle

---

[56] A herd of 2,000 in 1968 had been developed from 300 head imported to the zone between 1955 and 1960.

1,000 families on parcels of 50 ha each (including 5 ha of rubber) and to assist the 120 farmers already living in the area. Total employment generated in the region would amount to about 4,000 families.[57] In this case CONOMALI–a private company–would be contracted by the government to undertake a directed colonization project. The argument in favor of this action was that there was excess capacity in some investments that had already been made on Gleba Arinos and that for fourteen years the company had acquired invaluable experience in the zone. The rubber area would be doubled, with gross sales reaching $8 million by 1986. On the assumption that this was a limit on rubber imposed by physical and market conditions, the policy maker faces the problem of how to maximize the ratio of gross aggregate consumption in the region to value added by rubber, consistent with established minimum income criteria.

The application of the regional value added as the estimate of benefits with a zero opportunity cost of land and labor results in exceptional performance projections using the cost and return estimates from the Plano Aliança and CONOMALI's 1954-67 cash flow. If one uses a 15 percent discount rate on the estimated cash flow from 1954 to 1967 and projections from 1968 to 1984 (when the 13,000 ha of rubber were expected to be in full production), the supportable development investment (1954-72), yielding an IRR of 15 percent over 30 years (1954-84), would be approximately $10 million, exclusive of costs and benefits from nonrubber activities in the region. This figure is 1.4 times the projected requirement.[58] While tax, land, and labor costs may be sufficient to discourage private investment, the expected returns

---

[57]CONOMALI, "Plano Aliança de amplicacão dos trabalhos de colonizacão na Gleba Arinos" (March 1967, mimeo.).

[58]This is based on the following assumptions:

1. That 6,900 ha of rubber would be planted (767 ha annually from 1959 to 1967).
2. That an additional 6,100 ha of rubber would be planted under the Plano Aliança at the rate of 2,033 ha annually from 1968 to 1970.
3. Plantations would start producing in the eighth year, with a yield of 500 kilograms per ha and a farm gate value of $200.
4. Plantations would reach full production in the thirteenth year, with a gross sales value of $680 per ha.
5. Production inputs imported to the region would be $25 per ha on the accumulated area in plantations.
6. There would be 500 employed families in 1967, 1,500 in 1970, and 2,500 at full production of the 13,000 ha in 1984.
7. Labor would be valued at $250 per family per year, and all costs would be considered chargeable against the rubber enterprise.

The estimated total investment by CONOMALI and other rubber companies between 1954 and 1967 was $1.3 million, excluding transfer payments, such as land purchase, social security, taxes, interest, and amortization payments. The budget for the Plano Aliança for the period 1968-72 was $5.2 million, exclusive of transfer payments.

appear to have considerable social utility in a country with large areas of unexploited tropical lands and an underemployed rural labor force.

Since the Plano Aliança was not put into effect the issue is CONOMALI's expected performance on the basis of current operations. Private capital has been mobilized to develop land resources that otherwise undoubtedly would have remained idle for decades. This heroic leap beyond the forest frontier might have had important external effects in encouraging spontaneous settlement along the access road. After fifteen years such effects do not appear significant. But accepting the rubber price and yield projections of the Plano Aliança, financial viability seems assured. However, the social impact resulting from the generation of employment and the distribution of income—which was outstanding in Ivinheima and the CMNP operations—is likely to be minimal in Gleba Arinos.

Tournavista

The Tournavista experiment in Peru (map 3) offers some interesting insights into the relationship between private enterprise and a government in tropical land development. The contract setting up the project was signed by the Peruvian government and the R. G. Le Tourneau Corporation in 1953. Le Tourneau was to receive a concession of 400,000 ha of virgin jungle lands 800 km from Lima between the Pachitea River and the Huánuco-Pucallpa highway. The condition for this grant was that the corporation would construct 50 km of road to railroad specifications that were to be incorporated into the proposal for the Pucallpa–Tambo del Sol rail line to link the Ucayali River with the Pacific coast. Title to the first 60,000 ha was to be granted with the arrival in Peru of equipment and materials valued at $110,000 or more; a mercantile mortgage was to be retained on this area until satisfactory completion of the first 10 km of road. Subsequently title was to be granted to four more tracts of 60,000 ha with the completion of each 10 km of road. With final acceptance of the road, title would be delivered to the remaining 100,000 ha.

Within a few years the government abandoned plans for the railroad. In the meantime the construction of a highway roadbed to width, grade, and radius specifications for a railroad resulted in a worse highway at a greater cost than could have been obtained if the alignment and construction had been exclusively for a highway. The road that had cost $3.9 million was valued at only $1 million in 1966, and the investment required to put it in acceptable condition for year-round use was estimated at about $0.5 million. The question of the jurisdiction of the road remained under constant debate until the contract was rescinded in 1971. Although the contract specified the procedure whereby the government would approve and accept sections of the road as they were built, acceptance was avoided, especially after all interest was lost in the railroad.

Because Le Tourneau made no serious moves in the direction of colonization up to 1967, the government took the position that the road was essentially private and that therefore the company should bear the $20,000–$30,000 annual maintenance cost, but without the right to enforce closure in wet weather. The company was in a weak position to take any action in its interest that might have provoked reaction by influential truckers who used the road for logging and as a link with up-river trade on the Pachitea River.

Since the road was not formally accepted by the government, the only land transaction completed was the granting of title to the 60,000 ha subject to a mercantile mortgage. This situation contributed to the company's reluctance to comply with other clauses on colonization. With the granting of title, Le Tourneau was required to subdivide part of the lands for colonization, with a minimum lot size of 10 ha; to build the necessary urban infrastructure; to undertake agricultural research and extension for the colonists; and to maintain machinery and workshops that would sell services to the settlers. No time was specified for the colonization. There was no indication of how many hectares were to constitute "part" of the lands, nor was there an upper limit on the size of parcels.

Aside from the inevitable friction arising from attempts to execute such an imprecise contract and the waste of resources in constructing a road to railroad specifications, the company made errors in planning and carrying out the project. In the first place, a decision was made to construct the road starting from the Pachitea River and working back to the Pucallpa-Lima highway. This had a threefold effect:

1. Transporting machinery and supplies and the establishment of the base at Tournavista were more expensive than if construction had started at the Pucallpa road.
2. The company was forced to establish its center of operations at Tournavista, i.e., at the most distant point on the road. Thus transport costs again were higher and maintenance of the road became essential regardless of what policy the government took with respect to acceptance.
3. The company automatically started developing lands in the vicinity of its headquarters. As a result, the most valuable lands of its concession—the junction with the Pucallpa road—were neglected, and the area was irrevocably settled in an unplanned manner by spontaneous colonists.

The evident intent of the contract was that Le Tourneau should undertake extensive colonization; in the first fourteen years of operation the company made no move in this direction. In fact, opposition was shown to spontaneous settlers who located along the road. From the outset the company had no clear idea of what sort of land development could be undertaken or on what scale, how to organize and finance colonization, what sort of schedule might be appropriate for developing and settling 400,000 ha, or how to exploit the forest resources. The average exploitation of commercial timber from 1955 to 1967 was about 3 percent.[59]

One of the principal objectives of the Le Tourneau Corporation was to test forest-clearing machinery under humid tropical conditions. In the first twelve years the company cleared 3,000 ha with machinery worth about $200,000. Included in this machinery were two tree-crushers with a rated capacity of 1 ha per hour each. Thus, theoretically, at 200 working days per year these machines could clear about 40,000 ha in 12 years. Even allowing for repairs, bad weather, and the experimental nature of the machines, output equivalent to 7 percent of capacity was poor advertising.

Livestock Development Programs

It is evident from the foregoing survey that in many instances cattle are regarded as the panacea for tropical land development and are desired by most colonists. Beef production is the solution offered by government land development agencies when problems of marketing tropical crops are suspected or encountered—e.g., La Chontalpa and the coffee diversification programs in Guatemala and Mexico—or when soils turn out to be less fertile than indicated by original surveys, e.g., Yapacani. The World Bank and IDB have been prompted to lend extensively for the expansion of the livestock industry in the humid tropics of Latin America because of the apparent strong market for beef, intentions to close the "protein gap," the suitability of many tropical areas for cattle, improved breeds adapted to the tropics that have been developed in Brazil and some temperate regions, and advanced tropical pasture technology that has been developed in Australia and Africa. No evaluation has been made of any of the cattle development programs, but the principal elements that govern public policy in directing resources to this activity will be discussed briefly.[60]

Cattle development is governed by biological, technical, economic, and institutional factors.[61] The biological and technical factors control the rate at which a herd can be expanded, annual sales, and the weight per animal. Experiments with importing cattle on a large scale from Australia and North America have been conducted in some areas of Latin America but have not

[59] Manuel Abastos Gomez, *Inventario y evaluación de la concesión Tournavista, Pucallpa* (Lima, Perú: Le Tourneau del Perú, 1967), p. 87.

[60] In a letter to the author, May 25, 1970, Barry Nestel of FAO pointed out that since no evaluation has been made of tropical livestock programs in Latin America, it is in order to reserve judgment on the extensive market prospects and high rates of return that are claimed.

[61] P. J. Brumby, "The Planning and Implementation of Livestock Development Projects" (Working Paper no. 42, Sixth FAO Inter-American Conference on Animal Production and Health, Gainesville, Florida, September 10–20, 1967).

been seriously considered as the basis for significant expansion of a regional herd numbering about 250 million. The crucial variables in a buildup of herd numbers are the calving, mortality, and culling rates.[62] In some regions the calving rate is as low as 35 percent, and mortality is commonly 5 percent for mature animals and 10 percent for young stock. Improvement of performance both in increasing cattle numbers and in the rate of weight gain hinges primarily on nutrition and health and to a much lesser extent on animal breeding.

The institutional and economic factors in the development of tropical livestock are the same as those for any other agricultural activity: (1) political stability and security of tenure, which encourages forgoing present consumption in order to build herd numbers and asset values; (2) the availability of credit on suitable terms, accompanied by adequate extension or supervision; and (3) the availability of markets and a physical infrastructure that places costs of production inputs and farm prices of cattle in a range that provides an incentive to produce.

When the public policy maker receives proposals for channeling resources into the improvement of technical, economic, and institutional conditions, he faces a dilemma because of the apparent expectation of economic viability on the one hand and the extensive nature, scale economies,[63] and limited social

---

[62]The relationship between the variables is given by the formula

$$m = \frac{a}{2}[(1-d_e)(1-d_f)(1-d_g) - C_q(1-d_e)(1-d_f)] - (d_h + C_t)$$

where

m = annual percentage increase in the breeding herd, once the herd structure is stable. If one independent variable is changed, it may take one to three years to reach a new level of stability, depending on the variable;

a = calving percentage at weaning;

d_e = mortality in calves;

d_f = mortality in one-year heifers;

d_g = mortality in two-year heifers;

d_h = mortality in mature breeding cows;

C_q = culling percentage of two-year heifers;

C_t = culling percentage of mature breeding cows.

If d is constant for all age groups at 4 percent, C_q is 20 percent, and C_t is 17 percent, the breeding herd will be maintained, i.e., $m = 0$, with a 60 percent calving. With the same coefficients, the achievement of a 6 percent annual increase in the breeding herd would require a 74 percent calving. If mortality increases from 4 percent to 6 percent, m could be maintained at zero by increasing calving from 60 percent to 70 percent.

[63]IBRD estimates for the Bolivian cattle program indicate that development investments per cow in a 200-cow herd is triple that of a 1,000-cow herd.

and employment impact on the other. It has been suggested that an efficient breeding unit should have no less than 400 cows, with a total herd of about 1,000 head (excluding calves). This unit, together with some subsistence cropping, could be operated by three or four families.[64] In an area cleared from forest and sown to pasture with tropical legumes, 300–500 ha would be required. Mechanized land clearing and sowing, fencing, and other installations, plus the purchase of the basic herd, would involve an investment in excess of $30,000 per family, apart from operating capital and infrastructure to serve a new area and its population. If a government's goal is the settlement of landless campesinos, the procedure above, although possibly yielding a satisfactory economic return, hardly appears acceptable where income distribution enters into the decision.

The other extreme in cattle development is clearing the forest by hand with family labor at no cash cost, minimal purchase of cows, and a buildup in herd numbers thereafter exclusively through retention of breeding stock. The effective limit to the area and rate of development in this case is set by the total amount of family labor per hectare required for clearing, and the amount required per hectare to manage the enterprise. In the first year all family labor available during the clearing season can be devoted to removing the forest cover. With each successive year the area already cleared will be larger, therefore the labor required for management will also be larger, and the amount for clearing will be correspondingly smaller. The area limit thus is reached when all available family labor is required to manage the enterprise.[65] Expressed symbolically the area limit is given by M/m where

m = number of man-days of labor required to maintain farming operations on 1 ha of cleared land during the forest-clearing season, subject to the condition that $m \geqslant$ the maximum requirement in other seasons;

a = total number of working days available during the forest-clearing season;

b = total number of equivalent workers per family;

$M = ab$ = total labor available (man-days) for forest clearing and farm operations during the forest-clearing season;

d = number of man-days of labor required to clear forest from 1 ha;

[64] Discussions with P. J. Brumby, livestock specialist, FAO-IBRD Program.

[65] If hired labor is introduced into the equation the only constraints on the rate of development and the size of the operation are management ability and financing. Using an extreme case–the development of a herd of 400 cows with hired labor–development could conceivably be achieved at the same rate as mechanized clearing with an investment requirement of about $75,000.

$K = M/d$ = number of hectares cleared of forest in the first year, or the family's maximum land-clearing capacity without a land maintenance obligation;

$R = m/d$ = ratio between labor requirement for land maintenance and forest clearing;

k = minimum area in hectares that a family considers worth clearing in one season. This factor is introduced to prevent the clearing time (t) from going to infinity as the area cleared each season approaches an infinitely small plot;

L_i = area cleared (hectares) by family labor in year i, assuming that priority in the use of labor will always be given to maintenance of land already cleared = $K(1 - R)^{i-1}$;

t = number of years for the family to clear the maximum area, i.e., the time at which $M = mL_T$ subject to the condition that $L_i = L_t = k$;

L_T = maximum area (hectares) the family can clear and maintain with their own labor = $\Sigma K(i - R)^{t-1}$

The clearing time (t) required to solve for L_T is given by

$$t \geqslant \frac{(\log k - \log K)}{\log (1 - R)} + 1.$$

Substituting estimates in the formula gives the following results: with a clearing season of three months, i.e., $a = 90$ days, with $b = 1.8$ workers, $k = 0.25$ ha, $d = 60$ man-days, and $m = 10$ man-days, the maximum area is 16 ha in 14 years. Changing the clearing season to four months reduces the time for full development to 11 years.

Reducing the pasture maintenance requirement increases the maximum area and clearing time in an inverse proportion, e.g., where m is reduced to 2 man-days, the maximum area becomes 80 ha with a clearing time of 70 years. Under conditions of severe weed infestation like that in the Alto Turiaçu area in Brazil (map 3), increasing labor requirements for pasture maintenance subsequently may force a reduction in area.

The illustration serves to highlight the principal factors that must be taken into account in designing a livestock project of this nature: the minimum income requirements, the desirability of introducing hired labor or machinery into the clearing process to reduce n; the necessity of using seasonal hired labor if m is not constant throughout the year; and the desirability of introducing technology to reduce m and thus accelerate the land development rate and increase the maximum area.

Using a minimum cost approach in a tropical area like Tingo María, a colonist with 50 ha who receives $6,000 in credit could expect to have 12–15 head of cattle on 8–10 ha after two or three years. Capital for clearing the remaining 40 ha and building up the herd to 100 head would have to be generated through the settler's own labor and increments to the herd through breeding. Theoretically a settler with fifteen cows in the third year should reach full production by the fifteenth year. This represents a substantial sacrifice of present consumption in expectation of future earnings. Little income would be realized from cattle sales until the sixth year. In a model developed for a Caquetá family unit of 100 ha using hired labor in land clearing, 80 ha would be in pasture after ten years. Total loan disbursements over a twelve-year period would be $11,000, with a maximum outstanding indebtedness of $5,000 between the fourth to seventh years.[66]

Regardless of which procedure is adopted for developing forest for cattle, the on-farm investments per family must be judged as high. In consequence most livestock promotion programs in the humid tropics of Latin America have been directed to the savanna regions, such as the Colombian Llanos, the Beni plains, or the Bolivian or Paraguayan Chaco. Furthermore a greater impact is sought by orienting the programs to producers already in operation who have private funds available or a significant inventory—a cattleman in tropical eastern Bolivia with 400 cows has a herd value of about $50,000.

In spite of the relatively high cash costs of initiating cattle development there are certain mitigating factors. First, as a means of diversification livestock provides more security for the colonist and a basis for more rapid capital accumulation than would be possible with crops.[67] Second, to the extent that capital accumulation is more rapid in cattle raising than in tropical cropping enterprises, the long-term employment multipliers may be greater. Third, some lands are wholly unsuited to exploitation except for raising cattle.

Beni Cattle Operations

Cattle development in the Beni plains of eastern Bolivia is illustrative of the problems that may be encountered. In the department of Beni, estimates of land suitable for cattle range as high as 150 million ha. Currently there are 15 million ha of savanna that carry about 800,000 head and are capable of supporting about 5 million head without improvement of native pastures.[68]

[66] Derived from data prepared by W. Schaefer-Kehnert of the IBRD for the Caquetá region, 1967.

[67] Raanan Weitz, *From Peasant to Farmer* (Columbia University Press, 1971), pp. 17–18.

[68] CBF, *La situación ganadera en el trópico* (La Paz, Bolivia, 1964); and Percival Bono, "La situación ganadera en el altiplano y el trópico de Bolivia" (Grupo CEPAL/FAO, La Paz, Bolivia, February 1966, mimeo.).

Calving is estimated at 35-45 percent. This low figure is attributed to poor nutrition and lack of management in terms of weaning and segregation of the herd by sex and age group. Consequently many cows only calve once every two years, and the inadequate control of calving dates results in severe losses (up to 80 percent) among those born during the rainy season from January to April. Fifty percent of the savanna area is subject to annual flooding up to a depth of 1.6 meters during this period, and inept stock management resulted in disastrous flood losses in 1947 and again in 1957.

Animal health and sanitation is grossly neglected; there is a high incidence of external parasites, rabies, and aftosa. Even where vaccines are available there is no systematic procedure for administering them. Little attempt is made to improve the strain or to select high-yield animals for breeding.[69] There also is a tendency to "mine" herds, i.e., to reduce their reproductive capacity by selling breeding cows or heifers to obtain ready cash. This occurs partly because of irresponsible management and partly because of short loan periods (seven years) and high interest rates (12 percent) that may preclude a sufficient increase in production to cover amortization payments. Steers that should be held to three years are often sold at eighteen months, further lowering the stock on already underutilized pastures. Theft is prevalent due to ineffective police control and a lack of fencing. The slaughtering and marketing of cattle is disorganized; there has been a proliferation of slaughtering plants without sanitation, refrigeration, or quality control, and little opportunity exists for developing by-products.

In 1967 the World Bank and the Banco Agrícola Boliviana (BAB) initiated a phased program to improve Beni cattle production by using more fencing and corrals, increasing the supply of water for stock, vaccinating the stock, and importing a limited number of bulls and heifers. Under Phase I, $2 million was to be provided to 160 producers with 294,000 cattle; this was later expanded by $2 million for an additional 100 ranches. Phase II is programmed at $7 million for the remaining 315 ranches in the region. The projected direct impact of this program would be a 260 percent increase in herd by 1978 and a fivefold increase in beef production between 1968 and 1984.[70] Unquestionably a 10 percent rate of increase in production sustained over a seventeen-year period with IRR's on the order of 20-25 percent would be a creditable performance.[71] It remains to be seen whether the program will encounter institutional difficulties or problems related to administrative ca-

---

[69] Criollo cattle yield a dressed weight of about 170 kilograms at four years; animals crossed with improved breeds yield the same weight in three years. As long as there is excess pasture, this increased technical efficiency has little economic advantage.

[70] BAB, *Bolivian Livestock and Meat Marketing Situation and Possibilities for Its Development* (La Paz, September 1969).

[71] Latinconsult S.A. y M. Vivado y Asociados, *Fortalecimiento y desarrollo de la ganadería bovina de carne en el Oriente Boliviano* (La Paz, 1968), vol. 4, p. 204.

pacity, production, and marketing—all of which have caused a wide divergence between the projected and actual outcome of colonization.

State Enterprise in Agro-Industry

The experience in the development of an area of about 1 million ha north of Santa Cruz in the eastern Bolivian lowlands provides some insights into negative and positive elements encountered in the process of opening up new tropical lands. Aside from the Cochabama-Santa Cruz highway, opened to traffic in 1954 and paved in 1957, the main thrust of the government development program was directed toward sugar processing supported by colonization and a large-scale machinery pool. The first sugar mill in the region was established in 1944, and production prior to 1950 averaged 160 tons annually. Expectations of increased production, largely stemming from the progress on the highway link with Cochabamba and the highlands, resulted in plant expansion and a new mill in the early fifties; total production reached 4,500 tons by 1955. In 1956 the Corporación Boliviana de Fomento (CBF) inaugurated the Guabirá mill, and a fourth mill came into operation in 1957. By 1960 annual production had reached 25,000 tons. Imports that had averaged about 45,000 tons annually were reduced accordingly, and it became apparent that with existing installed capacity the national market would be saturated within a year or two, thus exceeding the most optimistic projections.

In support of agricultural development the Servicio Agrícola Interamericano operated a machinery pool from 1951 to 1958, which at its peak had 75 bulldozers, 230 wheel tractors, and 1,700 pieces of farm equipment, representing a total investment of about $5 million.[72] Between 1954 and 1963 the CBF established 4,350 families (including 870 foreign immigrants) on ten projects in the region occupying 200,000 ha.[73]

By 1961 there was some concern over the rapidly expanding agriculture in response to guaranteed sugar prices, improved corn varieties, and a sound domestic market for rice. It was recognized that corn and rice would also become surplus on the domestic market in an alarmingly short time. For this reason the CBF launched an ambitious diversification program in 1961-62 aimed at converting excess corn into marketable pork and lard, the latter being an import substitution item. Pedigreed hogs were imported from Argentina, and a breeding program was set up at Todos Santos (Guabirá) to provide improved stock to colonists. A freezing plant was constructed with a capacity of 250 hogs per eight-hour shift. Before this plant became operative it was

---

[72]José Kushner, "Posibilidades de diversificación agropecuaria en Santa Cruz," in Cámara de Comercio e Industria, *Ciclo de conferencias sobre desarrollo económico, Santa Cruz, Bolivia, July-September 1967* (1967), p. 84.

[73]Instituto Nacional de Colonización, Departamento de Promoción y Servicios Sociales, *Antecedentes de la colonización en Bolivia* (La Paz, Bolivia, 1966), p. 15.

decided there was a need for still more diversification to cope with potential market problems in the burgeoning agriculture. Thus in 1963 the CBF imported 600 cattle to provide the basis for improvement of local herds, and a program of artificial insemination was established. At the same time, an agreement was reached with foreign interests to set up a vegetable oil and balanced feed plant that would integrate the sugar by-products (molasses), soya, and corn to supply feed required for hog and cattle fattening and to provide a substitute for edible oil imports. In addition, plans were advanced for a milk condensation plant at Todos Santos that would further integrate the sugar and cattle industries.

In this manner a complex chain reaction had been set in motion based on a number of assumptions about institutional conditions and colonist behavior. In 1964 there was an abrupt change in government policy—plans for the feed plant were cancelled and the budget for Todos Santos was drastically cut. Many problems were experienced with the equipment for the freezing plant, and the hog-fattening program organized between the CBF and the colonists proved wholly inadequate to supply 250 head per day. The freezing plant was finally inaugurated in 1965 but with very limited funds to purchase hogs and virtually no plans for marketing. COMEBOL[74] was persuaded to accept a contract to supply the tin mines, but this was cancelled in 1966 mainly because of competition from low-priced beef. The CBF attempted to diversify into pork by-products with improvised machinery. The resultant low-quality production found little market acceptance, and processing was discontinued after a few months. Attempts to lease the facilities for cattle processing met with no success. The pedigreed hog operation was liquidated in 1968. No funds were available for the condensed milk plant, and the cattle improvement scheme met with only limited success due to credit restrictions, the unavailability of preferred breeds, and the movement of low-priced Brazilian cattle into the Bolivian market. The hog-freezing plant remained idle, and no state funds were available to buy, process, or market the output of the program to breed and fatten hogs.

While the complex Todos Santos scheme appears to have been poorly conceived and executed, the Guabirá mill has been a strong positive contribution to the development of the Santa Cruz region. The government commitment to the development of the sugar industry evidenced by the investment of $5.5 million in 1955–56 in a mill, plus the CBF colonization efforts and the machinery pool (particularly operations in land clearing and feeder road construction), provided strong incentive for expanding other mills. The guaranteed market at attractive prices induced a strong demand for cane contracts and fostered grower associations to negotiate with the mills.

---

[74] Comisión del Estaño Boliviana, the Bolivian state tin mining corporation.

It is estimated that by 1968 total investment in the three sugar mills amounted to $20–$25 million. Gross sales of sugar, alcohol, molasses, and feed concentrate were on the order of $20 million, of which about $17 million may be regarded as value added in the region. Plans exist to convert plants to gas, freeing the bagasse used as fuel for paper and fiberboard. Other by-product diversification plans include polyethylene derivatives from alcohol, solvents, balanced feeds, and the extraction of protein concentrate directly from cane for human consumption. The mills directly employ 800 permanent and 1,200 temporary workers representing a payroll, including fringe benefits, of $2.6 million; 2,200 farmers are involved in growing cane, and their sales amount to an average of $3,000 per grower; 5,500 cane cutters are employed for six months and earn an average of $200 over the period.[75] While there are no statistics available to test the multiplier effect of the sugar industry, it is to be expected that the generation of reliable income has had an important effect in consolidating agriculture. Furthermore the attraction of 6,700 temporary workers annually should result in expanded settlement in the region.

Whatever the positive impact of the sugar industry, the Guabirá mill must be granted a significant share of the credit. In 1969 the mill purchased 420,000 tons of cane ($2.3 million) from 1,260 independent producers, 1,110 of whom are organized into seven cooperatives or associations. On the average the 120 large growers (including 44 in a cooperative) each sold 1,800 tons; 80 medium-sized independent growers, 800 tons; and 1,060 members of small-grower cooperatives, 130 tons, representing a cash income of $750 per grower in the latter group. The mill has a permanent staff of 300 as well as 550 seasonal workers. A $1 million payroll, and other mill-operating expenditures are in large part responsible for the expansion of the town of Montero from a population of 4,000 in 1956 to 17,000 in 1969. Of the 4,700 families who have settled in the urban area during the thirteen-year period, 60 percent are from the department of Santa Cruz; the balance are from the altiplano and the intermontane valleys. This suggests a relatively strong rural-urban migration within the region and a considerable element of urbanization of the rural population, since a third of the labor force in Montero was directly employed in agriculture and forestry.[76]

It is difficult to be definitive about the role that state enterprise has played in the dynamic development of Santa Cruz agriculture during the decades of the fifties and sixties. The lessons from Todos Santos are clear. Inexperienced public administrators and technicians are apt to squander resources on overly

[75]Comisión Nacional de Estudio de la Caña y del Azúcar, *La industria azucarera Boliviana* (La Paz, Bolivia, 1964, 1965, and 1968).

[76]From a survey of 4,540 heads of families in Montero-Guabirá by the Comité de Obras Públicas, Santa Cruz, Bolivia, 1969.

ambitious and ill-prepared projects. Discontinuous policies for indivisible investments, such as those involving agricultural processing where lack of follow-through leads to idle capacity and discourages complementary private or public investment, reap undesirable consequences.

Documentation of the full impact of Guabirá presents innumerable problems. It is possible, however, to list the following positive results:

1. Expanded total agricultural production resulting from roads built by the CBF to give access to cane areas.
2. The provision of an assured cash income to small producers and the exposure of farmers to agricultural research in both cane and other crops.
3. The demonstration of the viability of producer associations and cooperatives.
4. Experimentation in processing, which has been useful to other mills.
5. Experience in the introduction and subsequent withdrawal of subsidized prices designed to stimulate production; there was a 20 percent subsidy in 1959 that was eliminated and replaced by formula pricing.[77]
6. A positive response to the challenge posed by overproduction manifested in effective organization for export, efforts to lower production costs, as well as self-imposed levies on producers and mills to cover export expenses.[78]
7. The creation of temporary wage employment, which provided the resources, experience, and exposure to the region needed to establish spontaneous colonists.

In spite of these positive indications there is latitude to ask whether the same policy on sugar would be reenacted if the clock were turned back. Agriculture in Santa Cruz developed at a rate of 7–8 percent annually over the period 1955–68. Further expansion, however, faces many problems. Sugar yields have declined from 60 tons per ha to a 35-ton average, and a price of $185 per ton, of which $40 is freight, is a strong disincentive for the use of fertilizer.[79] Import substitution, which provided the basis for dynamic increases in production in the early years, has been completed. Transport

[77] Carlos E. Chardón and Stephen Leigh, *Desarrollo de la industria azucarera en el Departamento de Santa Cruz*, Ministerio de Economía Nacional, Comisión Nacional de Estudio de la Caña y del Azúcar (La Paz, Bolivia, November 1959), p. 67.

[78] Rafael Deheza, "Resultados de la exportación de azúcar y sus perspectivas en el desarrollo económico regional y nacional," in Cámara de Comercio e Industria, *Ciclo de conferencias*, p. 200.

[79] The price of ammonium nitrate fertilizer in Santa Cruz is $180 per ton. Freight from Antofagasta to Cochabamba by rail is $22.70 per ton; from Cochabamba to Santa Cruz by truck, $12, and from Santa Cruz to Yapacani, $5.30.

costs from such a remote interior region, high-cost production (two to three times the world price), import substitution programs throughout all Latin American countries, and an inadeqate marketing structure, impose severe constraints on the export potential.

THE CONSERVATION
VI AND USE
OF NATURAL RESOURCES

The most important conservation issue in the humid tropics is that of the critical consequences of destroying the forest cover. Conservation in Latin America is speculative in large measure—little is known of the effect of large forest areas on climate, nor is there a thorough understanding of the complex hydrology of the vast river systems of the Orinoco and Amazon. There is no definitive analysis of the potential downstream effects of flooding and silting caused by accelerated runoff or erosion, and the distinction between man-induced and geological erosion in the headwaters is not clearly drawn. Nevertheless the words "runoff" and "erosion" applied to the humid tropics of Latin America evoke the same specter of evil that has haunted much of the discussion of conservation and clouded the formulation and implementation of resource policies in other parts of the world.[1]

Before proceeding to the evaluation of factors related to tropical land development, the reader should be aware of the definitions of "conservation" and "depletion" that have been adopted here. Wantrup defined the economic issue exclusively in terms of the pattern of resource use over time. Conservation is "redistribution of use in the direction of the future," and depletion is redistribution "in the direction of the present." He went on to say that "the concepts 'conservation,' 'depletion,' and 'state of conservation' carry no connotation of efficiency or waste." The measure of efficiency is gained from the present worths of the stream of expected private or social costs and benefits associated with a shift in the rate of resource use in one direction or the other. Clearly either may yield a favorable benefit-cost ratio, and therefore waste is not automatically correlated with depletion nor efficiency with conservation.[2] This definition is taken as the point of departure for the discussion in this chapter.

Edward Mason made a strong case for the inevitability of value judgments in setting conservation policy. He defined conservation as "the avoidance of

[1] See Morris Miller, "The Scope and Content of Resource Policy in Relation to Economic Development," *Land Economics*, vol. 37, no. 4 (November 1961), p. 29.

[2] S. V. Ciriacy-Wantrup, *Resource Conservation: Economics and Policies* (University of California Press, 1952), pp. 51–54.

wastes associated with a faulty time distribution of the use of resources," the wastes being those to be expected under a laissez-faire system. The operational issue then becomes government intervention in the public interest to avoid "the sacrifice of high-priority future uses in favor of low-priority present uses" of tropical lands and associated forest, wildlife, and water resources.[3] Phrased in this way the subjectivity is readily apparent. Who rules on what is the public interest? How will the distinction be made between intervention in response to pressure from special interest groups and intervention on behalf of public interest? Who is to say that the destruction of a hectare of tropical forest in order to produce corn to feed a campesino and his family is a low-priority present use and that harvesting of the same hectare for timber ten years hence is a high-priority future use? Or conversely who decides that clearing forest for farmlands in the headwaters of a river is a high-priority present use and that external diseconomies in the form of destruction wrought by floods downstream in twenty years' time constitute a low-priority consequence?

The resources of interest in this study are all renewable, therefore the primary concerns of conservation policy should be (1) an understanding of potential external economies and diseconomies of alternative patterns of land use; and (2) assurance that the resources, in fact, will be renewed. Thus attention should be directed to the conditions of replacement; in the case of soil erosion, this depends on the point of irreversibility within limits prescribed by costs, known technology, and the relevant planning period. For soils in particular a case can be made for adopting a long-term view where the applicable discount rate for benefit-cost analysis may approach zero.[4]

As indicated in chapter 1 public policy regarding the conservation of humid tropical land and associated resources should be guided by consideration of external economies or diseconomies that might be the result of specific programs designed to accelerate or retard the rate of resource use. The conservationist position (centered on the diseconomies) is that uncontrolled destruction of the virgin forest and wildlife, if allowed to continue, in a very few generations would reduce the greater part of the humid tropics of Latin America to a laterized and severely eroded condition capable at best of sustaining low brush cover and useless for commercial forestry (plantations), livestock, or cropping. Conservationists contend that if the jungle is removed, particularly on the steep upper catchment areas, the accelerated runoff and silting is likely to ruin valuable downstream urban and rural lands, require costly flood control structures, and create serious water supply problems for some of the urban complexes.

[3] Edward S. Mason, "The Political Economy of Resource Use," in Henry Jarrett, ed., *Perspectives on Conservation* (Johns Hopkins Press for Resources for the Future, 1958), pp. 158–59.
[4] Ibid., p. 185.

The depletionist position is exemplified in the policies of most countries with humid tropical lands in Latin America that have undertaken programs and investments to expand settlement in full knowledge that the potential settlers are technically and financially ill-equipped and that institutions are incapable of effectively controlling resource use. Public administrators lack any clear understanding of the ecological, social, or economic factors that should guide the type of control to be exercised.

The experience of tropical land development as evidence for or against either of these positions is inconclusive and serves to highlight once again the uncertainties and knowledge gaps that confront policy makers. To be sure, there are many problems—the destruction of trees that may have potential economic value, erosion, the depletion and leaching of soil nutrients, declining yields, reversion to shifting agriculture, abandonment of lands, weed infestation, and regrowth vegetation far inferior in quality to the virgin forest. What is difficult to prove or evaluate are the extent of total abandonment, the irreversibility of the erosion process, the nature and extent of downstream effects, the time horizon involved, and the potential impact of new technology on forestry, soil management, and agricultural production.

It is worthy of note that in the Florencia zone of Caquetá where significant settlement has been under way for over thirty years, 40 percent of the farm area remains in forest—on the group of farms having the smallest average size and the greatest average net income per hectare and per farm. (See table 14.) The limited area of cropland and the high proportion of pasture in Florencia indicate a change in land use as colonization matures. The evident higher incomes of colonists in the older settled area contradict the theory that erosion and fertility loss resulting from the removal of tropical forest leads to abandonment.

Sanguine technicians may not accept imperfect knowledge, at least with regard to physical potential, maintaining that programs should never be undertaken without "adequate" knowledge. This is not a very useful concept since the time required to assemble "adequate" knowledge can be infinite. The fact is that very few projects have worked out as planned, even those that apparently have been very carefully studied, e.g., Alexandre de Gusmão in Brazil.[5] Does this suggest a moratorium on tropical land development investments until more information has been gathered? Such an approach is unlikely to prove a viable policy alternative in view of the political commitments and substantial public investments that have already been made. On technical and economic grounds, public policy for the conservation and development of tropical lands should be conditioned by the expected effects of removing the forest cover. In turn, these effects are a function of the natural resource situation, the method of clearing, and subsequent management.

[5] "Aspectos de la reforma agraria en Brazil" (informe de la Misión de la FAO, May 1968, mimeo.), pp. 23 and 124.

The exploitation of some areas appears to be out of the question with existing technology.[6] For example, in the Guianas the properties of certain soils are such that once the forest is cleared the soils will not support even one crop and will immediately revert to grasses and scrub that are virtually worthless for grazing. In other areas—e.g., Alto Turiaçu—concretionary layers may be induced after the trees are removed that either restrict use to pasture or produce drainage problems precluding agriculture altogether. The principal aspects that are relevant to policies that may affect procedures for forest clearing and soil management are discussed in the remainder of this chapter.

Depletion and Waste of Forest and Wildlife Resources

Underutilization of Forests

High freight rates from remote areas; poor market acceptance of many little-known tropical timber species; the high cost of extraction and milling; and the lack of capital, entrepreneurs, and an effective market structure have resulted in the destruction of over 95 percent of the millable timber in most settlement areas. Hope for the improved utilization of the broadleaved forests rests on:

1. The classification of species into groups having similar properties to species that already are accepted in the world markets, thus increasing the percentage of saleable trees per hectare (for example, about forty species are sold in the United States as oak).
2. The introduction of management programs that will increase the percentage of commercial species in the natural forest or replace natural forest with plantations, such as the teak plantations in Indonesia.
3. The development of large-scale integrated industries that produce a range of products such as lumber, veneer, particle board, pulp, paper, and chemicals.
4. Technological breakthroughs that may permit economic conversion of wood fiber and leaves into edible products for animal and human consumption or into any of the synthetics and chemicals now derived from coal or petroleum.

When the tropical forest is cleared at the projected required average rate of 1.75 million hectares (ha) annually,[7] only a small fraction of the commercial-sized trees can expect to find a market. Estimates of the actual area of tropical forest that has been cleared in Latin America range from 5 million to

---

[6]The soil and climatic limitations on the development of tropical agriculture were reviewed in chap. 1.

[7]See chap. 1 for a discussion of the question of the potential utilization of forest resources.

10 million ha annually, although there is no indication what proportion of this area is second growth or is unsuited for pasture, annual cultivation, or tree crops.[8] These figures require little elaboration to show that some drastic changes of policy are called for if there is genuine concern about the importance of the percentage of forest utilization to the economic development of the region. Unless it is feasible to reduce the rate of land clearing to about a tenth of the current level, it is likely that the equation of wood demand and supply will be out of the question for the next decade or two.

Take, for example, the situation posed by mechanized land clearing that is receiving much attention in Latin America. A tree-crusher with a clearing capacity of 10 ha per day, or about 1,000 ha per year, would have to be accompanied by a milling capacity of 55,000 board feet per day (bf/d)[9] to handle an average of 40 cubic meters per hectare of "presently commercial" species or 200,000 bf/d to handle all commercial-sized or millable trees (45 centimeters in diameter at breast height and over), a volume of 150 cubic meters per hectare. With the mills having a capacity of 2,000–4,000 bf/d now used in frontier areas, the financial requirement would be 18 to 70 mills per tree-crusher, an investment of $125,000–$500,000.[10] With a more complex mill, such as the Iparía mill at Tournavista (discussed below), capable of higher recovery ratios and timber treatment and working a theoretical two shifts 200 days per year, the requirement would be 0.6 to 2.25 mills for such installations per tree-crusher, or an investment of $0.4–1.5 million, excluding logging machinery and trucks.

In areas such as the Alto Beni that are poorly located in regard to markets and that lack entrepreneurs with knowledge of production and marketing, even modest plans to extract about 5 percent of the commercial timber were not realized. On Gleba Arinos distance precluded any exploitation beyond the satisfaction of the local demand for construction materials and posts. At Ivinheima, however, access to markets and effective promotion by the development company in demonstrating viable lumber production from its own mill resulted in the installation of fifteen mills by 1968 with a total output of 40 cubic meters per day (about 50 percent of capacity). This has enabled colonists to follow the practice of leaving millable trees at the time of clearing. Trees that are killed in the burn must be cut within six to eight months; the remainder may be milled at will. Through this procedure colonists have been able to sell about 9–10 cubic meters of logs per hectare with a return of $20. Even at this level only about 10–20 percent of commercial-sized trees are exploited.

[8] *Unasylva*, vol. 20, nos. 80–81, p. 56.

[9] Based on 150 working days per year.

[10] The milling requirement for each crawler tractor of 250–300 horsepower employed in jungle clearing would be about three to fifteen installations with a capacity of 2,000–3,000 bf/d each.

It has been suggested that in isolated regions, where market possibilities for all but the most valuable species are nil and where the land has an alternative use in agriculture, consideration be given to setting aside reserves or to milling and storing lumber in the hope that prices in some future period will be sufficient to amortize costs or to compensate present income forgone. Such expectations would rest on increased demand, either locally or in export markets for the region; lowered freight rates from the region to export markets, and higher freight rates or production costs in competing regions. A further possibility is that the quality of the forest stand would be improved by management during the interim. Figure 1 illustrates the two situations.

In case A the land is cleared for agriculture in a situation where the price of lumber does not cover the cost of production. The justification for milling during the clearing process and storing for future sale, rather than burning, depends on

$$WXYZ \geq OABt^j + t^jCDt^m$$

when cash flows are expressed as net present value (NPV). This is given by the equation

$$\sum_{i=t^1}^{t^m} P_i h_i^d \ (1 + r)^{-i} \geq \sum_{i=1}^{t^j} c_i h_i^p \ (1 + r)^{-i} + \sum_{i=t^j+1}^{t^m} g_i h_i^s \ (1 + r)^{-i}$$

where

h_i^d = tons of lumber sold in year i,

h_i^p = tons of lumber produced in year i,

h_i^s = tons of lumber stored in year i,

c_i = lumber production cost per ton in year i,

P_i = FOB price of lumber per ton in the region in year i,

g_i = annual storage costs of lumber per ton in year i,

r = discount rate.

If it is assumed that the cost of producing lumber is $25 in t^j, that there is a 15 percent discount rate, that all sales occur in the fifth year, and that there are annual storage charges of 25¢ per ton, $P_{i=5}$ would have to exceed $52 to justify the procedure.

In case B some potential agricultural land is set aside as forest reserve, thus the agricultural benefits (OUX in case A) are lowered to OQ over the period t^1. With the harvesting of the reserve over t^1t^m, additional land is brought into agriculture and reaches full production (T) at t^n. Justification for reservation of the forest resources is given by

$$PQRS - A't^1t^mB' \geq OUTQ$$

expressed as NPV.[11] Given the same conditions as case A and a yield of 30 tons of lumber per hectare, if $P_{i=5} = \$52$, then reservation is justified if net benefits from agriculture are less than $120 per hectare per year over the five-year period (assuming constant agricultural production throughout).[12]

High Grading

High grading, i.e., the extraction of the most valuable forest species, such as mahogany, is a typical practice in areas having reasonable river or road access. To maximize profits the individual operator must balance the progressively lower prices against economies of scale from high extraction rates. In 1963, mills in Manaus, Brazil, paid $30 per cubic meter for first-grade mahogany logs, $20 for cedar, $2 for laurel, and an average of $1 for general utility species.[13] The 1968 statutory FOB export prices of logs shipped from Belém were $22 per cubic meter for general utility woods, $27 for durable construction woods, and $60 for furniture and decorative woods. The marked price differential, when taken in conjunction with the fixed cost of log transport and the relatively minor economies of scale from higher extraction rates, dictates high-grading practices.

A bid for mechanized exploitation of 10,000 ha of forest in the area of Santarém, Amazonia, illustrates the economies realizable from higher extraction rates. High grading of three species (about 10–20 percent of the commercial volume) at 23,000 cubic meters per year was estimated at a cost of $12 per cubic meter, and taking all the commercial species at 75,000 cubic meters per year, at $7 per cubic meter.[14]

---

[11]The level of indifference is given by

$$\sum_{i=t^1}^{t^m} h_i(P_i - c_i)(1 + r)^{-i} = \sum_{i=1}^{t^n-1} x_i(1 + r)^{-i}$$

where x_i = flow of additional agricultural benefits over t^n years from a given area if not reserved for forestry, i.e., $OUTQ$ in case B; it is assumed that $h_i = h_i^d = h_i^p$, $h_i^s = 0$ (immediate sale of production); and P_i, c_i, and r are as in case A.

[12]In this simplified calculation of a situation involving a single hectare, the flow of agricultural benefits forgone as a consequence of forest reservation becomes $U'XQQ'$ in case B, with t^j the delay in clearing and bringing the land into production.

[13]O. H. Knowles, *Produção e mercado de Madeira na Amazonia*, Ministerio do Interior, Superintendencia do Desenvolvimento de Amazonia (Belém, Brazil, 1967), pp. 32, 36, and 55.

[14]Ibid., pp. 56–57.

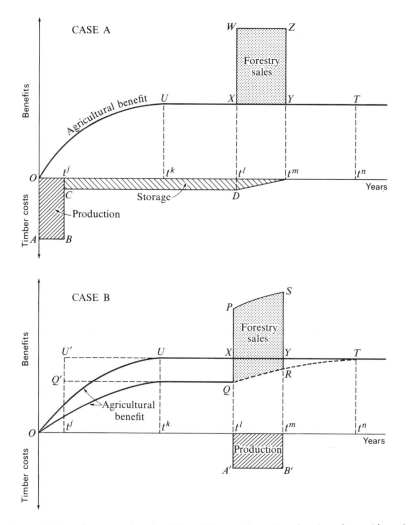

Figure 1. Benefits associated with milling and storing lumber (case A) and with setting aside forest reserves for future needs (case B).

Figure 2 shows the profit-maximizing level of extraction for an individual firm under short-run conditions with perfect competition, economies of scale to more intensive exploitation, and constant returns to extensive exploitation.[15] Under these circumstances the logging operator is faced with a discon-

[15] The assumption here is that the costs per hectare of log extraction will remain constant for a given intensity of exploitation (constant cubic meters per hectare) regardless of the area of the forest concession or the rate of exploitation.

tinuous and sharply declining marginal revenue curve and a moderately declining marginal cost curve with increased intensity of exploitation over the relevant range. A, B, and C are the prices of the highest grades within the preferred species. The slope in each step reflects declining quality within a species. The curve DE represents the prices of other commercial species in declining order—in practice this curve would also be stepped, but since prices in this group range from 2 to 10 percent of the preferred group in relative terms the steps will be negligible. With a stepped marginal revenue curve, equation with marginal cost at OD will occur with a complete extraction of one of the lower-priced preferred species, resulting in the exploitation of the commercial availability at q_1.

A procedure frequently advocated to increase forest utilization is to grant concessions that are conditional on the extraction of a given volume of timber. In this way it is hoped to mobilize profits from the valuable trees to finance the exploitation of nonpreferred species, thus increasing the net value added in forestry from any particular region.

The economic grounds for such a policy rest on the differences between private and social estimates of the opportunity costs of capital, labor, and entrepreneurship. Thus in social accounting terms the marginal cost curve (MC_2) becomes lower than OF at q_1, in which case the intensity of exploitation would be expanded to q_2, raising the issue of wage subsidies or state enterprise to approximate a social optimum. In fact steps in marginal revenue of the magnitude suggested above for the central Amazon region, plus the low

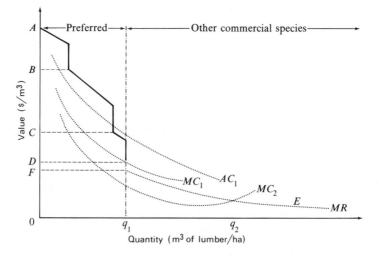

Figure 2. Profit maximization in tropical forest exploitation under conditions of a sharp price differential between preferred and other commercial species.

labor intensity of forestry, are likely to disqualify the forcing of higher levels of forest utilization on the grounds of social utility.

Large-Scale Enterprise

Small-scale milling operations in new colonization areas are highly inefficient and experience serious problems with the extraction of logs and transport to markets. A survey of twenty-four mills in the Tingo María area showed the average mill to have a one-shift capacity of 4,200 bf/d.[16] Fifty percent of these mills were able to obtain sufficient log supplies to operate throughout the year; the balance operated for six to eight months. The average operating time was 80 percent of the year, or 9.5 months, and output during operation was 30 percent of rated capacity; hence annual production was about 24 percent of capacity.

One of the available means to increase the utilization of forest resources, either prior to their ultimate destruction or in the achievement of sustained yields, is the introduction of large-scale horizontally and vertically integrated industrial complexes. Complexes such as the $100 million plant proposed for the department of Santander in Colombia for the production of lumber, plywood, chip-board, railroad ties, paper, and cardboard are an obvious solution. They provide capital and entrepreneurs (or capable state management) and have ready access to markets.

A less ambitious scheme was advanced for forestry development in association with the clearing and settlement of 50,000 ha of tropical forest in the Jengka Triangle project in Malaysia.[17] The net volume of merchantable timber—about 50,000–60,000 board feet (120–140 cubic meters) per hectare—was to be exploited over a twelve-year period. The proposal called for a mill with a capacity of 170,000 bf/d (eight-hour shift basis) working two ten-hour shifts, a veneer plant with an annual output of 95 million square feet of plywood (three-sixteenths of an inch), and a prefabrication plant with a capacity of 1,000 houses per year. The total investment was estimated at $5.7 million, with gross sales reaching $9 million annually after the third year and with a value added on the order of $7 million.[18] The project would have given direct employment to 240 in logging, 100 in the mill, 230 in the plywood operation, 150 in the prefabrication plant, and 60 in administration—a total of 780.

The principal objection to highly integrated forestry operations is the same as that already discussed in regard to tropical plantations—the combination of

[16] Office of the Departamento Forestal y Caza, Tingo María, Peru, 1967.

[17] TAMS and Hunting Technical Services, Ltd., *The Jengka Triangle Report: Resources and Development Planning*, Report to the Federal Land Development Agency, Malaysia (1967).

[18] Assuming 20 percent of production costs made up of inputs imported to the project area.

management skills, capital, and market contacts is often to be found only in foreign enterprises. Problems stem from the destination of profits, i.e., the reinvestment rate within the country, the political considerations connected with foreign ownership, and the inevitable conflict between any large organization and the interests of the small-mill operators. Such factors, together with market constraints, have undoubtedly contributed to the inability to put into practice the forest development plans for the Jengka Triangle. The trade-off between higher returns to entrepreneurial ability or scale and sociopolitical aspects, such as external dependency or income distribution, need to be made explicit in project design.

Nevertheless where it is assumed that the marginal opportunity cost of labor and forest resources is zero, a value added of the magnitude programmed for the Jengka Triangle during the first ten years of a colonization project is sufficient for economic justification of substantial infrastructure and services for the long-range development of agriculture. This situation is clearly illustrated in the La Joya project (Obispo–Mano Marques region) where subtraction of the costs and returns associated with the Pueblo Viejo mill in the first three years of the project reduces the estimated internal rate of return (IRR) from 25 percent to 7 percent.

The Need for Breakthroughs in Technology

As discussed in chapter 2, hopes for saving the forest from destruction through sustained-yield harvesting or for better utilization in the process of clearing for agriculture rest largely on the development of new technology, such as the economic extraction of hydrocarbons. At present there is no indication of the period that will be required to perfect such industrial processes. Immediate hopes focus on refinements that will make systems already in operation more economic—planing and molding mills; plants for the production of parquet, fine veneer, particle board, chemical pulp, treated or kiln-dried lumber; small-scale integrated wood-using industries; and forest management or plantations to upgrade the quality and density of marketable species and to lower extraction costs. Emphasis is placed on increasing the value added on the forest frontier itself to reduce the adverse impact of freight charges. An example is the recent advance in the manufacture of fine veneer whose value-weight ratio may even support the cost of airfreighting. The principal drawbacks are the limited opportunity to exploit by-products and the difficulty in persuading qualified management to live in isolated tropical forest regions. Largely as a result of these drawbacks, one company established a veneer plant in Lima, and its logs are trucked 800 km from the Pucallpa region. Considering a freight rate of $7.40 per metric ton[19] for the

[19]Based on a dry season freight rate of $37 per 1,000 board feet weighing 5,100 kilograms.

journey and a volume reduction of 84 percent[20] from the log to plywood, management and by-products appear highly valued to warrant an added freight charge of $38 per ton of finished product.

The difficulties encountered in operating a high-technology chip-board plant may be gauged from the experience of Madera Prensada, S.A., in Tingo María. The plant was installed in 1963 at a cost of about $2.2 million and has a capacity to handle 55 tons of logs daily. The operation is based on an initial concession to extract 2.36 million board feet (log volume) on 4,300 ha over a five-year period. Two hundred different types of wood were considered to be suitable raw material. Because the machines operate on the basis of chips with a 0.5 specific gravity, many complications arose in adjusting the process for each mixture of woods. Since the species were not classified and there was little transferable experience, much experimentation was required to test mixtures and glues. As a consequence the plant was in a "start-up" stage for two years. Once the plant was operating a problem arose in supplying and storing logs. Because of the nature of the process, logs stored more than three weeks dry out and become difficult to treat. Since many of the trees are diseased the logs tend to rot if kept in a pond. This inability to stockpile during the dry season makes it extremely difficult to maintain the supply of raw materials during the rainy season of four to six months. In 1968 the plant was operating at 60 percent of capacity.

Another attempt to introduce advanced technology into tropical forestry was made by the Peruvian Forestry Department when it established the Iparía mill at Tournavista. The fully automated plant with a capacity of 20,000 bf/d was completed in May 1967 at a total cost of $750,000. Its prime purpose was to demonstrate efficient exploitation of a wide range of tropical species from the 300,000-ha Iparía Forest, which had been set aside as a reserve in 1966 for sustained-yield management. The mill is designed for operation by about one-third of the work force actually employed. But the sophisticated machinery is beyond the training and experience of the local labor force. This complex equipment has caused considerable maintenance problems. Technicians capable of repairing the electronic controls and other electrical gear are not readily found in such an isolated area, and trained band saw sharpeners have been unavailable. A breakdown of one machine may paralyze the whole plant. As a result it became necessary to carry a large inventory of spare parts to avoid extensive delays in obtaining replacements from Lima or overseas. The problem was further aggravated by a lack of skilled machine operators and of experience in both management and the type of spare parts inventory that should be carried. In order to remedy this situation a Canadian

---

[20]On the average, a log volume of 1,000 cubic meters yields 520 cubic meters of raw veneer, giving 260 cubic meters in dried sheets ready for pressing, which, after pressing, results in 160 cubic meters of finished plywood.

firm was contracted in June 1968 to handle all logging and marketing and to advise on mill operation.

The most serious problem in operation has been obtaining an adequate supply of logs. The government had no funds to advance credit to local colonists and loggers to bring logs out and raft them down the river. Furthermore the antiquated logging machinery supplied under a contract with the Agency for International Development was unsatisfactory. Even with the new machinery that has been ordered, it is likely that there will be difficulties in stockpiling sufficient logs to keep the plant in full operation for twelve months. The logging season with trucks lasts five months—May to September. On the Pachitea River, logs are usually supplied between October and March; the trees are cut in the dry season and left till the small streams rise sufficiently to float logs to the main river. Most of the valuable cedar and mahogany has been cut out 2-4 km back from these streams. With better prices, upriver loggers have been able to use tractors in the dry season to haul logs from up to 7 km beyond the stream bank. If logging is sufficiently organized during the May–September period, if credit is made available, and if less valuable species are accepted, it should be possible to maintain raw material supplies via the river.

While marketing the lumber has presented no real problem, freight rates have prejudiced the mill's ability to compete. Freight rates are particularly high during the wet season in order to offset the threat of truck delays on the unsurfaced road in the event of rain. The freight rate to Lima may be as high as 8 cents per board foot, which amounts to 20 percent of the Lima price for export-grade mahogany and 50 percent of the price for lower-quality lumber or little-known varieties.

The cumulative effect of these various difficulties was a production of only 1.1 million board feet in the first eighteen months of operation, or 15 to 20 percent of the one-shift capacity. The mill was idled for repairs or lack of logs for approximately 30 percent of the time; when operating, its output ran at about 25 percent of capacity. As mentioned earlier the mill was set up specifically to upgrade the level of utilization of a humid tropical forest by handling a variety of timbers. In fact, production to date is over 95 percent in four species, with mahogany accounting for 60-70 percent. Disinterest in other species is evidenced by the fact that the drying kilns and treating plant to process such lumber were not completed.[21]

The foregoing highlights the difficulty of applying advanced technology as it has been developed in the industrialized countries of the temperate zones. The breakthrough element, then, must be either in a new technology suited to the physical, institutional, and human resource conditions under which it

[21]Russell C. Stadelman, "Feasibility of Utilizing Timber Resources at Tournavista" (report to Le Tourneau del Perú, October 1968, mimeo.).

will be applied or in adapting institutions and human resources to existing technology.

In the realm of forest and land management the development and application of new technology depends not only on biological knowledge about the area, but on the political-administrative system as well. The preparation of integrated management plans for selected tropical forest areas is under way in Ecuador, Venezuela, and Guyana. The feasibility of applying such plans to large areas and the institutional prerequisites are yet to be tested. There is little experience in tropical timber plantations that might guide policy on the issue of planting eroded watersheds—e.g., Caranavi—or of actually clearing forest that has little or no economic value and establishing pure stands of preferred species. Preferred species are almost invariably pine or araucaria, which are fast growing and have good market prospects as pulp and treated lumber. A study conducted in Chile indicates that in temperate zones pine may yield a better rate of return than either pasture or cropping under certain conditions.[22] Some coniferous species[23] are well adapted to the tropics, but it is yet to be demonstrated that they have characteristics enabling them to compete with temperate sources when produced in plantations.

Indonesia is experimenting with *Pinus mercusii* as the basis for a pulp and paper industry. The area planted by 1968 amounted to 150,000 ha, much of which had been cleared of native forest for the purpose. Among the broadleaf species, principal emphasis has been placed on teak and eucalyptus. Indonesia has a long history of teak plantations, which covered about 400,000 ha in 1968. The plantations are exploited on a sixty-to-eighty-year rotation plan.

Data on teak plantations in Trinidad indicate an annual production equivalent to 10 cubic meters per hectare (log volume) on a thirty-year rotation at a total cost of $175 per hectare in standing timber.[24] With a recovery ratio of 60 percent, an average mill price of $60 per cubic meter, a logging and milling cost of $22 per cubic meter (sawn lumber), and a zero opportunity cost of land, this kind of enterprise would yield an IRR of 15 percent.[25] Rotations that range from twenty to eighty years preclude smallholder participation in plantation ventures.

---

[22] John A. Menz, "Alternativas forestales del uso de las tierras en la reforma agraria y colonización" (paper presented at the Seminar on Forestry Development, Agrarian Reform and Colonization for Selected Countries of Latin America, Brazília, November 18–25, 1968).

[23] For example, *Pinus caribaea* and *Araucaria angustifolia*.

[24] "Forestry Plantations in Latin America: Development and Prospects" (Report of the Tenth Session of the Latin American Forestry Commission, Trinidad, 1967, mimeo.), p. 20.

[25] Based on costs of $100 per hectare in the first year for roads and planting, an annual average of $2.60 from the second to thirtieth year, and a net return of $6,800 in the thirtieth year.

Plans prepared by the Latin American Forestry Commission[26] called for an annual investment of approximately $6 million to establish the following plantations in the humid tropics over the period of 1968-85:

	hectares
Araucaria	275,000
Pinus caribaea	70,000
Eucalyptus	350,000
Teak	60,000
Other broadleaved species	75,000
Total	780,000

While this is not an inconsiderable effort, questions arise. On one hand, how do such activities relate to net annual additions of 5-10 million ha of cleared jungle land—an enormous extension of deforested land that is in need of regeneration for watershed protection? On the other hand, what are the market prospects?

Forestry Administration

In many countries administrative incapability to supervise concessions or to enforce forest conservation regulations is a major impediment to the achievement of rational forest use. In Bolivia a regulation prohibits the cutting of trees within 1 km of any river. Much of the area affected consists of alluvial flats, i.e., the prime agricultural land in the tropics. As a result no effort has been made to apply the law. The Papaloapan basin is a frontier area where strict conservationist regulation of permits, conditions for clearing, and the exploitation of forests are virtually unenforceable. The felling and burning of forests to open up lands for corn, rice, and cattle by individuals or ejidos proceeds on an extensive scale, largely without official approval. Most colonists and even some of the operators of small portable mills are not aware that regulations exist. In such uncharted and inaccessible areas the definition and policing of forestry concessions is beyond the staff capability of the agencies in charge. Where control is exercised the prime concerns are the total volume of wood extracted without regard to area and a maximum rather than a minimum rate of exploitation.

As shown on the La Joya project, where markets exist the sequence and rate of forestry development can strongly influence the economic viability of land development projects. There is a degree of indivisibility in infrastructure investments associated with land development and an inevitable production lag while the forest is progressively cleared and crops are sown. Since forestry

[26]"Forestry Plantations," p. 27.

precedes agriculture its production sequence is precisely scheduled to materially improve benefit-cost ratios. Thus from an economic standpoint, where agricultural development is either planned or deemed inevitable, forestry regulations should focus on minimum acceptable levels of exploitation (rather than on setting maximum limits) and be designed to maximize extraction rates and the concentration of lumbering activities in areas that lie in the path of colonists.

Forestry and Wildlife Reserves

In the humid tropics the classic case of the economic exploitation of forest and wildlife resources for tourism, recreation, and the controlled harvesting of game is in Africa in Botswana, where seventeen national parks were established between 1965 and 1968. Park entry fees, shooting permits, and the export of hides and meat increased the direct income from game and tourism from $200,000 to $3 million annually. In conservation of this type a zero rate of discount may be applicable on the grounds that a particular irreplaceable resource must be available to future generations. The belief that future generations will prize the services equally as much as the current generation is implicit in this approach.

Given the extent of existing virgin areas it seems unlikely that Latin America is faced with the prospect of early extinction of the jungle, though the risk may exist for certain wildlife species. In the meantime, therefore, it might be more appropriate to apply something approaching standard discount rates in evaluating the expected costs and benefits of forestry and wildlife reserves. A reserve has been proposed in the province of Madre de Dios in eastern Peru. As long as such areas are inaccessible the decision to establish a reserve is largely academic. The test comes when pressure builds up to develop forestry or agriculture. Where commercial exploitation of the forest is out of the question in the process of land clearing and where permanent agriculture could not be sustained (e.g., northeastern Senegal), a reservation appears to be reasonable—providing that national institutions are able to control entry and there are, in fact, indications of potential benefits. Obviously this does not rule out the reservation of other areas, such as the Ilha do Bananal on the Araguaia River in central Brazil, where immediate recreation benefits are possible.

Depletion of Barbasco in Mexico

Barbasco is a rhizome native to the jungles of southeastern Mexico. The chemical properties of the root of this plant were recognized in 1944, and since the early 1950s it has provided the raw material for a variety of organic chemicals, including the steroid used in birth control pills. In 1960 the Mexican government restricted the exportation of dried barbasco. Since then six processing laboratories have been established in the country. In 1966 the investment rate reached about $2 million; and in 1967 it was estimated that total profits amounted to $1.7 million. At that time Mexico produced 40–50 percent of the world's supply of birth control hormones. This source of wealth drew attention to the potential capacity of the raw material supply. Efforts to cultivate barbasco have been unsuccessful, though research is continuing along these lines. As a conservation measure the government established the maximum annual harvest at 5,000 tons. This product provided an important source of income to colonists; for example, the value of production from the southern forest fringe of the Papaloapan basin in the peak year 1963 amounted to about $0.4 million, with total shipments on the order of $2 million between 1955 and 1964.[27]

To what extent should conservation of barbasco be practiced, and how can production be controlled? The risk of exhausting the natural source of supply and thus eliminating an important national industry must be balanced against two possibilities: (1) through research, a species adaptable to cultivation either in Mexico or elsewhere will be developed, or (2) a competitive synthetic process for hormone production will be developed.[28] In a capital-hungry developing country with high interest rates, production now as opposed to production later is critical in an economic evaluation of performance.

Once a course of conservation is decided upon, the problem becomes that of exercising effective control over harvesting. Management approaching sustained yield involves a rest period without crops between harvests to allow for recuperation of the roots and for the replanting of the small rhizomes. Mechanical harvesting is a remote possibility to say the least; any attempt to supervise hundreds of individual colonists in scattered areas is out of the question. The only practical approach appears to be the posting of inspectors at barbasco drying plants who would reject small roots delivered by settlers. Action along these lines requires considerable staff and only provides a partial solution—the management of the barbasco lands would remain uncontrolled. Any move to regular cropping or permanent pasture will eliminate the plant. Production is dependent on hand labor as well as on continuing expansion with relatively primitive practices on the agricultural frontier.

A similar situation applied to the harvesting of chicle (resin used as a raw material for chewing gum) in Guatemala and quina (the bark of a tree containing quinine) in the Yungas region of Bolivia. In both cases sustained-yield management was possible by reducing the immediate harvest. For example, if the *quiñeros* cut the quina tree 0.5 meters above the ground, there would be

---

[27] Reports of the Papaloapan Commission, Ciudad Aleman, Veracruz, Mexico.

[28] See Jorge Vidal, *La tragedia del salitre* (Santiago, Chile: Editorial Universitaria 1953), for a discussion of the death blow dealt to the Chilean nitrate bonanza by the Haber-Bosch process.

rapid regrowth from the established root system. The stump, however, contains 25 percent of the total bark available from a single tree. In view of unstable prices (ranging from $370 per ton in 1954 to a peak of $760 in the early sixties, with a sharp drop to $260 in 1967), the dispersion of the trees, and the difficulty of access on foot, it is not surprising that the *quiñero* elected to kill the tree and obtain a higher immediate return per hour worked. As in the case of barbasco it is by no means certain that this depletion decision was wasteful or counterproductive in economic development. Any attempt by the government to control quina production would have been costly and hampered by formidable administrative problems. In practice the state only intervened to impose taxes.

Yield Decline, Erosion, and Downstream Effects

To discuss tropical soil management is to open Pandora's box. Tracing the sequence following clearing in selected instances, however, gives some idea of the range of possible consequences. In the Alto Turiacu area land is cropped for three to five years; at the end of this period the area is liable to be completely taken over by emperada, a dense tropical plant. Because of the availability of new lands, low product prices, and high-cost inputs, chemicals have not been used against this weed. Colonists faced with it must develop additional areas for crops, diversify into cattle, or leave their parcels to cattlemen. A similar situation prevails on Caquetá—where colonists find the soils will support two or three crops of rice; thereafter much of the area is turned over to cattle.

On Cihualtepec, yield declined about 50 percent by the third year of cropping, and the land was then left in bush-fallow for three to five years. Recovery depends on the fallow period and the quality of land, but yields seldom equal those of the first rotation. Declining fertility and a diminishing virgin forest area have encouraged the use of advanced techniques—fertilizers, pesticides, and hybrid varieties. The alternative to such capital-intensive practices appears to be the lengthening of the fallow period or a move to permanent pasture and livestock. Both involve the consolidation of properties to increase the land area per family; conversion to pasture and livestock requires substantial additional capital.

In many inaccessible areas, such as Chapare, high transport costs are likely to eliminate the possibility of using chemical inputs to maintain lands in permanent production. Expanding the area to offset declining yields or weed infestation may eventually lead to abandonment in cases where family labor is insufficient to handle the cultivation and harvesting on the more extensive crop area and the increasing demands for weed control and where cash income is insufficient to support hired labor. In the case of Chapare, where settlement has been under way more than forty years, the average cleared area is 4 ha per farm, which appears to approach the limit a family can handle when it must cope with weeds, regrowth forest, and rainfall of 3–4 meters annually.

The question of postponing the development of such areas depends on the possible economic returns to be had from delayed and improved exploitation of natural resources in the region; the potential losses or costs incurred downstream from erosion, sedimentation, and increased runoff; the external economies that might result from early development; and the immediate alternative investment opportunities available. Some of these aspects together with stability of settlement are discussed below for the case of the Yungas region of Bolivia.

Erosion and Settlement Stability in the Bolivian Yungas

The Yungas region consists of the subtropical lower foothills and valleys of the Bolivian Andes as typified by Caranavi where colonization has taken place under conditions of erosion and declining yields. It is steep country—80 percent has slopes with a gradient of more than 10 percent, and the altitude ranges from 200 to 900 meters. Average annual rainfall is 1,500 millimeters, and 90 percent of the rainfall occurs in the eight-month period from September to April. The maximum temperature range is 15° to 35°C.

On the basis of topography, soils, and climate, one would expect the area to be wholly unsuited to agriculture. Only 15 percent of the occupied land is classified as agricultural.[29] Thus it is not surprising that erosion, exhaustion of soil nutrients, and declining yields are the inevitable consequences of regular cropping and the absence of fertilizer use or conservation practices. The general land development practice followed to date has been to sow annual crops (rice, corn, or yucca) for the first two or three years after clearing the forest. At the same time permanent crops such as bananas, coffee, or citrus have been intersown in the second and third years. This has resulted in an intensive use of land and a slow rate of forest clearing after the third year; only 36 percent of the subdivided area had been cleared of forest in 1967. Thus over a period of ten to fifteen years the colonists have cleared about 3–4 ha each. The average property has 1 ha in annual crops and 2.5 ha in permanent crops. There is no widespread application of bush-fallow, although this probably is the next step in the evolution of agriculture in the area.

Since settlement has been in process for over twenty years the question of yield declines and their potential effects on the rate of abandonment or on management practices—such as increased capital and labor inputs for fertilizer and terracing or a switch from annual crops to tree crops and pasture— remains uncertain. There are no experimental results that isolate seasonal and

[29] INC, *Colonización espontánea en Caranavi: estudio socioeconómico* (La Paz, Bolivia, 1967), p. 9.

soil effects in yield variation. Land-use decisions will be governed by the rate of yield decline, the break-even point for abandoning land, output response to added capital and labor, the availability of capital, and short-run and long-run returns from various combinations of soil-depleting and soil-conserving practices. It has been estimated that up to 30 percent of the land now in cultivation may have to be abandoned within the next five to ten years; but there is no indication whether the bush-fallow should last two, five, or twenty-five years or whether the area should be permanent forest reserve.

Under the existing situation with respect to markets, the availability of virgin land, the agrarian structure, and physical and legal access to new land, yield levels at which producers either abandon the land or return it to bush-fallow appear to be 400 kilograms (kg) per hectare for rice and corn, 5,000 kg per hectare for yucca, and 400 stems of bananas per hectare. These yields represent a 60-75 percent decrease from the peak obtained in the first year or two after clearing the forest. In the case of citrus many of the orchards are essentially abandoned within five to ten years because of diseased plants or the lack of markets. There is no firm basis, however, for projecting the rate at which land will be abandoned, the length of the bush-fallow period, or the technical steps (within the constraints of economics, management ability, and the availability of capital and labor) that may be taken to avoid or reduce abandonment. It was estimated that 24,000 ha, or about 33 percent of the land in cultivation in Caranavi in 1967 would be abandoned within five to eight years.[30] These figures and the history of Caranavi since 1947 suggest that, on the average, land remains in production about ten or fifteen years.[31] Without a change in management practices the average area in cultivation that can be handled by a farm family is about 4-7 ha.

The general implication was that land would be abandoned at an accelerating rate of between 500 and 2,500 ha annually over the period 1966-70. At the same time it was estimated that the clearing of virgin forest was proceeding at the rate of 3,000-4,000 ha per year. Of this area, about 2,000 ha were being cleared by established colonists on their own lots. Thus it may be estimated that the net immigration was about 500-1,000 families annually (assuming that each colonist cleared 2 ha in the first year), though not all these families were new to the region, some being colonists who already lived in the valley and were preparing to abandon their properties.

It is asserted that fear of disastrous crop and livestock diseases, uncertainties about the ability of the land to support permanent agriculture, delays in titling, the lack of credit, and the lack of extension services to control

[30]Estimate by BAB and INC agents in Caranavi.

[31]On the basis of settlement and forest-clearing rates in the discussion of Caranavi in chap. 5, an estimated 9,000-10,000 ha were cleared in 1956. Assuming this to be the candidate area for early abandonment, it would constitute the approximately 8,000 ha (33 percent of 24,000 ha) projected to go out of production in 1966-70.

diseases and establish a more stable form of farming created a socioeconomic environment conducive to nomadic agriculture, i.e., a situation where total abandonment might be expected.[32] While these factors are unquestionably negative, there is evidence that the expectations of the settlers were actually based on permanent economic activity in the region. Many farmers have sown tree crops that have long-term pay-out periods. Particularly in urban areas, infrastructure other than highways has provided an important degree of stability. Settlers have independently built feeder roads and schools and have progressed from temporary palm-roofed housing to adobe construction. All of these activities are positive indications of initiative and permanence.

The fundamental policy question is whether Bolivia would have been better off in the long run if development in Caranavi had been delayed for perhaps twenty-five or thirty years until the country was both institutionally and technically capable of handling the development so that the timber resources could be harvested systematically and land use could be controlled to ensure watershed protection, permanent agriculture, or exclusion of agriculture where appropriate. Assuming that no diseconomies have resulted from the Caranavi development, a case can be made for delayed development if the alternative investment opportunities over the 1945–70 period could have yielded a 13–20 percent IRR with similar employment generation. If there were measurable and predictable external or secondary effects, then the IRR's associated with a delay could be higher or lower depending on whether these effects were positive or negative. At such time as the government feels itself capable of exercising the necessary control over resource use, the implication is that the IRR will be higher, if for no other reason than reduction in external diseconomies. Higher levels of timber extraction may also be expected to improve the benefit-cost ratio.

The problem posed is one of dynamic programming[33] –the benefit rate of the Caranavi project changes with calendar time, whereas costs (net of operation and maintenance) may be assumed to be unaffected by the date of investment.[34] The application of this concept not only involves quantification of the benefit flows for Caranavi with various starting dates and scheduling, but also the same quantification for alternative projects available for public investment. Admittedly theoretical the issue is nonetheless highly relevant to tropical land development policy. In practice there are no data on alternative investment opportunities either in 1945 or 1970.

External effects of the Caranavi settlement are not readily apparent. To date there has been no evidence of adverse downstream effects directly trace-

---

[32] INC, *Colonización espontánea*, p. 9.

[33] See Stephen A. Marglin, *Approaches to Dynamic Investment Planning* (Amsterdam: North-Holland Publishing Co., 1963).

[34] Since the Caranavi project is readily divisible, the investment schedule rather than the date is applicable.

able to deforestation in the Yungas region. Nor are there estimates of the cost of undertaking a study of sufficient depth to give a meaningful evaluation of the possible downstream consequences of an expansion of existing agricultural and forestry development practices over extensive areas of the precordillera, including the Yungas. In short, the development of tropical lands in Caranavi over a twenty-three-year period may be regarded as highly inconclusive in providing a clear indication of resource conservation policy. The irony of this is that by many traditional indicators (e.g., slope, erodability, adequacy for crops) the area would be ruled out for agricultural endeavor.

Fertilizers and High-Yielding Varieties

As indicated above, destruction of the forest can only be justified if it is to be followed by permanent agriculture or if there is a reasonable certainty that erosion will not proceed to the stage of irreversibility in a relevant planning period of, say, twenty years. This will require changes in the production pattern—more purchased inputs or more intensive use of labor for weed control, terracing, expanded forest clearing, and so on. Increasing demands on unpaid family labor may eventually become limiting. Thus if a solution exists to a potential labor shortage and the associated low per capita incomes, it lies in the use of machinery, fertilizers, improved seeds, pesticides, and herbicides. The adoption of such practices again opens up the questions of agrarian structure, relative prices, and the potential prerequisite of "balance" between a number of activities discussed above, notably (1) whether knowledge of available inputs and associated management will reach the producer without effective extension, (2) whether the producer is able to put the knowledge to use without credit, (3) whether the increased production is warranted without markets and marketing services, and (4) whether the larger producer will benefit to the detriment of the smaller.

In terms of production economics the level of technology and the composition of production is governed by the factor-product, factor-factor, and product-product relationships. These relationships for two tropical Latin American countries are compared with those in the United States in table 19. Some general conclusions about capital use and technology can be drawn from the figures. The Colombian cattleman is in a substantially better position than a Paraguayan cattleman to use fertilizer and machinery as well as labor-intensive methods in beef production. A day's wages in Paraguay, however, will buy twice as much beef as in Colombia. In beef equivalent the costs of buying and operating a tractor are about the same in Colombia and in the United States, but the same expenditure in Colombia will buy five times as much labor. These comparisons illustrate the dangers of generalizing about the economic feasibility of using more capital-intensive or labor-intensive methods in different countries in the humid tropics, even though the physical responses to such inputs may be similar.

While extensive plot testing of inputs has not been undertaken in the humid tropics of Latin America, there are some indications of the potential. Table 20 shows the results of fertilizer trials in four tropical areas. The response is highly variable and is based on relatively few observations. Nevertheless value-cost ratios on the order of two or three are not uncommon. Considering the risks involved in fertilizer use, a producer in a developed country may well require a 50 percent return. The rate will undoubtedly be much higher for a small producer with limited resources who is becoming established on the tropical forest frontier. But if yield responses can be demonstrated, such as 33 percent, or 600 kg of corn per hectare, to 45 kg of nitrogen fertilizer (giving a net increase in return of $50 per hectare and a value-cost ratio of 3:1 in the accessible rates already studied), there is little doubt that additional freight rates of $40 per ton, or $5 per hectare, for ammonium nitrate could be justified.

There is ample evidence that the use of high-yielding fertilizer-responsive varieties may compound these effects. Indications are that the response of

Table 19. Comparison of Factor and Product Price Relationships in Paraguay, Colombia, and the United States, Applied to Beef Production

Item	Factor unit[a]	Equivalent value of factor or product		
		Paraguay	Colombia	U.S.
Factor-product price ratios				
		Beef (*kg, liveweight*)		
Unskilled labor	1 month	231	109	534
Skilled farm labor[b]	1 month	431	143	688
Tractor[c]	1 hp	725	197	168
Diesel fuel	1 m^3	625	97	88
Nitrogen fertilizer[d]	1 ton N	3,310	710	520
Feed concentrates[e]	1 ton	625	246	166
Product-product price ratios				
Milk	1 ton	625	371	274
Pork (liveweight)	1 ton	1,000	1,429	920
Factor-factor price ratios				
		Unskilled labor (*man-days*)		
Tractor	1 hp	78	45	8
Diesel fuel	1 m^3	68	22	4

Source: W. Schaefer-Kehnert, IBRD.

[a]Calculated on the basis of unit prices converted to U.S. dollars at the 1967 official exchange rate.
[b]Tractor driver or boundary rider for twenty-five man-days per month.
[c]Tractor of 40–65 hp.
[d]Expressed in pure nutrients of nitrogen.
[e]Feed with 20 percent protein content.

Table 20. Yield Response and Returns from Fertilizer Trials in
Humid Tropical Areas of Honduras, Panama, Nicaragua, and Ecuador

Crop	Country	Fertilizer treatment (kg/ha)			Yield increase (percent)	Net return ($/ha)	Value/cost ratio
		N	P_2O_5	K_2O			
Corn	Honduras[a]	45			26	33	2.8
		90	90	45	49	20	1.3
	Panama[b]	45			47	78	7.0
		45	90	45	50	57	2.4
	Ecuador	45			36	56	3.4
		45	90	45	4	−54	0.1
Rice	Panama[b]	68			10	5	1.2
		68	68	68	59	127	3.4
Beans	Honduras[a]		45		21	12	1.7
		90	90	45	53	−4	0.9
	Nicaragua		45		62	73	6.9
		45	90	45	94	79	2.6
Cotton	Ecuador[c]	45			21	−11	0.5
		90	90	90	290	88	1.9

Source: FAO, Review of Trial and Demonstration Results, 1965/66, FFHC Fertilizer
Program (Rome, 1968).

[a]Caribbean coast region.
[b]Colón-Panama region.
[c]Pacific coast region.

traditional varieties of rice may tail off above 40–50 kg of nitrogen per
hectare, whereas improved varieties may continue to show yield increases
with up to twice this rate of fertilizer application. The IR-8 rice variety has
given 6–10 tons per hectare (relative to 1–3 tons for traditional varieties in
the Latin American tropics) and in a trial with three successive crops in one
year yielded 20 tons per hectare. There are many technical and institutional
obstacles to the large-scale introduction of such practices. Pests and diseases
may become increasing problems and quality may be sacrificed. Greatly improved management is required in cultivation, fertilizer placement, use of
crop protection chemicals, and grain drying. Institutional bottlenecks may be
expected in plant breeding; seed certification; the supply and distribution of
fertilizers and other inputs; price administration; and transport, storage, and
marketing of the product.[35]

The Australian Bureau of Agricultural Economics generally discounts the
results of experiment stations by 30 percent. In view of experiences such as

[35] "Strategy of Agricultural Development, FAO Areas of Concentration" (staff position paper, Item 16 (b), FAO Conference, Rome, November 8–27, 1969).

Bataan, perhaps twice this figure would be more appropriate in jungle colonization areas of Latin America. In the absence of plot testing, colonists have considerable reason for skepticism—marked variation in soil and climate, uncertainty of prices of inputs and products from year to year, inflation, and potential side effects. Even discounting at a rate of 60 percent, however, the possibility of achieving a response acceptable to the colonist—50 percent, for instance—still appears to be within range.

The work of the Commonwealth Scientific and Industrial Research Organization in developing pasture species, fertilizer programs, and mechanized forest clearing for the Wallum region of southeastern Queensland, Australia, is a classic example of the application of technology to problem soils in the humid subtropics. Conditions are comparable to those in some of the poorer zones of the Latin American humid tropics. The sandy soils, which support relatively dense eucalypt forests, have a low water-holding capacity and extremely low fertility and are subject to both waterlogging and drought. Rainfall ranges from 1,000 to 1,750 millimeters annually, with 50 percent occurring in the three-month period December to March.

A combination of medium-heavy weight crawler tractors, chains, and bulldozer blades with "stinger" attached is used to clear the land and prepare it for pasture at a cost of $50–$70 per hectare. Technology for the area was based on the premise that as long as there is sufficient rainfall the only limitation is plant nutrition. Attention was directed to pasture and selection from hundreds of varieties of tropical grasses and legumes. Tropical grasses, such as pangola, are able to utilize carbon dioxide twice as efficiently as temperate grasses. Assuming no other nutrient deficiencies, the only constraint on production and feed value is nitrogen, which may be supplied directly as fertilizer or through legumes. Since legumes alone are unable to supply the enormous nitrogen requirements of the grasses, research was oriented to rhizobium bacteriology and the use of phosphate and potassium fertilizer to increase legume growth and the nitrogen-fixing capacity.

Experimentation led to the use of fertilizer on a grass-legume pasture at a rate unheard of in temperate agriculture. The initial dressing per hectare contained 630 kg of superphosphate, 630 kg of lime, 125 kg of muriate of potash, 8 kg of copper sulfate, 8 kg of zinc sulfate, and 0.15 kg of elemental molybdenum. This was followed by an annual application of 250 kg of superphosphate and 125 kg of muriate of potash. Stocking after the fourth year was sustained at 2.5 head of cattle per hectare with an average annual liveweight gain of 340 kg per hectare. Tests with nitrogen on all-grass pastures indicate a yield approaching a liveweight gain of 680 kg per hectare using 1,400 kg of ammonium nitrate per hectare annually.[36]

The application of such techniques on a large scale in the tropics of Latin America is probably out of the question in the near future. Nevertheless the

---

[36] Data from the Beerwah Pasture Research Station, CSIRO, Queensland, Australia.

possibility that depleted lands may be restored, that production from existing land may be increased, or that lands with such potentials may be eroded to the point of irreversibility all enter into current conservation policy.

Mechanization

Mechanization is one of the many controversial issues in tropical land development. It is capital intensive and saves labor in countries where capital is severely rationed and labor is underemployed. In forested areas mechanized felling and windrowing, followed by burning, can cause damage to the already fragile soil structure. Yet there are compelling arguments in favor of using machinery to tame the humid tropical environment.

The principal machines currently employed in clearing jungle and preparing new lands for crops and pasture include diesel crawler tractors of 100–280 horsepower (hp) equipped with a range of attachments, such as a bulldozer with or without shearing blades, a root rake, a tree-pusher bar, a chain, and giant discs; diesel-electric tree crushers of up to 1,000 hp; and 900–1,000 hp diesel-electric rubber-tired tractors mounted with a root rake or bulldozer blade. These machines are normally employed in combination to achieve a balance between the stages in the clearing sequence. The operational capacity and costs associated with selected combinations are shown in table 21.

The selection of machinery for felling depends on the type of forest. Where there are significant areas of light growth, the use of two medium-powered tractors for chaining is feasible at rates of up to 1.2 ha per tractor-hour. Where there are some larger trees (up to 60 centimeters in diameter at breast height), a heavy tractor with a tree-pusher bar may support a chaining team. Similarly, support may be provided by a tractor mounted with a shearing blade capable of felling a tree of any size. In heavier forest the clearing may be accomplished by the use of the shearing blade units with or without a tree-pusher bar—e.g., Cariari and Tocache where felling rates of 0.25 ha per tractor-hour were achieved. The diesel-electric tree crushers normally weigh between 40 and 70 tons, though some units have been built up to 120 tons. The machine is a tricycle design mounted on steel roller drums up to 2.5 meters wide with a diameter of 2 meters and employing the principle of the tree-pusher bar plus subsequent rolling and crushing. The machine is normally powered by one or two diesel generating units of 480 hp each and has a capacity to crush 0.8–1.3 ha per machine-hour when operating at 2–3 miles per hour cutting a 7-meter swath in the jungle. The advantage of this apparatus is its ability to operate under wet conditions, since it rides on a cushion of crushed vegetation. In fact the wetter the ground, the easier it is for the machine to fell the forest. In addition its weight and power enable it to push over large trees having shallow root systems and buttressed trunks of up to 3 meters in diameter at ground level. Such trees are time-consuming for a shearing blade.

Table 21. Capacity of Equipment and Costs of Mechanized

Machinery in the clearing unit	Area of project	Type of forest[c]	Annual rainfall[d] (mm)	Land clearing and preparation capacity[a]	
				Ha per hour[e]	Ha per year[f]
A. 4 270-hp tractors with shearing blades[k] 1 160-hp tractor with tree-pusher bar 4 giant discs	Tingo María- Tocache, Peru	Medium	2,400	0.60	800[l]
B. 1 180-hp tractor with shearing blade 1 180-hp tractor with tree-pusher bar 1 95-hp tractor with bulldozer blade 2 giant discs	Cariari, Costa Rica	Medium- dense	4,000	0.26	500[m]
C. 2 235-hp tractors with shearing blades 1 235-hp tractor with angle-dozer blade 2 tree-pusher bars 2 root rakes 1 100-meter chain 1 giant disc	Peru	Medium	–	0.21	200
D. 2 90-hp tractors with angle-dozer blades 2 tree-pusher bars 2 root rakes 1 100-meter chain 1 giant disc	Peru	Light	–	0.22	300
E. 1 475-hp tree-crusher 1 tree-crusher tender 3 240-hp tractors with bulldozer blades 2 giant discs	Ivory Coast	Medium	–	0.80	800
F. 1 475-hp tree-crusher 1 960-hp tree-crusher 1 tree-crusher tender 1 960-hp diesel-electric rubber-tired tractor 1 635-hp diesel-electric rubber-tired tractor 1 root rake 2 giant discs	Pucallpa, Peru	Medium	1,800	0.85[p]	2,000[q]
G. 1 960-hp tree-crusher with root rake 1 170-hp tractor with root rake 1 giant disc	British Honduras	Medium	1,300	0.90[t]	900
H. 2 960-hp tree-crushers 2 960-hp diesel-electric tractors with root rakes 2 635-hp diesel-electric tractors with root rakes 2 270-hp tractors with bulldozer blades 2 giant discs	(Theoretical)	Medium	–	2.50	3,900[w]
I. Combination of 230-270-hp, 150-170-hp, and 93-115-hp tractors equipped with shearing and bulldozer blades, root rakes, and giant discs	Ivory Coast	Dense Medium Light	– – –	– – –	– – –
J. 4 180-hp tractors with bulldozer blades 2 giant discs 1 100-meter chain	La Chontalpa	Medium- light	–	–	–

Sources: Enrique Ferrayros y Cía., S.A., *Operación Tocache* (Lima, February 1968), p. 68; Manuel Abastos Gómez, *Inventario y evaluación de la concesión Tournavista*, R. G. Le Tourneau, Inc. (Lima, July 1967); files of the Comisión de Grijalva, Cárdenas, Tabasco, Mexico; files of UNDP Huallaga Central Project, Tarapoto, Peru; and *Oleagineaux*, November 1966.

Note: Dashes indicate "not available."

[a]Land clearing and preparation includes felling, windrowing (either after burning in place or without burning) with 50- or 100-meter centers, reburning in the windrow, and two giant discings.

[b]Investment is based on the price of machinery at the port of entry, excluding taxes and including 10 percent allowance for inventory of replacement parts, with costs of transport to the site added.

[c]Dense forest is taken as that with 600–1,000 trees per hectare with over 100 being more than 60 cm DBH. Medium is defined as an average of 50–99 trees per ha of more than 60 cm DBH. Light is second growth or dry land forest of the xerophytic, caatinga, or cerrado type.

[d]The volume and distribution of rainfall together with the consistency and drying rate of the soil will have a significant effect on idle time of machinery and consequently on unit costs.

[e]Based on the assumption that machinery is working at 100 percent efficiency.

[f]Unless otherwise stated, it is assumed that machinery will average 1,000 hours at 100 percent efficiency annually.

[g]Operation and maintenance includes labor, fuel and oil, spare parts, and workshop expenses.

[h]Depreciation is based on a 10,000-hour life of machinery with no salvage value.

[i]Includes technical supervision, administration, on-the-job transport of machinery, operation of supporting vehicles, and interest on initial investment at 10 percent.

[j]Unless otherwise stated, owner's profit is assumed at 15 percent of total costs.

[k]Shearing blades, such as the Rome Plough Company's 4-ton model K-G, are bulldozer blades equipped with a horizontal knife edge along the base and a vertical stinger, or wedge, on one edge used for splitting standing trees.

Equipment investment[b] ($)			Cost per ha ($)					
Total	Per 1 ha/hour capacity	Per 100 ha/year capacity	Operation & maintenance[g]	Depreciation allowance[h]	Administration overhead[i]	Total (excluding profit)	Owner's profit[j]	Equivalent contract price
400,000	667,000	50,000	120	80	40	240	35	275
160,000	615,000	32,000	90	50	30	170	25	195
230,000	1,095,000	115,000	120	65	55	250[n]	40	290
90,000	410,000	30,000	45	30	25	100[o]	15	115
450,000	560,000	56,000	–	–	–	–	–	–
400,000	470,000	20,000	40	30	25	95[r]	–	210[s]
–	–	–	–	–	–	60[u]	20[v]	80
680,000	270,000	17,000	–	–	–	–	–	–
–	–	–	–	–	–	–	–	450–670[x]
–	–	–	–	–	–	–	–	290–450[x]
–	–	–	–	–	–	–	–	180–290[x]
–	–	–	–	–	–	125	–	250[y]

[l]In two months 200 ha were cleared, giving an annual rate of 1,000 ha. However, since the average rainfall during the period–180 mm per month–was only 80 percent of the average for the other nine months of the year, it is unlikely that this rate of clearing could be sustained.

[m]In eleven weeks 100 ha were cleared and 8 km of road were built by the clearing unit. Clearing and discing required 1,022 tractor hours and the road required 100 tractor hours; i.e., each tractor averaged 35 hours per week, and the clearing rate of the unit was 10 ha per week. Since rainfall averaged 350 mm per month during the test, equal to the average annual rate, it is justified to assume an annual clearing rate of $50 \times 10 = 500$ ha.

[n]Based on 14.5 tractor (235 hp) hours per ha at $20 per hour.

[o]Based on 9 tractor (90 hp) hours per ha at $11 per hour.

[p]Based on approximately 1,000 hours by tree-crushers to clear 850 ha.

[q]In three months 850 ha were cleared and during that time each machine averaged forty hours per week in operation; i.e., an annual rate of 3,400 ha. However, since work was accomplished during the dry season this figure has been scaled down to 2,000 ha.

[r]Based on crushing and burning in place at $40 per ha, windrowing at $30, and discing at $25.

[s]Approximate contract price for similar unit in the Pucallpa region. Price for crushing, burning in place, windrowing and reburning–$185 per ha.

[t]Crushing rate alone, 1.4 ha per hour.

[u]Assumed cost of root raking after windrowing, reburning, and two giant discings–$25 per ha.

[v]Based on a margin of 30 percent for crushing, removal of stumps, windrowing, and burning.

[w]Based on a ten-hour working day, ten-month season, and twenty working days per month, of which 25 percent are unsuitable because of rain. During actual available working time, machines work at 75 percent efficiency. Lost time is due to servicing, repairs, running out of fuel or getting stuck–i.e., total operation at 100 percent efficiency is 1,125 hours annually.

[x]Contract quotations.

[y]Contract price on the La Chontalpa project, not necessarily with the same equipment.

169

Windrowing is normally carried out by teams of two or three heavy crawler tractors mounted with bulldozer blades or root rakes. A tractor's capacity when sweeping felled trees into rows 50 meters apart is 0.2–0.5 ha per tractor-hour. If it is possible to burn the felled forest in place, the total volume of vegetation can be reduced by up to 60 percent, greatly facilitating the windrowing. A process of burning and re-piling in the windrows may reduce the total volume to 5 or 10 percent of the original volume; repetition may permit discing in of the remnants of the windrows after a year or two. In many climates burning is impossible. Where it is feasible the use of the tree-crusher leaves the mat of vegetation in better condition to dry out over a three-to-four-week period than do other methods, and therefore the vegetation burns more thoroughly. A 960-hp diesel-electric tractor mounted on rubber tires and carrying a 5-ton root rake can windrow up to 0.8 ha per hour if a good burn has been obtained. Rubber-tired tractors are much faster than the track-laying type but limited in their capacity to operate on wet ground. Thus their use may be precluded in areas or seasons of frequent rain.

In order to lower clearing costs and employ more unskilled labor, an experiment was conducted on La Chontalpa using hand methods for felling followed by mechanized windrowing. Because of serious problems the cost of windrowing per hectare was higher than it would have been if felling and windrowing had been fully mechanized. The requirement to hand-fell a block of sufficient size to warrant bringing in machinery (about 100 ha) resulted in the work extending over the entire dry season. By the following year re-growth had obscured the stumps and trunks, causing difficulties for the tractor operators. The removal of stumps required as much time as felling virgin forest. In addition the trunks of smaller trees had to be removed with shearing blades or bulldozers; in standing forest the trunks could have been pushed over.

The final step in land preparation is giant discing where medium-powered crawler tractors are employed. Two workings are normally required, one with giant discs and one with a lighter model. The average capacity for this step (two cultivations) ranges from 0.5 to 1.5 ha per tractor-hour.

There can be no real argument about soil damage being caused by machine clearing. Heavy machines working on wet ground (which is virtually unavoidable in much of the humid tropics except during parts of a three-to-four-month dry season) may well impair soil structure. The uprooting of enormous trees by tree-crushers or of smaller trees by chaining and tree-pusher bars leaves holes that will fill with the thin topsoil in the process of windrowing and cultivation. A further consequence is that much soil is carried by the roots into the windrows, together with soil pushed by the heavy trunks in the windrowing operation. Where there is windrowing prior to burning all the organic matter from the vegetation is lost to the soil; even with burning in place there is still extensive loss. The total removal of trunks accentuates the laterizing effects of heavy rains and hot sun on the bare ground.

The case in favor of mechanization rests on the following propositions:

1. The minimum acceptable unit of cattle is considered to be about 400 head, requiring 150 to 200 ha of pasture. The clearing and maintenance of such an area by hand would be impossible for a colonist of limited resources. Thus it is reasoned that land at the time it is turned over to the new settler must be largely cleared and sown to pasture, enabling him to direct most of his efforts to pasture maintenance, fencing, and livestock management.

2. In the case of annual or perennial cropping where there is strong forest regrowth or weed invasion, a vicious cycle is likely to develop where yields decline and demands on labor mount. As indicated above the farmer must resort to chemicals and mechanized farming to stay in business. If the lands are to be worked with machinery it is essential that the forest, even if felled by hand, be stumped and windrowed mechanically.

3. Mechanized clearing and farming offers the only solution for large-scale operations, especially where integrated processing is involved requiring an assured supply of raw material. Seasonal labor in sufficient quantity may not be available, particularly if account is taken of short harvesting seasons or the scheduling requirements for a multiple-cropping system. Even if labor were available the housing, feeding, and supervision of such large numbers would present excessive administrative problems.

4. It is estimated that as much as 25 percent of land cleared by hand may be unavailable for production for ten years or more until the stumps and trunks decay.[37] Windrows cover only about 5 percent of the land, and if reburning is practiced even this small percentage may be eliminated within two or three years. Where a shearing blade is used stump bases may occupy something like 5-10 percent of the area, rendering this fraction unsuitable for cropping for several years.

5. Where heavy indivisible investments are made in basic infrastructure—as in the La Chontalpa project—the economic justification demands that the lands within the area of influence of such infrastructure be brought into production as soon as possible. This can be achieved only through mechanized clearing. The economics of mechanization as a substitute for hand clearing is governed by:

  a) The opportunity cost of labor and capital and the requirements of these two factors.
  b) Diseconomies of scale in handling large numbers of workers in an operation such as jungle clearing.

[37] Enrique Ferrayros y Cía, S.A., *Operación Tocache* (February 1968), p. 84.

c) Reduction in yield (or added cost of inputs) as a consequence of the soil damage wrought by machinery.

d) Increased production due to higher land utilization made possible by mechanized clearing.

e) The difference in the rate at which land can be brought into full production under the two farming systems.

f) The rate at which land would be abandoned without the application of advanced technology and the timing of abandonment.

g) The cost of advanced technology.

Although this generalization of the problem covers elements about which little is known and therefore has little relevance to policy formulation, it does suggest some lines for further research. For example, no information is available on the negative or positive effects of mechanized land clearing on yields.[38] Similarly, diseconomies of scale in labor use have not been measured (contract piecework may have constant returns to scale). Little is known about the rate of abandonment of land, nor is there much information on the returns that might be expected from more advanced technology under the wide variety of soils, climates, and institutional conditions to be found in the humid tropics of Latin America.

The conditions that must be satisfied to justify mechanization are illustrated in figure 3. The curve $t^j WX$ represents the flow of benefits with hand methods. In figure 3 it has been assumed that the lag between starting to clear land and first production will be less in the case of hand clearing (t_j) than with mechanization (t^k). The greater lag expected with machinery is due to the indivisibility of the operation, i.e., relatively large blocks are cleared at one time, and there is added time for windrowing. Hand clearing is highly divisible and logs are not windrowed, thus planting can begin immediately after the burn or two to three weeks after starting to fell the forest. In both cases it is assumed that benefits at full production (b) will be identical. $OQRt^l$ represents the added costs of mechanized over hand methods. Justification for mechanization is given when:

$SUW - t^j t^k S > OQRt^l$ discounted to NPV. The point of indifference is given by the following formula:

$$\sum_{i=1}^{t^l} m_i(1 + r)^{-i} = \sum_{i=t^k}^{t^m} b_i (1 + r)^{-i} - \sum_{i=t^j}^{t^n} h_i(1 + r)^{-i}$$

where:

m_i = the added cost of mechanized land clearing in year i,

[38] Research is under way in Kenya to determine the yield effect of mechanized versus animal and hand cultivation practices. See IBRD Pemanent Mission in Eastern Africa, *Agricultural Mechanization in East African Countries* (Nairobi, Kenya, July 1966).

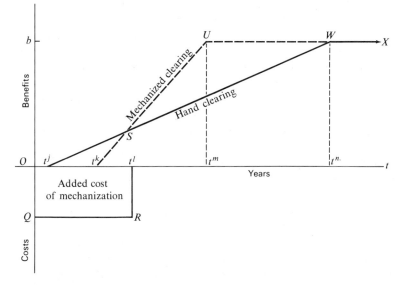

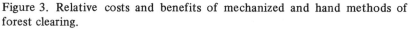

Figure 3. Relative costs and benefits of mechanized and hand methods of forest clearing.

t^j = first year of production with hand clearing,

t^k = first year of production with mechanized clearing,

t^l = year of completion of mechanized clearing,

t^m = year of reaching full production (b) with mechanized clearing,

t^n = year of reaching full production (b) with hand clearing,

b_i = benefits with mechanization,

h_i = benefits with hand methods,

r = discount rate.

Substituting values in the equation gives an indication of the sensitive elements. It may be safely assumed that O, t^j, t^k, and t^l will be relatively close together, and thus differences in the values will not materially affect the results. With $t^m = 6$ years, $t^n = 15$ years, and $b = 200 per hectare, the supportable cost of mechanized clearing is not highly sensitive to the discount rate—increasing r from 4 percent to 50 percent lowers M[39] from $880 per hectare to $420.[40] On the other hand the outcome is sensitive to the value of

[39] $M = \Sigma\ m_i$, i.e., $OQRT^l$ expressed as NPV in figure 3.

[40] Calculations based on the assumptions implied in figure 3 with linearity in all variables.

b. In the case above, if b is reduced from \$200 to \$40 with $r = 15$ percent, the justifiable level of M is reduced from \$680 to \$130 per hectare. Similarly, the delay in the realization of b–i.e., $t^n - t^m$–is of considerable importance. Taking b as \$200 per hectare, r at 15 percent with $t^m = 6$ years, and increasing t^n from 15 to 25 years raises the supportable M from \$680 to \$1,100 per hectare.

The problem posed by La Chontalpa is clearly illustrated by the example above: the government has a heavy fixed investment in infrastructure (\$650 per hectare) that is chargeable exclusively to the project regardless of which method of clearing is employed; the expectation is a high value for b; probabilities are high that the delay ($t^n - t^m$) will be an extended period, and further chances are that with hand methods production will not reach the level of b at t^n or thereafter.

Summary

The conflicts and complementarities between the negative and positive theories of tropical land development reviewed in chapter 2 in large measure center on the conservation of natural resources and the level of technology applied in resource exploitation. In all programs to expand the tropical agricultural land area it has been accepted that forests must be destroyed. Further, the position implicitly adopted with respect to soil erosion and potential downstream effects is that the expediency of generating present consumption overrides consideration of losses or benefits forgone in the future. One can hardly condone continuance of public decision making on such a vague basis. This is not to underestimate the importance of political expediency. But if the issues—future losses and benefits; feasible levels of technology given market, management, and capital constraints; and expectations of new technology—are squarely confronted, there will be a sounder basis for policy formulation.

Evidence of the effects of erosion and of technology that might reverse the process or increase productivity is inconclusive. Since such technology obviates the need for rapid forest clearing, this suggests that priority be given to research on degradation and recuperation of soils, hydrology, runoff effects, and conditions of plant growth in the humid tropics.

FACTORS AFFECTING DEVELOPMENT POLICY: 1. AREA SELECTION, BENEFICIARIES, AND INFRASTRUCTURE

VII

The survey in chapter 5 revealed immense diversity rather than consistent points of similarity in the situation and performance of the land development projects that were studied. Past experience therefore is not always useful as a guide for policy makers. Nonetheless it is possible to single out a number of factors that are crucial in formulating policies to expand the tropical land frontier. In this chapter the project histories are drawn upon to illustrate those elements bearing on the selection of areas and beneficiaries in tropical land development and on decisions for investment in infrastructure to expand the forest frontier.

Area Selection and Preinvestment Studies

In every decision to undertake investment or other programs to promote the development of new lands there is the probability of underestimating costs and overestimating benefits. In order to reduce these probabilities to an acceptable level some type of preinvestment study is made. The study may include physical resource inventories; engineering estimates of infrastructure or forest industry investment and maintenance costs; techno-economic studies of soil management, production patterns, markets, credit, extension, costs of production, transport, and marketing; or investigation into such social aspects as the source of potential colonists, the demand for tropical farmlands, the adaptability of new settlers, the quantity and quality of entrepreneurial talent that will be attracted to undertake development, the amount of capital that will be available, and the social organization and services needed in isolated frontier areas.

There are at least two levels of preinvestment study. The first is designed to identify the most promising areas for further investigation and to establish some order of priority among them. The second, a feasibility study, is used as the basis for an investment decision. Between these two levels project analysts identify a range of progressively more detailed preliminary studies.

Indications are that neither countries nor international financing institutions have adopted the first level. Projects appear to be selected (1) on the basis of their potential economic viability without regard to alternatives,

(2) as side effects of other projects, (3) because of national security considerations, (4) as a result of the existence of an unoccupied block of fiscal land, or (5) because of the availability of a completed resource survey. For example, the Papaloapan Commission in Mexico was formed as a direct response to the disastrous floods in the Papaloapan basin in 1944. In addition to flood control works the commission proposed a subproject for the settlement of "hundreds of thousands of people."[1] The Grijalva Commission became involved in land settlement as a by-product of the Malpaso Dam, which was constructed for power and flood control purposes. The Carretera Marginal de la Selva, actively promoted by former President Fernando Belaunde Terry of Peru, has become the focus of much government-sponsored colonization activity in Ecuador, Peru, and Bolivia. The alignment of this highway was not designed specifically to open up the most favorable areas for settlement in the countries through which it passes nor to open up priority areas on some planned schedule. But the road has tended to become an important force in shaping government settlement policies. If it had been the other way around there well might have been different alignments and scheduling.

The most systematic approach to colonization has probably occurred in the case of settlement for national security reasons, in particular by Brazil along the border of the Amapá territory, by Peru on the northern frontier, by Paraguay in the Chaco, and by Guatemala in the frontier province of Petén. In addition both Paraguay and Brazil have carried out extensive penetration road programs in virgin tropical regions. A prime purpose of these programs was the consolidation of sovereignty through the subsequent occupation and development of lands made accessible by the roads.

Much of the blame for the failures in tropical land development has been placed on inadequate technical, economic, and social planning. The extent of the analysis that can precede a given project, however, is without limit. At issue is whether countries must be condemned to undertake an endless succession of studies that only point to the need for further study before a decision can be made.

Natural Resource Information

In itself the gathering of information on natural resources clearly involves an economizing process.[2] How much information is required about land, forest, and water resources in order to identify promising areas for development? How much of the available virgin tropical lands should be subjected to survey before a preliminary selection of priority areas is made? How much more data would be required on the preliminary areas selected to establish a

[1] Thomas Poleman, *The Papaloapan Project* (Stanford University Press, 1964), p. 136.

[2] Orris C. Herfindahl, *Natural Resource Information for Economic Development* (Johns Hopkins Press for Resources for the Future, 1969), pp. 122–26.

priority for undertaking feasibility studies? What degree of precision in natural resource data is required to support a final feasibility study?

When confronted by virgin areas of the magnitude found in tropical Latin America, decision makers may be tempted to commit heavy outlays merely to identify the potential. Many soil, forestry, and integrated resource surveys have been undertaken. For example, since 1960 the United Nations Development Programme (UNDP) has supported tropical forest inventories of 90,000 square kilometers (km) in the region with a total investment of $10.3 million. Costs range from $50 to $700 per square kilometer, with an average of $116.[3] At this price, Ecuador, with the smallest tropical forest area in South America, would have to spend $15 million to $20 million for complete coverage without regard to soils, and Brazil would have to spend forty times this amount. Such surveys are not contemplated, but these figures give an indication of the size of potential investments.

In Bolivia a study was undertaken of the soil capability of 190,000 square kilometers along the proposed route of the Carretera Marginal de la Selva. The selection of colonization projects, however, and the final choice of highway alignment were made prior to the completion of the study. Preliminary identification of promising colonization areas (Alto Beni I and II, Chimoré, and Yapacani)[4] was made despite the absence of any systematic compilation of data on natural resources. Then a survey of resources was made on each area and all were found suitable for development. The precision of the Chimoré and Yapacani surveys was wholly inadequate for an investment decision; it was subsequently found that about 60 percent of the original area programmed for settlement on these two projects was subject to extensive annual flooding and therefore was unsuited to settlement. Moreover insufficient study of the hydrology of the Yapacani River resulted in the loss of the eastern abutment of the bridge giving access to the project, requiring the expenditure of an additional $1.6 million, or $950 per family.[5]

Peru has been particularly active in promoting new-land development. Since 1958 the government has undertaken a relatively intensive series of resource surveys designed to lay the foundations for the extensive settlement and development of the selva region, with the Carretera Marginal as the axis. In 1960 a general survey was made of 75,000 square kilometers in the Ceja de la Montaña area to identify colonization areas.[6] This was followed up by

[3] Ibid., pp. 85–93.

[4] In the case of the Alto Beni the decision appears to have been strongly influenced by the existence of an aerial survey made by the Instituto Geográfico Militar in 1954 in connection with a proposed hydroelectric plant at Bala, plus interest in a highway link with the Beni plains for national integration purposes. Chimoré and Yapacani are both along the proposed alignment of the Carretera Marginal de la Selva.

[5] Based on a figure of 1,700 settlers west of the river in 1969.

[6] OAS, *Integración económica y social de Perú Central* (Washington, 1961).

fifteen separate general resource surveys covering 60,000 square kilometers in the Andean Piedmont and upper Amazon plain, and plans exist for the completion of a survey of an additional 25,000 square kilometers by the end of 1970. The cost of these surveys has been around $22 per square kilometer.[7]

One of the studies identified a potential for developing 100,000 ha and settling about 10,000 colonists in the department of San Martín.[8] The report led to one of the most ambitious and detailed integrated resource surveys undertaken in the humid tropics of Latin America—a six-to-seven-year program known as the Huallaga Central Project, covering 33,600 square km and having a budget of about $4 million.[9]

The Huallaga Central Project. Closer examination of the Huallaga Central Project is warranted since it represents one of the most detailed natural resource evaluations undertaken in a humid tropical region of Latin America. The principal objectives of the project are as follows:

1. A land survey program (see table 22).
2. Investigations of climate, including the installation of nineteen weather stations.
3. A hydrology survey, including the installation of eleven hydrological stations and the evaluation of the potential for hydroelectric generation, groundwater, city water supply, irrigation, and drainage.
4. Soil conservation, irrigation, and drainage projects.
5. An analysis of the agricultural production potential and the preparation of development promotion programs in extension, credit, and research.
6. A census of land tenancy.
7. A survey of human resources.
8. A diagnosis of the economy of the region and the formulation of a general plan for medium- and long-term development, including specific projects in irrigation, forest industries, highways, urban infrastructure, social services, hydroelectricity, agricultural experiment stations, livestock promotion, agricultural promotion programs, and agricultural processing and other industries.

The principal thrust of the project has been toward agricultural development and the preparation of plans for the settlement of population from the

[7] Based on data provided by José Lizarraga for ONERN surveys of Rio Tambo, Rio Pachitea, and Perené-Satipo-Ene (letter to the author, December 6, 1968).

[8] SCIF, *Estudio del potencial agropecuario del Departamento de San Martín para justificar el financiamiento de su red vial* (Lima, 1960).

[9] The original project was initiated in 1965 as a five-year, $3.5 million program ($1.3 million funded by the UNDP). The scope of the project was subsequently expanded, the termination date was extended to 1971, and an additional budget of $0.4 million was granted. See ONRA and UNDP/FAO, "Preliminary Report on the Area of the Project Development of the Central Huallaga, Chiriyacu and Nieva River Basins" (Lima, 1966, mimeo.).

Table 22. Land Survey Program for the Huallaga Central Project

Survey	(*hectares*) Area
Aerial photography at 1 : 40,000	2,110,000
Aerial photography at 1 : 20,000	765,000
Controlled photo mosaics at 1 : 40,000	2,110,000
Geomorphological photo maps at 1 : 40,000	2,110,000
Mosaics at 1 : 20,000	630,000
Topographic maps at 1 : 10,000	280,000
Cadastral maps	19,336[a]
Soil map at 1 : 100,000	2,110,000
Soil studies at 1 : 10,000	280,000
Reconnaissance forest survey at 1 : 500,000	3,000,000
Forest inventory at 1 : 20,000	128,000
Forest management plan	128,000
Detailed agricultural development plan	280,000

Source: UNDP/FAO, Huallaga Central Project, Tarapoto, Peru.

[a]Properties.

sierra on new lands in the region. After the project got under way it was discovered that if tenancy and production were rationalized for the existing 28,000 settlers[10] on the 400,000 ha suitable for agriculture (giving an average of 14 ha per family) there would be little or no land available for new settlers. The original survey, however, had indicated a potential for 10,000 new colonists.

The project is in sharp contrast to the Bolivian colonization venture, which lacked a general reconnaissance survey to aid in the selection of areas for settlement and adequate natural resource surveys at the project level. There can be little doubt that such deficiencies will be remedied in the Huallaga Central region. But is there justification for study expenditures amounting to $140 per potential colonist, or $10 per hectare of agricultural land? It may be argued that the studies will have impact far beyond the 28,000–30,000 farm families affected in terms of forest and agricultural industries, other resources, and urban development. Full justification rests on the probability and timing of development in the region, the extent to which development can be directly attributed to the studies, and the degree to which the experience will contribute to the design of future surveys adapted to the critical requirements for effective implementation of a development plan.

An alternative to these costly studies would be a phased approach. Since the Huallaga Central Project is itself a second phase, the question may be asked: Was the original survey sufficiently detailed or should intermediate phases have been undertaken? In view of the findings of the second phase,

[10]Eleven thousand with title, 11,000 with titles pending, and 6,000 in precarious occupancy.

the margin of error in the first phase was probably too great to justify a decision on a step involving $4 million, since the new settlement capacity (which largely motivated the second phase) is now considered to be perhaps 5-10 percent of the original estimate. The colonization consolidation objectives that evolved from the second survey are perfectly acceptable and may be of high priority, but the fact that they bear little relationship to the original new settlement objectives suggests that study programming could have been more systematic.

A major problem encountered in the Huallaga Central, and which is common to many tropical settlement projects, is the rationalization of land tenure. The cadastral survey, the resettlement of 28,000 families, and titling, will be a herculean task. What criteria will be used to establish the minimum farm unit? How will the expensive soil surveys be used in this operation? Is a soil map of scale 1:10,000 sufficient to determine cropping patterns, management practices, and the boundaries of a minimum-sized lot? Is the establishment of legal tenancy a prerequisite to the implementation of any agricultural development program or new colonization? What will a cadastral survey cost?

The thesis has been advanced that the crucial issue in agricultural development of the Huallaga Central is prices, which in turn depend on markets—i.e., attractive product prices will elicit production, and inputs such as fertilizer and machinery will be used at the "right" price. The lack of road access has resulted in low product prices and high input costs. The regional economy has been insufficient to generate demand for agricultural products or to warrant the local manufacture of inputs. Moreover with improved price conditions, farm access roads, a workable land tenure law, and credit granted in support of such a law, the demand for land will rise. Spontaneous colonists will bring pressure to bear on existing owners to intensify. Under these conditions the occupants of the land would have substantial incentive to rearrange property boundaries and establish title within the constraints of the law.[11]

Precision of Resource Data. The question of costs and of the detail of resource information is brought into sharp focus by the Huallaga Central Project. In determining the resource potential, surveys may be undertaken at various levels of precision—exploratory, reconnaissance, semidetailed inventories, and detailed studies.[12] Data are presented in table 23 to illustrate a typical range of costs that apply to gathering resource data in humid tropical areas. Costs rise sharply as the scale of mapping increases.

Given the objectives and the course of the Huallaga Central Project, one might ask whether such projects should be undertaken sequentially across the

[11] Discussion with Fernando Rozensweig, economist for UNDP Huallaga Central Project.

[12] Estevam Strauss, "Algunos aspectos de la investigación y explotación de recursos naturales en América Latina relacionados con la planificación económica," pt. 1 (Santiago, Chile: ILPES, July 1965, mimeo.), p. 11.

Table 23. Estimated Range of Costs of Natural Resource Surveys in
Humid Tropical Lowland Areas

(dollars per square kilometer)

Type of Survey	Scale	Cost		
		Low	High	Average
Aerial photography[a]	1 : 40,000	1	3	2
	1 : 20,000	3	8	6
	1 : 10,000	5	25	15
Topographic mapping[b]	1 : 250,000	7	12	10
	1 : 100,000	15	25	20
	1 : 25,000	20	60	35
Reconnaissance, soils capability	1 : 100,000	2	10	6
Semidetailed, soils capability	1 : 50,000	30	70	50
Detailed, soils capability	1 : 10,000	100	225	150
Reconnaissance, forest inventory	1 : 50,000	6	18	12
Forest inventory and development plan		50	500	100

Sources: Estimates based on data from Orris C. Herfindahl, *Natural Resource Information for Economic Development* (Johns Hopkins Press for Resources for the Future, 1969), pp. 55–74, and Huallaga Central Project.

Note: Surveys based on an area of approximately 2,000 square km.

[a]Excluding ground control. Cost varies significantly according to size and shape of area, distance of airport, and frequency of days suitable for photography.

[b]Twenty-meter contour intervals.

entire tropical forest frontier region of Latin America, or even in isolated virgin areas. Although it would be heresy to be against the accumulation of knowledge on the physical and human environment, the economist has the unenviable task of raising the issue of whether expected benefits from surveys of humid tropical lands are commensurate with costs. The Huallaga Central experience raises three fundamental considerations with respect to the justification of detailed data collection and planning:

1. The application of Hirschman's doctrine to the identification of those items in development that cannot be determined through previous study, i.e., where answers are found only in the actual process of development.[13]
2. The evaluation of the institutional capability of a government to implement even apparently flawless land tenure laws and detailed development plans.

[13]A. O. Hirschman, *Development Projects Observed* (Brookings Institution, 1967), pp. 128–59.

3. The identification of the political forces for and against the survey or plan to be undertaken and the potential influence of these forces on eventual action.

To venture an opinion that the Huallaga Central Project has a high probability of being uneconomic would be wholly unwarranted. The possibility of directly attributing future development to the project appears somewhat tenuous, but a number of important positive external effects may result from it, such as training and research that can be applied to other areas. Conceivably one result could be that no further projects of this nature will be mounted.

If the government is considering directed colonization or resettlement there may well be a case for expenditures in soil mapping to the level required for management planning, e.g., 1:5,000. The presumption is that through credit operations, control of land tenure conditions, or some other mechanism, the government can effectively influence the pattern of land use on each parcel. It is axiomatic that the value of soil mapping depends on how and by whom it is used. Given the type of colonists and the nature of agriculture under spontaneous settlement as well as the lack of institutional support that frequently prevails, there is doubt that an expenditure of $1.50 per hectare on a survey useful to the farmer will be justified.

If the government intends to influence land use at the farm level, it is only logical to take into account the size of the parcel in relation to the resource endowment and the proposed management program. Otherwise there is an automatic favoring of those with better lands or those permitted to grow the more profitable crops. In the La Chontalpa project the requisite degree of control is being exercised. On other projects detailed programming of production and subdivision according to soil capability has not been attempted except for consolidated plantation areas. In fact on most projects only two classes of land are identified—crop and pasture—with the assumption that returns per hectare from crops will be three to five times those from pastures. Within each class, parcels are generally of identical size. This probably provides the closest approach to equity, given the high cost of detailed soil mapping required and the unknowns regarding the selection of crops, prices, and technology that may well change the order of profitability of different soil classes over time; and the motivation, management ability, and capital resources of the individual colonist.

What indicators are available to guide policy on gathering resource information as a basis for future decisions to open new lands in the humid tropics? Turning first to the level of information required to identify promising development opportunities, there already is a considerable body of knowledge on virgin areas in Latin America. This is evidenced by the systematic compilation of topographic, climatic, geologic, and soils data by FAO as the basis for the soil map of South America.[14] Some of this knowledge is held by pioneer colonists, speculators, and land developers. The systematic assemblage and verification of the information may well provide valuable insights into resource potential. In addition there are a significant number of detailed studies that, combined with more general data available, increase understanding of the potential range of resource capabilities in unsurveyed areas. Using this approach, Holdridge has developed an inexpensive technique to measure a minimum number of parameters as a basis for mapping vegetation and land capability.[15] Plath also has used simple procedures for making estimates of land capability from sparse physical data.[16]

Ivinheima, which appears to be a highly successful project, was selected and is being developed without any formal resource survey. It was first identified because it was the only large area of virgin forest in southern Mato Grosso. Preliminary observations from the air indicated an acceptable proportion of lands suitable for intensive colonization. The natural resource elements of the decision depended on local knowledge; comparison of the topography with adjacent developed areas in the state of Paraná; the use of certain trees as indicators of good, bad, or poorly drained soils; and spot checking of soils and commercial timber species. A similar situation characterized the spontaneous expansion of settlement in the La Lana-La Trinidad basin. These examples support the thesis that further general surveys are often unnecessary if the objectives are clear and a systematic appraisal is made of available data on resources and location.[17] Illustrating simple and effective resource identification, they are in sharp contrast to the formal surveys of Yapacani and Chimoré where serious errors were made.

Since one can say with a reasonable degree of confidence that the greater part of the humid tropical lands of the region will not be developed in this century (FAO estimates that 6 percent of the potential cropland will be exploited by 1985),[18] systematic resource surveys on a grid system or by province are unlikely to be justified in economic terms. The chances are slim that surveys will reveal some hitherto undreamed of block of fertile land or valuable timber stand. In the Huallaga Central it was found that the best lands

[14]K. J. Beek, *Soil Map of South America 1:5,000,000*, FAO/UNESCO Project, World Soil Resources Report no. 18 (Rome: FAO, 1965), pp. 6–12.

[15]L. R. Holdridge, *Life Zone Ecology* (San José, Costa Rica: Tropical Science Center, 1967).

[16]C. V. Plath, *Uso potencial de la tierra, informe a los gobiernos de: Costa Rica, El Salvador, Guatemala, Honduras, Nicaragua, Panama* (Rome: FAO, 1966).

[17]In a letter to the author, September 29, 1971, Paul I. Mandell of Stanford University pointed out that "there has been absolutely no significant surveying in the important Triángulo Minero, Southern Goiás and Southern Mato Grosso areas that in any way affected development."

[18]FAO, *Indicative World Plan for Agricultural Development to 1975 and 1985, South America*, vol. 1 (Rome, 1968).

had already been identified and settled. Surveys such as the $8 million program in eastern Bolivia must be justified by objectives other than new-land development—on strategic grounds or on the expectation of immediately exploitable minerals. If, as a result of these investigations, roads are built to give access to frontiers or mines, the investment clearly contributes to new-land development, but this must be viewed as a by-product and not as a basic justification of the original survey. The assertion that such surveys are multipurpose serves to cloud the issue unless the expected benefits from various sources are at least identified.

If it is accepted that opening up new lands in the region on an extensive scale is improbable over the next thirty years, a suggested approach to decisions on expansion of the tropical agricultural frontier is:

1. Approximate the amount of new agricultural land that may be needed, e.g., it has been estimated that the maximum new-land requirement in the Peruvian selva by 1990 will be 1.7 million ha.[19]
2. From existing data, estimate where such lands may be available, giving particular emphasis to areas that are adjacent to existing settlements and to penetration roads.
3. Retain flexibility to take advantage of any new possibility for new-land development that may be offered by highways or new population centers stemming from regional developments in minerals, forestry, or energy; e.g., the Transoceánica Highway in eastern Ecuador that is expected to be built by an international petroleum consortium to give access to oil fields 300 km from any existing road or settlement.[20]
4. Any resource studies that are undertaken should be carefully prescribed and restricted to areas that are believed to have potential on the basis of a screening of available data.

This conservative procedure is governed by two factors. First, since it is likely that suitable areas for development will be dispersed, general surveys would produce information on vast areas that have little possibility of exploitation. Second, since the areas expected to be developed in the immediate future will be small (2–3 million ha per year) in relation to available unexploited lands (perhaps 700 million ha), it would be easy to collect data prematurely.

The accumulation of detailed information about natural resources that have no immediate prospect of development constitutes a serious misuse of

[19] Estevam Strauss, *Reestructuración del espacio económico Latinoamericano* (Santiago, Chile: ILPES, May 6, 1969), p. 47.

[20] The project's 413 km of new highway will give access to Puerto Putamayo on the Putamayo River, which is a navigable tributary of the Amazon. See Comisión Mixta Ecuador-Brazil, Subcomisión Técnica de Transportes, *Via Interoceánica* (Quito, Ecuador, 1966).

scarce investment funds. It is to be assumed that survey techniques will be improved, permitting greater precision and lowered unit costs. In the future, information may be required on items that are now considered to have no commercial value. The data may become obsolete, the forest inventory may have to be redone, or the soil survey may no longer be useful because of changes in markets, the technology of soil management, or transportation. In any case the unused information represents an idle investment that would have had a higher earning capacity in other alternatives.

For instance in 1966 Bolivia initiated an extensive general survey program in the humid tropics for mapping 490,000 square km of the eastern tropical lowlands over a seven-year period at a cost of $8.5 million ($17 per square kilometer).[21] If no development takes place in eastern Bolivia prior to 1982 that may be directly attributed to the survey, and assuming the opportunity cost of capital to be 15 percent, the loss to the economy in income forgone would amount to $32 million. In addition there would be the extra costs or losses due to collecting data in 1972 that will not be applicable in 1982, collecting additional data in 1982 on items that may be unknown or thought to be valueless in 1972, and the expected cheaper techniques for obtaining the same degree of precision by 1982. This is not to discredit the value of research in tropical forestry, soils, hydrology, and wildlife to enhance the supply of knowledge that can be applied to specific areas as the need arises.

Where project identification surveys are concerned there are compelling reasons to be cautious in the extensive use of procedures listed in table 23 that may cost $5 to $10 per square kilometer even for minimal reconnaissance-level inventories. The extent to which the government should reduce the degree of uncertainty about tropical land and forest resources is conditioned by the expectation of when and how development will take place and the source of labor, capital, and enterprise needed. The relevant issue is: In the light of available experience, how much better are the returns on capital invested in new-land development than on marginal alternative opportunities in the achievement of social and economic development goals? Ideally the approach is the equation of costs and benefits. If the expected internal rate of return (IRR) on a particular survey investment is higher than the opportunity cost of capital, there appears to be no reason not to undertake it unless some even more attractive prospects were offered. The quantification of variables is not feasible, however; thus as an aid to public policy it is necessary to fall back on cost effectiveness, i.e., certain goals must be established regarding how much new land will be needed in production over a five- or ten-year period. The information flow would then be organized so that priority areas sufficient to meet the targets could be identified within an acceptable margin of error and at minimum cost.

[21] The program includes aerial photography, magnetic survey, triangulations and levels, gravity measurement, some photo interpretation, field classification, and preparation of topographic maps at 1:50,000 with 20–meter contours.

If this approach is adopted the project would become the principal focus of resource surveys. These surveys could be progressively more detailed until the decision maker would be satisfied that the margin of error had been reduced to the point where he could either proceed with development investment or abandon the project. There would be two types of data: those that are essential prerequisites to any decision—data on soils, flooding, and climate would fall in this category—and those whose incremental refinement improves the basis for decision by reducing the expected margin of error, e.g., data on economic and social aspects.

The sequence of data collection is illustrated in figure 4. The investment OA is accumulation of data to point X where probabilities of a successful project are sufficient to warrant selection of the area as a priority for more detailed investigation. Additional expenditures AB are made in requisite natural resource data. In figure 4 the survey is considered indivisible, i.e., until the investment AB has been made there is no improvement in the basis for decision. At that point, however, there is step XY, and a decision must be made on accumulation of further data. Due to the wide confidence limits inherent in the social science data, it is unlikely that further refinement of the physical data will be warranted. If it is required it will probably again be of the step type. The principal latitude for flexibility in resource data collection is in the reduction or expansion of the geographic area.

In figure 4 cost per hectare has been taken as an index of data volume and quality. Undoubtedly there are difficulties in generalizing on this basis since location, economies of scale, the amount of data already on hand, the quality of personnel, and the new techniques available will have a significant impact on unit costs for a given level of precision. The Bolivian piedmont area is an example. In the early 1960s when the soil surveys of the Alto Beni, Chimoré, and Yapacani areas were undertaken there were no aerial photos available, and the costs were in the range of $40 to $50 per square kilometer. As indicated earlier, from hindsight the margin of error in the surveys on Yapacani and Chimoré must be judged unacceptable. In 1966-67 a survey was made of the whole piedmont area but with the benefit of the original surveys, local experience accumulated between 1962 and 1967, aerial photos taken in the course of petroleum exploration, and personnel capable of photo interpretation. The result was a cost of $2 to $3 per square kilometer for information that is likely to be considerably more reliable than the earlier surveys.

Three aspects of land settlement discussed later in this chapter bear on resource data collection—the slow rate at which the land is taken up by new settlers, the slow rate at which the individual parcels are developed, and economies of scale associated with the integrated development of large contiguous areas. The point here is that the preliminary screening should result in the selection of large areas where a high proportion of the land is expected to

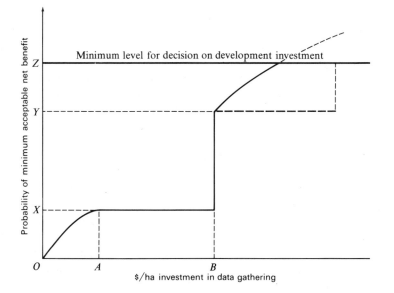

Figure 4. Illustration of the data accumulation and costs for an investment decision in tropical land development. Net benefits expressed as present value =

$$\sum_{i=1}^{n} (1 + r)^{-1} B_i$$

where B_i is the expected net benefit in year i per ha of gross area surveyed.

be suited to intensive development, and subsequent detailed resource surveys should be phased according to the expected scheduling of settlement so that data are not collected on areas that may not be occupied for five or ten years or on areas where sufficient local knowledge will be accumulated before settlement to preclude the need for additional surveys.

Feasibility Studies

It has been mentioned that survey programs are conditioned by the expectation that the resources identified will have sufficient economic value within a time period (allowing for discounting) to justify the investment. Thus there is an implicit interrelationship between the physical and economic aspects throughout the process of identifying investment opportunities in land resource development. But economic rather than physical attributes will generally govern the initial screening of areas, particularly with respect to location. At some stage after the resource survey it becomes necessary to establish engineering estimates of infrastructure investment and maintenance costs. On the fourteen colonization projects listed in table 24, highways accounted for 56 percent of the public investment (excluding credit to colonists). Consequently the accuracy of these estimates is critical to any projection of economic return. Indications are that problems associated with highway construction and maintenance have not been well understood. As a result project estimates tend to be substantially below actual investments in construction and above actual expenditures for maintenance.

A lack of reliable rainfall data makes it difficult to estimate drainage requirements. This, combined with rough terrain covered by dense forest, poses difficult problems for the cost estimator. On one section of the Carretera Marginal de la Selva the contractor spent more than $1 million over the budget merely to clear slips from the completed portion in order to maintain supplies for the machinery and crews working at the roadhead.

Construction problems on highway project 7 (part of which provides access to the Yapacani project) in northwestern Santa Cruz, Bolivia, exemplify those that can arise in the humid tropics. The original budget was $6.1 million—an estimate based on two passes with machinery to consolidate semi-dry fill. In fact twelve passes were required to consolidate wet fill. Unskilled labor cost 80 percent more than budgeted because of wage increases and the Bolivian law requiring severance pay equivalent to five months' salary. Down time during working hours was 37 percent—in nontropical areas the average runs 15 percent. The isolation of the highway project made it impossible to withdraw equipment for use in drier areas during the wet season. Isolation also made it necessary to carry a large inventory of spare parts, and what remained after completion of the contract had little value. As a result of these circumstances actual costs were about 80 percent over the budget.

Annual highway maintenance costs established by consulting engineers range from $260 to $1,000 per kilometer in the piedmont area of Bolivia. Actual expenditures in Ecuador and Bolivia in recent years have averaged from $60 to $125 in tropical areas.[22] The economics of low levels of maintenance is discussed under infrastructure; the essential point to be made here is the effect of these discrepancies between theory and practice on the feasibility study and investment decisions.

The feasibility study is dependent on improved resource and engineering data and on calculations to show the following:

---

[22]Tudor Engineering Company, *Estudio comparativo y analitico de las dos rutas propuestas de acceso al Valle del Rio Upano* (San Francisco, 1967), p. III-15; and the Dirección Nacional de Caminos, La Paz, Bolivia.

1. The land-clearing sequence.
2. Crop rotations.
3. The evolution of physical production on average parcels as the forest is replaced by annual or perennial crops and as the latter gradually reach maturity.
4. Production inputs such as unpaid family labor and hired labor and other items according to whether they originate in the region itself or elsewhere in the country or are imported.
5. Man-days per hectare per crop, labor distribution throughout the year, and man-land ratios.
6. Input and transport costs and projected markets and prices.
7. The distribution of projected production between reuse on the farm and home consumption and sales in the region or elsewhere in the country or exports.
8. The propensity of colonists to save and the consequent effect on reinvestment and credit requirements.

The question of the refinement of such estimates was discussed in chapter 4; brief reference is made to it here because these estimates are decisive in the findings of the feasibility study and at the same time are probably subject to the greatest margin of error.

The reader is referred to the discussion in chapter 5 of differences between actual and projected production and scheduling in the individual projects. There is no need to look further for evidence of the uncertainties associated with new-land development in the humid tropics—uncertainties created by a lack of knowledge on almost every facet of the problem—institutional, social, economic, and physical. Nor is it assured that the mounting of expensive preinvestment studies, such as that for the Rigoberto Cabezas settlement project on the Atlantic coast of Nicaragua ($500,000 to prepare a program for 4,500 colonists), will solve the problem.

Aside from the temptation to undertake extensive integrated surveys of virgin tropical areas to identify development possibilities, the lure of international loans provides a strong incentive to amass elaborate project feasibility reports containing multicolored maps, detailed projections of production and cash flows, and invariably favorable benefit-cost ratios. Glamour is endlessly associated with the "last frontier."

The importance of preinvestment studies is further emphasized when consideration is given to the sequence of events following their completion. It is rare to find negative recommendations; thus a project is launched on a "programmed" course whose velocity and direction depend on the influence of the government agency involved. An agency that has staked its prestige on a costly exercise—a natural resource survey or a feasibility study—will find it imperative to act on the findings if they are favorable. The more expensive

Table 24. Commitments of Public Funds in Fourteen Tropical Colonization Projects

($ thousand)

Project	Number of colonists[a]	Roads			Credit			Other activities	Total
		Trunk and access	Feeder	Total	Housing and subsistence[b]	Agriculture	Total		
				($ thousand)					
Alto Beni I		1,710	180	1,890	140	100	240	1,110	3,240
Alto Beni II		280	500	780	540	400	940	1,510	3,230
Bataan		0	0	0	60	520	580	1,440	2,020[c]
Cariari		220	330	550	260	950	1,210	460	2,220
Chimoré		5,200	580	5,780	450	400	850	810	7,440
Cihualtepec		270	0	270	180	170	350	400	1,020
La Chontalpa		0	28,400	28,400	2,790	23,000	25,790	31,310	85,500
La Joya		240	0	240	130	100	230	340	810
Nuevo Ixcatlán		340	0	340	380	330	710	720	1,770
Puerto Pdte. Stroessner		0	110	110	290	170	460	610	1,180[d]
Santo Domingo de los Colorados		0	1,350	1,350	1,120	1,280	2,400	1,050	4,800
Tingo María		8,920	2,210	11,130	4,590	9,380	13,970	5,200	30,300
Upano		3,150[e]	780	3,930	0[f]	1,230	1,230	840	6,000
Yapacani		5,500	470	5,970	750	340	1,090	1,820	8,880
Total		25,830	34,910	60,740	11,680	38,370	50,050	47,620	158,410

Unit cost per family ($)

	Number of farmers[a]								Total
Alto Beni I	520	3,290	350	3,640	270	190	460	2,130	6,230
Alto Beni II	1,500	190	330	520	360	270	630	1,010	2,160
Bataan	600	0	0	0	100	870	970	2,400	3,370
Cariari	400	550	830	1,380	650	2,380	3,030	1,150	5,560
Chimoré	1,000	5,200	580	5,780	450	400	850	810	7,440
Cihualtepec	500	540	0	540	360	340	700	800	2,040
La Chontalpa	4,800	0	5,920	5,920	580	4,790	5,370	6,520	17,810
La Joya	285	840	0	840	630	350	980	1,190	3,010
Nuevo Ixcatlán	700	490	0	490	540	470	1,010	1,030	2,530
Puerto Pdte. Stroessner	1,200	0	90	90	240	140	380	510	980
Santo Domingo de los Colorados	12,000								
Tingo María	6,300	1,420	350	1,770	730	1,490	2,220	830	4,820
Upano	2,900	1,090	270	1,360	0	420	420	290	2,070
Yapacani	2,400	2,290	200	2,490	310	140	450	760	3,700
Total and average	35,105	730	990	1,720	330	1,090	1,420	1,360	4,500

Note: Based on revisions and adjustments in plans or actual expenditures to 1968.

[a] Includes total number of farmers (projected or in residence in 1968) within the project area. In Puerto Presidente Stroessner, Santo Domingo de los Colorados, Tingo María, Upano, and Yapacani many colonists are not direct beneficiaries in terms of credit and some "other activities," thus averages are misleading.

[b] Includes domestic water supply and food provided on credit through WFP.

[c] Excludes cost of land purchased by the government.

[d] Excludes value imputed to colonist labor.

[e] Includes estimate of $0.4 million for unbudgeted sections.

[f] Included in agricultural credit.

the study, the higher the pressures to recommend positive action will be. If the project is not implemented, the funds will appear to have been wasted.

Providing that the recommendations are well founded, the use of pressure to get action is admirable. But when the high percentage of favorable feasibility studies is set against evident discrepancies between expectation and practice and the dismal literature on the failure of tropical settlement, doubt is cast on the efficacy of the system. Where virgin humid tropical lands are concerned, there is a need to consider totally new products and production technology and new modes of organization, a consideration that increases the degree of risk and uncertainty associated with projects in these regions. This suggests a more cautious approach in project design, using such procedures as carefully staged development or pilot programs.[23]

Clientele

This discussion is restricted to the beneficiaries of government programs that are designed to achieve either the settlement of new lands or consolidation in frontier areas. The motivation for the program is a combination of production, employment generation, and income distribution. Programs oriented to medium- and large-scale cattle enterprises must be regarded as special cases of consolidation where the goal is exclusively production. In virtually all other instances the principal goal is employment generation, which is automatically related to income distribution in that those in need of employment are per se in the lower income brackets.

Aside from programs in Paraguay and Brazil, government colonization schemes in the humid tropics are explicitly designed to transfer people out of overpopulated depressed rural areas. The Bajo Aguan in Honduras was designed to accommodate excess population from the western highlands. Throughout the Andean region there have been over twenty government-sponsored settlements in the past twenty years whose objective was transmigration from the altiplano and intermontane valleys to the Orinoco and Amazon plains. Where consolidation of tropical settlement is the purpose, such as La Chontalpa or Tingo María, the zones selected are occupied by subsistence farmers who do not have title to their lands, and there is an expectation that peripheral areas can be opened for new settlement. The clientele for pioneer projects are generally landless peasants; occasionally they are displaced miners or marginal urban dwellers.

The selection of beneficiaries is political in nature. Two systems are employed universally: (1) applicants are screened by checking their qualifications against a list of prerequisites, or (2) settlers are recruited in specific geographic areas or from among special groups. The first system is more manageable, providing the campesinos have a reasonable expectation of bet-

[23]Herfindahl, *Natural Resource Information*, p. 199.

tering their position by migrating. This presupposes some mechanism for a flow of information on potential opportunities. In many cases sufficient subsidy is involved to make migration highly attractive, even if only on a temporary basis. The use of points to score the attributes of prospective colonists, developed in Malaysia, represents one of the most sophisticated applications of the screening system. The applicant is judged on four criteria: age, number of children, area of land already owned, and farming experience. He is graded on the basis of how many of a maximum of twenty-four points he is able to achieve (see table 25).

The second system is more likely to satisfy the political aspirations of administrators and has been attempted in most cases of directed colonization under pioneer conditions in Latin America. Settlers for the Quintana Roo and Río Candelaria projects in Mexico were recruited from restricted localities in the state of Chihuahua. The Peruvian government undertook the La Morada project in order to demonstrate the viability of migration of the marginal urban population from Lima to the tropical land frontier. The most formal efforts in recruitment have been made by the Bolivian government for settlement of the Alto Beni, Chimoré, and Yapacani projects. For example, the state tin mining corporation, Comisión de Estaño Boliviana, found it necessary to lay off workers in order to streamline its operations, and a target was set of locating 600 ex-miners on the projects. Promoters were sent out to communities on the altiplano with quotas to fill by stated dates. It is not surprising that extravagant promises were made in order to meet deadlines. Even if the real conditions had been fully explained by the promoters, it is

Table 25. Criteria-Weighting System for Settler Selection in Malaysia

Criteria	No. of points	Criteria	No. of points
Age of applicant		Area of land owned	
21	3	Less than 1 acre	5
22–24	5	1–2 acres	4
25–27	8	2–3 acres	3
28–30	10	3–4 acres	2
31–33	8	4–5 acres	1
34–36	3	5 acres plus	0
37–42	3		
43–45	1	Field experience	
Number of children		Rubber cultivation	4
		Oil palm cultivation	4
5	5	Vegetable cultivation	1
4	4	Animal husbandry	1
3	3		
2	2		
1	1		

Source: Federal Land Development Authority, *Conditions and Acceptance of Candidates to FLDA Schemes* (Kuala Lumpur, Malaysia, 1967).

hardly likely that the forty-eight Chipaya Indians—from a semidesertic zone at 13,000 feet on the Chilean border—who signed up for Yapacani could have had any conception of such a drastic change in environment.

The eligibility requirements for taking up new land on the Tingo María project illustrate some of the selection criteria. The prospective colonist must be a Peruvian citizen, be physically fit, have a knowledge of agriculture, hold no more than 2 ha of land elsewhere, and be eighteen to sixty years of age. He has a five-year grace period on land purchase; thereafter payments are to be made in twenty annual quotas including 2 percent interest. The land is inalienable for five years and in any subsequent sale the new buyer must fulfill the requirements listed above. Once the contract of sale is delivered the colonist is eligible for a maximum of $6,000 in credit over a four-year period. The land price charged by the government ranges from 50 cents per hectare for inferior land suited only to pasture to $15 for good-quality cropland. Since land prices in adjacent settled areas are two to three times this level and 2 percent interest is well below the commercial market, the conditions clearly favor new settlers. With adequate promotion a vigorous selection process could be enforced so that only those with the highest qualifications, or those most worthy for other reasons, would be accepted.

In both the Bolivian and Peruvian cases the system of selecting colonists from the altiplano, whether by screening or recruiting, has broken down in practice. The problem faced by the administrative agencies changed from alleviation of unemployment in the sierra to one of performance statistics. As justification for extensive public investments, it became necessary to show a more rapid occupation of the lands, more production, and a higher level of stability among settlers. To this end certain modifications were made in the rules and therefore in the clientele. Promotion was directed to attracting colonists from other tropical areas who would have prior knowledge of the living conditions and management practices. More spontaneous applicants were accepted regardless of their origin or other qualifications. Programs were changed or expanded to incorporate spontaneous settlements already in operation, i.e., pioneer programs were directed toward consolidation.

A number of conflicts are inherent in the identification of beneficiaries. In the first place there is the danger that by granting significant privileges to attract settlers to new lands an elite group may be created in an area whose periphery later becomes settled (or is already settled) by spontaneous subsistence farmers. It would be out of the question for the state to offer equal incentives on a massive scale. Justification must rest on the formation of a cadre that can demonstrate what can be done. On the other hand if a government program becomes associated with low levels of living for those who take up lands under its auspices, there is immediate concern over the unchecked expansion of subsistence agriculture without a positive attempt to use public money to break the vicious circle of stagnation in the rural sector.

The usual requirement that the beneficiary must live permanently on his farm and not own other lands poses a dilemma. The uncertainties in the minds of prospective settlers weigh heavily in their decisions and, in view of experience, are by no means unfounded. Understandably they are extremely reluctant to irrevocably cut all ties with their original means of livelihood. In spontaneous areas such as Caranavi this situation gives rise to the *pendulares*—those who simultaneously farm in the tropics and on the altiplano until they gain confidence and until the expected advantages of specialization are high enough to persuade them to opt for the lowlands.

A study of the Yapacani project in 1965 showed that 70 percent of the colonists had not felt sufficiently committed to the tropics to bring their families.[24] This type of instability may be perfectly normal in the process of settling frontier areas; the problem arises where public funds are used in the unproductive transfer of population. It has proved impossible to recoup these expenses. In order to balance the books the Bolivian government accumulated outstanding charges against the land—thus the new occupant of an abandoned lot was obliged to assume all the defaulted debts of his predecessors. Any attempt to enforce such a condition would have institutionalized instability and resulted in regular abandonment of properties as the loans fell due.

One report lists among the principles of successful settlement: "Selection of settlers who adapt readily to the new locale, can farm successfully, and can live harmoniously with other colonists."[25] Such a utopian situation may be difficult to approximate, and it is evident from experience in Mexico, Peru, and Bolivia that there is room for more flexibility in the choice of beneficiaries for programs aimed at extending the land frontiers.

There may be advantages in attracting capital and management into new areas—the 800-ha tea plantation of the Sociedad Ecuatoriana de Desarrollo Industria Agropecuaria (SEDIA) in eastern Ecuador, for example. The development of some medium-scale or even large-scale enterprises provides a supplemental labor market that is important to pioneers struggling to get established. The provision of wage employment whereby landless workers accumulate experience in the tropics may be a useful first step in creating independent producers. Sometimes larger operations serve to demonstrate management practices that small farmers are unwilling to risk untested.

If title to land is highly prized the authorities may impose certain conditions such as maximum or minimum size, residence, or level of exploitation, before granting title. The standardization of lot sizes at 10 or 15 ha of arable land has certain limitations. If frontier settlement is to be dynamic, those

---

[24] Richard W. Patch, "Aspectos sociales del programa de colonización CBF-BID en Bolivia (Lima, Peru: American Universities Field Staff, July 1965, mimeo.).

[25] Milton Jacobs, Alexander R. Askenasy, and Norita P. Scott, *Resettlement in Latin America: An Analysis of 35 Cases* (Center for Research in Social Systems, American University, April 1967), p. 10.

with the ability to develop land and to accumulate capital will abandon the region unless there is opportunity to rent, buy additional land, sell, and buy a larger property or develop more new land. Unless settlers see these possibilities they may not be attracted in the first place. This degree of flexibility seems to have been introduced by the Companhía Melhoramentos Norte do Paraná (CMNP) in their subdivision and settlement of over 1 million ha in lots ranging from 10 to 200 ha with an overall average of 33 ha. The conditions for the purchase of lots between 5 and 40 ha on the Ivinheima project provide another point of reference:

1. Payment of 40 percent of the price at the time of occupancy, with the balance due in three annual quotas.
2. Minimum development of 2 ha in the first year to avoid speculation.
3. Prohibition on purchases of adjoining property.

On all projects examined the recruitment of settlers has been a failure, the governments have not achieved their political objectives, and the dissatisfaction of those who felt they had been moved under false pretenses has been an unsettling influence in what were already fragile experiments in transferring population. A basic knowledge gap exists on the circumstances surrounding migration decisions and the phenomena that precipitate these decisions. The apparent immobility of the highland population, at least with respect to transfer to the humid tropics, presumably rests on a lack of information on alternatives or noneconomic factors.[26]

Experience in Bolivia illustrates the paradoxical situation arising from the interplay of recruitment programs; eligibility requirements; indebtedness; and the technical, economic, and institutional uncertainties inherent in tropical agriculture. To be eligible for a directed program a colonist must renounce his rights to other property, thus eliminating any element of insurance in a risky venture; he may become saddled with excessive debts and title to the new land is by no means assured. While the laws governing spontaneous colonization contain the same requirement, there is not the same automatic incurrence of debt. Furthermore, land may be held without any official declaration until viable exploitation has been tested. Thereafter, when the settler pays his survey fees to the Instituto Nacional de Colonización, title application may be initiated with reasonable assurance that it will be delivered in due course. Under such circumstances anyone who has land, feels some need for security, or has a sense of responsibility to repay loans would find little reason to elect directed rather than spontaneous settlement.

[26]For a discussion of these aspects see Craig L. Dozier, *Land Development and Colonization in Latin America* (Praeger, 1969); and Donald Sawyer, "Penetration Roads and Population Growth, Patterns of Migration and Settlement on the Belém-Brazília Highway" (Harvard University, March 1969, mimeo.).

Who then are the colonists who are recruited on the basis of quotas and deadlines? They are those who do not know or believe the conditions and obligations, are prepared to gamble on a remission of debts, have nothing to lose, or are in search of a change. A greater degree of stability is to be expected from settlers who take up virgin lands of their own volition rather than on the basis of exaggerated expectations.

It is frequently argued that if tropical settlement is to be viable the settler (1) must be granted sufficient land to yield an "acceptable" income when the land is fully developed, (2) must either be granted sufficient capital to clear the land rapidly or be granted land cleared by the government prior to distribution, and (3) must be supplied with sufficient capital and extension and marketing services to enable management to approach optimum efficiency. Aside from the management capability of the prospective colonists, institutional conditions governing production and marketing, and the definition of such terms as "acceptable income" and "optimum efficiency," one of the fundamental issues is how much indebtedness the producer can support, assuming he has no resources of his own—a typical situation faced by colonists in directed and semidirected government settlement programs in Latin America. (This is discussed later under credit and capitalization of agriculture.)

In appraising policy on colonist selection, it is well to ask: What is the advisability of undertaking tropical land development under difficult conditions of technical production and marketing, when recruited colonists lack resources and experience in tropical agriculture and decision making, and when recuperation to be expected from direct beneficiaries probably does not exceed 10-20 percent of the government investment?

The shortcomings inherent in the system of deliberate colonist selection are the risk of excessive incentives creating a small privileged group, the need for surveillance after settlement to ensure compliance, and the likelihood of abuse in both the selection and subsequent monitoring. There is a need to clearly establish the objectives of land settlement so that the amount of migration required or expected can be estimated. Once this is determined the incentives and selection criteria can be systematically evaluated. If objectives were established the state would be in a position to apply eligibility criteria in the selection of spontaneous colonists, to seek the transfer of predetermined groups identified by region or class, to impose restrictions on farm size or to require collective action, and to establish the total new area to be exploited consistent with population transfer goals. Implementation will require consideration of the mechanisms for identifying and qualifying spontaneous colonists, for determining the feasibility of transferring whole communities in order to achieve stability or communal enterprise, and for providing ancillary employment in new areas and determining how access to this employment may be achieved.

Relocation of a selected clientele through directed or semidirected colonization over the past twenty years in the Latin American tropics probably has involved not more than 40,000 families; assistance has been given to perhaps an equal number already occupying lands within project areas—a total population of 400,000–500,000. In 1970 the rural population of the countries in which these programs have been undertaken was 109 million (about 70 million in the subsistence sector), an increase of 25 million over the twenty-year period. Thus colonization affected only 0.5 percent of the total, or 2 percent of the increase, in rural population over the period and cannot be regarded as having made any significant contribution to rural welfare.

Infrastructure

For the purposes of this discussion infrastructure is regarded as government investments in physical structures for communication or the provision of productive and social services to the population in new areas. Typically these investments include civil works such as highways; drainage and irrigation; utility systems in urban areas; and public buildings to house such services as health, education, police, banking, extension, research, land titling, municipal government, or project administration. It is evident that beyond this point there is a gray area where physical facilities covering the whole range of housing, rural utilities, community centers or recreation, commercial services (retail outlets, warehouses, machine shops, hotels, canteens, etc.), and industry may be financed publicly or privately. No single project has involved public investment in every one of the infrastructure categories, but taking the projects studied as a whole, public funds have been applied directly or indirectly to all of the categories. Thus they must be included in an evaluation of public policy.

It is necessary, however, to make a clear distinction between those items that the state (or a private development entity like the Sociedade de Melhoramentos e Colonizaçaõ) must finance as a general rule in order to accelerate expansion of the land frontier and those that may be financed by private interests with or without some form of government subsidy. Much of the discussion of the viability of tropical land development and the proper role for government hinges on this division of financing and capital formation. The fundamental questions facing the government decision maker are (1) the quality, quantity, timing, sequence, and range of infrastructure facilities that must be provided with public funds; and (2) who must be expected to pay. In most of the pioneer zones studied the only private funds forthcoming for infrastructure in the early years were essentially in the form of labor for the construction of houses; water supply; or community projects such as roads, bridges, and schools, plus minimal outlays for retail establishments. Notable exceptions are the full-range infrastructure built by land development and plantation companies and private investment in penetration routes for mineral exploration, e.g., oil in the case of Caquetá and Puyo-Tena and manganese in the case of the 200-km railroad from Pôrto Santana to Serra do Navio, Amapá.

In the consolidation phase autonomous private investment is to be expected in commercial activities, in forestry and agricultural processing (e.g., Caranavi), and in accelerated community activities such as the construction of 120 km of feeder roads by the colonists in the La Lana–La Trinidad basin between 1954 and 1967. In some countries effective local government may be permitted to develop with the power of taxing and investing within its area of jurisdiction, e.g., Ivinheima. The type of urban infrastructure developed in the case of Londrina on the area opened up by the CMNP represents a final stage of private investment and local government activity.

Highways

In both directed and semidirected settlement projects, roads are the major public investment item, averaging 38 percent for the fourteen projects listed in table 24.[27] The allocation of these costs is a major source of ambiguity in project analysis. The essential distinction is between access or trunk roads, which may not be chargeable entirely to land development, and feeder roads, which normally must be justified by agricultural and forestry development. Highways, transport costs, and new-land development are interdependent. The issue is not whether to build roads but, having selected an area, how far should they reach, how fast should they be built, to what standard should they be constructed and maintained, and what complementary investments are required?

Access Roads–The Carretera Marginal de la Selva. Map 11 shows the existing and planned highways oriented to penetration of the virgin tropical lands of South America. Seven of the colonization projects discussed in chapter 5 are served by the proposed Carretera Marginal de la Selva. It is readily apparent on map 11 that this 5,500-km road does not open up the great virgin heartland of the enormous continent but looks more like a coastal highway. Nevertheless this project has gained much more attention as the potential dynamo of jungle development than the radial system of roads emanating from Brasília that is planned to penetrate the remotest corners of the region.

An expenditure of $350 million for the highway and $140 million for colonization and other development programs is expected to result in the settlement of 1.6 million people, with the incorporation of 7.4 million ha of virgin land[28] yielding an annual agricultural output of $134 million at full

---

[27]Excluding special credit for the colonists in these projects, highways account for 56 percent.

[28]FAO estimates call for 39 million ha to be cleared from forest over the twenty-three-year period 1962–85 (see table 3).

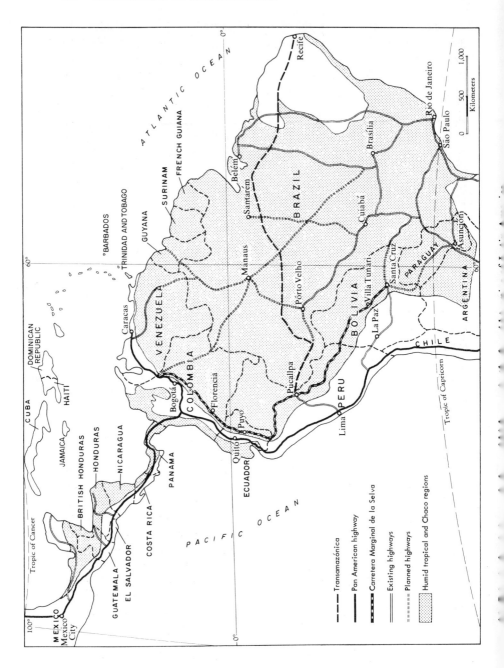

Transamazónica

Pan American highway

Carretera Marginal de la Selva

Existing highways

Planned highways

Humid tropical and Chaco regions

production.[29] If these estimates are accepted and a ten-year construction period with a further ten-year lag in reaching full production (where value added is 80 percent of gross output) is assumed—the project may be regarded as justified with an internal rate of return of 13 percent. Aside from these direct benefits many other positive aspects are attributed to the highway—it "opens to penetration the largest undeveloped tropical areas in the world," makes possible a more balanced economic growth process and political integration, and "lays the basis for a more effective common market. . .[with] long-run influence upon the attainment of peace and understanding."[30]

Economics is known as the dismal science; true to form, the question arises: How sanguine can one be about the probabilities of realizing these projections? Hirschman[31] argues convincingly that if the analyst becomes too preoccupied with such matters few projects would be initiated, and it is probable that imaginative projects (which the Carretera Marginal undoubtedly is) would never see the light of day. Nevertheless, in view of tropical land development experience, some further examination of the project's justification may be warranted. Given transference of population to the tropics as the objective of the four countries concerned, is the construction of this highway the most effective use of resources to achieve this end? The highway is located to minimize the distance between the projects and existing centers of population. But it does not follow that transport costs from a specific area served to a major market will be less than if the road penetrated farther into the Amazon plain.

Integrated development of the tropical lands has been stressed; in the case of the Carretera Marginal distance from current market centers has been subordinated to the quality and combination of natural resources. There is no reason to believe that the most promising resources in each country are made accessible. In the case of Bolivia the most appropriate lands for settlement lie to the east of the proposed alignment.[32] Distance should not be correlated automatically with freight rates and the ability of areas to compete for markets—the level of management, natural resources, the market structure, and the highway standard all enter in. For example, rice from Santa Cruz in Bolivia is hauled 900 km to La Paz and can compete in the market with rice from the Alto Beni, which is only 200 km from La Paz. The freight rate from Santa Cruz is 5 cents per ton-kilometer, or $45 per ton; from the Alto Beni it is 8 cents per ton-kilometer, or $16 per ton. The ability of Santa Cruz to

[29]Charles J. Stokes, *Transportation and Economic Development in Latin America* (Praeger, 1968), p. 116.

[30]Ibid., p. 115.

[31]A. O. Hirschman, *Development Projects Observed*, pp. 130–31.

[32]T. T. Cochrane, *Land Systems Map of Central Tropical Bolivia*, Ministerio de Agricultura, British Tropical Mission (Santa Cruz, Bolivia, 1967), p. 3.

overcome the differential must be attributed to the conditions of production and marketing.

What are the probabilities that the costs and benefits will be as projected? Under the assumptions made above about 200,000 farm families would have an average of 37 ha in production with a gross annual output of $700 on reaching full capacity. Project experience indicates that the gross output per family is readily attainable, though there is considerable doubt that 37 ha could be maintained in production without major changes in technology that would raise production, investment, and inputs. (Mention has been made of the uncertainties with respect to sustaining yields.) The migration of 1 million to 1.2 million people over a twenty-year period appears reasonable, but considerable uncertainty surrounds the availability of 7.4 million ha of suitable land and whether it can be made accessible and brought into full production with a public investment of $500 million, i.e., $65 per ha. Estimates for colonization projects in the Andean piedmont area discussed in chapter 5 range from $100 to $400 per ha.[33]

The highway unquestionably would influence national integration, but since about three-quarters of the eastern tropics in the four countries concerned would remain unserved by roads, the possibility exists that an alternative highway pattern might contribute more to this objective. The principal cargo originating along this route will be tropical agricultural and forest products common to all areas. Thus significant international trade is unlikely.[34]

It is evident that the Carretera Marginal was conceived without regard to alternatives or to any national or multinational development strategy. The fact that it is a highly imaginative and ambitious project and that it is directed toward the mobilization of idle resources may account for its appeal. The existence of the highway feasibility study in itself has focused the attention of ministries of public works in the various countries. Thus a chain reaction is set in motion and scarce capital is directed not only to the road, but also to supporting projects such as colonization—and neither the road nor the projects may be in the best interests of economic development or political integration in the individual countries. This evidently has been the case in Bolivia where major resources have been diverted to highway construction and colonization oriented around the Carretera Marginal alignment to the exclusion of promising land resources in northern and eastern Santa Cruz.[35] The role of transportation (not only highways, but also their integration with fluvial and air modes) in opening new lands is susceptible to evaluation

---

[33] Assuming the inclusion of all infrastructure, settlement costs, and credit and excluding the value of family labor. For a discussion of settler costs see the section in this chapter on costs and cost allocation.

[34] Montague Yudelman and Frederic Howard, *Agricultural Development and Economic Development in Latin America* (Washington: IDB, April 1969), p. 179.

[35] Cochrane, *Land Systems Map*, pp. 1–3.

through system models (linear programming, simulation, and so on) that permit consideration of possible outcomes from a wide range of alternatives, plus sensitivity analysis where reliable data are scarce.[36] The application of this technique to the 160 million ha making up the eastern tropical regions of Colombia, Ecuador, Peru, and Bolivia might have resulted in a configuration of development different from that expected from a proposed expenditure of $500 million.

If the Carretera Marginal is in fact of questionable priority for the development of new lands and Latin American integration, what then are the attributes of access road projects that should have priority? The answer depends more on the objectives for national and international integration and for the populating of the unoccupied jungle hinterland than on the economics of new-land development. Projections of the food, fiber, and forestry products that will be required from this region in the next few decades are insufficient to justify massive investment in penetration highways.[37] The existence of a resource complex that may result in an urban growth pole must be regarded as the exception. Nevertheless recent studies show that a $118 million investment over a three-to-five year period in 3,780 km of trunk highways in the central western Brazilian Amazon region is economically feasible.[38] Another example is the recently announced 5,300-km Transamazónica, with 3,500 km of new construction to be associated with opening up 7 million ha of new land.[39] One is left with the impression that infeasibility is impossible and that the number of highways that could crisscross the Amazon and Orinoco basins is unlimited.

Feeder Roads. Feeder roads tend to be neglected in programs to open up new lands since trunk roads carry more political appeal. In most of the major trunk road programs, such as the Trans-Chaco, Brazília-Acre, Puyo-Tena, Huánuco-Pucallpa and Brazília-Belém, feeder roads have received little attention. In many areas there is no urgency for additional penetration roads; the requirement is consolidation and expansion of settlement in areas already served by highways such as those listed above.

On colonization projects financed by the Inter-American Development Bank, feeder roads are an important element. The most concentrated network

[36]Wilfred Owen, *Distance and Development* (The Brookings Institution, 1968), p. 74. As an example, see Roy E. Lave and Donald W. Kyle, *A System Study of Transportation in Northeast Brazil*, Institute of Engineering–Economic Systems (Stanford University Press, March 1966).

[37]Robert T. Brown, *Transport and the Economic Integration of South America* (The Brookings Institution, 1966), p. 225.

[38]Transcon-Berger, Inc., *Transport Master Plan for the State of Amazonas* (1968), pp. 481–83; and Baker Wibberley and Associates, Inc., *Technical and Economic Feasibility Report, Brazil-Peru Highway* (1966), pp. 259–78.

[39]Fernando Morais, Ricardo Gontijo, and Roberto de Oliveira Campos, *Transamazónica* (São Paulo: Editora Brazilienese, 1970).

is on La Chontalpa—0.7 km per 100 ha at a cost of $225 per hectare of agricultural land. In more extensive development for cattle and cropping, such as the Valle del Upano, farm access roads amounted to 0.2 km per 100 ha. Farm-to-market roads in Europe and the United States average about 2.5 km per 100 ha; in Taiwan, 1.8 km; in the Philippines, 0.6 km; and in Malaysia, 0.4 km.[40] There is considerable scope for more systematic examination of the density and standard of feeder roads under pioneer, consolidation, or growth conditions and of the balance between penetration and feeder roads.

One of the principal problems of feeder roads is maintenance. The case of La Joya in Mexico illustrates the consequence of no maintenance in a humid tropical climate. The Papaloapan Commission abandoned the 12-km road in 1960 and within two years the road was impassable. This case also highlights an additional problem in many countries—the inability of local organizations or municipalities to undertake maintenance operations. It is likely that distant sparsely populated frontier areas will receive little attention from the central government. Only three of the tropical countries of Latin America have any significant decentralization of public expenditure. In Brazil the central government controls 60 percent of public expenditures; Colombia, 70 percent; and Ecuador, 80 percent. In the remainder the average is 90-95 percent. In these same three countries, municipalities handle 10-20 percent of all public monies; elsewhere the figure is 2-3 percent.[41]

In pioneer areas it is unlikely that social organization will have progressed to the stage of forming a municipality; even if it has, resources available for highway maintenace will be minimal. Thus if the central government is not actively concerned, feeder roads are likely to deteriorate rapidly. Exceptions are: (1) Ivinheima, where municipal government was established four years after the first settlers arrived, and which is adequately financed to buy and operate its own highway equipment; and (2) San Juan in Bolivia and Filadelfia in the Paraguayan Chaco, where organized foreign settlers have shown themselves capable of both building and maintaining road networks with extra-national assistance. In Caranavi and the lower La Lana-La Trinidad basin colonists and logging interests collaborate in using local hand labor to construct and maintain feeder roads. This is an example of the oft promoted scheme of creating capital goods by using resources with a low or zero opportunity cost.

Highway Standards—The Yapacani Case. The derivation of highway standards in tropical forest frontier areas appears to be governed by three factors. The first is the probability that new economic opportunity will in fact be created by a highway, that there will be awareness of this potential, and that

[40] Owen, *Distance and Development*, p. 61.

[41] Walter Stohr, "Regional Development in Latin America: Experience and Prospects" (paper presented to the second Seminario Interamericano; Instituto Panamericano de Geografía e Historia, La Regionalización de las Políticas de Desarrollo en América Latina, Santiago, Chile, September 8-12, 1969), p. 30.

those exploiting the potential will have the required financial capacity and mobility. A related aspect is the elasticity of supply in response to transport cost savings and the extent to which reduced vehicle-operating costs will be reflected as increased prices to producers. A graphic example of the possible impact of all-weather access is provided by the production hopes the Mennonites at Filadelfia are staking on the 427-km Trans-Chaco highway—if the highway is paved. The whole output pattern would be changed toward high-value perishable items such as milk, eggs, pork, and broilers, with a higher proportion of value added in the zone; e.g., sausages and prepackaged meat and poultry, cheese, and butter. The projected increase in gross output in ten years is $10 million to $12 million (quadruple the 1968 level) with an investment by the Mennonite community of about $3.8 million in land clearing, water supply, processing plants, and power.[42]

Second, there is a need to understand the relationship between road standard costs and vehicle-operating costs, and between standard and investment costs plus subsequent maintenance costs. The institutional capability for highway construction and maintenance is crucial. Theoretically low-standard dirt roads may be perfectly serviceable with preventative maintenance and closure after rain. This has been demonstrated by the San Juan colonists whose average closure is thirty days annually. Similar procedures have been effectively followed on the Filadelfia settlement and by the Paraguayan army, which controls the use of the Trans-Chaco highway, where closure ranges from 120 to 150 days annually. Where this type of capability or discipline does not exist, a case may be made for construction to high standards with low maintenance to avoid either totally unserviceable roads or excessive investment in reconstruction.[43]

A third factor is the substitutability of highway investments by processing or storage facilities; for example, settlers in the Alto Beni II project suffered severe losses from mildewed and sprouted rice because they did not have all-weather access to drying plants in Caranavi. One alternative to an all-weather road in resolving this problem would be the installation of a drying plant on the project itself.

The Yapacani project serves as a good example for a discussion of the elements in deriving highway standards for colonization. In Yapacani 70 km of access highway were improved and paved, a major bridge was built to

---

[42] De Leuw, Cather and Company of Canada, Ltd., *Estudio de factibilidad para la Ruta Trans-Chaco* (Toronto, March 1969), pp. 71–78.

[43] For additional discussion of highway standards, see Ministerio de Obras Públicas, Dirección General de Vialidad, *Sub-programa de caminos vecinales—metodología* (Caracas, 1971); Kampsax, Inc., *Brazil Transport Survey, Highway Studies, Coordination of Studies, Principles, Methodologies, and Procedures*, vol. 12-B (Rio de Janeiro, 1969); IBRD, *Reappraisal of a Road Project in Iran*, World Bank Occasional Staff Papers no. 7 (Washington, 1968); Richard M. Soberman, *Economic Analysis of Highway Design in Developing Countries*, NAS-NRC, Highway Research Record no. 115 (Washington, 1966); and Arturo Israel, *Appraisal Methodology for Feeder Road Projects*, IBRD, Economics Department Working Paper no. 70 (Washington, March 1970).

replace a ferry on the boundary of the project, and 63 km of new arterial road and necessary feeder roads were to be constructed. Alternative standards of construction can be postulated for each of these three components as follows:

1. (a) Improve the 70-km access road to a 10-meter-wide asphalt surface at a cost of $1.8 million, with an annual maintenance cost of $25,000 and a transport cost of 2.7 cents per ton-kilometer (70-km haul = $1.69 per ton).

   (b) Maintain the access road at the present standard at a cost of $70,000 annually, with a transport cost of 5.7 cents per ton-kilometer (70-km haul = $4 per ton).

2. (a) Build the Yapacani bridge, budgeted at $910,000 with an annual maintenance cost of $20,000 (no toll and negligible vehicle-operating costs over the span).

   (b) Retain the existing ferry service with $2 per ton in charges, including freight transfer costs.

3. (a) Build the 63-km arterial highway to a specification of a 9-meter-wide gravel surface, including all structures—bridges, culverts, and drains—at $2.22 million plus $50,000 annual maintenance costs, with a transport cost of 6 cents per ton-kilometer (average haul of 30 km = $1.8 per ton).

   (b) Build the arterial highway to a 9-meter width with a 6-meter single bituminous surface treatment and the same structures as in (a) above at an investment of $2.44 million with an annual maintenance cost of $60,000 and transport costs of 2.5 cents per ton-kilometer (75 cents per ton for 30 km).

   (c) Build only structures at $625,000 and maintain the existing dirt road (first 40 km open ten months and the remaining 23 km open five months per year) at an annual cost of $110,000, with transport costs of 8 cents per ton-kilometer ($2.40 per ton for 30 km).[44]

4. It is assumed that the feeder roads will be built to the specifications in 3 (a) above regardless of the main road specifications. Thus feeder road investment is treated in the same way as any of the other associated development measures that must earn the opportunity cost of capital.

With the cost parameters above, twelve combinations of investment and transport service are available. Determination of the highest IRR on highway expenditures is given by solving the following equation for r:[45]

[44]TAMS, *Proposed Highway Yapacani to Puerto Grether and Yapacani Bridge*, prepared for AID and Ministerio de Economía (Cochabamba, Bolivia, April 1963).

[45]The more general formulation is given by:

$$\sum_{i=m}^{i=t} X_i^k (1 + r)^{-i} = \sum_{i=1}^{i=t} C_i^k (1 + r)^{-i}$$

$$\sum_{i=m}^{s-1} X_i^k (1 + r)^{-i} + \sum_{i=s}^{t} X_s^k (1 + r)^{-i} = \sum_{i=1}^{p} C_{c_i}^k (1 + r)^{-i}$$

$$+ \sum_{i=q}^{i=t} [C_{m_i}^k (1 + r)^{-i} + C_{q_i}^k (1 + r)^{-i}]$$

where

$X_i^k =$ value added in the area of influence in year i with highway combination k,

$m =$ first year with value added,

$s =$ year in which full production is reached. X_i^k beyond s is assumed constant at X_s^k. The values for X_i^k over the period m to $(s - 1)$ would be defined by a function or calculated by budget.

$r =$ discount rate,

$t =$ effective life of the project,

$C_{c_i}^k =$ construction cost of highway combination k in year i

$p =$ last year of highway construction,

$C_m^k =$ annual maintenance cost of highway combination k,

$q =$ first year maintenance is required,

$C_{q_i}^k =$ nonhighway costs associated with the development of X_i^k.

For purposes of this discussion C_q^k is assumed to be zero and the critical independent variable is X_i^k, which is a function of

$w =$ rate of settlement (families per year) $= 0$ after reaching X_s^k,

$x =$ rate of land clearing (hectares per family per year) $= 0$ after reaching X_s^k,

$y =$ average value of production (dollars per hectare),

$z =$ average value of inputs imported to the zone (dollars per hectare),

$A =$ the physical limitation on expansion of the area of influence.

In order to evaluate the transport implications it is necessary to define X_i in terms of physical freight inbound and outbound. If it is assumed that in-

---

where

$$C_i^k = C_c^k + C_m^k + C_q^k .$$

bound freight rates on production inputs have no influence on production, the focus becomes the volume of outbound freight (Q_k) with each highway combination k.

$$Q_k = \frac{Y_k - D_k}{P_k} \quad ,$$

$Y_k = X_i^k a =$ gross value of production

where

$a =$ gross value of production (sold or consumed by the owner's family or other farm labor) as a percentage of value added expressed in farm gate prices with highway combination k,

$D_k =$ gross value of on-farm consumption of farm products expressed in farm gate prices with highway combination k,

$P_k = (p - t_k)_n =$ weighted average farm gate price per ton of d products sold under highway combination k,

$p =$ average weighted price per ton of d products sold at the delivery point on the highway,

$t_k =$ freight rate per ton farm to market with highway combination k.

Aside from the development benefits assignable to the highway project (combination k) that have been assumed at X_i^k, there would also be user benefits and development benefits attributable to eventual through traffic on both the access and trunk road through the projects. If these development benefits are disregarded and no change in product proportions is assumed, the increase in production resulting from an incremental improvement from any highway combination k to any other highway combination k' depends on the price elasticity of supply ($E_{k-k'}$). This can be written

$$E_{k-k'} = \frac{\dfrac{Q_{k_i} - Q_k}{Q_k}}{\dfrac{P_{k_i} - P_k}{P_k}} = \frac{\Delta Q_k}{\Delta P_k}\left(\frac{Q_k}{P_k}\right).$$

Since project production is assumed to be small relative to the total market, p is assumed to be constant.[46] Transport services are assumed to be

[46] With large-scale development it would become necessary to take account of the price elasticity of demand that would govern the proportion of transport savings accruing to the consumer.

available under competitive conditions; hence any saving in transport costs is passed on to project farmers. In addition, aside from price influence, the transition from a seasonal highway (or one subject to intermittent closure) to an all-weather road may have an important impact on the type of products where perishables are involved.

When the issue is expressed in the form above the analyst is placed in the difficult position of having to attach numbers to a great many variables for which there is little or no corroborating statistical evidence. The question is whether the rate of return on the project investment is improved by adopting highway combination k' rather than k. If there is some doubt about the predictability of $E_{k-k'}$, as well there may be, aside from assigning a probability distribution to this parameter, consideration can be given to the phasing of construction leading to a higher total outlay per kilometer. On a present value basis, however, the cost may be less; even if it is more, the procedure could be justified by improving the chances of achieving an acceptable return.

Faith in the use of benefit-cost analysis as an aid in such decisions is not improved if account is taken of changes in projections or actual events during the first four years of the Yapacani project. The cost of the access road was 15–20 percent more than budgeted; an unplanned river control works together with additional spans almost tripled the cost of the Yapacani bridge and expected annual maintenance expenses. Sixty percent of the original planned settlement area was found unsuitable for intensive agriculture, and there was a corresponding reduction in the length of the arterial highway and the number of settlers. Also, the average annual rate of settlement on the original area was only 17 percent of the projected level. In spite of the unreliability of cost estimates and projected benefits from new-land development in the humid tropics, there is some value in applying the formula above. First, it forces consideration of alternatives and, second, it allows solution for the values that must be achieved for independent variables (excluding highway expenditures) if any given combination of the highway components is to break even.

In the formulas above, data for highway projects 3 and 7 (serving Yapacani) in Santa Cruz, Bolivia, have been substituted in order to calculate the break-even values for benefits (X_i) and the elasticity of supply $(E_{k-k'})$ as shown in table 26. In the table the area of influence (A) is assumed to be unconstrained, which is a violation of most project specifications where both A and the number of settlers are stipulated. The assumption could also be made that A is finite, and thus column 3 would reflect the increased yields required to justify incremental improvements in highway standards.[47] The

---

[47] If A is fixed the increasing yields force adoption of a functional relationship between a and Y_k rather than the constant assumed for calculations in table 26. Further, since sales (Q_k) involve both Y and D_k some assumption is required with respect to D_k. In table 26, D_k has been taken as a constant proportion of Y_k (20 percent), carrying the

essential point is that column 11 indicates the theoretical elasticities required if this justification is to be sought exclusively through a supply response from agriculture. Since an elasticity of 29 is patently impossible the project analyst is given an indication of the magnitude of user benefits or attributable non-agricultural development required to support a recommendation to move from k to k^1 (which corresponds to moving from combination A to combination B in table 26).

It is evident that a number of elements in the formulas require further examination. What is the scale variable with respect to $C_{c_i}^k$ that may suggest alternative design standards and construction schedules to satisfy budget constraints? How important is the level of gross sales (Y_k-D_k) as an incentive to settlement? Conceivably the investment in highways could be justified by home consumption (D_k) alone. What minimum service is required? Under alternative A there may be no settlement at all, and it is to be expected that the rate of settlement (w), individual rate of clearing (x), and product composition affecting y and z will vary with alternative standards. The area of influence (A) cannot be considered static. Certain highway services may induce autonomous investment by the colonists themselves to expand the feeder road network. The structure of the trucking industry may be such that little of the reduced vehicle-operating cost is reflected in tariffs.

In the case of the Yapacani project where $5.5 million, or 70 percent of the total public expenditure on the original area, eventually will be tied up in the bridge and trunk road, the principal issues are (1) to what extent production from the area served would be affected by bridge access as opposed to ferry service, and (2) to what other development the bridge and trunk road might be charged. Ferry service would be intermittent and additional transport cost represents 1-2 percent of the producer price for rice and 5-8 percent for bananas or yucca. The impact of all-weather access on the rate of settlement and land development, the extent to which transport cost savings would be passed on to the producers, and supply elasticity have not been evaluated. The case for charging the bridge and trunk road to other developments rests on the completion of the 110-km section to Puerto Villaroel, which would then provide an alternative link between Santa Cruz and Cochabamba with lower transport costs. It would also provide an outlet for cargo from the Mamoré River system to the Santa Cruz area and, theoretically, would open up additional lands for settlement. The misallocation of

---

implication that the supply response is achieved by attracting a greater number of settlers to an expandable project area. If A is fixed, then D_k is assumed constant, i.e., the same number of settlers increase output under more attractive price situations. The latter assumption would yield somewhat higher elasticities since the requirement in value added will be the same in each alternative, and since D_k is not increasing (as it would where D_k/Y_k is constant), total sales must increase faster in response to the same price changes.

Table 26. Estimated Benefits and Supply Elasticities Justifying
Alternative Highway Standards for the Yapacani Project

	(1)	(2)	(3)	(4)	(5)	(6)	(7)	(8)	(9)	(10)	(11)
	Highway costs		Value-added required to justify project $(X_i^k)^a$	Required gross value of sales $(Y_k-D_k)^b$	Freight rate (t_k)	Value of sales at farm gate $(P_k)^c$	Required total sales (Q_k)	Incremental change in sales $(\Delta Q_k)^d$	Change in sales^d	Change in farm gate price^d	Elasticity of supply $(E_{k-k'})$
Alternative highway combinations (k)	Construction C_c^k	Annual maintenance C_m^k									
	(------- $ thousand -------)				(--- $ ton ---)		(------ tons ------)		(----- percent -----)		
A^e	625	180	425	377	8.40	26.97	13,980	-	-	-	-
B^f	2,220	120	714	634	7.80	27.57	23,000	9,020	64.5	2.2	29.3
C^g	2,440	130	782	695	6.75	28.62	24,280	1,280	5.8	3.8	1.5
D^h	3,130	140	962	855	5.80	29.57	28,910	4,630	16.0	3.3	4.8
E^i	4,930	95	1,320	1,172	3.40	31.97	36,660	7,750	26.8	8.1	3.3
F^j	5,150	105	1,390	1,234	2.35	33.02	37,370	710	1.9	3.3	0.6k

Sources: TAMS, *Proposed Proposed Highway Yapacani to Puerto Grether and Yapacani Bridge*, prepared for AID and the Ministerio de Economía (Cochabamba, Bolivia, April 1963); and INC.

a Based on the assumption of no restriction on the area of influence (A) and a lineal rate of increase in value added from zero in the first year to full production in the tenth year (s). The figures given are the requirement for the full-production level yielding a 15 percent internal rate of return (r) over a project life of twenty-five years (t).

b Based on the assumption that value added is 90 percent of gross value (a = 1.11) and sales are 80 percent of gross value ($D_k = 0.2Y_k$).

c Market price (p) = $35.37. Value of sales at farm gate = $P - t_k$.

d The change in each case is B-A, C-B, D-C, E-D, and F-E, respectively.

e Maintenance of 70-km access road and Yapacani ferry at existing standard, building structures on the 63-km trunk road, and maintaining a dirt road giving seasonal access.

f Same as A with 63-km trunk road constructed to 9-meter width and all-weather standard.

g Same as B with bituminous surface on 63-km trunk road.

h Same as B with bridge substituting for Yapacani ferry.

i Same as D with construction of 70-km access road to 10-meter width and asphalt surface.

j Same as E with construction of 63-km trunk road to the standard in C.

k Elasticities for AB = 29.3; AC = 12.0; AD = 11.08; AE = 8.75; and AF = 7.46.

resources that may stem from assumptions of such secondary benefits is discussed at the end of this section.

Accepting the production relationships under highway combination A in Table 26, it is evident that an enormous response is required to justify improvement to level B. The improvement from A to B permits a 2.2 percent increase in farm gate prices. This price improvement must be sufficient to call forth a 65 percent increase in gross sales from the area served. Thus justification for undertaking B rather than A hinges on the assessment of the probability of attracting additional settlers through improved service and prices, the production response of existing settlers, and additional attributable benefits from outside the project area—e.g., additional traffic generated through river connections. If combination B is accepted, then the incremental improvements to combinations C, D, and so on, become much easier to justify in terms of the required elasticity of supply. A priori it appears that if a case can be made for E, an elasticity of 0.6 from E to F would readily justify the additional investment of $220,000 to move to combination F.

The foregoing exercise serves to highlight the critical variables in highway investment decisions related to opening up new lands in the humid tropics. In directed and semidirected colonization projects examined in this study no attempt was made to derive a highway standard and a phasing or construction schedule. The standards were established a priori, no phasing was contemplated, the construction schedule was generally set to permit a minimum cost contract, and there was no quantification of a gradually expanding area of influence.

Measurement and Allocation of Benefits. The standard procedure for the justification of highway investment for colonization is benefit-cost analysis where certain specifications are postulated with respect to rate, scale, standard, or phasing of construction. For each condition an estimate is made of costs (including maintenance); the impact on settlement (either directed or spontaneous), total production, net value added in the area of influence, and physical movement of goods; and the transport cost per ton per kilometer. The benefits attributable to each condition fall into two classes—user and development. The user benefit is only applicable if a highway already exists. While, typically, new-land development would spring from a new road, thus involving only development benefits, the improvement of existing access to colonies might well be more important than new roads, assuming that the reduced vehicle-operating costs are reflected in higher prices to producers. It will be remembered from chapter 5 that the bases for the projections of net value added and the related growth in average daily traffic can be somewhat tenuous. Further, the surplus in the area of influence is implicitly attributed to the highway investment, since it is assumed that all other private and public investment associated with the development of the new lands will earn its opportunity cost. The question of how the expected surplus should be allocated to various investments in land development is obviated if an integrated approach is taken to project evaluation and if it is recognized that, as a minimum, additional investment by the colonists themselves will be a prerequisite.

Aside from direct economic benefits there is obvious social utility associated with better communications. Access to amenities in other centers reduces isolation, improves living conditions, and makes frontier areas more attractive to qualified teachers, doctors, and other professional personnel. Evidence from studies in Malaysia reinforces the thesis that improved access accelerates the rate of immigration to pioneer areas. In five zones that were settled in the 1930s and received highway access in 1960-61, the net addition to population was an average of 50 families per year from 1935 to 1959, 300 families annually in 1960-61, and 600 during the period 1962-64.[48] Similar road-related population increases occurred in the spontaneous settlements examined in this study—Caranavi, Caquetá, Puyo-Tena, Upano, and the La Lana-La Trinidad basin.

The Case for Balanced Investment. Where highways are built into new areas a strong case can be made that there will be little or no development without complementary programs.[49] According to G. W. Wilson: "Where there is no initial growth or development, a single transportation project cannot be expected to accomplish much. It is in this type of situation that a coordinated set of investments, inducements, and policies is most essential and where prospects of success from a single project of any kind are very low. The *initiation* of growth is a fundamentally different and more difficult task than its facilitation and normally requires a more careful appraisal of noneconomic factors as well."[50]

In order to take into account the coordinated approach it has been suggested that highway investments should be evaluated within a completely integrated framework of associated activities including the interindustry multiplier effects.[51] Empirical proof of the relationship between highway investments and associated private and public activities would be extremely difficult to obtain, given the wide range of physical, economic, and social conditions that determine the course of new-land development. There are instances

---

[48] William Hughes, "Social Benefits through Improved Transport in Malaya," in Edwin T. Haefele, ed., *Transport and National Goals* (Brookings Institution, 1969), pp. 112-14.

[49] Hans A. Adler, *Sector and Project Planning in Transportation*, IBRD, World Bank Occasional Staff Papers no. 4 (Washington, 1967), pp. 54-57.

[50] George W. Wilson, "Toward a Theory of Transport and Development," in George W. Wilson and others, *The Impact of Highway Investment on Development* (Brookings Institution, 1966), p. 212.

[51] Willis W. Shaner, "Economic Evaluation of Investments in Agricultural Penetration Roads in Developing Countries: A Case Study of the Tingo María-Tocache Project in Peru" (Report EEP-22, Institute in Engineering-Economic Systems, Stanford University, August 1966, mimeo.).

of development—the La Lana–La Trinidad basin, Caranavi, Puyo-Tena, the Guayas banana boom in Ecuador, or the Brazília-Belém highway—where significant development in areas served by new penetration roads has proceeded essentially in the absence of any effective complementary services, at least in the early stages. On the other hand projects such as Quintana Roo in Mexico or Cotoca in Bolivia have been abandoned for all intents and purposes in spite of extensive complementary programs in association with access roads. Nevertheless the land titling, extension, credit, and feeder road programs in support of the major trunk highways through the Santo Domingo de los Colorados project appear to have had an important (though unmeasurable) impact on development.

Paradoxically the evidence from projects discussed in chapter 5 indicates that the associated services may have less impact in the pioneer than in the consolidation phase. This suggests that where the objective is the opening up of wholly virgin areas that are not on the periphery of existing settlements, such as much of the region served by the 2,670-km Acre highway in Brazil, it may be advisable to keep associated programs at a low level until the spontaneous settlement enters the consolidation stage. The suggestion that penetration highways having few or no supporting development programs should be the spearhead for new-land development is clearly controversial:

1. On the basis that this demands unnecessary sacrifice on the part of early settlers whose lives could be made more comfortable and rewarding through certain production and social services.
2. On the economic grounds that unless steps are taken to accelerate expansion of settlement, production, and traffic growth the investment cannot be justified.
3. Because uncontrolled settlement will lead to unwarranted forest and soil destruction in areas adjacent to the road.

Providing the road penetrates an area with real economic potential, the experience at Caquetá, Upano, Santo Domingo de los Colorados, Puerto Presidente Stroessner, and Tingo María indicates that rapid spontaneous settlement will follow. Then a "coordinated set of investments, inducements and policies"[52] will be likely to have significant impact. An inherent risk in this approach stems from the potential incapacity of public institutions to regulate settlement in such a way as to assure that colonists originate from the group in society that is to be benefited and that colonists observe regulations designed to prevent resource destruction.

Programming Highway Investments. Mention has been made of the user benefits and development benefits that can result from access to other areas

---

[52] Wilson, "Toward a Theory of Transport," p. 212.

(currently unoccupied or partially developed) that gives rise to through traffic. This leads into the whole question of programmed transport investment as part of an integrated plan for development. As indicated in the discussion of criteria for area selection, areas served by integration highways designed to join developed regions (e.g., the Belém-Brazília highway) or highways built for the exploitation of natural resources other than land—principally minerals—(e.g., the Transoceánico) become a prime target for land settlement or forestry programs. In such cases the economic justification rests largely on the economic activity induced either by lower transport costs or by the opportunity for interregional specialization and trade.

Roads that penetrate deeper and deeper into virgin territory where the eventuality of major through traffic is remote—e.g., the La Paz–Caranavi–Alto Beni highway in Bolivia—of necessity must be justified by agricultural and forestry development; expected external economies generally take the form of more such development. Without the Caranavi road the settlement of Alto Beni I probably would not have been seriously contemplated, nor of Alto Beni II if the road to Alto Beni I had not been in existence. Thus the Caranavi highway investment may create external economies that make Alto Beni I and II feasible.

The question of sunk costs is relevant to this issue. The government decision maker faced with a major indivisible investment in an access road finds all his costs variable. In seeking the economic justification he may call on external economies if the projected direct benefits are insufficient. Once the road is built the only cost related to it that enters into subsequent decisions to extend the road or to stimulate development and traffic by colonization is the annual maintenance charge. Miscalculation of benefits may lead to a chain reaction in the form of additional investments made to justify the initial project; but since these investments are marginal costs they require justification only on the basis of marginal benefits. Clearly there is a danger of major misallocation of funds through this procedure, particularly in the case of highways, since the investments normally are relatively large and indivisible.

The colonization-highway complex associated with development programs for the Bolivian piedmont region between the Chapare and Yapacani rivers is an example of this potential situation. Total investments in the Chimoré and Yapacani colonization projects, including trunk roads and the improvements of their immediate access, will amount to about $17 million. Settlement on these two areas is now projected to reach 2,500 families, i.e., 40 percent of the number in the original plan, and expected associated spontaneous settlement over the first five years has been insignificant. In order to improve the conditions for production in the Chimoré-Chapare region a $51 million contract was signed for the realignment of the Cochabamba-Chapare access road. Attributable benefits needed to justify such an investment with a 15 percent discount rate, assuming a linear expansion to 1990, would have to reach eight times the 1968 net value added from the 7,200 families in Chapare and Chimoré.[53]

Regardless of the probability of realizing such development through reduced isolation and the reduction of transport costs from $14 to $4.50 per ton,[54] justification of further investment can be expected for the 110-km Chimoré-Yapacani section that would complete an alternative route from Santa Cruz to Cochabamba. Since the state will have $65 million to $70 million tied up in the Chapare-Yapacani complex it is to be presumed that any marginal investment that might help to amortize this enormous sum, or at least show a more significant impact overall, would receive favorable consideration. The existing Santa Cruz-Cochabamba highway was built between 1945 and 1956 at a cost of $44 million and was resurfaced in 1968-70 at a cost of $3.1 million. Diversion of traffic from the existing highway may yield user benefits on the order of $5-$10 per ton.

Incremental expansions of this sort are not necessarily bad. The potential danger stems from the possibility that those seeking to vindicate an investment that was made on the basis of faulty projections will pour in additional resources—without particular attention to whether benefits are commensurate with costs—in an attempt to show an impact of significant magnitude. This phenomenon is not peculiar to investments in tropical land development. Because of the demonstrable uncertainties in development, however, and the overwhelming dominance of highways in the public investment component, the chances of aberrations in resource allocation are probably greater.

Ideally land development and highways should be jointly programmed; but given the institutional structure of most Latin American countries, it appears likely that the highway-colonization syndrome will continue—either highways will be built in response to colonization pressures or colonization will be attempted to justify highway plans.

Housing, Utilities, and Urban Services

In cases of directed and semidirected settlement the institutions that finance and carry out the projects generally take the stand that they cannot be associated with any program that permits traditional housing. As a result provision is usually made for $100 to $500 per colonist for building housing to a standard design with a concrete floor and a corrugated iron roof. In a number of instances colonists have been reluctant to accept housing loans and have indicated a preference for being granted the equivalent sum as production credit (e.g., Tingo María). In most directed government projects—e.g., La Chontalpa, Alto Beni I, and Nuevo Ixcatlán—the executing authority was not

[53] Excluding user benefits.

[54] Based on preproject operating costs of $83 (1964) per 6-ton truck from Villa Tunari to Cochabamba and $27 with the proposed new alignment. TAMS, *Proposed Highway Cochabamba to Villa Tunari and Isiboro River* (Cochabamba, January 1964).

empowered to make such substitutions. It appears that self-reliant pioneers are perfectly capable of meeting their own temporary housing requirements in the initial years when they are uncertain about the length of their stay in the new environment. As colonists become established and enter the consolidation stage with a reasonable expectation of receiving title to their lands, they change to permanent structures.

On the basis of the projects observed it appears that housing is one of the least important infrastructure items deserving special government assistance in opening up new lands. This is especially true if public investment per colonist is to be minimized. On the forest frontier, basic materials for housing are essentially free to an enterprising settler. In the consolidation phase, credit for housing may be warranted—particularly to encourage location in urban centers.

In all but the special case of the ejido in Mexico, settlers have shown a preference to live on their own parcel of land. This tendency toward dispersion rather than concentration of population complicates the provision of utilities and social services. It follows that where capital is relatively scarce, utilities such as water, sewerage, and electricity can be provided only in urban centers. Moreover the quality of health, police, and education services, as well as recreation facilities, will be far superior.

An elaborate scheme for the concentration of population is being undertaken at La Chontalpa. All settlers are obliged to live in planned urban units, from which they go out to farm the lands allotted to them. Each unit consists of 200 identical houses, a school, a medical post, a recreation center, a warehouse, paved streets, space available for churches, and commercial establishments. All utilities are provided. It is no surprise that adults resisted this change in their traditional environment, but the urban units have had a notable effect on the children. Many new horizons are open to the children because of the greatly improved quality of their education and their much wider field of experience, and it is likely that their opportunities and aspirations will differ markedly from those of their parents. In addition improved social services should make it easier to generate more effective community action in municipal utilities, production management, and marketing. The principal drawback is that the formation of urban centers requires a degree of coercion. In spite of this some consideration might be given to introducing a requirement that colonists, directed and spontaneous, take up residence in a prescribed urban center serving a specific area available for settlement. If the advantages are real rather than merely imagined by the planners, there should be no need to enforce such regulations after the first few centers have been established. The social and economic efficiency of the La Chontalpa experiment is yet to be tested.

The model of urbanization applied on Ivinheima represents another approach to reducing the degree of dispersion. The urban center is planned prior to any land settlement, subdivision is designed so that the maximum number of farmers can live in or near the town, and lots of 2–5 ha are laid out around the planned commercial and industrial center. These lots are offered at low prices to attract laborers and potential buyers of farm property. Every effort is made to attract commerce, forest industry, and government services to locate in the center. The company itself builds the initial timber mill, hotel, warehouse, and machine shop and provides utilities as the nucleus for subsequent growth. The whole effort is oriented to the creation of a consumption, service, and recreation center for agriculture by making the area a more attractive place in which to live. The effects are, first, an increasing demand and price for farmland and, second, the higher rental values of commercial urban property that remains in company ownership.

A degree of dispersed settlement (especially spontaneous) is inevitable, but there is little doubt that the role of a government in accelerating new-land development should be oriented toward the promotion of urban centers. In particular the government should have a hand in (1) the siting and physical planning of towns; (2) setting up health, education, titling, and forestry services in the early years; (3) establishing other public services in the consolidation stage—extension, banking, utilities, and other urban infrastructure; and (4) offering credit and subsidized utilities to encourage the concentration of housing, industry, and commerce.

The provision of rural infrastructure (excluding roads) and social services in a newly developing area of a country with limited financial and administrative capabilities poses severe problems. While schools or health centers can be built, retention of an adequate staff and effective maintenance of the buildings, equipment, and supplies have been impossible in many cases (e.g., Tingo María and Chimoré). Suitable water is not always available on a farm-by-farm basis; where pumps have been installed the colonists often have neither the capability nor the resources to maintain them (e.g., Alto Beni II). Given these limitations no formula is apparent in the pioneer stage of development for the provision of rural infrastructure and services.

As an area enters the consolidation stage, when there is a possibility of community action and responsibility, the activity of the government might be along the line of supporting and cooperating with local organizations in order to meet their needs for education, health, recreation, water supply, and access. Caranavi provides examples of effective community initiative to obtain such services in seventy communities that have independently built and staffed their own schools. In a number of areas such as Puyo-Tena and Caquetá the WFP has attempted to strengthen group action by giving food in payment for labor used in the construction of bridges, schools, and so forth. These efforts have not always met with outstanding success since the distribution of food is often cumbersome and difficult to supervise.

Summary

The question of preinvestment information about tropical lands—resource surveys and feasibility studies—is without doubt highly controversial. One can hardly argue against the position that with better knowledge the problems of new-land development would be reduced. The composition of the knowledge accumulated, however, appears to have been influenced by the institutions involved and the techniques available for assembling data. Thus certain imbalances in the information flow have arisen. Although in some cases natural resource surveys have left much to be desired, considerably more is known about resources than about the interaction among institutions, agrarian structure, markets, and colonist decisions on migration and production. Experience indicates a need to keep data requirements in perspective in regard to overall expectations from the settlement of new lands, budget limitations, and the real knowledge gaps that have constrained performance in the past.

Behavioral characteristics of prospective or existing settlers have been one of the prime unknowns in new-land development. The clientele for the great majority of state-directed or semidirected settlements consists of landless peasants or *minifundistas*. Efforts to identify a specific underprivileged community or social group as a target for recruiting programs have failed. This must be attributed to a lack of understanding of campesino decision making and to political interests of the institutions concerned that were incompatible with the process of migration and development. The system of screening applicants for land in order to obtain the best colonists—while sound in theory—has broken down in practice because of a lack of applicants and the incapacity of state agencies to effectively regulate the flow of colonists. A lack of perspective has characterized decisions about which people and how many should be benefited in the process of pushing agriculture out into the jungle.

The role of infrastructure is universally accepted as both basic and crucial to success in the development of new lands. However, the standard of this infrastructure, the phasing of its construction, the relationship between components (e.g., trunk versus feeder roads), and maintenance requirements have not been systematically analyzed before project execution. As a result it has proved to be a bottleneck in development in some cases and has represented an overinvestment in others.

VIII

FACTORS AFFECTING DEVELOPMENT POLICY: 2. ECONOMIC, TECHNICAL, AND ADMINISTRATIVE

Once the specific area has been chosen for development, the potential clientele identified, and basic requirements for infrastructure specified, it is necessary to examine a number of technical and economic elements in project design relating to settlement, land development, agricultural and forestry production, and marketing. Consideration also must be given to organization and administration in the formulation of policy to expand agriculture into humid forested regions. Discussion in this chapter focuses on how such factors impinge on project performance.

Settlement Organization

The question of organization for the settlement and development of new lands can be examined within the general framework outlined in chapter 4, according to the stage of development and the degree of government control. Where the intent is to open up wholly new areas, i.e., pioneer development, three types of organization have been used: (1) directed colonization, (2) spontaneous settlement generally associated with penetration highways,[1] and (3) the integrated plantation, a variation of the directed form of organization where the processing plant and central management are in the hands of the state or a cooperative and parcels are owned individually. The classic example of this type of plantation organization is the Jengka Triangle project in Malaysia where 2,800 families are being established in an 11,000-ha oil palm plantation, which has three government mills, and are being given an additional 0.7 ha of cropland each. On a smaller scale similar plans exist for 2,000 ha of export bananas on La Chontalpa and 3,000 ha of oil palm on Tingo María.

Where the purpose of a project is consolidation and the expansion of settlement in an area already partially occupied, the approach can vary from a formal semidirected government project, such as Santo Domingo de los Colorados, through any combination and intensity of normal rural development

---

[1] See chap. 5 for discussions of directed and spontaneous colonization.

activities—credit, extension, titling, or the installation of agricultural processing plants that operate on the basis of contracts with small and medium producers. Semidirected projects tend to follow the same pattern as directed projects in their orientation to minimum family units.

The utilization of tropical lands for agriculture is characterized by:

1. Relatively high costs of land preparation (except where unpaid family labor is used), which necessitates high-value production per hectare.
2. Isolation from markets, which dictates a high value-to-weight ratio in order to justify transport charges.
3. A high potential for products that tend to be in surplus supply and that require specialized quality control and international marketing.
4. Special problems of declining soil fertility, climate, weed infestation, plant and animal diseases, and handling of perishable products, all of which call for a high level of technology and management.

Points 3 and 4 indicate a tendency to economies of scale.

Such economies have been explicitly recognized in the design of the plantation operations on the La Chontalpa, Tingo María, and Jengka Triangle projects. There is some conflict, however, between the general practice followed in Latin America of establishing minimum units on the one hand and certain scale economies in production and marketing on the other that suggest consideration should be given to modifying the standard formula for settlement organization. The cases examined (aside from cooperatives, which are discussed later in this chapter) indicate that three avenues to settlement organization might warrant testing: (1) agro-industry, (2) a joint venture between government and private enterprise, and (3) subdivision with a variety of farm sizes. Foreign colonization of the San Juan or Filadelfia type is irrelevant to future policy.

As indicated in chapter 3 the traditional plantation is unlikely to be an acceptable form of land development organization. There are certain modifications of the system, however, that bear examination. One modification is to operate processing plants that have established market channels where the supply of primary products is handled through contracts to small producers backed up by credit and technical assistance, e.g., the Guabirá mill. This form of organization provides a relatively secure market and the ability to carry out effective agricultural extension in all aspects of farm management when a guaranteed market is provided for one of the products. Its incorporation into project plans is worth consideration, since marketing and extension are two of the most troublesome problems in colonization.

Another variant of the plantation system is when infrastructure installed by a private forestry or agricultural company results in spontaneous settlement. The company may also provide employment while the colonists are becoming established, e.g., the tea plantations of the Sociedad Ecuatoriana de Desarrollo Industria Agropecuaria in eastern Ecuador. In state or private enterprises that include plans for extensive infrastructure or plant investments that may provide the nucleus for an urban center; may generate employment; and may bring management, extension, and marketing skills into a frontier region, there appears to be good reason to consider associating the plans with land settlement. An example is the tea plantation of the Compañía Ecuatoriana de Té in Ecuador whose market contacts and technical knowledge were mobilized by the Banco de Fomento through a contract to set up a nursery and supervise the planting and management of 1-2 ha of tea on 600 small holdings, with a guarantee to buy the total production.

In cases where the requirement is a high level of technical management skill combined with marketing experience and contacts, the possibility of cooperative or state enterprise with contract management is by no means precluded. An example is the Iparía timber mill at Tournavista where management and marketing have been contracted to a Canadian company.

Consideration might be given to combining some of the promotional and financial aspects of private enterprise with government services and controls in undertaking land development and settlement. Organization of this sort is probably best handled on the basis of a contractual agreement like that between Le Tourneau del Peru and the Banco de Fomento Agrícola for the El Pimental project near Pucallpa. In this case the company financed the land, land clearing, and highways, and the bank granted the credit for housing, pepper plantations, and the rice- and pepper-processing plants.

A further adaption of quasi-government enterprise to carry out colonization would be the division of activities between a development financing and promotion agency, such as the Sociedade de Melhoramentos e Colonização (SOMECO), and the government. In this case the government would construct most of the basic infrastructure or would accept infrastructure from the company (e.g., the trunk highway on Ivinheima), control subdivision plans and titling, and provide credit and social services. The company would be responsible for creating a demand for land and for urbanization, financing industries, productive services, and land clearing in the initial stages. An alternative procedure would be for a national development corporation—e.g., the National Financiera, the Corporación Boliviana de Fomento, or a regional authority such as the Superintendencia do Desinvolvimento da Amazonia or the Corporación Venezolana de Guayana to hold an equity interest. An additional possibility is government contracting of private developers for the execution of specific functions. The state of Goiás, in fact, contracted with SOMECO for identification of colonization areas with the understanding of follow-through on some of the development and promotional activities.

On the one hand the staff of most government agencies connected with land and forestry are suspicious of the methods and motives of a private company operating in the colonization field. On the other hand private companies are skeptical of excessive government delays in approving land titles, land subdivision plans, or infrastructure and of constantly changing policies and personnel where the minimum pay-out period is fifteen to twenty years. In the future, governments probably will be more restrictive on private enterprise than in the past. With a resource as politically delicate as land, the state will want to exercise a substantial degree of control over the planning and even over many of the operating decisions of the executing company. There are potential advantages in permitting a range of farm sizes in a newly developing area regardless of whether the organization is directed, semidirected, or spontaneous. It is likely that there will be more mobilization of private capital. Where a few operators of larger farms or cattle ranches are attracted to invest, a supplementary labor market and a basis for testing and demonstrating advanced technology are provided.

Centralized Management—The La Chontalpa Case

Centralized management was introduced by the Grijalva Commission on La Chontalpa solely to assure reaching a level of production in a sufficiently short period of time to justify the enormous infrastructure investment.[2] Although it may be five or ten years before an evaluation can be made of this management experiment, it contains some interesting potential implications for colonization projects in general. The principal question is: How and when could the commission extricate itself from management without causing any serious decline in the volume and quality of production or a deterioration of the marketing procedures? Possible organizational changes that might follow such a move are:

1. The creation of a quasi-ejidal agricultural enterprise in which management would be appointed by the state and ejidatarios would have a vote in major policy decisions either through a general assembly or an elected executive committee. A variation of this might be that only the processing plants, cattle operation, plantations, machinery pool, and certain marketing and purchasing functions would remain under the jurisdiction of the state-ejidal corporation. Other farming would be done on individually operated parcels.
2. The creation of a private agricultural enterprise in which the ejidatarios would be the sole stockholders; the government would provide advice but would retain no management authority. The variations and functions would be the same as in 1 above. Or the management of certain specialized operations, such as the processing plants, machinery pool, or the banana plantation, might be contracted to the government or to

[2] See the section on La Chontalpa in chap. 5.

private concerns. The success of this form of organization would require a high degree of sophistication on the part of the ejidatarios.

If a corporate structure is not retained, at least for those parts of the operation in which communal management is essential, the ejidatarios would have to sell their interests in the processing plants and machinery pool. Subdivision of the communal cattle operation would present a number of complications. The cattle would be liquidated and the area would be subdivided into lots of 2–4 ha assigned to each ejidatario. The fences and yards would probably have no salvage value and the area would be converted into crops. Some of the plantations would be operated by the individual owners; in the case of export bananas, the management of the plantation would have to be retained by the owners of the packing plant.

If the 15-ha parcels now allotted to each ejidatario were given over totally to individual management, it is an open question whether production would decline. It is likely that sharp differences would arise among the ejidatarios because some would have more capital and would be more capable and diligent than others. The current position of the commission is that unless there is a high level of technology and mechanization, both gross production and value added would be lower. The outcome would depend on the knowledge, work discipline, entrepreneurial ability, and motivation of the ejidatario at the time he assumed responsibility for the management of his own parcel or became a shareholder in a communal enterprise.

One feature of centralized management on La Chontalpa is the absence of any serious thought as to how management might be transferred to the ejidatarios and over what period of time. The paternalistic approach taken to date is not conducive to the development of managerial qualities. In the somewhat artificial environment where credit is made available on the recommendation of the technicians of the Instituto Nacional de Investigación Agraria and cash is received for all work performed in the fields either as a loan or as salary, entrepreneurial ability is likely to atrophy rather than to develop.

It is tacitly assumed by the commission that over the long run lands must be operated as a corporate enterprise with specialization of labor. It will be necessary to train a few people for managerial positions and some for specialized positions such as mechanics, machine operators, or plant foremen. The great mass of the ejidatarios would remain unskilled farm laborers without any need to make decisions. This type of organization could result in income disparities that eventually could lead to dissolution of the communal enterprise. If members receive sufficient education they undoubtedly will recognize the advantages of joint ownership and specialization for the common good.

Although the experiment of exposing ejidatarios to modern technology is well advanced on La Chontalpa, there are no definite programs to create either (1) a group of ejidatarios who would retain relatively advanced management if given responsibility for their individual parcels or (2) the conditions necessary for an efficient communal agricultural enterprise managed by the ejidatarios themselves.

Credit and Capitalization of Agriculture

Capital flow is one of the most controversial issues in formulating public policy for the development of new lands. Debate centers on such aspects as mechanized versus hand clearing, the requirement for high levels of inputs, technology and management versus the settlement of inexperienced colonists who lack funds, economies of scale versus the creation of minimum farm units, and the key role played by the interrelated structural factors that influence credit, extension, marketing, and land titling. These factors affect both the amount and the source of the capital required. For example, mechanized forest clearing requires a cash outlay of $150-$250 per hectare relative to $50-$100 for contract hand felling and burning and less than $10 for clearing done by unpaid family labor. Furthermore if development is undertaken by large concerns the necessary cash will be forthcoming from regular channels—corporate and private savings or commercial banks. Where ownership is in the hands of colonists who have little or no resources of their own, it follows that the government would have to become heavily involved in credit operations, probably subsidized, if agriculture is to be developed beyond the subsistence level. The extent of state involvement in this case would be governed by:

1. The nature of the clientele—personal resources; access to nongovernment credit channels; experience in humid tropical agriculture; and education, motivation, management ability and propensity to save and reinvest.
2. The rate of development required, which in turn is dependent on the cash investment per hectare in basic infrastructure and land preparation and the income conditions set in points 3, 4, and 5 below.
3. The minimum income level to be achieved at full development.
4. The minimum tolerable subsistence level until the minimum income is reached.
5. The maximum lag that can be tolerated in reaching the minimum income.

The discussion here centers on capitalization and state credit where development is not undertaken by commercial enterprises. Although the government may elect to finance such enterprises, funds are usually supplied by the state agricultural bank, which applies standard loan conditions. (The nature of the noncommercial clientele was reviewed earlier.) In examining the level of capitalization one might argue that a government cannot deliberately associate itself with a project that will merely be an extension of subsistence agriculture. In these circumstances governments must seek a compromise between acceptable income levels and the number of beneficiaries encompassed by public programs with limited funding. Thus income distribution is involved to the extent that the state has the option of spreading its programs thinner. The alternative consequences of compromise are:

1. Colonists may be required to have some minimum resources of their own, e.g., Ivinheima, where a family needs approximately $1,000 to get started.
2. Colonists may be granted significant privileges in comparison with the average campesino in terms of credit and the quality of extension services.

The rate of land development is prescribed by land-clearing procedures and production technology. In cases such as La Chontalpa where the investment in subdivision, feeder roads, and drainage amounts to $650 per hectare, economic justification imposes the course of action taken by the Grijalva Commission—i.e., mechanized removal of the forest cover on a massive scale and intensive high-technology agriculture. Experience on projects such as Nuevo Ixcatlán indicates that it would take a colonist five to eight years to clear 10–15 ha and even then he would probably adopt a bush-fallow system whereby only 3–5 ha were in production annually. Assuming a net addition to land in production of 2 ha per year per colonist on a 12-ha plot, annual net value added per hectare would have to average $150 if an infrastructure investment of $650 per hectare is to show a 15 percent return.

While this figure is well within the range of intensive cropping, returns are prejudiced if only about one-third of the area is in production, as is common in many projects. Thus the Grijalva Commission was obliged to invest an additional $150–$200 per hectare for clearing with bulldozers, reinforcing the need for intensive exploitation to justify cash outlays. An investment of $10,000 per farm[3] is clearly beyond the financial capability of the type of beneficiary generally selected for colonization.[4] For this reason the Mexican government is prepared to write off up to 75 percent of this sum for the La

[3] The total cost of infrastructure and land preparation is $870 per hectare. At 12–13 ha per family, total investment is $10,000 (see chap. 5). The total outlay on La Chontalpa is estimated at $17,800 per family (see table 5).

[4] In a situation where a colonist is saddled with a $10,000 debt in his first year (with a twenty-five-year repayment period and five years' grace at 8 percent) and $1,000 per year for the following five years in production credit, he must have a propensity to save, after allowing $300 for annual family subsistence, on the order of 0.9 from the sixth to the twenty-fifth year. That is, effective family income is restricted to $500 for twenty-five years. These conditions appear incompatible with reality.

Chontalpa settlers and to grant the remainder as twenty-five-year credit with a five-year grace period.[5] Annual production credit requirements for the planned intensive exploitation sequence increase from $200 to $2,500 per colonist during the ten-year development period.

This example suggests that the combination of high-cost land development and the requirement that the beneficiaries be landless campesinos without capital leads to an inevitable train of events if economic return is taken as an important criterion in project evaluation—mechanized land clearing as the only method of preparing the land for crops fast enough; mechanized high-technology farming with central management and 100 percent state-financed production credit in order to achieve rapid development and sustained high levels of production; the marginal participation of beneficiaries in either management decisions or gainful employment; and heavily subsidized development costs, since the colonists' agricultural labor contribution is relatively minor and no allowance is made for nonfarm income.

The application of minimum income conditions as a criterion in the design of credit programs in support of new-land development and the question of who pays—i.e., what will be considered credit and what will be considered subsidy—are taken up in later sections of this chapter. Table 24 shows the importance of state credit in directed and semidirected settlement projects; this item averages 32 percent of the total public funds allocated.

When the degree of subsidy that will be applied in new-land development is known, i.e., the amount of the investment not directly recoupable from the colonists, the level of supportable individual indebtedness (P) is given by the following:[6]

$$P = \sum_{i=h+1}^{j} a_i (1 + r)^{-i}$$

where

$P =$ credit granted,

[5] Secretaría de Recursos Hidráulicos, Comisión de Grijalva, ¿Qué es el plan de la Chontalpa? (Cárdenas, Tabasco, Mexico, February 1967), p. 8.

[6] The formula is derived from $1 + (1 + r)^{-i}/r$, which defines the present value of a fixed annual payment at compound interest, with the introduction of a grace period and flexible amortization quotas, where P is the accumulated debt over a given term for establishment (normally the grace period) expressed as NPV. Thus if $P'_i =$ annual additions to the colonists' debt over h years they must be distributed so that

$$P = \sum_{k=1}^{h} P'_i (1 + r)^{-i}.$$

If $r > 0$, then $\Sigma P'_i = P$.

r = rate of interest,

h = grace period (years),

j = term of loan (years),

$a_i = k(y_i - \bar{y})$ = amortization quota paid in the ith year,

y_i = real annual family income,

$\bar{y}$ = minimum annual family subsistence (dollars),

$y_i - \bar{y}$ = income available to service debts,

k = percentage of $(y_i - \bar{y})$ actually assigned to servicing debts, i.e., propensity for repayment.

On the assumption that the colonist has minimal resources of his own, the volume of credit required to give certain amenities, such as housing or water supply, and to meet a production schedule yielding income y_i, can be readily calculated. The extent to which this credit plus other investments (e.g., feeder roads or drainage) may be recouped can be calculated from the formula above, providing that values are placed on $\bar{y}$ and k.

In the case of Chimoré, assuming y_i at \$2,000, $\bar{y}$ at \$300, and k at 50 percent, a colonist could handle an accumulated debt of \$7,000–\$8,000, which is sufficient to cover housing, subsistence, land development, livestock, and production credit, plus all state investments in the project over a five-year development period.[7] The volume of supportable indebtedness is directly related to the value of k if y and $\bar{y}$ remain constant. In the case of Alto Beni I colonists have demonstrated a value of k approaching zero over the first ten years of the project. In addition to k there is a question of the colonists' interpretation of "minimum subsistence" ($\bar{y}$). In the five cases in table 11 consumption ranged from \$400 to \$800 per family, and only in the case of Alto Beni I were any savings registered. Under such conditions the value of k becomes academic. If state finance is to be an important element in policy for new land development, it is essential to attach probabilities to the levels of $\bar{y}$ and k.

Almost without exception credit operations in colonization have experienced serious difficulties in the projects studied. In directed pioneer settlement the purpose of a credit program is to assure compliance with an established production schedule. Overly optimistic production plans and institutional pressure to comply with the credit disbursement rates have resulted in loans to colonists who were technically unprepared. Further, constantly

---

[7] To simplify the calculation all loans have been assumed to have the following terms: r = 6 percent, h = 5 years, j = 20 years, and lineal expansion of y_i from zero to \$2,000 in the tenth year.

changing production plans and the resulting high level of uncertainty made the agricultural banks wary of the risks of nonrecuperation. Consequently experimentation with production plans was largely at the expense of the colonist.

In a number of cases the demand for credit has been accelerated by emphasis in the early years on the establishment of permanent plantations instead of on annual crops that would provide immediate income to meet living expenses and possibly to reinvest in accelerated land clearing.[8] The state lending agencies tend to apply the same loan conditions to a colonist as to any other agricultural producer. This combined with short amortization periods quickly reduces the colonists' capacity to absorb further credit, especially if they have followed a production program heavily weighted to permanent crops in the early years—e.g., on Tingo María the ratio of credit for long-range production plantations and cattle to annual cropping was 16:1; on Alto Beni II, Chimoré, and Yapacani, it was 8:1. Instead, when the initial credit is given, emphasis should be on helping the settlers to generate a rapid cash income and on providing incentive to reinvest. If colonists at the outset are without cash, management experience, or knowledge of tropical agriculture, a case can usually be made for a subsidized interest rate.

On the other hand agricultural banks are reluctant to consider colonists as clients even under standard interest rates and amortization. The credit recuperation record of government-directed colonization projects is extremely poor. On Alto Beni I all loans were, in effect, canceled. The best performance was achieved by the Ecuadorian Banco Nacional de Fomento, which had only 20 percent delinquency on Santo Domingo de los Colorados. As a result it becomes difficult to persuade a banking organization that credit should be granted on preferential terms in order to generate a viable and responsible clientele that will play an important role in stimulating commercial operations through its impact on the socioeconomic development of the country over the long run.

High-cost loan administration to small producers is not unique to agriculture in new areas. The lack of settler organization, however, and the high risks associated with development in humid tropical frontier areas compound the normal problems. Where colonists are without resources and credit is unavailable for contract land clearing or production inputs, the development process must necessarily be slow. In Caranavi, development has occurred under these conditions, and even in the stage of consolidation only 3 percent of the settlers are serviced by the Banco Agrícola Boliviano. Recourse has been to channel credit through cooperatives in order to reduce loan-handling costs

---

[8] If colonists can be persuaded to invest in permanent crops that part of their labor not needed for annual crops, the advantages are obvious as long as credit is not expected in lieu of wages. In this case, plantations represent additional saving and contribute to the stability of settlement.

and improve the recuperation rate through group action. In practice it is unlikely that the colonists in the pioneer phase will have the experience and mutual confidence to effectively operate a cooperative credit program. The experience of Alto Beni I, Chimoré, and Yapacani in Bolivia has shown the inappropriateness of credit cooperatives in the pioneer stage. (See the later section in this chapter on cooperatives.)

In order to improve the loan recuperation record on La Chontalpa the Banco Agrícola instituted a system of *crédito solidario* whereby groups of ten or twenty ejidatarios receive credit collectively and are made collectively responsible for its repayment. It is hoped that the "internal" control introduced will discourage individuals from defaulting and, at the same time, that unless there is deliberate collusion by the group repayment will be virtually assured (assuming adequate management).

Under consolidation conditions the Instituto Colombiano de la Reforma Agraria (INCORA) carried out a successful program in Caquetá, disbursing $4 million in credit to 2,700 farmers between 1963 and 1967. Of total disbursements averaging $1,400 per settler, production credit was 15 percent, cattle purchase 70 percent, and machinery and permanent improvements 15 percent. Loans were carefully supervised—there was one field officer for every sixty borrowers—and were granted on the basis of standards of credit worthiness established by the agency rather than on mere occupancy, a criterion used in some settlement projects. In a study of participants in the credit program, INCORA estimated that after two years average gross farm output was increased by 121 percent, from $340 to $750, with net income raised from $25 to $300. The principal drawbacks of the program were the heavy requirement for trained loan supervisors and the drain on available funds where 70 percent is tied up in seven-year loans for the build-up of cattle herds. As a consequence only 12 percent of the settlers were reached.

Institutional aspects that complicate the flow of capital to new-land development are apparent from the cases studied—notably the extreme delays in granting titles in many countries, such as Bolivia, Paraguay, Brazil, and Peru, and the loan requirement for many tropical products, the term of which is beyond that allowed by many state credit systems. In a number of instances (e.g., Nuevo Ixcatlán and Alto Beni I) the credit agencies have failed to establish any effective relationship between lending and extension. Institutional barriers have prevented the vesting of responsibility for both activities in the same organization.

Some of the credit problems are evident in the Papaloapan projects where the ejidal system was applied. In the area of international financing, questions have been raised about the credit worthiness of ejidos where the land is inalienable from the state. Reluctance to finance or to guarantee financing is most evident in the case of long-term loans—five years—where a mortgage is normally required. At the national level the Banco Ejidal was not disposed to move into the La Lana–La Trinidad basin, possibly because of the difficult access and the relatively small loans that may be authorized. The Banco Agrícola y Ganadero has provided credit on a modest scale to individual cattlemen. Excessive delay in processing title registration for individual colonists or ejidos has been blamed for the lack of interest by the commercial banks. The Mexican agricultural credit system provides loans on the basis of three terms, 180 days, 18 months, and 5 years, with the first two having a priority claim on available state funds. Many tropical crops require financing on much longer terms, e.g., the twelve-year loans for rubber plantations granted by the Mexican Coffee Institute under the coffee diversification program.

Extension and Research

Research and extension in support of credit and other programs, particularly the promotion of cooperatives, have been two of the most difficult activities in the acceleration of new-land development. The gap between theory and practice in tropical agriculture and forestry, especially in the case of small producers, is amply demonstrated by the cases studied. The fundamental questions are:

1. How correct is the theory in the first place; i.e., how transferable is experience from one tropical area to another and from the experiment station to the farm?
2. Once the degree of technical transferability has been established, what are the economic and social barriers to transference?
3. What sort of extension in combination with structural changes and economic incentives is required to overcome these barriers?

In effect these questions are a restatement of the tropical land development problem.

The lack of an objective basis for projecting agricultural production stems in part from the great variation in soils and climate and in part from the failure to systematically examine available experimental and field data to establish bench mark conditions—these may be technical, economic, or social. Agencies in the business of promoting tropical land settlement are generally aware of the divergence of expectations from actual performance. The problems faced are how to make research findings more indicative of the technical and economic potential in new project areas and how to obtain actual production that approaches the economic potential.

It is evident that experience from other tropical areas is only partially transferable to a new colonization zone. The extent to which this situation is attributable to technical, economic, or social factors is not understood, and it is important that this be explicitly recognized in formulating public policy for expanded land exploitation in the humid tropics. Even at the technical level of agricultural research and farm management, where a relatively high degree of transferability might be expected, there appear to be limitations; e.g., many crop varieties and management practices developed at the El Palmar tropical station in Veracruz gave unsatisfactory results 200 km away on La Chontalpa, which is located in the same tropical coast region along the Gulf of Mexico.

Experiment stations have been established on most directed settlement projects. Perhaps such stations or pilot farms should be established to develop data over a period of three to five years as a prerequisite to a decision on whether or not to invest public funds in colonization. Experimentation on this scale might be a far more prudent procedure for tropical land development than the recent "experiments" involving thousands of families and millions of dollars. The issue is the extent to which the probability of a wrong decision is reduced by research (either scientific or through practical demonstration farms) beyond the level of natural resource surveys and feasibility studies. The value of research or demonstration programs is seriously reduced in areas that have a wide variety of soils and climate; e.g., on the Tingo María project rainfall changes from 1,000 millimeters (mm) to 2,000 mm in 100 km. Further, the decision maker is faced with the prospect of data obsolescence and the possibility that structural and social factors will overshadow technical considerations in the production response of a given project. An alternative would be to center research in established experiment stations or in universities and to conduct systematic plot testing of proven tropical varieties of crops and grasses and of fertilizer and disease control practices over the range of soil and climatic types found in areas scheduled for development.

It is evident that experimental work, demonstration plots, or pilot farms are complementary to resource surveys and to a degree may be considered as alternatives. In addition it is to be hoped that research would focus systematically on some of the structural, cultural, or motivational aspects governing migration, supply elasticity, and the adoption of technology.

Even if adequate credit and some research results are available there are a number of standard problems in the provision of extension services, namely:

1. Technicians, either from preference or because of the bureaucratic demands of office work, find little time to visit the colonists.
2. Due to the absence of road access the number of colonists who can be reached is limited.
3. Advice of the extension agent is not adequately supported by experience; thus colonists may feel that the agent's agricultural experience is being gained at their expense—with credit that they are expected to repay.
4. Most extension agents willing to live in frontier areas are young and do not inspire confidence in the colonists.

5. Visits made by technicians to the parcels are often related to bureaucratic requirements, such as the completion of forms, questionnaires, or routine inspections, and little or no advice is given.
6. Because of his educational and cultural level the colonist is slow to accept technical advice and to act on it. He is suspicious of new ideas. If inexperience, lack of research support, or unforeseeable weather or plant disease cause the extension agent's advice to result in failure there can be a strong reaction in the community and mistrust can deepen.
7. Since a colonization program may threaten certain established interests, such as produce buyers or large landowners who may be holding property on speculation, attempts may be made to sabotage relations between the government and the colonists.
8. A paternalistic approach by technicians toward colonists may cause resentment and resistance, leading to a breakdown of communications.
9. The planning of technical assistance may be inadequate because insufficient account has been taken of available credit and markets and the capacity of the colonist to amortize loans. Thus technical assistance may be given when the colonist does not have the economic or management resources to execute a production program or, vice versa, credit may be advanced without technical assistance.
10. The extension staff may not be adequately involved in the decisions of the head office and may become discouraged by programs and objectives that are regarded as inappropriate or unrealistic.

Extension agents must be cognizant of the limitations of available technical data and of the importance of working systematically to accumulate experience without imposing an undue risk of losses on the colonist. When neither the most productive seed varieties nor the control measures for diseases are known, customary management practices and any local variety will most probably give results. In many cases the colonist's requirements in the early years for growing the standard tropical crops—corn, yucca, and rice—are such that the extension agent's prime contribution is common sense, not the application of advanced technical knowledge. As a general rule extension will be provided only to those receiving production or marketing credit.

Extension was available on the resettlement projects of the Papaloapan Commission, but because the settlers lacked credit, confidence in the marketing system, and adequate access, it had little impact. On the La Joya project there were fifty families per extension agent in the early years. The commission made specific efforts to introduce permanent crops—coffee, rubber, citrus, and mangos—to provide the basic cash income. Nursery stock was provided free of charge. In large part the program was rejected by the colonists principally because of (1) the limited land available, which they used primarily for subsistence production; (2) the long-term nature of the program; (3) a general feeling of insecurity that manifested itself in the failure of the ejidos to allocate specific parcels of land to individual members; and (4) the destruction of some of the early rubber plantations by pests. The latter situation raises the issue of the extent to which programs should be coordinated for land development. If the development is to be market oriented, which is the implicit objective in most cases, there is a readily distinguishable interdependence between land titling, credit, extension, penetration roads, and markets, and some effort is warranted by planners or administrators to keep these factors in balance as far as possible. Alternatively, if plans for the settlement of new lands emphasize employment generation and a predetermined subsistence level of production becomes the objective, the interdependence becomes weaker—assuming that such a procedure is politically viable.

The quantity and quality of extension agents are aspects of colonization project design about which it is almost impossible to set ground rules. For example, on Tingo María saturation extension has been applied with one extension agent per 180 families, compared with the Peruvian average of 1 to 3,500 families. On Ivinheima the ratio is 1:1,200. No standard basis can be established to justify a ratio of 1:100 over 1:1,000. Critical factors include the nature of the clientele, the volume of supporting credit, and the quality and availability of extension agents. Where resources are scarce and a sufficient quantity of extension agents is not available, extension services can be directed to leaders in the community or effort can be concentrated on group demonstration.

The foregoing implies that some objective criteria might be defined for the design of extension programs. In fact, with the institutional, technical, and social unknowns in the tropical land development equation, it is difficult to visualize an extension plan whose performance can be evaluated meaningfully without a control situation. One firm point of reference is the quality of the personnel. The best possibility of getting a good, stable field staff, not only in extension but in all phases of colonization implementation, appears to rest on placing executive responsibility with a prestigious agency that can offer both salary and career advancement incentives and that has a policy of delegating major authority and responsibility to the field office (e.g., the Grijalva Commission). Where processing industries can be established they can provide satisfactory extension services as part of their contract and credit relationships with settlers.

Marketing

Marketing problems are in no way unique to colonization projects, but because of the lack of producer organization, low-volume production, difficulty in attracting qualified entrepreneurs, high freight rates from distant jungle frontiers with a low back-haul ratio, and poorly maintained and hazardous roads, the difficulties as a rule are acute. Justifiable criticism has been leveled at government programs in land settlement for giving insufficient attention to marketing aspects.[9] In spontaneous colonization areas, such as Caranavi and Chapare, producers have been largely left to fend for themselves; a gradual buildup of the marketing structure has occurred without government encouragement or control. The structure takes the form of storage and processing facilities, trucker-buyers, commission agents, and merchants who advance production credit and buy total available output. Under the model of pure competition this process should maximize economic efficiency. Under the institutional and structural conditions that prevail in most tropical countries of Latin America, however, free operation of the market mechanism is unlikely to evolve spontaneously in frontier areas. In general this situation is characterized by a few market elements that create a monopsonistic situation in which such elements are integrated with production and consumer credit and trucking services and in which colonists have difficulty in organizing themselves.

The case of Nuevo Ixcatlán illustrates the consequences of default by government agencies in providing credit, education, and assistance to settlers in the organization and effective regulation of the commercial sector. A severe shortage of credit developed and the commercial banks were not disposed to lend to small producers, partly because of the insecurity of land titles. The government suspended its credit operations in the project in 1960 because of (1) difficulties with the colonists, who complained of excessive problems in applying; (2) delayed disbursement; (3) unnecessary controls on the sale of products; (4) loan defaults; and (5) declining rice prices. As a result well-organized intermediaries were able to move into the unorganized credit market and to earn interest at rates as high as 6 percent a month. The colonists have shown themselves incapable of setting up any effective cooperative to break the merchants' control over credit, interest rates, and the prices of goods purchased and sold. It is estimated that this situation has enabled the group controlling credit and marketing (which constitutes 5 percent of the labor force) to appropriate about half the value added on the project.[10]

In La Joya the gross return from sesame was about $150 per hectare, four times that from corn. Because of difficult access and uncertain markets, however, the colonists used the major portion of their scarce land resources for corn, in order to assure their food supplies. A similar situation characterized the tobacco promotion program on Cihualtepec, which failed in spite of yielding a net return to the owner of $80 per hectare over and above the standard wage for his own labor input. An equivalent income would have

[9] See Instituto de Colonización, *Mesa redonda sobre colonización* (La Paz, Bolivia, 1967); and Oficina Nacional de Reforma Agraria, *Seminario de colonizaciones de selva* (Lima, Peru, July 1967).

[10] Juan Ballesteros, Matthew Edel, and Michael Nelson, *Colonización del Papaloapan*, Centro de Investigaciones Agrarias (Mexico, D.F.: Editorial Imprenta Casas, S.A., 1970), p. 103.

required per hectare yields of 3.5 tons for corn and 3.7 tons for rice, levels that were 50–100 percent above 1967 averages. The failure can be attributed to the insecurity inherent in reduced subsistence production, the difficulty with credit transactions, the inability of state and private agencies to convince the producer of the potential for improved yields and quality, and the uncertain prices of the product and inputs.

Caranavi provides another example of the development limitations imposed by the interplay of the physical crop potential and the transport and market structure. The area suffers from the traditional defects of tropical regions. Products are highly perishable and in oversupply; bananas, citrus, papaya, and avocados account for 70 percent of the area cultivated. Because of the high costs of transport over difficult mountain highways there is little opportunity to compete in export markets, and prices in La Paz itself are depressed by excess supply from other tropical areas. Products such as rice and corn that do have a market are not well suited to the region and are severely damaging to the soil except on the limited alluvial flats.

Of 207 colonies only 45 have direct highway access; 44 are more than 5 km from roads that are often difficult to reach because of broken terrain and unbridged rivers. Only 10 percent of the settlers have draft animals, thus a large percentage must carry products for sale on their backs for up to 30 km.

The marketing structure is often highly prejudicial to the producer. He has little opportunity to reject the buyer's price since in many cases he may have taken a day to walk to the road with a perishable product. Even if his product is not perishable there are inadequate storage facilities, and he has little desire to carry the product back to his farm. Given the relatively low level of organization and education of the producers in the area there has been little development of marketing cooperatives, and government agencies responsible for the control of marketing practices and the promotion of cooperatives have shown little interest in the region.[11]

Market imperfections in frontier areas diminish as development occurs and competition increases between commercial interests. There can be little doubt, however, that in many cases these imperfections act as a serious brake on development.

The precarious production-marketing situation of the colonists in Chapare highlights the need for marketing programs. Distance and climate have forced a majority of the settlers to become dependent on coca as a basic cash crop.

---

[11] In spite of all the drawbacks listed above, Caranavi must still be regarded as a relatively successful settlement when consideration is given to performance in other areas and to the alternative opportunities available to the colonists. This is not to deny that it would have been vastly more successful if the region had rich agricultural lands with ready access to large markets and with a highly competitive transport and marketing system.

Because of the distance from markets a high ratio of value to weight is required to offset the freight charges, and the difficulty of keeping land cleared where forest regrowth is strong dictates a high value of output per hectare. Coca fulfills these requisites. However, recent legislation for the elimination of coca production demands a major effort by the authorities to develop and promote substitute products.

Aside from providing highways, the principal ways in which the state can intervene to improve marketing conditions in support of new-land settlement are: (1) the promotion of enterprises to perform marketing functions, particularly in urban centers; (2) the provision of credit to buying agents; and (3) the fostering of planned urban development plus services to attract business interests to locate in the region, thus encouraging the expansion of the urban population and increasing local demand for agricultural and forestry products. The promotion of marketing organizations may take the form of state enterprise (such as the Comisión Nacional de Subsistencias Populares in Mexico, which handles all the corn from La Chontalpa); credit granted to producer cooperatives and private, industrial, and commercial interests or to any of these interests working cooperatively with the state; subsidized freight rates or utilities; government purchasing contracts and tax concessions.

In cases where the government finances buying agents, credit may be advanced on preferential terms against evidence of purchase in a colonization zone. Alternatively the limit on credit granted to individual agents or processing industries may be extended on the basis of evidence of a minimum percentage of total purchases or a quota from a given project area. Similarly state banks might provide a line of credit for disbursement on security of merchandise stored by colonists in registered warehouses.

The questions of the tendency to low-market orientation, i.e., subsistence agriculture, and ceilings imposed on tropical land development by domestic and export market constraints are taken up in chapter 9.

Cooperatives

The system universally accepted by governments in either the pioneer or consolidation phase of settlement for the solution of problems in credit, machinery pools, marketing, and processing is the cooperative. While in theory the cooperative may be the ideal form of colonist organization, in practice it has been difficult to put into effect.

Colonization agencies usually neglect to make a distinction between the voluntary cooperative—which follows the principles of the Rochdale plan[12]

[12] A consumer cooperative plan initiated in Rochdale, England, in 1844. Members contributed the capital, but each member received only one vote regardless of the amount of his contribution. The legal rate governed the return on capital, sales were at prevailing market prices, and the surplus was either distributed to members or held in reserve.

—and imposed "cooperatives." Under pioneer conditions the true cooperative has proved almost impossible to implement except in colonies established by ethnic or religious groups. As a consequence the position generally taken on directed and semidirected projects is (1) that colonists are individualistic and unwilling to cooperate because of their suspicions about corruption and mismanagement; and (2) that the colonists' limited education prevents them from understanding the meaning of economies of scale and of recognizing the benefits to be derived from collective bargaining—therefore, the only solution rests in obligatory membership in "cooperatives" for the colonists' own good. While this line of reasoning is eminently paternalistic and coercive, it may be supportable on efficiency grounds to the extent that there are real economies of scale and a need to introduce outside management for their realization. The crucial element is management.

Cases of effective cooperation are rare in the pioneer and consolidation stages of colonization. Adequate administrative capacity is unlikely to be found in the membership ranks. Cooperatives, particularly in marketing, require good managers who in turn normally require good salaries or profit-sharing incentives. Among a membership with meager resources, limited education, and little experience, this need is likely to carry little weight. On Santo Domingo de los Colorados, colonists formed cooperatives principally because they were prerequisites for the receipt of a land title, which in turn was the prime requirement for obtaining credit. Beyond this point some of the more dynamic cooperatives have achieved advantages through collective bargaining, i.e., they have obtained access roads, schools, or recreation facilities. The Santo Domingo consortium of ninety cooperatives with a total of 5,000 members is primarily a political organization representing the interests of the colonists before government agencies. It also functions in support of member cooperatives in disputes with neighboring land owners. However, despite this relatively successful primary and secondary cooperation, no headway has been made in improving credit, marketing, and processing or in the organization of communal production, such as palm oil or rubber, where clear economies of scale may be expected.

INCORA has actively promoted a consumer and marketing cooperative in Caquetá. In its early years of operation the cooperative was widely distrusted on the grounds that prices received for products were lower and the costs of items purchased were higher than those available through private commercial channels.[13] Special education on cooperatives and management training programs were carried out for several years. By 1968 the cooperative had 2,500 members, a capital of $100,000, and agencies in eight urban centers. In spite of this progress the cooperative movement still remained a relatively unim-

---

[13] Ronald L. Tinnermeir, *New Land Settlement in the Eastern Lowlands of Colombia*, Research Paper no. 13 (Land Tenure Center, University of Wisconsin, December 1964), p. 41.

portant element in the economy of the region—barely 12 percent of the farmers were members and only 2 percent of the members' rice output (the principal product) was marketed through the organization, which can only be attributed to lack of confidence.

Some viable cooperatives exist in the consolidation stage. A case in point is the Naranjillo Cooperative on Tingo María, which was founded in 1964 and has demonstrated the ability to provide substantive service to members in marketing their coffee. The membership of 275 consists mainly of spontaneous settlers.

Cooperatives formed by disciplined ethnic or religious groups are indicative of the potential benefits of this system and may lend support to the "coercion" school of thought. One of the most outstanding examples is the Mennonite colony in the Paraguayan Chaco, which in all probability would not have survived the early pioneer years without rigorous cooperation. Through a high degree of organization these settlers were able to develop one of the most isolated and inhospitable natural environments in the humid tropics of South America. Between 1927 and 1968 the Mennonites built their economic infrastructure, developed agriculture and industries, and provided social services and utilities for a population that had reached 20,000 by 1968. The entire enterprise is organized into three diversified cooperatives that handle the construction and maintenance of all feeder roads; the generation and distribution of power plus other utilities in principal urban centers; a centralized consumer outlet; the construction and operation of schools and hospitals; a machinery pool; a trucking service to Asunción; the operation of all processing industries (seven plants); underground water exploration and development; the education and settlement of local Indians; and the marketing of all processed items and those agricultural products sold outside the colonies ($2.6 million in 1968).

The Cooperativa Agrícola Mista de Tomé Açú in the Brazilian state of Pará was formed in 1949 by 70 Japanese colonists remaining in the zone from the original group of 370 families who were unsuccessful in developing a viable agriculture prior to World War II. Membership in 1967 was 515, with operations based exclusively on the communal production of pepper. In 1964 the organization reached an agreement with a Japanese chemical firm to establish a plant on the project for the extraction of oil resin from pepper. Assets amount to $1.5 million, including offices and a warehouse in Belém; gross sales in 1967 were about $4 million. The cooperative maintains a sales office in São Paulo and handles all the pepper marketing (domestic and export), central purchasing, and transport on the Acará River—270 km between Belém and Tomé Açú.

The generally unsatisfactory performance of cooperatives formed as a result of government pressure—e.g., Tingo María, Alto Beni II, Chimoré, and Yapacani—can be attributed not so much to excessive state intervention, but rather to the fact that the agencies have been anxious to demonstrate a semblance of genuine cooperation and colonist participation. Thus membership in credit or marketing cooperatives has been imposed on reluctant settlers, and the project authority has then vested management responsibility in people elected from the membership who are unprepared for administration. In many instances the results have confirmed the colonists' worst fears of corruption and mismanagement. On the directed Bolivian projects, funds advanced to cooperatives for relending as production credit were largely absorbed in overhead expenses. As a result of this type of experience the Banco Agrícola Boliviana ceased lending to cooperatives in colonization zones in 1969, changing to a system whereby credit is advanced to a small group of farmers who jointly accept responsibility.

The cooperative promotion program on Tingo María met with disappointing results attributed to a lack of education and cooperative spirit among members; weak campesino leadership; limited and, on occasion, misguided technical assistance; and inadequate program management. Seven cooperatives were formed within the project area. Two—Naranjillo and La Morada—were founded in 1964 without promotion. Table 27 summarizes the cooperative history to 1968. All failed—with the exception of Naranjillo and possibly El Progreso and Lanjemak, two cooperatives established for a consolidated rubber plantation—and a number of loans were not fully repaid. These early failures were cumulative in their effect and make doubly difficult the establishment of a strong cooperative movement.

Where economies are to be derived from group action, their realization in a pioneer situation could well require the obligatory organization of settlers under management either contracted or provided by the state. The issue

Table 27. Cooperative Membership on the
Tingo María–Tocache Colonization Project

Cooperative	Year founded	Foundation membership	Membership 1967–68		Financing 1968	
			Official	Active	Paid-in capital ($)	Reserve funds ($)
Naranjillo	1964	86	274	274	1,600	4,900
La Morada	1964	30	36	0	300	0
Azul de Magdalena	1965	23	23	0	200	0
San Martín de Pucate	1965	36	20	0	200	0
Mariscal Sucre	1966	25	23	0	0	0
El Progreso	1967	25	33	12	100	400
Lanjemak	1968	25	24	12	0	0
Total		250	433	298	2,400	5,300

Source: ONRA, Aucayacú, Peru, 1968.

should not be allowed to become confused by considering such an organization a cooperative. This procedure was followed effectively for the settlement of 1,700 families in the Sele Valley on the Italian Mezzo Giorno project.[14] In this case the managers of the producer cooperatives and of the second-order processing cooperative were government employees. Membership was obligatory for all who took up lands on the project. After 10 years' residence settlers were free to resign from the cooperative; the great majority retained their membership since they were able to obtain credit at about one-third the commercial interest rate. In addition the fruit-processing plant was in effect a gift to the second-order cooperative. This demonstration of the advantages of group action, of the education of colonists in cooperative endeavors, and of management training of selected farmers with leadership ability, suggests that such procedures might be the prerequisites for viable cooperatives.

Where the objective is the promotion of voluntary cooperatives early in the colonization process, the following appear to be minimum conditions if in fact there are economies of scale, collective bargaining, or other real benefits to be derived from the cooperative organization:

1. That the operation undertaken by the cooperative be viable even with a very limited membership of perhaps twenty-five or thirty; in some instances it may be necessary to demonstrate such viability through state or private enterprise.
2. That membership not only be voluntary but that members be allowed to keep their options open to obtain some of the service provided by the cooperative through other channels; in this way there is a controlled test of cooperative efficiency.
3. That the service offered by the cooperative in the initial stages be simple, requiring a minimum of overhead and administration; proliferation of services may come later. Operations of this sort should provide the opportunity to identify and train leaders as well as provide a practical basis for education in cooperative organization.

Control exercised by a state agency in support of settler associations should guarantee as far as possible the right of free entry and the democratic control of cooperatives, unions, or any other form of organization chosen by the colonists. Control should also ensure sound administrative and accounting practices. In addition every effort should be made to reinforce and improve traditional peasant organizations (such as the *sindicatos* in Bolivia, which were specifically prohibited in Alto Beni II, Chimoré, and Yapacani) and

[14]Pietro Morselli, "Procedures for Settlement of Farmers on New Land" (paper presented at the Seventh International Congress for International Development, Mexico City, April 1969).

other manifestations of communal action, e.g., the *ayni* in Bolivia, and *minga* in Ecuador.

Land Tenure and Subdivision

It is apparent that either political resistance or a lack of administrative capacity impedes the processing of land titles in newly occupied areas of most tropical countries of Latin America. Notable exceptions are Ecuador and Mexico. In Caranavi, where settlement has been underway for over twenty years, only 50 percent of the 8,200 colonists had received title in 1967. In Chapare, where about 5,500 families took up lands between 1920 and 1967, no definitive titles had been granted and only 18 percent of the families had applications in process by 1968.

Even in directed and semidirected projects, governments have shown considerable reluctance to grant titles. On eight projects[15] where specific government settlement programs were initiated between 1964 and 1966, less than a quarter of the 10,000 colonists in occupation during 1968 could prove ownership. This reticence on the part of the state in confirming ownership represents a disincentive to investment and precludes the granting of credit where a mortgage may be applicable. In a number of countries, however, resources are insufficient to provide credit for the majority of small-scale farmers even if they had title. Further, in areas such as Caranavi and Chapare, it would be extremely difficult to prove a relationship between production level and title— in both areas about 70 percent of the cultivated land is in permanent crops, which may be interpreted as an indication of at least a five-to-ten-year expectation of secure tenure. One may speculate that withholding title would encourage a more irresponsible exploitation of natural resources and would lead to nomadic agriculture. While there was a degree of irresponsible forest and soil destruction plus shifting agriculture in the cases studied, there is little evidence that lack of title was the cause. On projects such as Ivinheima, where significant initial investments are made by the colonists, it follows that title is virtually a prerequisite to development.

It has been mentioned that where roads or other programs open up areas whose location and natural resources offer prospects for economic exploitation, spontaneous settlement is unavoidable, even when the plan calls for controlled colonization (e.g., Tingo María and Upano). Also, in such areas a degree of colonization may already have taken place without highway access. Thus programs aimed at opening up new lands inevitably become involved in the question of tenure for those people already in residence. In the case of Tingo María the Oficina Nacional de Reforma Agraria considered the titling of the 2,150 spontaneous settlers in accordance with the law to be the basic

---

[15] Bataan, Tingo María, Alto Beni I and II, Chimoré, Yapacani, Upano, and Puerto Presidente Stroessner.

prerequisite to development. Regulations specified eligibility conditions for land ownership[16] and defined the minimum unit as 15 ha for cropping and 50 ha for livestock. Project officials discovered that *minifundistas* with from 2 to 10 ha numbered over 5,000 rather than the 2,000 to 3,000 expected, and conducting a cadastral survey and arranging land transfers and indemnizations led to abrasive encounters with colonists and was time-consuming and costly—$10-$15 per hectare.

Attempts were made to impose a 15-ha parcel in which 6 ha would be held individually and 9 ha cooperatively. This plan was dictated in part by the necessity of coping with the *minifundia* problem. Over 75 percent of the colonists, however, were opposed to the procedure, and there was much resistance to cooperative land ownership of any area because of doubts about management and the fair distribution of work and profits. In a few areas where the majority of settlers had less than 6 ha the plan was accepted. As a result of campesino resistance, subdivision plans were changed to provide a 10-ha minimum individual unit with 2 ha in cooperative plantations and 3 ha in reserve.

It became apparent that the program of titling could be carried through faithfully only if the spontaneous occupation of lands were checked. Otherwise it would be quite impossible to meet the objectives of the project in terms of the budget, scheduling, and settlement of "selected" colonists from the sierra. The whole project would degenerate into a never-ending exercise in restructuring the ownership pattern where colonists, one jump ahead of the survey teams, would be constantly taking up lands that did not meet the legal requirements. Accordingly in 1967 ONRA put an end to unauthorized settlement of new lands. In addition the program was modified to exclude some of the more densely settled *minifundia* areas and to establish conditions, such as the granting of credit and the provision of new units, whereby the settlers would have an incentive to take the necessary steps to establish their land claims within the provisions of the law.

The question was raised earlier whether a cadastral survey and legal titling of resident spontaneous colonists are essential prior conditions for new-land development in tropical frontier areas. It can be argued that as infrastructure, services, and credit are made available the trend will be toward commercial agriculture with increasingly intensive management of land, and it will then be in the interests of the colonist to establish title and comply with the property laws.

Where the value of land is enormously increased as a result of public infrastructure investments (e.g., $650 per hectare on La Chontalpa), it is probable that a cadastral survey will be undertaken and that either the land will be expropriated with indemnization or a capital gains tax will be levied. In

[16] See the section on clientele in chap. 7.

theory this procedure is automatic, but in practice it has presented certain problems that are illustrated by the La Chontalpa case. Initially the Grijalva Commission experienced difficulty in convincing the campesinos to accept the program involving highways, forest clearing, drainage and irrigation, the dissolution and restructuring of existing ejidos, the relocation of all families in urban centers, and the granting of rights to parcels of 10-15 ha for which credit and management would be provided to assure intensive production.

In the first place the campesinos found it almost impossible to visualize such a complete change in the landscape, their homes, work habits, services, and agricultural practices. Many of the concepts were completely unknown to them. Many had the natural reaction that the changes, especially the breaking up of their ejidos and resettlement in urban centers, would be for the worse, although in the early stages they did not understand that they would also lose the right of management decision over the use of their lands. In addition there was an inclination to mistrust the promises of officials about credit, amenities, services, and potential income.

The commission employed the strategy of pushing one 2,500-ha unit (including a 200-family urban center) with all speed as a demonstration area. No effort was spared to overcome the resistance of private landowners, to persuade or entice ejidatarios, and to assure successful relocation and production on this unit. As a result it was possible to streamline subsequent operations. Standards for crop valuation were established along with routine procedures for settling disputes between ejidatarios over exchanged crops, and the commission was able to take a more severe line in its dealings with recalcitrant campesinos. Little time was wasted in persuasion—the settler was given an ultimatum to review the demonstration unit. If he was not interested in the improved health services, education, and opportunity for higher consumption levels, he was advised to accept 100 percent indemnization and leave the project.

An opinion widely held in the commission as a result of this experience is that coercion must be used in cases where campesinos have no standard of comparison to evaluate whether or not to accept a proposal to improve their well-being. While the practices applied may appear to have a ruthless cast, they have nevertheless been effective in dealing with a complex problem of restructuring land tenure conditions.

Where entry into virgin areas can be controlled effectively the question of subdivision and tenure is greatly simplified. The procedure on Ivinheima is representative of such a situation. A colonization unit on the order of 2,000-3,000 ha was selected, and the perimeter and internal rivers were surveyed first. The average unit was established at about 20 ha. Then the roads were surveyed, following high ground as far as possible (0.15 km per lot), to divide the unit into sections of 300-400 ha each. The final subdivision was done to maximize the number of lots with access to rivers and to give all the lots road frontage. This averaged from 1 to 1.5 km of surveying per lot at a cost of about $5-$8 per hectare. The principal problem in this instance was the equation of the flow of colonists to the number of surveyed units. If occupation is delayed more than six months after subdivision, the boundary lines become overgrown and have to be resurveyed.

The establishment of acceptable tenure conditions and subdivision in disorganized forest fringe areas has proved to be a formidable obstacle in the development of new land and the achievement of stable settlement. Cash costs of surveys and indemnities in settlement reorganization probably preclude serious consideration of a large-scale program (e.g., the Huallaga Central area). The implementation of regulations designed to achieve the same objectives without heavy public expenditure is likely to founder because of institutional constraints. Theoretically settlers should comply with the legal requirements for title through either incentives or coercion. Once such requirements are met, either in a consolidation or in a pioneer area, granting the title should be automatic, simultaneously fulfilling the minimum prerequisite for credit. Where virgin fiscal lands are distributed, it appears that title should be granted on occupancy subject to a minimum payment or mortgage, plus any other conditions related to use, resale, aggregation, owner's residence, and so on, that may be deemed necessary.

Level and Distribution of Income and Farm Size

Most public programs for the development of new lands in the humid tropics are prefaced by a discussion of the social implications of improving income levels for landless peasants and *minifundistas*. The programs generally do not make explicit the degree of income improvement sought nor the possibility of conflict between income distribution and productivity objectives. Minimum income criteria are ignored by government agencies. In no project studied was minimum income used as a design criterion; subdivision, capitalization, and production programs were not specifically designed to maximize the number of beneficiaries within constraints imposed by the availability of public funds and the necessity to provide reasonable assurance that the colonist would achieve an acceptable minimum income level. If it is assumed that it is politically feasible to establish a minimum income level, then the size of the farms and of capital assistance would depend on the weight assigned to maximizing beneficiaries per unit of public investment. The choice is between quantity (more people with lower incomes) and quality (less people with higher incomes). Having established the income level, the man-land and capital-land ratios can be determined mathematically, given some knowledge of the quality of lands and climate and of assumptions about production costs and prices of potential products.

In practice the layout of colonization projects has been little affected by soil maps,[17] and farm size has been institutionally determined. Within this framework capital requirements are calculated for a theoretical production pattern on the assumption that the colonist will have no resources of his own and only limited management skills. The average income established by this exercise becomes the objective of the project.

In the formulation of the policy or design of projects the only controllable factors affecting settler income are size of farm, credit (together with extension and marketing), and capital requirement for eligibility.[18] It has been assumed in most directed and semidirected projects that the closest approach to equity will be obtained by giving each colonist 10-15 ha of arable land or 30-50 ha of pastureland. Whether or not these are appropriate areas for a farm, the system of standard units is probably as efficient as any other given the following:

1. The high cost of soil mapping at a scale approaching 1:2,000. Such mapping would be necessary for any meaningful modification of the subdivision plan on the basis of differences in productivity and suitability for various crops.
2. The unknowns with respect to the selection of crops, prices, and technology that over time may reverse the profitability of different soil classes.
3. The differences in the colonists' motivation, management ability, and capital resources, which inevitably lead to income disparities.

The area of the standard unit has given rise to a strong feeling in many quarters that the cause of Latin American economic and social development will not be advanced by the proliferation of minimum-size farms in humid tropical areas. It is evident that equity aspects cannot be divorced from production objectives in setting farm size. With respect to income distribution the question arises whether the areas are too large, since in a number of cases the per capita income objectives are more than five times the 1960-65 national averages for the group to be assisted by such programs (see table 28). On La Chontalpa it was deemed necessary to use the most advanced technology available in order to get sufficient production fast enough to justify the $45 million investment in infrastructure. Family income in the project area is projected to be raised from $300 to $2,200. When the average income of Mexican campesinos is $300-$400 it is clear that minimum income and income distribution had little to do with project design.

[17]Property size tends to be standardized regardless of differences in soils.

[18]Infrastructure and social services influence the real income of the colonist—the focus of this discussion is farm income.

If production and economic efficiency are to be achieved, new-land development cannot be viewed within a static framework. As the region evolves the system must be flexible enough for those with ability and savings to put these assets to productive use in the form of expanded agricultural operations. In theory the structure of land tenure, exchange and sale of property, renting, labor regulations, extension, and credit should not be directed toward retaining a rigid relationship between land, labor, and capital. The Paraná Land Company's approach to this problem in the initial stages was to attempt to subdivide into various farm sizes, up to a maximum of 200 hectares, basing the size-groups on the expected demand for land. The application of mixed enterprises and variable farm sizes and the creation of wage employment as a means of introducing dynamic elements were discussed earlier.

The effect of yield decline further complicates the determination of farm size. Where settlement takes place on tropical soil of only moderate or low fertility, a change from annual cropping to pasture and tree crops becomes inevitable (e.g., Caquetá). The consequences of this restructuring are twofold. First, if the change is to pasture and cattle, either in a rotation or as a specialization activity, holdings of a larger size than the original subdivision may be required. Second, considerable additional capital is required.

In practice it is likely that there will be institutional factors limiting the adoption and implementation of flexible programs. The execution of such programs requires a level of administrative capacity and a degree of continuity that may not be forthcoming for some time in many tropical countries of Latin America. A rigid system is much easier to supervise. Further, political opposition may be expected due to fears that a freewheeling operation would be subject to abuse or exploitation by the existing, or an emerging, oligarchy. While these rigidities may be conducive to a smoother-running bureaucracy, their inevitable cost is reduced efficiency and less settler participation. The latter point once again reinforces the argument in favor of spontaneous settlement.

Costs and Cost Allocation

Costs per colonist or per hectare of new land developed are figures sought by development planners in the application of cost effectiveness when objectives other than economic or financial return are involved. International finance agencies and government departments scrutinize projected costs per family—La Chontalpa, $18,000; Jengka, $10,000; Alto Beni I, $6,000; Alto Beni II, $2,000; and the Ethiopian Walamo project, $600—for the income distribution implications. The projects, however, are often approved in spite of apparent disparities. Before examining this point further it may be well to note that such unit costs have absolutely no relevance in either economic or

Table 28. Comparison of Family Incomes on Selected Colonization Projects, with National Averages for the Agricultural and Subsistence Sectors

Country and project	Average value added per family ($/yr)					Ratio of value added by project families in 1967–68 to national averages		Ratio of full production project goals (per family) to national averages	
	Project beneficiaries[a]			National average[b]		Subsist- ence sector	Agricul- tural sector	Subsist- ence sector	Agricul- tural sector
	Before project	1967–68	Goal at full production	Subsist- ence sector	Agricul- tural sector				
Bolivia				170	380				
Alto Beni I	–	400	1,950			1.4	1.1	11.5	5.1
Alto Beni II	–	390	1,940			2.3	1.0	11.4	5.1
Chimoré	–	290	1,230			1.7	0.8	7.2	3.2
Yapacani	–	320	2,030			1.9	0.8	11.9	5.3
Chapare	–	450	–			2.6	1.2	–	–
Caranavi	–	400	–			2.4	1.1	–	–
Brazil				330	720				
Alto Turiaçu	400	600	–			1.8	0.8	–	–
Ivinheima	–	–	1,740			–	–	5.3	2.4
Guamá	–	–	12,500			–	–	37.9	17.4
Colombia				450	1,370				

[illegible]		[illegible]	[illegible]			[illegible]	[illegible]	[illegible]	[illegible]
Coto Brus	450	530	920			1.0	0.3	1.7	0.5
Cariari	–	–	1,280			–	–	2.4	0.8
Ecuador				430	880				
Santo Domingo de los Colorados	–	560	1,700			1.3	0.6	4.0	1.9
Upano	180	750	2,750			1.7	0.9	6.4	3.1
Mexico				310	910				
La Chontalpa	300	–	2,200			–	–	7.1	2.4
La Joya	–	220	–			0.7	0.2	–	–
Nuevo Ixcatlán	–	490	–			1.6	0.5	–	–
Cihualtepec	–	370	–			1.2	0.4	–	–
La Lana–La Trinidad	–	880	–			2.8	1.0	–	–
Mano Marquez	–	330	–			1.1	0.4	–	–
Paraguay				320	710				
Puerto Pdte. Stroessner	110	380	2,250			1.2	0.5	7.0	3.2
Peru				310	720				
Tingo María	–	700	2,300			2.3	1.0	7.4	3.2

Sources: UN, *Demographic Yearbook*, 1955, 1962, and 1963; and OAS, *América en cifras 1965–situación social* (Washington, 1967), chap. 5, table 6.

Note: Dashes indicate "not applicable."

[a]Calculated on the basis of the number of families who are property owners within the project.

[b]National averages are estimated from data on productivity per member of the active population in each sector, multiplied by the average number of workers per family in each country.

financial analysis.[19] Their importance is predicated solely on employment or income distribution.

The interest of national and international agencies in unit costs stems largely from concern that public funds be used to benefit the widest possible number of people. The underlying premise is that farms created through colonization will be either family or collective units. Thus almost all farm jobs generated by a project will be essentially of the self-employed variety. The concern over high public investment per family established is either (1) that the family will earn an excessively high income that could have been better distributed by reducing the area or the capital intensity of the operation, or (2) that the owner will receive a high income and employ a large number of peons who will earn a subsistence wage.

What is a low unit cost and what is high? Some argue that the cost is immaterial because of the enormous external economies to be expected. It has been maintained throughout that unless external economies can be quantified and some probability distributions can be attached to them, the concept is not useful in evaluating policy or projects for new-land development. Public costs per primary (or even secondary) beneficiary, however, are relevant to policy. It was suggested in chapter 2 that public outlays of $2,000-$5,000 per family in directed or semidirected colonization preclude the possibility of massive population transfer by this means. Dozier maintains that the expenditure of $1,350 per family on Alto Beni II is relatively low;[20] a figure of $2,700 for Caicara in Venezuela is also considered low by Jaspersen.[21]

The application of these figures as an index for public policy assessment and interproject comparison requires careful qualification. In the first place there must be a definition of costs with a clear distinction made between economic and financial costs. These costs must be allocated according to policy objectives—economic return or income distribution. Second, the number of families and hectares and their distribution over time must be prescribed. It is meaningless to use figures for the public cost per family as a basis for project selection or to establish some maximum investment level as a policy criterion if the conditions governing the numerator and denominator in the calculation are not specified. Some of the problems in specification are discussed below.

At the project level many colonization agencies are vague and inconsistent in their definition of costs. Sometimes an arbitrary value of state lands is included—in Alto Beni II, Chimoré, and Yapacani $10 million was considered

---

[19] The essential distinction here is between unit and total costs. Obviously total costs constitute half the benefit-cost ratio, but a ratio between two factors of production, when three are involved, is not very illuminating with respect to economic efficiency.

[20] Dozier, *Land Development*, p. 150.

[21] Frederick Z. Jaspersen, "The Economic Impact of the Venezuelan Agrarian Reform" (Ph.D. dissertation, Indiana University, 1968), p. 211.

the cost of the government property to be occupied. In most cases such resources are valued at zero. Discussion may center on whether to include historical public investments in a proposed project area. Expenditures for access highways and arterial roads through projects are excluded or included at random. The operation and maintenance of infrastructure and services during an arbitrary "development" period may be considered a cost; thereafter such expenses are dropped from the cash flow. It may be argued that basic social services are not legitimate charges against a project since such services would be provided to the population regardless of location. The question is one of existing excess capacity and the standard of such services in other areas.

Interest and service charges on foreign loans may be added in. Special programs not directly paid for by a project authority may or may not be regarded as costs—e.g., construction by army engineers; foreign gifts of food, machinery, vehicles, or medical supplies; and the services and overhead of other government agencies or foreign volunteers. Special government credit programs for housing, land development, food and subsistence, and production are frequently counted, as are public investments in timber mills, storage, processing and retailing facilities, and so on. Private investments in such facilities are normally excluded, however, together with cash investments by the colonists themselves and the value of production items (livestock, tools, or machinery) the colonists may bring with them. On occasion an arbitrary value is placed on unpaid family labor expected to be applied in capital formation activities (buildings, forest clearing, drainage, irrigation, fencing) and added to costs.

With respect to cost allocation the questions are:

1. How much of a project investment should be recouped from the direct beneficiaries?
2. How much should be written off as substitute welfare payments or income distribution?
3. How much should be allocated to long-run economic and social development?

In practical terms the only concern is the expected recovery of cash investments from the colonists; the balance automatically will be allocated to national development with benefits accruing in due time through expanded economic activity in forestry, manufacturing, and services both in the project area and outside. It follows that the higher the percentage recuperation from the colonists is, the more financially viable the project becomes, since the expectation of long-run secondary and external effects is present in all cases.

While it may be desirable to trace the employment linkages of a given project investment and to add the families involved to the denominator, meaningful results could hardly be expected given the huge influence of well-directed or misdirected macro-economic policies. Even when the impact is restricted to direct beneficiaries and the land area of a project, there are still problems in definition. The most obvious question is whether to include local employment induced by agricultural and forestry activities plus forest industry itself. In consolidation projects existing residents cannot be separated from new colonists nor land being exploited from new land to be brought into production. There is also the question of how to treat extensive areas in bush-fallow. Since those making policies for new-land development must weigh consolidation versus pioneer settlement this inseparability restricts the use of unit costs for interproject comparisons. One would expect to find unit costs in the consolidation stage lower than those in the pioneer stage. In general this is true, but sometimes production objectives overshadow the stage of development. This was the case in La Chontalpa, a consolidation project where over 95 percent of the beneficiaries were residents in the area prior to the project, and costs per settler were nine times those on the pioneer Alto Beni II project where only 4 percent of the beneficiaries were residents prior to formal settlement.

In order for unit costs to be useful in evaluating a consolidation project it becomes necessary to further allocate costs between existing and new colonists and between improved production from lands already farmed and new lands. The bases for this reassignment of costs are likely to be even more tenuous than the assumptions underlying the original allocation. The simplest and most arbitrary way out of the dilemma is to allocate costs in direct proportion to the ratio of existing to new settlers (or land area). In this case, figures for consolidation and pioneer development become directly comparable. This is likely to prejudice consolidation since it might be argued that the incidence of costs should fall more heavily on new colonists and new lands.

The problem created by the flow of costs and beneficiaries can be illustrated by Caranavi. Between 1945 and 1967 it is estimated that the Bolivian government spent about $7 million on infrastructure and services in the region. In those twenty-three years 8,200 families were settled at a public cost per family of $850, of which $600 was accounted for by highway construction and maintenance. It is evident that there is no way of expressing this figure in such a way as to reflect the timing of the migration, which is of prime importance to planners in designing programs and investment projects for the expansion of settlement in humid tropical areas. Where settlement is expected to occur within a period of three or four years, which is the case with most directed and semidirected projects, the rate is not important. Experience, however, shows that the period is not standard, and if spontaneous colonization is to be considered an alternative a long-term view must be taken.

The evaluation of project costs requires a breakdown of the components according to their application to financial or economic analysis and the de-

gree to which they may be allocated to and recouped from the direct beneficiaries. An example of the theoretical breakdown of costs is shown in table 29 for the Tingo María project. Unit costs to the state are derived in
table 30 and range from $1,800 to $5,700 per settler and $110 to $350 per
hectare of land developed, depending on the use of financial or economic
measures, cost allocation assumptions, and the division of investment between public and private sources. No attempt is made here to justify the cost
allocation assumptions. Table 24 shows total and unit costs for fourteen projects that demonstrate a wide spectrum of directed and semidirected tropical
land development procedures drawn from the cases included in this inquiry.

Returning to the interest of development planners in settlement costs—the
coefficient sought is the public investment per hectare of new land and per
unit of new employment generated. Generalization about such figures is hazardous, since enormous differences may be introduced by indivisible infrastructure investment—e.g., the Yapacaní bridge alone cost over $2,000 per
colonist in the project zone served—and by cost allocation assumptions—e.g.,
the same bridge investment may be charged wholly against expected developments outside the project. In a pioneer situation with spontaneous settlement
this public investment may be on the order of $100 per hectare[22] and $700
per family, with private cash outlays of $500 to $800 per family distributed
over a development period of fifteen to twenty years. Pioneer directed settlement may require $500 per hectare[23] and $5,000 per family, with negligible
private cash investment (excluding government credit) over a period of five to
ten years.

The principal advantage of going through the exercise of calculating unit
costs as a basis for public policy on new lands lies in the requirement for
explicit definition of the people and area benefited, the cost components
(implying standardized accounting procedures), and the assumptions underlying cost allocation. While reference to such an advantage may appear to be a
gratuitous statement of the obvious, no systematic approach had been taken
on the question of costs by the agencies responsible for the projects examined
here.

Public Administration

The technical and economic feasibility of all the different approaches to
the development and settlement of new lands depends on the effectiveness of
public administration, especially as administration relates to the control of
resource use, land aggregation and type of beneficiary, the construction and
maintenance of infrastructure, the provision of production and social services,

---

[22] Land cleared regardless of whether it is in production or bush-fallow.
[23] Assuming 10 ha per family.

Table 29.   New-Land Development Costs and Cost Allocation on the Tingo María Colonization Project

Cost item	Total costs and revenues ($ million)	Recoupment of financial costs		Allocation of economic costs	
		Direct recoupment[a] (percent)	Total nonrecoupable cost ($ million)	Allocable to project (percent)	Total allocable to project ($ thousand)
Government financial balance					
Expenditures[b]					
Land aquisition and indemnity	–	100	0	–	–
Infrastructure					
Trunk roads	8.4	0	8.4	–	–
Feeder roads, drainage, irrigation	2.2	100	0	–	–
Social services[c]	1.3	0	1.3	–	–
Operation and maintenance of infrastructure					
Trunk roads	0.3[d]	0	0.3	–	–
Feeder roads, drainage, irrigation	0.3	100	0	–	–
Social services[e]	2.5	0	2.5	–	–
Land clearing	0.0	100	0	–	–
State marketing and processing facilities	0.1	0	0.1	–	–
Credit					
Housing and subsistence	4.6	100	0	–	–
Production	2.4	100	0	–	–
Development	7.0	100	0	–	–
Project administration and overhead[f]	0.9	0	0.9	–	–
Total expenditures	30.0	55	13.5	–	–
Revenues[b]					
Land sales	g	0	g	–	–
Survey and registration fees, stumpage, etc.	g	0	g	–	–
Taxes	g	0	g	–	–
Total revenues	g	0	g	–	–

Government				
Construction, operation, and maintenance of infrastructure and social services	15.0	–	50	7.5
State marketing and processing facilities	0.1	–	75	0.1
Land clearing	0.0	–	100	0
Subsidy provided through credit and gifts[h]	1.4	–	100	1.4
Overhead	0.6	–	50	0.3
Total government costs	17.1	–	55	9.3
Private				
Development credit[i]	7.0	–	100	7.0
Housing credit	4.6	–	50	2.3
Unpaid family labor[j]	3.1	–	100	3.1
Cash and production items transferred[k]	0.8	–	100	0.8
Commerce and industry	[g]	–	100	0
Total private costs	15.5	–	–	13.2
Total costs	32.6	–	70	22.5

Sources: ONRA and IDB.

Note: Dashes indicate "not applicable."

[a] Expenses expected to be covered by the direct beneficiaries either through land purchase, fees, cash payment, or loan amortization.

[b] Relates only to expenditures and revenues that accrue during a predetermined "development" period (5 years).

[c] Includes facilities for administration and equipment purchased during the development period.

[d] Highway maintenance budget of $582,000 prorated between 163 km of trunk road and 630 km of feeder road, assuming costs for feeder road maintenance at 20 percent of trunk road.

[e] Includes land subdivision, health, police, education.

[f] Includes studies, special training of technicians, and interest charges on loans.

[g] Not estimated.

[h] Credit is granted at 8 percent. Assuming 12 percent as the opportunity cost of capital and assuming the $14 million in credit is disbursed over a five-year development period, the total subsidy may be calculated as $14 million $\times$ 0.5 $\times$ 5 $\times$ 4/100 = $1.4 million.

[i] It is assumed that production credit of one year or less is not an investment chargeable to the project, and other development credit is an obligation assumed by the colonist.

[j] ONRA estimate.

[k] Assumed that 1,000 new colonists will bring in $100 each in productive assets during the development period. Further, 5,250 colonists will reinvest an average of $25 per year during the development period, i.e., $0.7 million.

Table 30. Theoretical Costs per Settler and per Hectare on the
Tingo María Colonization Project

(dollars)

Cost item	Cost	
	Per settler[a]	Per ha[b]
Public financial cost		
Total	5,700	350
Nonrecoupable costs	2,600	150
Economic cost		
Public–total	3,300	200
Public–allocable to project	1,800	110
Private–total	3,000	180
Private–allocable to project	2,500	160
Total public and private costs	6,300	380
Total costs allocable to project	4,300	270

Source: ONRA.

[a] Based on 5,250 settlers in the project area.
[b] Based on a productive potential area of 85,000 ha.

taxation, and execution of the projects (principally in forestry and agriculture). Attention here is directed to project execution.

It is possible to cite a list of instances of misguided administration that have led to excessive expenditures, nonrealization of prospective benefits, or injustices to settlers. Examples of more serious faults are lack of flexibility and follow-through in project execution and inattention to marketing problems. Most of the institutional deficiencies responsible for these difficulties can be corrected only over the long run. Hence the problem becomes that of identifying projects where such deficiencies can do the least harm in economic and social terms.

In chapters 4 and 5 emphasis was placed on techniques for project evaluation oriented primarily to making a rational selection from an array of projects. While it is evident that there is plenty of scope to improve the reality or quality of evaluation for new-land development projects, the argument that the really significant advances are to be made in the area of administration carries considerable weight. In other words, rather than seeking a refined ranking of project priorities, more effort should be directed to the efficient execution of whatever is actually undertaken. Tropical land development, characterized by a high degree of uncertainty and a long-range perspective, requires exceptionally perceptive administration and continuity of personnel with experience. With the exception of military projects and some of the operations of regional development agencies, land settlement typically appears to be in the hands of weak government agencies. This situation combined with political instability makes it difficult to build a cadre of experienced professionals and technicians in tropical land development. Further consequences are listed in an annual report of ONRA with respect to carrying out the Tingo María project:

1. Discontinuity of field management.
2. Difficulty in obtaining qualified field staff.
3. A scarcity of vehicles as a result of insufficient maintenance.
4. A lack of a clear legal framework for the adjudication of lands.
5. Campesino and landowner resistance to the objectives of the program and to the methods of executing them.
6. Bureaucratic bottlenecks leading to unnecessary delays and inefficient scheduling of disbursements, materials, personnel, and so on.
7. Breakdowns in interagency coordination reflected in the disinterest of the provincial government in processing land titles, the inability of the agricultural extension and research service to carry out the rubber tree propagation program on schedule, the inflexibility of the Banco de Fomento Agrícola in reacting to the requirements of the project administration, and delays by the Ministry of Health in staffing clinics.[24]

Major decisions regarding most colonization schemes are generally made in the capital city. The project supervisor visits the area every few weeks for a few days and in between has many other unrelated duties to perform within the agency. The project manager in the field has little say about expenditure or staffing decisions and has no control over disbursements.

The structure of the La Chontalpa project is in marked contrast to this pattern, since the Grijalva Commission has shown itself to be an effective instrument for executing land development. While the commission has been criticized for giving insufficient attention to social problems, it is probable that if well-conceived social development programs had been provided the management could have executed them with the same drive and flexibility demonstrated in other aspects of the project. In this case efficiency must be attributed in large part to the fact that the Grijalva Commission is a dependency of the Secretaría de Recursos Hidráulicos (SRH) one of the most powerful and prestigious agencies in the Mexican government. It is a relatively autonomous agency with adequate funds, and it is therefore free of the torpid bureaucracy that shackles most colonization projects with delayed decisions, interagency rivalry, cuts in approved allocations, remote control from the capital, and excessive reporting requirements—all of which breed inflexibility and inefficiency. The nature of the Grijalva Commission enables it to attract capable administrators and staff. The commission's headquarters are on the project, and the executive director and his staff are residents and dedicate

---

[24] ONRA, *Memoria, 1967—Colonizaciones de selva* (Lima, Peru, 1968).

themselves exclusively to the project.[25] Once the budget is approved for the commission within the SRH, it cannot be reduced without the express order of the Secretaría de Hacienda. All decisions with respect to expenditures and program execution are made on the project itself.

A hypothesis may be advanced that state agencies with the most prestige—and therefore the financial position to follow through on long-term projects and to attract capable administrators—are those associated with construction; e.g., highways, dams, electric power, ports, or irrigation. The implication of this thesis is that new-land development would have a better chance of success if responsibility for a given program or project were vested in such an agency—perhaps a highway department, the ministry of public works, or a regional agency with a construction orientation; e.g., the Grijalva Commission, the Corporación Venezolana de Guayana, or the Corporación Boliviana de Fomento (CBF).

Although the potential advantages of this type of organization for new-land development appear great, there may be correspondingly large risks. The engineering orientation may result in the neglect of the social aspects to which new-land settlements are sensitive, and potentially disastrous effects would follow a major change in national priorities. The withdrawal, or even the reduction, of the funds for management of a complex and expensive land development operation could result in serious economic losses to the country and hardship to the prospective beneficiaries. The operations of the Papaloapan Commission in the 1950s provide an example of this type of situation.[26]

None of the cases studied sheds light on the question of transferring administrative responsibilities for a developing area from a powerful agency to other agencies or to a local government. In Bolivia the transfer of responsibility for colonization from the CBF to the Instituto Nacional de Colonización (INC), an affiliate of the Ministry of Agriculture, can hardly be judged an administrative success. It is evident that in some countries—Brazil, for instance—the institutional structure is more conducive to the formation of viable municipal and local government, which should be able to develop sufficient finances and political leverage to assure the provision of necessary services, e.g., Ivinheima.[27] In the case of La Chontalpa one of the major imponderables is how to achieve the transition of management of what is, in effect, an integrated corporate land development and farming enterprise from

[25] A small office is maintained in Mexico City to handle interagency matters, contracts, and purchases.

[26] See Poleman, *The Papaloapan Project*.

[27] Spontaneous colonization in Brazil has been accomplished in large part by transferring the socioeconomic structure from the consolidation areas to the pioneer frontier. The leaders in this process constitute an elite who have consistently acquired local recognition and the attendant economic and political power. (Letter, Paul Mandell to the author, September 29, 1971.)

the Grijalva Commission, with its sophisticated staff of technicians and administrators, to 4,000 ejidatarios whose training and experience are limited.

In view of the complexity of colonization ventures and the limited administrative capacity of many state agencies, it appears desirable to orient new-land development policy in such a way as to simplify administration. The cases examined in chapter 5 give some indication of how this might be achieved. To summarize these points:

1. In the design of projects, provision should be made for systematic feedback and for the evaluation of performance as measured against the original objectives. In addition administration will be facilitated if there is explicit allowance for flexibility, contingency elements, and an experimental approach to accumulate knowledge about the unknown elements—soil management; forest utilization; transport; the storage and processing of agricultural and forestry products; administrative skill; the forces behind migration to tropical frontier areas; the capability of migrants and their consumption, saving, and reinvestment objectives; urbanization; regional development, and external effects.

2. Management errors would be reduced under phased implementation, which, in pioneer areas, would result in a much slower rate of development than has been contemplated for many projects to date. The expectation that 8,000 families could be transferred to the CBF-INC projects in two-and-a-half years proved wholly unrealistic, given the institutional situation.

3. Administration would be greatly simplified if the elements of land settlement that are most susceptible to paternalism could be reduced or eliminated—e.g., the construction and maintenance of houses and community centers or the creation of cooperatives for forestry, marketing, machinery pools, and credit, where subsequent management is provided by the executive agency. It may well be necessary for the state to provide such services, but administration is complicated by efforts to do this in the guise of cooperatives. This suggests the desirability of orienting programs away from highly directed colonization and toward support for spontaneous settlement.

4. Administrative problems are compounded by geographic dispersion. Where the proper physical conditions exist, it seems advisable to concentrate colonization in a single area. During the development of a significant project the administrators should reside in the area and should have full authority to decide on personnel and the disbursement of funds. These circumstances provide a better possibility of attracting qualified professionals to remain in day-to-day contact with project operations. Supervision from distant capital cities is hardly conducive to flexible and decisive administration.

The foregoing suggests that flexibility is the essence in programs for developing new lands in humid tropical forest areas. Where governments elect to follow the route of directed colonization, however, expected weakness in administration dictates a rigid plan of operations that can be audited easily.

Given these two diametrically opposed concepts, directed settlement is a collision course.

Summary

The interrelationships among the many factors bearing on the performance of deliberate programs to develop new lands in the humid tropics preclude any priority ranking. But there is a sequence to be followed in formulating policy that gives a clue to relative importance. Clearly the prerequisite is the establishment of the criteria against which success will be measured. It is evident that the specification of clientele, farm size, and cost allocation is derived primarily from income distribution considerations. It will be equally evident that these may prescribe performance in certain other objectives such as economic return. The question of natural resource depletion forces consideration of present versus future consumption in setting goals.

After goals have been established, the primary decisions relate to the choice of area—i.e., the land and forest capability, access, and the stage of development at the time any given program is implemented; markets and marketing as influenced by location and agrarian structure; the level of government involvement in the organization of new settlement; and the source of nongovernment capital and enterprise. While correct decisions are crucial to success, they are nevertheless conditioned by a group of factors that are basic to program execution: (1) conservation and control in the exploitation of soil and forest resources; (2) the level of capitalization in agriculture, particularly with respect to mechanization and other technology; and (3) the programming and standards of highway and urban infrastructure. Another category closer to the operating level can be identified that includes the principal public services in support of agriculture, forestry, processing industries and commercial activities—marketing regulation and facilities, credit, promotion of cooperatives, extension, research, and land titling. The extent to which these elements govern performance and thus enter into policy determination and project design is discussed in chapter 9.

IX POLICY IMPLICATIONS AND PROJECT DESIGN

The principal policy issues concerning the area of new land that should be brought into production over a given planning period in order to meet production, employment, or income distribution objectives are governed by alternatives in national development strategy. If it is assumed that a systematic approach, with a progressively improving basis for decisions, is adopted to equate goals with available resources so that the location and quality of the more suitable lands can be established simultaneously with projected requirements in annual additions to land in production, then the crucial question is how should such development be achieved? Which characteristics of new-land development have been associated with failure and are therefore to be avoided? Which characteristics appear to be related to success and are therefore to be emphasized?

Project Success and Failure

In this inquiry the measures of success are restricted to economic return, employment generation, and self-sustaining regional growth. The question of income distribution has been treated by indirection in terms of the economic status of beneficiaries of the various programs examined. The characteristics and performance of the twenty-four projects evaluated are summarized in table 31. Since employment generation[1] ranks high among the criteria of success, the primary rating has been based on evidence of dynamic rural and urban growth (column 15 of the table). The projects have also been classified in terms of high, medium, or low expectations of economic viability (column 14). In table 32 it is readily apparent that the performance of the directed projects is inferior to the rest.

No directed colonization projects appear among the dynamic group. The nine projects classified as dynamic have had a major impact on employment and, to the extent that analysis permits using gross regional product as a

[1] Employment generation tends to carry an implicit income distribution connotation since it can be assumed that most of those who gain employment will come from the lower-income strata and will be better off as a result of any given project.

261

Table 31. Characteristics of Twenty-four

Level of government participation and project	Country	Date of project initiation	Stage of development		Date of first settlement	Gross area (*ha*)
			At time project was initiated	1967–68		
	(1)	(2)	(3)	(4)	(5)	(6)
Directed colonization						
Nuevo Ixcatlán	Mexico	1955	Pioneer	Consolidation	1955	13,400
Cihualtepec	Mexico	1957	Pioneer	Pioneer	1957	18,600
La Joya	Mexico	1956	Pioneer	Pioneer	1956	8,000
La Chontalpa	Mexico	1965	Consolidation	Consolidation	1900–20	83,000
Bataan	Costa Rica	1964	Consolidation	Consolidation	1930	10,500
Alto Beni I	Bolivia	1959	Pioneer	Pioneer	1960	7,000
Alto Beni II	Bolivia	1963	Pioneer	Pioneer	1964	36,000
Chimoré	Bolivia	1963	Pioneer	Pioneer	1964	120,000
Yapacani	Bolivia	1963	Pioneer	Pioneer	1964	110,000[f]
Semidirected colonization						
Santo Domingo de los Colorados	Ecuador	1964	Consolidation	Consolid./growth	1940–50	210,000
Valle del Upano	Ecuador	1964	Consolidation	Consolidation	1800s	170,000
Tingo María–Tocache	Peru	1966	Consolidation	Consolidation	1947	127,500
Puerto Presidente Stroessner	Paraguay	1963	Consolidation	Consolidation	1945	45,000
Spontaneous colonization						
Caranavi	Bolivia	1945	Pioneer	Consolidation	1945	500,000
Chapare	Bolivia	1920	Pioneer	Consolidation	1920–40	185,000
Caquetá	Colombia	1932	Pioneer	Consolidation	1932	1,050,000
Puyo-Tena	Ecuador	1940	Pioneer	Consolidation	1940	220,000
Private subdivision and development						
Ivinheima (SOMECO)	Brazil	1958	Pioneer	Pioneer/growth	1962	1,000,000
Cia. Melhoramentos Norte do Paraná	Brazil	1930	Pioneer	Growth	1930	1,250,000
Gleba Arinos (CONOMALI)	Brazil	1954	Pioneer	Pioneer	1955	200,000
Tournavista	Peru	1954	Pioneer	Pioneer	1955	410,000
Foreign colonization						
San Juan	Bolivia	1957	Pioneer	Consolidation	1955	35,000
Okinawa	Bolivia	1957	Pioneer	Consolidation	1957	55,000
Filadelfia	Paraguay	1927	Pioneer	Growth	1927	500,000
Total: 24 projects						6,364,000

Note: Data are for 1967–68. Dashes indicate "not available."

[a] T = tropical, S = subtropical, r = rain, w = wet, m = moist, d = dry.
[b] Author's judgment: a = good, b = fair, c = poor.
[c] H = high, M = medium, L = low.

Tropical Land Development Projects

Area cleared (*ha*)	No. of farms	Rural and urban population in project area	Ecological zone[a]	Quality of the physical and institutional environment[b]			Expectation of economic viability[c]	Association with dynamic rural and urban development[b]
				Location	Natural resources	Institutional and administrative conditions		
(7)	(8)	(9)	(10)	(11)	(12)	(13)	(14)	(15)
6,000[d]	703	3,000	Sw	a	b	c	L[e]	b
3,000[d]	476	1,700	Sm	a	b	c	L[e]	b
2,200	285	1,400	Sm	b	c	c	L	c
40,000	4,900	22,000	Tm	a	a	a	L	b
–	265	1,300	Tw	a	c	c	L	c
–	520	2,500	Tm	c	b	c	L	c
4,200	1,400	6,500	Tm	c	b	c	M	c
1,600	700	3,400	Tr	c	c	c	L	c
11,100	1,900	9,500	Sm	b	c	c	M	c
67,000	5,200	40,000	S/Tm	a	b	b	H	a
–	1,400	7,150	Sr	b	b	b	H	b
–	2,150	30,000	Sw	b	b	b	M	b
–	900	4,500	Sm	a	a	b	H	a
36,000	8,250	39,000	Sm	c	c	c	H	a
23,000	5,460	18,600	Tr	c	c	c	L	c
90,000[d]	22,000	175,000	Tw	c	b	b	H	a
105,000	4,000	30,000	Sr	b	b	b	H	a
–	1,600	28,000	Sm	a	a	a	H	a
–	39,000	1,700,000	Sm	a	a	a	H	a
8,000	120	600	Tw	c	b	b	M	c
3,000	100	600	Tw	b	b	c	L	c
9,500	280	1,580	Sm	b	b	a	H	b
20,000[d]	600	4,000	Sm	b	b	a	H	b
100,000[d]	1,500	20,000	Sd	c	c	a	H	a
–	103,709	2,150,330						

[d] Estimate based on average per farm data on crops, pasture, and bush-fallow.
[e] When evaluated within the La Lana–La Trinidad basin expectation is H.
[f] Includes estimate of areas incorporated beyond the original project area of 90,000 ha.

Table 32.   Performance Ranking of Twenty-four
Tropical Land Development Projects

Level of government participation	Project performance[a]		
	Dynamic	Acceptable	Poor
Directed colonization		Nuevo Ixcatlán (L) Cihualtepec (L) La Chontalpa (L)	La Joya (L) Bataan (L) Alto Beni I (L) Alto Beni II (M) Chimoré (L) Yapacani (M)

Semidirected colonization	Santo Domingo de
	   los Colorados (H)
	Puerte Presidente
	   Stroessner (H)
		Upano (H)
		
		Tingo María (M)	

Spontaneous colonization	Caquetá (H) Caranavi (H) Puyo-Tena (H)		Chapare (L)
Private subdivision	Ivinheima (H) CMNP (H)		Gleba Arinos (M) Tournavista (L)
Foreign colonization	Filadelfia (H)	San Juan (H) Okinawa (H)	

[a]Basis for performance rating taken from table 31 (see footnotes d and e). Expectation of economic viability: H=high, M=medium, and L=low.

measure of benefits, appear to have good prospects of being economically viable.

Seven projects are classed as acceptable. Since there is little urban development associated with the acceptable group, employment generation is less than in the dynamic group. The expected economic performance of the seven projects is highly variable. Considered in isolation, Nuevo Ixcatlán and Cihualtepec appear wholly uneconomic, but taken within the context of the La Lana–La Trinidad basin acceptable returns are indicated. La Chontalpa appears to have a low probability of being economic due to the enormous initial cash outlay and expected delays in the achievement of a high-valued multi-cropping system. The other four projects in this group are all expected to yield a satisfactory economic return.

The nine projects with poor performance are characterized as stagnant or slow growing in relation to the massive doses of public or private capital applied to the respective regions. The employment impact of projects in this group has been restricted by an inability to generate either peripheral spontaneous settlement or urbanization. La Joya, Bataan, and Tournavista are expected to show a net loss. Reasonable internal rates of return (IRR) in the range of 10-15 percent may be obtained from Alto Beni II, Yapacani, and Gleba Arinos. Less than 5 percent is expected from the other projects—a poor showing if the opportunity cost capital in most of the countries concerned is taken to be 15 percent plus.

It must be emphasized that the foregoing sample is biased since no real failures are included.[2] But few spheres of economic development have a history of, or reputation for, failure to match that of government-sponsored colonization in humid tropical zones. Horror stories abound about expensive ventures that resulted in colonies where few if any settlers remained after several years—e.g., the first attempt by the Corporación Boliviana de Fomento to colonize Yapacani, Cotoca in Bolivia, and the Bajo Aguan in northern Honduras. The evidence is irrefutable, and failure can be attributed only to the institutions responsible for selecting the area and the colonists, planning and executing the development program, and subsequently maintaining or abandoning the infrastructure and services in the region. The jungle has also taken its toll of private investors. Among the more spectacular disasters is the Fordlândia project in Amazonia. In the early fifties the Ford Motor Company, seeking vertical integration, took up about 200,000 hectares (ha) of virgin jungle land along the Amazon 700 kilometers (km) inland. A rubber plantation of 1.6 million trees was established and within a decade the entire plantation was wiped out by a fungus disease.[3] Undoubtedly there also are cases where spontaneous settlers have been forced to abandon their hard-won lands in the face of starvation when weed infestation, soil fertility loss, or plant and animal disease reduced their output.

The history of tropical land development and the case studies in chapter 5 suggest that failure is directly related to the degree of government involvement in a project, transport costs, and the degree of pioneer colonization involved relative to consolidation with peripheral expansion into new areas. Although one might expect the natural resource endowment of a development area to be an overriding factor, it would be difficult to sustain the thesis that a settlement is doomed to failure in one ecological situation or bound to succeed in another. Filadelfia and Caranavi reasonably could be regarded as unsuited to intensive exploitation on ecological grounds, but they have been relatively successful. On the other hand alluvial flats in the Bajo Aguan that were colonized in the fifties have been abandoned.

Nonetheless the natural resource endowment is obviously important when planners must deal with a fixed quantity or quality of capital, human re-

---

[2] The reader will appreciate that there are difficulties in obtaining data on abandoned projects. No settlers remain to provide information, and government agencies connected with a fiasco are understandably reluctant to divulge information.

[3] F. M. Foland, "A Profile of Amazonia," *Journal of Inter-American Studies and World Affairs*, vol. 13, no. 1 (January 1971), p. 69.

sources, and administrative capability. The starting point in any program of new-land development is an inventory of available information on natural resources. To date, however, land development has been characterized by a piecemeal approach, wide geographic dispersion, and the lack of a relationship to major development goals of the countries concerned. For example, Peru planned to place 1 million ha of tropical forest under cultivation over a twenty-year period, with a public investment of about $300 million.[4] No formal consideration was given to alternative areas; the requirements for creating employment; complementary investments needed in forestry, industries, and services in colonization areas to generate a multiplier effect; or the question of the efficiency of concentration versus dispersion of settlement in five unrelated areas scattered over a 1,200-km forest frontier. In no case does national planning appear to have had any meaningful effect either on project selection or on the level of effort applied to tropical land development.

Within the general context sketched above—the level of state direction in colonization, the stage of development at the time programs are launched, and natural resource endowment—two factors appear to be crucial to success: markets with associated highway access and organization for settlement. A universal assumption in land settlement ventures has been that markets exist and that the cost of producing and transporting commodities to these markets will be low enough to yield a competitive price. This assumption has proved to be the *bête noire* of many projects. Markets are the principal bottleneck in new-land development, and frequently the situation is aggravated by an inefficient or monopolistic marketing structure and high-cost transport stemming from poorly constructed and maintained roads. In the case of La Chontalpa, gross output projections were scaled down by about a third because of potential market surpluses in some of the more intensive crops that were not perceived at the time the original plan was formulated.

Plantation crops have considerable attraction for the planners of public programs because (1) these crops can be produced under centralized management or in cooperatives, and (2) they have a well-known technology that makes it possible to predict the physical production function—characteristics that are not typical of most nonplantation tropical products. The danger here arises from the high costs of establishing plantations and long-term payout periods in a situation where many countries (acting independently) have the capability for large-scale production. Under such supply conditions, market saturation may force prices down to a level approaching the producers' variable costs. Returns on the fixed investment approach zero, as do savings. While there may be a return in a social accounting sense, abandonment of

---

[4]Ministerio de Agricultura, *Inventario de proyectos para incrementar el area cultivada en un millón de hectáreas* (Lima, 1965).

plantations and pressure to keep wages low could reduce the consumption generated by the original investment.

The marketing problem is of institutional origin. Market projections made in support of land development investment are often cursory. The state finds itself incapable of regulating private marketing agents, who sometimes exploit disorganized colonists in isolated forest frontiers—e.g., in Nuevo Ixcatlán. Further, the limited technical and financial capacity of the government usually precludes its providing effective marketing services and credit. In general a more balanced development of production and marketing evolves with spontaneous settlement.

The role of the government is of primary importance in the development process. Practically all recorded colonization failures have been state-directed projects. The inadequate technical and administrative capacity of government agencies has been evident in all phases of the process—e.g., faulty resource surveys on Chimoré, inadequate market analysis for La Chontalpa, insufficient hydrology study for the Yapacani bridge, an inoperable development plan for Bataan, and ineffective project execution on Alto Beni I.

There is little doubt that directed colonization has been a highly uncertain and risky venture, both socially and economically. It is more susceptible than most state programs to the vagaries of political maneuvering, discontinuity of effort, and poor administration. In contrast the three semidirected projects examined were notable for their relatively smooth operation. One positive factor is the simplified administration of semidirected projects made possible by the virtual removal of the elements of uncertainty in regard to natural resources, the stability of settlement, the quality of management, and the economic viability of agriculture that characterize directed colonization in virgin areas. A positive contribution of directed government projects in recent years has been the opportunity to learn, even though learning has been a slow and often expensive process. Many people have acquired experience in a difficult and complex endeavor, and this should help to improve decision making in various branches of government.

Rigidities introduced by a high level of state involvement in the settlement process have led to the misallocation of resources. Governments, and to a greater extent international lending agencies, are faced with a dilemma. On the one hand a rigid plan that is easily audited has obvious advantages in situations characterized by staff and institutional instability. On the other hand precise plans for subdivision, production composition and scheduling, credit disbursement, and infrastructure programming may be both unnecessary and undesirable because they may compound inflexibility when the institutions that draw up the plans also have responsibility for their execution. This suggests the diversion of resources to activities that are less susceptible to uncertainties than the fragile socioeconomic experiments in the directed transfer of population to the tropical land frontier. The alternative lies in more emphasis on services to spontaneous settlement in the consolidation or growth stage or, where pioneer colonization is desired, on orienting programs to penetration roads or private subdivision.

If a high level of government participation is deemed necessary or unavoidable, the long-term nature and uncertainties inherent in tropical land settlement dictate an administrative organization that is flexible, responsive to changing conditions, perceptive of new opportunities, and powerful enough to follow through on extended programs. Within the hierarchy of government, ministries of agriculture have tended to rank low, and, within these ministries, sections or institutes connected with colonization are often among the least important. If an assumption is made that ministries of agriculture will continue to be unstable and underfinanced, the complexities of colonization dictate a search for a stronger agency to take the lead. The most effective institutions appear to be those with an engineering orientation, such as ministries of public works, development corporations, river basin authorities, or hydraulic resource development agencies. Institutions of this kind frequently have the prestige and funds to undertake a long-range integrated approach in a new area. The Grijalva Commission, for example, effectively contracted with other government agencies for the nonengineering inputs in the La Chontalpa project. Although there is the obvious risk that land development might become secondary to the engineering operations, this would be a small price to pay if the project is carried out efficiently.

In the case of spontaneous settlement, as the degree of government participation lessens, a significant portion of the capital and enterprise derives from the colonists themselves. For pioneer development, state participation could be limited to the construction of penetration highways, where chances of error are much reduced. Again in this instance the bottleneck in successful development is institutional: (1) in the selection of areas to be served by penetration roads; (2) in the definition of appropriate resource use and the enforcement of regulations concerning such use; and (3) in the temptation to extend highways at the expense of the maintenance, feeder roads, and public services that should be provided as regions enter the consolidation stage.

As a means of overcoming some of the financial and administrative constraints on new-land development, governments could associate themselves with private corporate enterprise or could foster foreign colonization. Formal arrangements made between the state (to provide infrastructure and agricultural credit), private interests in processing and marketing, and small individual producers offer a possible solution to the problems of undercapitalization, administration, marketing, and extension encountered in many newly developing areas of the Latin American tropics. The agreement between the Ecuadorian Banco Nacional de Fomento (BNF) and the Sociedad Ecuatoriana de Desarrollo Industria Agropecuaria (SEDIA) for tea production is illustrative of this situation.

Brazilian experience offers some interesting insights into the application of private settlement schemes. Between 1950 and 1965, thirty-six projects covering an area of 590,000 ha[5] were initiated officially by nongovernment agencies. While a number of these ventures were based on little more than speculation, the success elements in the cases of the Sociedade de Melhoramentos e Colonização (SOMECO) and the Companhía Melhoramentos Norte do Paraná (CMNP) bear examination. Entrepreneurial talent with perception of economic opportunity, sound administrative ability, and access to capital markets has been marshaled for the settlement of small and medium producers. The policy question is: Under what conditions could such enterprises be replicated? Political conditions changed markedly in the sixties, and state arrangements with private interests are undoubtedly controversial and suspect in many quarters. Formulas acceptable to both governments and development promoters will be difficult to identify, given the long-term nature of the venture.

In the case of foreign colonization it is unlikely that factor proportions in the tropical agriculture of Latin America are such that increments to labor will increase efficiency in total resource use. Massive immigration is not considered. Thus the question is: Will the settlement of small pilot groups, well-trained and highly motivated, have an important impact on land development in surrounding areas, and, if so, how can this impact be maximized? It goes without saying that the ability of individual farmers to assume leadership, take risks, and demonstrate viable production is necessary in new-land development in the humid tropics. Japanese colonists on San Juan and Okinawa have had such a demonstration effect in northwestern Santa Cruz. The experience of Filadelfia provides strong support to those who propose cooperatives as a basis for tropical land development. The Mennonites have demonstrated that with diligent settlers and collective action it is possible to surmount many of the problems stemming from isolation and poor soil and climatic resources. The transferability of these attributes, however, is another matter, and quantification of the impact as a justification for projects presents considerable problems.

The principal elements related to project success and failure are summarized in table 33. The evaluations in this table are based on study of the thirty-seven projects shown earlier in figure 3 and reflect the institutional conditions prevailing in the eleven countries in which the projects were undertaken. Necessarily, a degree of value judgment has been unavoidable in the

[5] Fernando A. Genschow, *O plano nacional de colonização—A colonização do Brazil* (Rio de Janeiro: INDA, April 1967), pp. 8–12.

Table 33. Factors Affecting Performance in Tropical Land Development

Elements influencing project performance	Pioneer			Consolidation			Growth		
	Suc-cess	Neu-tral	Fail-ure	Suc-cess	Neu-tral	Fail-ure	Suc-cess	Neu-tral	Fail-ure
Settlement organization									
Directed			X*	not applicable			not applicable		
Semidirected	not applicable			X			not applicable		
Spontaneous	X*			X*			X*		
Highways									
Access	X*			X*			X		
Feeder	X*			X*			X*		
Maintenance	X			X			X		
Planning									
Existence of a national plan		X			X			X	
Existence of resource inventory		X			X			X	
Existence of project feasibility study		X			X			X	
Application of colonist recruitment procedures		X				X	not applicable		
Forest industry	X*			X*			X		
Rural development activities									
Research		X			X		X		
Extension		X			X		X		
Credit		X		X			X		
Marketing services		X					X		
Cooperative promotion			X		X			X	
Titling		X			X			X	
Housing		X			X			X	
Water supply		X			X			X	
Community development		X			X			X	
Mechanization									
–large-scale commercial enterprises	X			X			X		
–small holdings			X			X			X
Promotion of urban centers (infrastructure and concentration of services, industry, and population)	X*			X*			X*		
Farm size									
Establishment of standard minimum unit (10–15 ha)		X			X			X	
Subdivision in variable sizes	X			X			X		
Reorganization and consolidation of *minifundia*	not applicable					X			X
Balanced development "Package" projects			X*	not applicable			not applicable		

Table 33. (Continued)

Simultaneous rural-urban development	X*	X*	X*
Association of agro-industry and rural development	not applicable	X*	X*
Association of commercial enterprises and small holdings	X	X	X

*High impact on success or failure.

interpretation. Both public administration and conservation issues have been omitted from the list since their influence is, in effect, pervasive throughout the land development process. The elements that characterize failure or are neutral in their impact are due to the technical and administrative deficiencies of public agencies. It will be appreciated that where activities have a neutral impact, resources are largely wasted, and therefore economic returns are lowered.

The project elements that can be manipulated to improve the probability of success are area selection, highways, urbanization, and supporting government services. The interaction between the physical natural resource endowment of an area, the soil technology and forest management applied, and the restrictions imposed on use are not sufficiently understood to provide clear guidelines in area selection.

The destruction of natural resources that have no immediate market in order to provide transitory subsistence for a fraction of the population poses a highly complex problem. While project performance may be unaffected over the short run, the problem must be viewed in the context of a geometric expansion of the area affected, the long-run external diseconomies, and expected increased returns by postponing resource use. National planning, resource surveys, and feasibility studies, as they have been applied in the cases examined, appear to have contributed little to the resolution of this problem, to area selection, or to project success. It is axiomatic that if the planning, surveys, and studies are efficiently carried out the chance of successful tropical land development will be greatly enhanced.

If a single element is to be isolated as the prerequisite to success in new-land development, it must be highways. Even though settlers in isolated areas may have river or air communication with the outside, their foremost concern is roads. For the great majority, prior highway access or the firm expectation of such access, as at Upano, is a condition for settlement. Spontaneous colonists who follow penetration routes and frequently organize feeder roads on their own account are basically market oriented. This attracts truckers and commercial interests who, although unscrupulous in many cases, introduce a dynamism into frontier development, paving the way for effective public measures to regulate, orient, and support production and marketing in these areas. But little systematic thought appears to have been given to the standard, or staged, construction of penetration roads; to whom the benefits of lowered vehicle-operating costs would accrue; or to the relationship between feeder roads and the penetration road in efforts to concentrate development and achieve higher employment, production, and benefit-cost (B/C) ratios from the total highway investment. The importance of roads is illustrated by the negative impact of highway abandonment on La Joya and the positive impact of the Trans-Chaco on Filadelfia and of the feeder roads constructed by the colonists themselves on Caranavi, Caquetá, and the lower La Lana-La Trinidad basin.

The outstanding success of the CMNP in large measure must be attributed to the urbanization policy adopted in the process of occupying new lands. The focus is on critical mass, i.e., concentration versus dispersion, and balance in the package of activities that are to be financed or promoted. Emphasis is placed on integrated investments that will create a labor market in the region. The economic incentive is sufficient to attract private capital and management capacity into a proportion of medium- or large-scale agricultural enterprises, plus agricultural processing and forest industries. Population is concentrated at one point rather than at several points simultaneously along a wide forest frontier.

An urban center must be promoted through the construction of infrastructure and utilities, the centralization of government services and industries, and—to the extent possible—the provision of incentives to the farm population to settle in such areas. Feeder roads should be laid out to concentrate population relative to the center. The size of the farms should be sufficient to maximize aggregate consumption of those goods and services that will create employment in the region. Baldwin made the point that the technological nature of the production functions of the export commodities (he contrasted plantation crops with those suited to family farms) influences the potential for dynamic development in newly settled regions through their impact on: the nature of factor migration, early distribution of income within a region, and the subsequent multiplier effect on the volume of trade.[6] This thesis is borne out by the SOMECO experience. Development along the lines suggested here is clearly favored when the political structure permits the formation of a viable local government.

An alternative to the Brazilian cases mentioned above is a 100 percent application of state enterprise, as in La Chontalpa. In La Chontalpa the

[6] Robert E. Baldwin, "Patterns of Development in Newly Settled Regions," *The Manchester School of Economic and Social Studies*, vol. 24, no. 2 (May 1956), pp. 161–179.

approach was taken one stage further; the farm population was totally urbanized. The experiment is not sufficiently advanced to evaluate, but the public administrative capacity needed for the successful execution of such complex projects is a scarce resource indeed.

Deliberate programs for settler recruitment have constituted a failure element; self-reliant pioneer colonists are not necessarily attracted by the programs, and the executive agency tends to be drawn into expensive paternalistic operations. A set of criteria and mechanisms are required to qualify or disqualify spontaneous settlers or any entity or group taking up new lands.

While government services in support of production research, extension, credit, promotion of cooperatives, and marketing are all to be desired, they have not been prime movers in opening the forest frontier. In theory these services should play a major role in assuring success. In practice the efforts have been largely ineffective; a majority of colonists have not been reached by such services, and those that have been reached frequently show little response in terms of output. The discrepancy between theory and practice must be ascribed to structural factors affecting the distribution of benefits from increased output and to the limited technical and administrative capacity of the agencies involved. Again it must be taken as self-evident that efficient provision of these services together with structural change will be most beneficial to project performance.

The effectiveness of credit is intimately related to the marketability of the product and the capacity of bank personnel to assess the credit worthiness of clients. The practice of granting credit indiscriminately on many directed projects is conducive to failure in economic terms. While a number of selective credit programs under consolidation conditions appear to have been successful, such as that of the Instituto Columbiana de la Reforma Agraria in Caquetá and of the BNF in Santo Domingo de los Colorados, the proportion of producers participating tends to be limited—3 percent in Caranavi, 10 percent in Santo Domingo de los Colorados, and 25 percent in Caquetá. It is axiomatic that capital is a bottleneck in new-land development when policy is oriented to the settlement of families who have little or no resources of their own. Because of the high incidence of credit delinquency in pioneer areas and the limited financial resources of most governments, credit should be reserved for the consolidation or growth stages to achieve the greatest impact on per capita incomes. Where markets are assured—e.g., for sugar in Santa Cruz—producers have shown themselves more than willing to form cooperatives, to accept advice from extension agents, and to manage credit in order to take full advantage of their opportunities. The problem faced by the government is to find products and a marketing mechanism that will assure attractive prices without undue subsidy.

Social services—education, health, land titling, community development, housing, and utilities—would be expected to have a favorable impact on productivity and stability of settlement. Their effect on project success, however, has been similar to that of the production services mentioned above. It must be taken for granted that education and health services must be provided; the other services have not been critical to success.

Project Appraisal and Design

Perhaps the most difficult problem in tropical land development in the past has been to define the technical constraints: (1) the measurement of the physical potential, use of "miracle" crop varieties, side effects from chemical or sustained cultivation, and the production function for agriculture; (2) the soil and hydraulic factors that govern the costs of highway construction and maintenance; (3) the conservation implications in terms of wasted forest reserves, soil erosion and yield decline, and downstream effects of accelerated runoff; and (4) the costs of corrective conservation measures. The analyst may well ask: How can an investment be undertaken in the absence of such elementary data? Project design presents a dismal prospect when one adds to the physical data uncertainties—which are theoretically quantifiable within rather narrow confidence limits (albeit a costly exercise)—the qualitative factors related to social behavior, institutions, and markets.

The principal characteristic of the directed and semidirected projects that have been evaluated is the consistent discrepancy between the initial projections and the results after three to five years of execution. On the basis of projections that have been revised in light of the experience to date, the expected IRR's are reduced by about two-thirds. Admittedly these revisions are still projections; however, the deviations from planned operation are sufficiently sharp to cast considerable doubt on the probability of realizing even revised twenty-year plans. The Chimoré settlement in 1968 had reached only 20 percent of the project target for that year and 10 percent of gross production.

There has been a tendency to underestimate costs and overestimate benefits. This situation stems from such aspects as deficient engineering, inadequate resource and marketing studies, and unrealistic production plans—e.g., Bataan, where projected yields were double or triple those actually achieved. Other examples are Puerto Presidente Stroessner, where additional mill machinery and technical assistance were assumed capable of reducing unit production costs of lumber to 8 percent of the preproject level, and Alto Beni II, where only about 5 percent of the projected marketable timber was actually harvested. This optimism results in extremely high projected IRR's— Upano, 60 percent; Bataan, 30 percent; Alto Beni II, 50 percent. If returns of this magnitude are to be taken seriously, it must be asked why governments did not divert major resources to colonization.

On what basis have these decisions been reached? There is little evidence that a systematic approach has been used. Penetration roads such as Caranavi,

Belém-Brazília, or Cuiabá-Acre have been constructed essentially without regard to the development of the area through which they passed. In pioneer projects, total failures such as the Bajo Aguan appear to be more attributable to isolation and poor access than to error in technical information. Indications are that the degree of ignorance about the physical, social, and economic factors in new-land development was similar in most cases of pioneer settlement. Theoretically, at least, there should have been information on natural resources in the directed cases. But at the time original pioneer settlements were launched at Caranavi, Chapare, Puyo-Tena, Tingo María, Belém-Brazília, Tournavista, Caquetá, Nuevo Ixcatlán, La Joya, Cihualtepec, Puerto Presidente Stroessner, and Santo Domingo de los Colorados, available information was minimal on any of the factors above. In all of these cases, as in the directed pioneer projects, viable agriculture proved to be possible. The success or failure of the projects depended on the institutional conditions that guided the proportions of the production factors in the exploitation of the regions. The directed projects were saddled with high public expenditures and a rigid design based on information that could not be as accurate as assumed without excessive expenditures for studies on hydrology, sociology, anthropology, soils, and so on. Spontaneous pioneer settlement was not burdened by high overhead, and projects launched in the consolidation phase had the benefit of a considerable accumulation of information on the factors listed above.

The exceptionally high degree of uncertainty associated with humid tropical land development, combined with multiple objectives, suggests that when projects are appraised probability distributions should be assigned to relevant factors that can then be aggregated to yield estimates of the probability distribution of net present value (NPV) or IRR.[7] Projects of this type are affected by a number of basic events and parameters that are stochastic, such as rainfall, floods, production coefficients, supply elasticities, or price. While the problem of quantifying variables is undeniable, recognition of this very fact justifies mathematical formulation and analysis. Sensitivity analysis can be used to identify minimum conditions for acceptability and those elements whose deviation from projections is most likely to affect outcome, thus requiring that contingency elements be built into the design from the outset. The mathematical approach facilitates flexible programming, which is the essence of project execution in this area, and simplifies the incorporation of improved data as they come to hand. It is hoped that this will lead to a better definition of bench mark situations.

In B/C analysis the results are sensitive to those elements that constitute a relatively high proportion of total benefits or costs or to those whose values

[7]Shlomo Reutlinger, *Techniques for Project Appraisal Under Uncertainty*, IBRD, World Bank Staff Occasional Papers no. 10 (Washington 1970).

are high in the early years of the project. The relative impact on the IRR's of changes in costs and benefits whose incidence over time is increasing or decreasing is illustrated in figure 5. Where initial benefits are high and decreasing with time (curve B_2)—e.g., forestry—the IRR is sensitive to small changes in benefits. The situation is similar for costs (curve C_1) having the same configuration—e.g., expensive infrastructure projects in highways, drainage, irrigation, or directed colonization that is financed 100 percent. Curves C_2 and B_1, representing increasing costs (e.g., social services) and increasing benefits (e.g., agriculture), indicate the relative insensitivity of the IRR to changes in elements with this type of time pattern. For instance the IRR in figure 5 can be increased from r to r' with an x percent increase in B_2 or a $7x$ percent increase in B_1.

Typically, in project analysis for new-land development it has been assumed that the flow of benefits and costs would be the same regardless of when the project was initiated. There may be no basis for forecasting changes

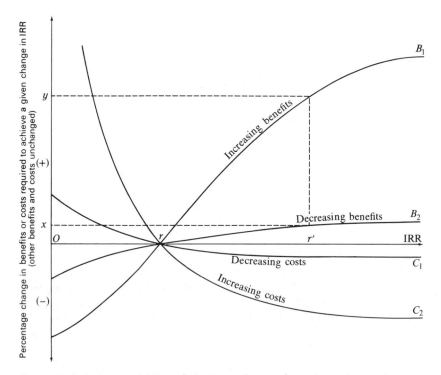

Figure 5. Relative sensitivity of the internal rate of return to changes in costs and benefits whose distribution over time is decreasing or increasing. The curves are merely illustrative; $r = 15$ percent is used as the point equating the various cost and benefit flows.

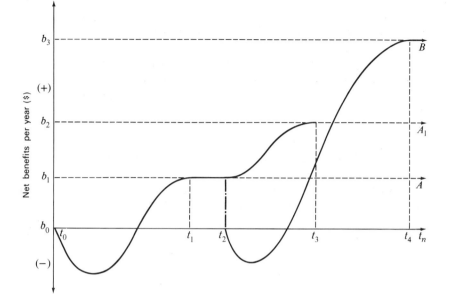

Figure 6. Benefit rates over calendar time under two assumptions on the efficiency of resource use and the project starting time.

in demand for project inputs and products that alter prices and change the benefit rate over time from constant physical output. It was suggested in chapter 2, however, that institutional and technical aspects that influence project performance may improve over time. A potential situation is illustrated in figure 6. For a given project initiated at t_0—on the assumption of significant destruction of forests and soils because of the lack of suitable technology or administrative capacity to control the use of natural resources—the benefit flow is t_0A reaching a stable level b_1 at t_1. This static condition can be replaced by an assumption that at t_2 the government achieves a major advance in its administrative capacity with or without an improvement in technology. As a result project benefits are raised to b_2 over the period $t_2 t_3$ and remain constant thereafter to t_n. Prior destruction, however, precludes reaching a benefit level higher than b_2. If the conditions above are expected over the period t_n, an alternative is to delay the project until t_2, in which case a benefit flow t_2B clearly yields a higher return than either t_0A or t_0A_1. Initiation of the project prior to t_2 will reduce the NPV or IRR progressively as the date approaches t_0, assuming that the same capital could earn its opportunity cost in another project.

Aside from the possibility of postponing investment, scheduling and capital intensity are of major importance in the design of tropical land development projects. The question of capital intensity, particularly in mechanization, is closely tied to the labor value and employment issues that were discussed in chapter 4. Concern is frequently expressed about the competition between men and machines in developing countries.[8] The excessive use of machinery may result from undervalued foreign exchange, overvalued labor, the rising aspirations of colonists with access to subsidized state credit, or "the ambition of some Governments to acquire prestige through spectacular spending."[9] The mechanization of highway construction and major drainage schemes is apparently accepted as beyond argument and is not treated here. The focus, then, is forest clearing and subsequent operations in farming or forest industry. Aside from shadow pricing the primary considerations are (1) markets; (2) minimum conditions for attracting settlers in terms of the type and hours of work and consumption expectations; (3) land requirements to meet minimum consumption expectations and the capacity of the colonists to maintain this land in production without machinery whether or not mechanization increases or decreases production per unit area; and (4) economies of scale related to investments, such as infrastructure, as a consequence of more or less intensive exploitation of the land. If there are no market constraints, employment might well be increased through mechanization. The same would be true if significant forward linkages from agriculture are expected—e.g., labor-intensive processing for export—or in cases where land would otherwise be abandoned.

In a situation where capital and markets are limiting with weak backward and forward linkages from mechanization and where underemployment and income distribution are weighted among the objectives, it becomes difficult to justify mechanized land clearing for massive settlement in the tropics. Of course, without mechanization, it is necessary that unpaid family labor be willing to undertake the task of clearing. In individual projects, such as La Chontalpa, that have a high-cost infrastructure, acceptable IRR's can be attained only through the rapid and intensive exploitation that mechanization makes possible. But if the conditions above prevail, this is not a model for extensive land settlement.

Livestock poses a similar problem in mechanizing a project. Cattle enterprises are not intensive in the use of labor; thus new employment generated per unit of investment in infrastructure, land development, and animals is much less than in cropping. Nevertheless cattle offer a solution in tropical areas that are unsuitable for crops, and there appears to be sufficient demand to maintain prices that reflect the high freight charges from isolated jungle

---

[8] See Estevam Strauss, *Metodología de evaluación de los recursos naturales*, Cuadernos del ILPES, Serie II, no. 4 (Santiago, 1969), p. 19.

[9] W. A. Lewis, *Development Planning: The Essentials of Economic Policy* (Harper & Row, 1966), p. 66.

frontiers. The issue is further complicated by the colonist's expectation that returns on an investment in cattle, where scale will permit adequate management, are more secure than in traditional crops.

In developing new areas, balance among complementary activities, both within and without the project area, is widely advocated. If markets are limiting, it is argued, new-land development must be matched by programs that give incentives for expanded demand either by final consumers or processing industries. This requires tracing the multiplier effect of the increased primary production through an interindustry model to identify where bottlenecks might be expected to occur. If bottlenecks are found, the original project must be adapted and expanded to induce investments to achieve complementarity, economies of scale, and external economies—i.e., internalizing such economies.[10]

In the absence of a general equilibrium model of the economy, little contribution can be made to clarifying the question of balance at the national level. The prime concern, therefore, is the package of activities within the project. Many government attempts at comprehensive colonization schemes have been wasteful of resources. This has been due to the conviction of project planners that the information necessary to program various inputs and outputs was available and to inflexibility in project execution when the original information was found to be faulty. The quest for balance at the project level in the pioneer stage tends to complicate an already complex activity fraught with uncertainties. It is much easier to locate bottlenecks in the consolidation or growth stages.

In the original plans an integrated approach to project design was rarely adopted as a basis for economic evaluation. In many cases clear definitions were lacking on such aspects as the starting date and sunk costs; preproject production and occupancy; the gross and net project area; new colonists to be settled; the virgin forest area to be developed; the reinvestment rate and the colonists' prospensity to save; supply elasticity; the source of public and private investment; investment requirements for forestry development and the output and costs of production of timber products; access highways; and annual maintenance costs during and after development. Explicit treatment of the employment implications and the opportunity costs of labor, capital, and natural resources were lacking in project statements. Only in the case of La Chontalpa did the original plan include any consideration of labor needed in addition to that which could be drawn from colonists' families. Upano was the only case where a value was placed on family labor. In no case was any effort made to measure urban employment associated with colonization.

---

[10]Willis W. Shaner, "Economic Evaluation of Investments in Agricultural Penetration Roads in Developing Countries: A Case Study of the Tingo María-Tocache Project in Peru" (Report EEP-22, Institute of Engineering-Economic Systems, Stanford University, California, August 1966, mimeo.).

The exclusion or inclusion of highway investments as a project cost is frequently debated. A case may be made to charge investment in, and maintenance of, trunk roads to national and international integration and long-term economic development. As long as the project itself will bear the cost of the trunk road, this is academic. If a chance exists, however, that the project benefits will not justify the inclusion of highway costs, then more serious attention must be given to the exact nature and timing of the expected benefits and to the probability of their realization.

Government costs per settler have become a principal issue in the selection and design of colonization projects. Evaluation requires clarification of what will be considered project costs, of shadow prices, of cost allocation, of who constitutes a settler, and of what multiplier effects can be measured and included. The range of experience and project outcomes demonstrates the inappropriateness of unqualified costs per colonist as an index useful in decision making.

Meaningful evaluation criteria are difficult to establish where programs are applied in the consolidation stage of development. The imponderable is what would have happened without the project. In such complex situations an attempt to attribute impact to any of the various investment components is open to criticism. But such a determination is an essential element in the allocation of scarce resources and the establishment of the correct combination of complementary programs.

External economies in pioneer tropical settlement are slow in making their appearance. The expansive and unquantifiable references to these external economies in original plans are of doubtful assistance in project decisions and such economies have not been apparent to the point of being useful indicators for future policy. Although any well-conceived project offers the opportunity for government officials to acquire experience in new-land development, the application of this experience to other development areas is often vague and a long time in coming. No useful attempt can be made to delimit the areas to which the experience will apply or to establish when it might be applied.[11] There is little indication to date that state projects in directed colonization have been truly pilot projects in that they have demonstrated the viability of tropical agriculture and thus have spearheaded a self-sustaining wave of spontaneous immigration and land development that has resulted in subsequent urban growth. In view of the rate at which technology is advancing, the apparent limitation on the transferability of knowledge from one

---

[11] An exception may be La Chontalpa. Much of the early justification for undertaking the El Limón project was its pilot nature. Insofar as the Grijalva Commission undertakes development of the remaining 170,000 ha in the balance of phases I and II, the experience gained will be invaluable. The whole basin of the Grijalva and Usumasinta rivers contains almost 1 million ha of similar lands to which the development and production experience on La Chontalpa can be applied.

tropical area to another, extended lags in the realization of external effects of the type mentioned here, and difficulties of measurement, it is concluded that these external effects should carry little weight in the evaluation of tropical land development investments.

Some General Policy Considerations

It has been stressed throughout that the development of new lands in Latin America is an inevitable and irreversible process that has considerable momentum. Government funds are committed; land concessions are granted; and international loans are approved for highways, colonization, forestry, large-scale mechanized agriculture, and livestock. There is a political commitment that constitutes both a potential danger, in terms of wasted resources, and a dynamic force that can be harnessed and directed toward seeking more effective procedures for accelerating development.

The prerequisite for policy formulation is the establishment of who benefits and who pays. As a general rule the primary beneficiaries of public programs to open new lands must be landless campesinos. Benefits that accrue from associated construction, processing, or marketing may be channeled to small landowners or the state through cooperative or public enterprise. Without such organizations, and when structural deficiencies in taxation or other state regulatory mechanisms (price, freight rate, monopoly) are present, the principal benefits may be reaped by factors in secondary or tertiary activities. When it comes to the question of who pays, the focus is on how much of the public investment will be recovered from those who receive new lands, i.e., the direct beneficiaries. Recovery from indirect beneficiaries must be expected through regular tax channels and is hardly accountable on a project basis. The implication of most land settlement projects is that wealth will be transferred, through subsidized development, from the rest of the economy, to the direct and indirect beneficiaries, thus the incidence of nonrecoupable costs depends on the national taxation and price control system. The immediate objective is usually the flow of population and private and public capital to forest frontier areas in the expectation of employment generation (income distribution effects), foreign exchange saving, and economic returns higher than the next best alternative. Other motivations for developing idle tropical lands might include the fulfillment of "national destiny," defense, the establishment of sovereignty, or aspirations to take "full advantage" of the natural resource endowment.

The essential conclusion to be drawn from both the negative and positive theories discussed in chapter 2 is that new-land development should be postponed pending improved knowledge and institutional structures—i.e., the conservationist position is reinforced. Since the positive theory is largely speculative and requires wholly new approaches, an examination of past experience throws little light on the probability of overcoming current institutional and technological bottlenecks through such approaches. On the other hand experience does bear out much of the negative theory. Costs of penetration roads are unquestionably high—e.g., $51 million for the Chapare access road and $44 million for the Santa Cruz highway, which require massive and rapid benefits for economic justification. Relatively high infrastructure costs coupled with an objective of developing an agriculture above the subsistence level may dictate the use of large-scale capital-intensive methods for forest clearance or drainage. If colonists are drawn from the subsistence sector there is no possibility of financing such methods from their own resources. In consequence limited public funds may be used to subsidize the deliberate creation of small favored groups. In theory this subsidization may be unintentional since full recuperation of government loans is expected. However, repayments by colonists have been minimal or zero in many cases. As an alternative the necessary investment could be made either through a state enterprise (La Chontalpa) or by vertically integrated agricultural corporations (SEDIA) and land development promotion organizations (SOMECO). But because of the existing political climate in Latin America, the acceptability of the two latter forms of private investment appears to be progressively diminishing.

Evidence of soil erosion, laterization, and the destruction of forest and wildlife resources, while not quantified, is undeniable. But emotive discussion of the consequences—the creation of wastelands, downstream flooding, silting, weather changes, or reduced carbon dioxide exchange—is of little help. If policy makers are to be convinced, considerably more hard data are required to establish the probability of long-term benefits from forgoing present consumption. For instance, twenty years' evidence of yield declines, forest destruction, erosion, and downstream effects in the cases of Caranavi and Caquetá does not lead to a conclusion that development should have been delayed.

Countries that looked to their extensive virgin tropical forest lands as a basis for accelerating economic development have found themselves constrained by markets. Virtually all tropical exports originate in the coastal regions—a small fraction of Latin America's humid tropics. Limited quantities of beef, mahogany, Brazil nuts, and coffee from the central and upper Amazon find their way into international trade. While a number of individual projects oriented to export are economically viable (SEDIA's 1,800 ha of tea or the 2,000 ha of bananas on La Chontalpa), it is abundantly clear that the development of plantations on any significant scale is out of the question. Thus if a massive investment in agriculture is seen as a solution to the problems of underdevelopment, the contribution of tropical plantations will be limited. The principal hope for a solution rests on the ability of settlers in virgin tropical areas to gain an expanding share of the world market for animal products, fibers, and vegetable oils at the expense of suppliers in temperate regions.

The domestic market for most tropical food products can be readily supplied if there are minor expansions in area and employment. This is illustrated by Santa Cruz, which, within five or six years of the completion of the access highway, was able to saturate the Bolivian market for rice and sugar through the development of about 50,000 ha—a drop in the bucket compared with the land available and the country's need to generate productive employment. On the El Pimental project at Tournavista, by 1971 forty colonists with 10 ha of pepper each were expected to produce three times the volume of pepper imported by Peru in 1968.[12]

The improved income distribution implicit in reform programs will have only a slight effect on total per capita food consumption. Although major shifts in the consumption pattern could occur, it is unlikely that the land and labor resources required to provide tropical food items would be significantly increased on a per capita basis. Industrial tropical crops, such as vegetable oils, fibers, and rubber, will also encounter limited national markets. The long-run prospects for a major expansion of these crops are governed by the development of domestic industries that are competitive in international markets.

Where the opening of new tropical lands is seen as the avenue to the relief of rural poverty, the approach is constrained by (1) the public investment required to make major transfers of population; (2) the degree to which the state carries out its objective of improving the level of living—an improvement that must be sufficient to attract the necessary migration; and (3) the market orientation necessary to yield the prescribed level of living and the relationship between marketable surplus generated and the total market opportunities. Extensive application of directed colonization, where nonrecoupable government investments range up to $3,000 per family, cannot be sustained. For example, for Bolivia to have achieved the stated objective of establishing 100,000 families between 1961 and 1970 on directed settlements would have required 40 percent of state revenues for the immediate benefit of about 10 percent of the population, but about 90 percent of the population was equally in need of assistance.

When the range of issues is considered, philosophical questions arise about the degree of coercion that can or should be applied by the government and the extent to which the state should stand by and allow coercion to be imposed by private interest groups or by the natural environment itself. If a serious goal is occupancy of vacant tropical lands and the population is unresponsive to the incentives provided, resort must be taken to such measures as military settlement. If economic return on public investment becomes paramount and there is no faith in campesino motivation or management capacity, then individual or collective decision making must be suppressed in

[12]BFA, "Colonización El Pimental—Un programa piloto para la promoción del cultivo de la pimienta en el Peru" (Pucallpa, Peru, July 1968, mimeo.).

favor of a technocratic solution. At the other end of the scale the degree of government inaction reflects an implicit policy of allowing inexperienced colonists to be exploited by predatory private interests or of leaving the colonists to battle the elements unaided by the provision of housing or social services. Policy formulation on new-land development in the humid tropics has not involved any formal evaluation of these extreme positions in order to arrive at some balance consistent with national goals. Any move in this direction would appear to be advantageous.

What of the Future?

Without exception government agencies lament the indiscriminate destruction of tropical forests and the irresponsible mining of the soil. For decades, however, they have remained impotent, and they even may have aggravated the situation with their road-building policies.

The enormous gaps in the knowledge needed for formulating policy for the development of new lands in Latin America's humid tropics can be filled only if research is used to identify and then to elucidate the critical elements and if projects are designed specifically to yield data based on experience. There is clearly a need for research into the institutional factors that bear on government impotence and the administrative inability to effectively orient or control resource use. On the technical side, questions that bear examination include the possibility of processing wood and foliage for food or hydrocarbons, the hydrology and downstream effects of accelerated runoff, the conditions contributing to yield decline and the technology for halting the decline, and the irreversibility of soil erosion. What motivates people to take up new lands is very imprecisely understood—i.e., how the supply of settlers is affected by such incentives as the expectation of improved consumption levels, land ownership and independence, and social services. What is the elasticity of supply in relation to roads and other services provided in frontier areas?

The foregoing is not to suggest a massive crash program of resource inventories, sociological studies, and the like. First, some thought must be given to *why* developments should be pressed forward in the jungle; to how, where, and when to develop; and to available alternatives. The present study, which is based on an examination of actual projects, is an attempt to clarify some of the issues in order to contribute to laying the framework needed to answer the why and how of development.

The positive theory holds that public institutions will generate the necessary financial and administrative capabilities needed to undertake massive integrated jungle development projects. These institutions will provide a sufficient flow of knowledge and capital to potential beneficiaries to assure marketable production, the necessary rate of migration, and an efficient cooperative organization. Given this proposition and excluding the question of whether or not to develop the tropical forest frontier, the policy issues disappear.

If the principal tenets of the negative theory concerning constraints imposed by markets, the ability to generate employment, and government financial and administrative capability are accepted, what avenues are available to use the untapped land and forest resources of the humid tropics to further economic development? Three suggest themselves:

1. The expansion of subsistence agriculture.
2. The creation of local or regional markets by forming production-consumption centers, or growth poles, in the tropical interior.
3. Phased expansion onto new lands, in line with minimum income criteria and consistent with projected markets (without radical change in their spatial distribution).

A deliberate program of investments having as its specific objective the massive expansion of subsistence agriculture is conceivable only after careful evaluation of the alternatives. No public agency could risk making such an objective explicit, even with solid economic justification for the approach as an intermediate step in the development process that would at least sustain rural per capita consumption levels until urban areas could create enough jobs to absorb accelerated rural migration. According to Yudelman and Howard: "The modest subsidy programme, which contributes to retaining self-sustaining underemployed in the rural areas would appear to be more beneficial to the economy at this time than a much higher-cost programme to maintain unemployed in the urban areas."[13] The actual capacity to retain population in subsistence agricultural activities will depend on the families' evaluation of the probability of improvement if they move to a town.[14]

The cases studied indicate that highways and the minimal social services associated with spontaneous colonization in peripheral frontier areas can result in relatively low-cost settlement at subsistence levels higher than the lower strata in the more densely populated rural areas. Whether the application of such policies could achieve a transference of population to the virgin jungle regions on a sufficient scale to stem the tide of urban migration is highly unlikely. Whether economic or social considerations dictate the massive expansion of subsistence agriculture—with, it is hoped, higher per capita consumption levels—requires broader analysis than has been adopted in this inquiry.

[13]Montague Yudelman and Frederic Howard, *Agricultural Development and Economic Development in Latin America* (Washington: IDB, April 1969), p. 178.

[14]John R. Harris and Michael P. Todaro, "Migration, Unemployment and Development," *American Economic Review*, vol. 60, no. 1 (March 1970), pp. 127-28.

The "growth pole" hypothesis requires the region to develop an exportable surplus that becomes the economic base for autonomous expansion of local employment and consumption. Thus market constraints apply. If producer incomes approach the subsistence level the multiplier effect will be negligible. Unless settlers have viable farm units and the technical and financial means to develop them, little economic growth can be expected. If a national program for the settlement of new lands is adopted, however, and the technical and financial means must be provided by the government, it follows that the creation of privileged groups by granting excessive subsidies or incentives should be avoided. The development of a growth pole based on tropical agriculture and forestry would appear to require special conditions. For example, the base of the Londrina project was coffee—the leading industry during the postwar boom in that commodity. The project also had a substantial injection of capital and entrepreneurial talent and was a satellite within the São Paulo market complex. A more typical case is that of Santa Cruz where the prime movers were petroleum and gas, supported by mahogany exports and a sharp increase in import-substituting agricultural products, some of which were amenable to vertical integration. While the experience of the cases studied points toward emphasis on urban development in association with new-land settlement, the partial approach that has been used precludes any meaningful test of the hypothesis that interior growth poles in the tropics will lead to the most effective use of available resources for economic development.[15]

In review, without a model of the national economy little can be drawn from the cases studied that illuminates the theses on the expansion of subsistence farming or new growth poles. Aside from these two approaches the primary issues governing policy on the extension of the agricultural land frontier center on (1) the cautious pilot approach versus the big push, with or without balanced activities, to achieve a critical mass yielding external economies; (2) geographic dispersion versus concentration of effort; (3) the market prospects in combination with minimum income, employment, and income distribution requirements; (4) conservation versus depletion; (5) the source of capital and enterprise—i.e., public or private, foreign or domestic; and (6) the stage of development of the region selected to apply measures for expansion of new lands.

The view taken of these issues will be conditioned by whether the decision maker is a private investor, a government administrator, or a loan committee chairman from an international financing agency. Each will have differing and possibly conflicting objectives. It can be assumed that the private entrepreneur will be a profit-maximizer. Undoubtedly it will be a long time before the

[15]Carlos Matus Romo, "El desarrollo del interior de América Latina," in ILPES, *Dos polémicas sobre el desarrollo de América Latina* (Santiago, Chile: Editorial Universitaria, S. A., October 1970), pp. 3–85.

government decision maker enjoys the benefit of reliable parameters that prescribe national policy objectives—e.g., weighting factors on income distribution or social accounting prices for labor, foreign exchange, and capital. An international institution for development financing would be concerned with the borrower's capacity to repay the loan, obtaining leverage on wider policies than those directly affecting any given project, and the execution of the project in accordance with the loan agreement.

An important factor governing success in tropical land development is the source of capital and enterprise. The record shows that government-directed settlement has given poor results and has failed completely in a number of cases. In such projects no mechanism has been available to attract private capital and management ability in support of development. Further, the involvement of international financing agencies has introduced rigidities for monitoring purposes that have impaired the execution of what were already overly complex operations.

Failure has a high cost—little if any of the state expenditure in infrastructure, housing, land clearing, moving expenses, subsistence, or credit can be salvaged. A high degree of uncertainty is associated with tropical land expansion and settlement ventures and is compounded when responsibility is vested in weak institutions. Under these circumstances, attempts at complex "big push" or "balanced package" approaches almost inevitably will founder under the weight of market constraints, mismanagement, constantly changing personnel, and policy reversals. The less the state has interfered in the settlement process and the more it has concentrated on providing services demanded by the colonists, the better the result has been in economic and social terms. Given land reform objectives throughout Latin America and increased political instability, the investment climate for private capital must be judged as poor, especially considering ten-to-twenty-year pay-out periods on such ventures as plantations or settlement promotion.

There are many aspects of tropical agriculture and forestry that are subject to economies of scale. For example, plantation crops are generally more competitive in markets outside the local region if production is both vertically and horizontally integrated. Forest industry also may benefit from vertical integration. Successful sustained crop and livestock production require high levels of technology. The management skills needed to apply such technology frequently must be imported to the region at a high price and therefore are justified only for large enterprises. Further, the risks involved (weather, disease, price, input costs) in production for the market may be too great for the small farmer. Cooperatives are universally promoted to achieve these economies, but the performance record is dismal. An alternative is state enterprise. Again the bottleneck is management—few government agencies can provide the needed talent on a sustained basis.

Where there are real market constraints, as is the case for most tropical products, and where rural labor is underemployed, as it is in all tropical countries of Latin America, the use of scarce capital for mechanized forest clearing and farming makes neither economic nor social sense. On financial grounds, a capital-intensive operation for specialty export production may be readily justifiable. However, limitations on the market dictate that land and labor resources dedicated to such activities wil! be inconsequential. The prime importance of these resources will be as catalysts for associated small-scale, labor-intensive settlement and service employment, if the use of idle natural resources is seen as a means of making a major contribution to employment and consumption.

In spite of the evil reputation spontaneous settlement has acquired because of natural resource destruction and shifting subsistence agriculture, it offers the best chance of success in developing new lands where capital and administrative resources are scarce. The key element is highway access, preferably to areas on the periphery of an existing settlement where soil is reasonably good. The pioneer settlers who follow such roads will better match the development task than those who come as a result of elaborate promotional and selection procedures.

As settlers become established, the next step is phased and flexible state support for consolidation and expansion through deliberate programs in marketing, feeder roads, urban centers, forestry industry, agro-industry, and services. These efforts should be concentrated geographically rather than follow the usual practice of dispersion, with the aim of creating a major urban center and labor market in the region and giving impetus to the formation of a viable municipal government.

To these ends the establishment of medium or large corporate entities (private, public, or quasi-public) in both agriculture and industry is essential. Such enterprises will test and demonstrate new farming techniques, introduce needed management skills, provide employment and the basis for an expanding market for service and local agricultural production, and may mobilize private capital and entrepreneurial talent. The primary drawback to this type of development stems from the governments' inability (1) to identify areas that should not be used for agriculture, that should be reserved for forestry prior to agricultural development, or that should be reserved for other reasons; (2) to exercise effective control over land and forest use, even if these areas were identified; and (3) to strike a balance in the regulation of commercial enterprise.

This approach may be criticized as the application of an inadmissible social law of survival of the fittest. In addition it appears to condemn a generation of colonists to a life of deprivation. The idea that pioneer settlers need not be universally provided with credit and a full range of social services from the date of entry into new areas seems to reflect a complete disregard for social costs. Justification rests on the premise that massive support to colonization areas frequently has been largely wasted—benefits have been short-lived, the social infrastructure has fallen into disrepair and become inoperative, colonist turnover has been high, and per capita production has been low. Consequently public funds would have been better used in other endeavors to achieve social goals.

The planner is constantly striving to place decision making in the widest possible context. He argues that unless any given program, such as new-land development in the humid tropics, is viewed within both a continental and a national framework, there is no rational basis for setting objectives. At the national level the political motivation has been to secure territorial sovereignty through the geographic distribution of population and to allay pressures for agrarian reform in the guise of aid to landless campesinos through the mobilization of unused natural resources. Seen in these terms it is small wonder that deliberate government programs in tropical land settlement have lacked a development focus. Outside Brazil few of these efforts have made a significant contribution to economic growth.

This situation is changing. There is more concern with development, and all tropical countries of Latin America are firmly dedicated to the continued expansion of the jungle frontier. The international lending agencies possess certain attributes that qualify them to play a role in achieving a more systematic expansion onto new lands, especially when the development planners' goal is to introduce order and procedures for the evaluation of alternatives. These agencies bring to the scene a diverse and qualified technical capacity in natural resources, engineering, sociology, economics, and public administration. Their wide experience is reflected in realistic project design and implementation, and in a rigorous performance that can seldom be matched by governments wary of making unpopular decisions. When these lending agencies are involved in a project, they achieve a continuity that transcends the political instability of individual countries. Moreover their experience, long-range perspectives, and worldwide view of potentials and objectives lead to flexibility in program and project administration. In new-land development the initial responsibility of the international lending agencies is to assign financial and technical resources to assist countries in defining land development goals and in identifying the most appropriate areas for achieving these goals. The next step is to place land development programs within the context of Latin American trade; domestic markets for agricultural and forestry products; and plans for infrastructure and a mineral or forestry industry in the tropical interior.

Having set the stage for individual project financing, the first priority would be phased assistance for the consolidation of present spontaneous settlement. The second priority would be to establish a forest industry and to build feeder roads on the periphery of existing viable settlements in areas already opened up by trunk highways, or in regions having a potential for multiple resource (particularly mineral) exploitation aimed at creating a major urban center.[16] All the financed activities would require a perspective of ten to fifteen years and a specific provision for the feedback of data to be used for continuous evaluation and reorientation. Financing should be linked with powerful government agencies or regional authorities in order to bring appropriate management and capital in support of spontaneous colonization and the creation of associated industrial and service activities.

If there is merit in attracting private capital, management, technical expertise, promotion, and marketing into the development of lands that will be farmed by small and medium producers, the drawbacks associated with private companies operating in the colonization field might be overcome where an international financing agency is involved. Commitments by such an agency could provide the element of stability required by private investors, while assuring the controls and income distribution required by government—the specification of development rates and minimum investment levels, compliance with labor laws, and restriction on land aggregation. The realization of full benefits from such activities will require reorientation of the entrenched ideas held by both governments and private enterprise.

The tenor of this analysis is by all odds negative. Little in the record sustains the theses that the tropical countries are metaphorically "floating on a lake of oil" in the form of their huge virgin forest lands; that these resources represent an infinite sponge that can absorb unlimited population in primary production and the multiplier effects of such production; or that the key to rapid economic development is a large infusion of capital for flattening the jungle so that bananas, cattle, or corn can be grown and processed.

It goes without saying that it is better to have than not to have these resources, but to equate them with Argentina's pampas or Venezuela's oil is indeed wishful thinking. None can deny that with yet-to-be-developed technology enormous wealth might be derived from this region. In the meantime it can be argued that these unexploited areas have some potentially negative features in that euphoria over their development prospects causes nations to divert resources and energy from the really crucial problems to be solved.

Employment is undoubtedly one of the primary issues facing developing countries. But the idea that a government can take a preselected underemployed group, say, 100,000 families from city x, region y, or industry z, transfer them to the jungle, and expect economic or social success is patently ridiculous. By all means information on opportunities of all types should be channeled to those in need of assistance, with preference given to those who apply for tropical lands.

It can be asserted with some confidence that over the next decade or so expansion of the agricultural frontier inevitably will result in the destruction of natural resources. Extension services will be inadequate. The majority of

---

[16] Recent oil discoveries in the upper Amazon basin may change the complexion of tropical land development.

colonists will not be capable of effectively using credit and, even if they were, sufficient credit would not be available. Markets and freight rates will constrain the flow of private capital into agricultural, forestry, and industrial enterprises. It is axiomatic that the level of effort should be dictated by available alternatives. If there were truly few, if any, alternatives, one could propose the expansion of subsistence agriculture.

If it is assumed that alternatives exist, the weight of evidence is on the side of those who would restrain expansion in the hope that higher returns would result from a sequence that places initial emphasis on consolidation, education, the accumulation of knowledge, and improvement in public administration. The prudent approach to movement into pioneer areas is a gradual one designed to attract spontaneous settlers and, within the limits prescribed above, private investment and enterprise. The caution reflected here will be put to the acid test over the next decade by Brazil's ambitious program to achieve a massive population shift from the south and northeast into the north and northwest, spearheaded by 15,000 km of penetration roads into the heart of the Amazon.

LIST OF ABBREVIATIONS

AID	Agency for International Development (U.S.)
BAB	Banco Agrícola Boliviano
B/C	Benefit cost
BFA	Banco de Fomento Agrícola (Peru)
bf/d	Board feet per day
BNF	Banco Nacional de Fomento (Paraguay and Ecuador)
CAPPS	Comisión de Administración de Puerto Presidente Stroessner (Paraguay)
CBF	Corporación Boliviana de Fomento
CELADE	Centro de Estudios Latinoamericanos de Demografía
CEPAL	Comisión Económica para América Latina
CETCA	Compañía Ecuatoriana de Té
CIDA	Comité Interamericano de Desarrollo Agrícola
cm	Centimeter
CMNP	Companhía Melhoramentos Norte do Paraná
COMEBOL	Comisión de Estano Boliviana
CONASUPO	Comisión Nacional de Subsistencias Populares (Mexico)
CONOMALI	Colonizadora Noroeste Matogrossense Ltda. (Brazil)
CORFIRA	Corporación de Financiamiento de la Reforma Agraria (Peru)
CREA	Centro de Reconversión Económica del Azuay, Cañar y Morona Santiago (Ecuador)
CSIRO	Commonwealth Scientific and Industrial Research Organization (Australia)
CVC	Corporación Valle del Cauca (Colombia)
CVG	Corporación Venezolana de Guayana
DBH	Diameter at breast height
FAO	Food and Agriculture Organization of the United Nations
GRP	Gross regional product
ha	Hectare
IBGE	Instituto Braziliero de Geografía y Estadística
IBRA	Instituto Braziliero de Reforma Agraria

IBRD	International Bank for Reconstruction and Development (World Bank)
ICIRA	Instituto de Capacitación e Investigación en Reforma Agraria (Chile)
IDB	Inter-American Development Bank
IERAC	Instituto Ecuatoriano de Reforma Agraria y Colonización
IICA	Instituto Interamericano de Ciencias Agrícolas
ILO	International Labour Office
ILPES	Instituto Latinamericano de Planificación Económica y Social
IMF	International Monetary Fund
INC	Instituto Nacional de Colonización (Bolivia)
INCODES	Instituto de Colonización y Desarrollo de Comunidades Rurales (Bolivia)
INCORA	Instituto Colombiano de la Reforma Agraria
INDA	Instituto Nacional de Desenvolvimento Agrario (Brazil)
INI	Instituto Nacional Indigenista (Mexico)
INIA	Instituto Nacional de Investigaciones Agrícolas (Mexico)
IPEAN	Instituto de Pesquisas e Experimentação Agropecuarias do Norte (Brazil)
IRDA	Instituto Regional de Desenvolvimento do Amapá (Brazil)
IRR	Internal rate of return
ITCO	Instituto de Tierras y Colonización (Costa Rica)
km	Kilometer
MVP	Marginal value product
NAS-NRC	National Academy of Sciences-National Research Council (U.S.)
NPV	Net present value
OAS	Organization of American States
ONERN	Oficina Nacional de Evaluación de Recursos Naturales (Peru)
ONRA	Oficina Nacional de Reforma Agraria (Peru)
RFF	Resources for the Future
SAI	Servicio Agrícola Interamericano (Bolivia)
SCIF	Servicio Cooperativo Interamericano de Fomento (Peru)
SEDIA	Sociedad Ecuatoriana de Desarrollo Industria Agropecuaria
SIECA	Secretaría de Integración Económica Centro-Americana
SIPA	Servicio de Investigación y Promoción Agropecuaria (Peru)
SOMECO	Sociedade de Melhoramentos e Colonização (Brazil)
SRH	Secretaría de Recursos Hidráulicos (Mexico)
SUDAM	Superintendencia do Desenvolvimento da Amazonia (Brazil)
SUDENE	Superintendencia do Desenvolvimento do Nordeste (Brazil)
TAMS	Tibbetts, Abbot, McCarthy, Stratton, Inc.
UN	United Nations
UNDP	United Nations Development Programme

UNESCO	United Nations Economic and Social Council
UNIDO	United Nations Industrial Development Organization
USDA	United States Department of Agriculture
WFP	World Food Programme

INDEX

THE JOHNS HOPKINS UNIVERSITY PRESS

This book was composed in Press Roman text and Optima Bold display by
Jones Composition Company, Inc. from a design by Harriet Sickler. It
was printed by Universal Lithographers, Inc., on Warren's 60-lb. Sebago,
regular finish, and bound by L. H. Jenkins, Inc., in Columbia Bayside Vellum.

Library of Congress Cataloging in Publication Data

Nelson, Michael, 1928–
    The development of tropical lands.

    Includes bibliographical references.
    1. Land–Latin America.   2. Land settlement–Latin America.   3. Tropics.
4. Agricultural colonies–Latin America.   I. Resources for the Future.
II. Title.
HD320.5.Z63N47   330.9′8′003   72–12363
ISBN 0–8018–1488–X